Barbarians and Bishops

Army, Church, and State
in the Age of
Arcadius and Chrysostom

J. H. W. G. Liebeschuetz

CLARENDON PRESS · OXFORD
1990

Oxford University Press, Walton Street, Oxford OX2 6DP

Oxford New York Toronto
Delhi Bombay Calcutta Madras Karachi
Petaling Jaya Singapore Hong Kong Tokyo
Nairobi Dar es Salaam Cape Town
Melbourne Auckland
and associated companies in
Berlin Ibadan

Oxford is a trade mark of Oxford University Press

Published in the United States
by Oxford University Press, New York

British Library Cataloguing in Publication Data
Liebeschuetz, J. H. W. G.
Barbarians and bishops: army, church, and state in the
age of Arcadius and Chrysostom
1. Roman Empire, 395–407
I. Title
937'.09
ISBN 0–19–814886–0

Library of Congress Cataloging in Publication Data
Liebeschuetz, J. H. W. G. (John Hugo Wolfgang Gideon)
Barbarians and bishops: army, church, and state in the age of
Arcadius and Chrysostom / J.H.W.G. Liebeschuetz.
Includes bibliographical references.
1. German mercenaries—Byzantine Empire. 2. John Chrysostom,
Saint, d. 407—Adversaries. 3. Byzantine Empire—History—Arcadius,
395–407. I. Title.
DF543.L33 1990   949.5'01—dc20   89–37625
ISBN 0–19–814886–0

Printed in Great Britain by
Courier International Ltd,
Tiptree, Essex

for my mother
Rachel Liebeschuetz

Preface

While working on the book I have received much help and inspiration from friends and colleagues. Edward Thompson nourished my interest in Late Roman barbarians with numerous off-prints. Conversations with Robert Markus were invariably stimulating and encouraging. I want to thank Timothy Barnes, Maria Cesa, Barrie Jones and John Matthews for informing me of results of their work. I learnt much from Peter Heather's still unpublished Oxford D.Phil. thesis. Conversations with Keith Hopwood about nomads greatly influenced my views of Germanic warrior bands. Alan Cameron sent me a copy of his almost complete *Barbarians and Politics at the Court of Arcadius*. Richard Schofield, Ruth Rubinstein and Mme Monbeig-Goguel helped with problems of Arcadius' column. I must thank the Library of Trinity College, Cambridge, the Bibliothèque Nationale, and the Louvre for giving permission to reproduce drawings from their collections, and the British Academy for a grant to pay for photographs. My book owes more to Averil Cameron than is acknowledged in foot-notes and bibliography. Text and notes were typed by Adrienne Edwards and Lena Cavanagh. They as well as Alan Sommerstein did their best to eliminate effects of my carelessness. I am very grateful to Janet Hamilton for giving her time and experience to read the proofs. John Cordy encouraged me to persist with the project and eventually saw the volume through the press with his well-known thoroughness and insight. My family for many years shared the house with barbarians and bishops. I am grateful to all and hope that they will be reasonably pleased with the book they helped bring into being. Errors and omissions that remain must be my own.

Nottingham   J.H.W.G.L.
August 1989

Contents

List of Plates   xi
Abbreviations   xiii

Introduction: Demilitarization and Christianization   1

PART I: AN ARMY OF MERCENARIES AND ITS PROBLEMS

 1. Barbarian Officers and Generals   7
 2. Reasons for the Recruiting of Barbarians   11
 3. The Consequences of Adrianople: Rebuilding the Army   26
 4. Regulars, Federates, and *Bucellarii*   32
 5. The Visigoths and Alaric's Goths   48

PART II: THE EASTERN GOVERNMENT AND ITS ARMY

 6. The Murder of Rufinus   89
 7. The Rulers of the East and their Military Policy   93
 8. The Age of Eutropius   96
 9. The Fall of Eutropius and the Prefecture of Aurelian   104
10. The Fall of Gainas   111
11. After Gainas   126
12. The Arcadian Estabishment, AD 392–412   132
13. Legislation against Heretics, Pagans, and Jews   146

PART III: CHRYSOSTOM AND THE POLITICIANS

14. Orthodoxy Imposed at Constantinople   157
15. The Election and Preaching of John Chrysostom   166
16. Chrysostom in the Gainas Crisis   189
17. Enemies and Friends of John Chrysostom: The Problem   195
18. The Three Bishops and Eudoxia   198
19. Theophilus   203
20. Clerical Opposition in Constantinople and in
    Neighbouring Provinces   208

21. Enemies in the Establishment   217
22. The Rich, the Poor, and the West   223
23. Bishop and Public Life in the Cyrenaica of Synesius   228

Conclusion: The Historians' Post-Mortem   236

Appendix I: The Identity of Typhos in Synesius'
  De Providentia   253
Appendix II: Arcadius' Column   273
Bibliography   279
Index   305

List of Plates

(at end)

1–2. 1–3. Freshfield drawings of the narrative bands 1–13 of the West, South, and East aspects of the column of Arcadius.

3. 1. Bibliothèque Nationale drawing of North aspect of band 9: the failure of Gainas' attempt to cross the Hellespont.
2. Freshfield drawing of the South side of the base of the column: chi/rho symbol and the harmony of the two emperors.

4. 1–3. Freshfield drawings of all three aspects of band 2: Goths leaving Constantinople.

5. 1. Bibliothèque Nationale drawing of South aspect of band 2: the hovering angel and the figure standing in the gate.
2. Louvre drawing: a very free adaptation of part of band 2.

6. 1–2. Freshfield drawing of band 8 of the West and South aspects.
3. Bibliothèque Nationale drawing of the same carving.

7. 1. Freshfield drawing of bands 12 and 13 from the South.
2. Bibliothèque Nationale drawing of part of the same bands.

Abbreviations

AASS	*Acta Sanctorum*
ACO	*Acta Conciliorum Oecumenicorum*, ed. E. Schwartz
AES	*Annales: Économies, Sociétés, Civilisations*
AJA	*American Journal of Archaeology*
AJP	*American Journal of Philology*
ANRW	*Aufstieg und Niedergang der römischen Welt*, ed. H. Temporini
BAR Int. Ser.	British Archaeological Reports International Series
BASOR	*Bulletin of the American Schools of Oriental Research*
BIFAO	*Bulletin de l'Institut français d'archéologie orientale*
BRGK	*Bericht der Römisch-Germanischen Kommission*
BROB	*Berichten van de Rijksdienst voor het oudheidkundig Bodemonderzoek*
CE	*Chronique d'Égypte*
CJ	*Codex Justinianus*
Cl. Phil.	*Classical Philology*
Chron. Min.	*Chronica Minora*, ed. Th. Mommsen
Com. Sac. Larg.	*comes sacrarum largitionum*
CQ	*Classical Quarterly*
CR	*Classical Review*
CRAI	*Comptes rendus de l'Académie des Inscriptions et Belles-Lettres*
CSCO	*Corpus Scriptorum Christianorum Orientalium*
CSEL	*Corpus Scriptorum Ecclesiasticorum Latinorum*
CT	*Codex Theodosianus*
DCB	*Dictionary of Christian Biography and Literature*, ed. H. Wace & W. C. Piercy
DOP	*Dumbarton Oaks Papers*
FHG	*Fragmenta Historicorum Graecorum* (1841–70), ed. C. Müller
FIEC	Fédération internationale des Associations des Études classiques
GRBS	*Greek, Roman and Byzantine Studies*
JCPh	*Jahrbücher für Classische Philologie*
JEH	*Journal of Ecclesiastical History*
JHS	*Journal of Hellenic Studies*

Jones *LRE*	A. H. M. Jones, *The Later Roman Empire*
JRS	*Journal of Roman Studies*
JThS	*Journal of Theological Studies*
Mag. Offic.	*magister officiorum*
Mansi	*Sacrorum Conciliorum Nova et Amplissima Collectio*
MIÖG	*Mitteilungen des Instituts für Österreichische Geschichtsforschung*
Mus. Helv.	*Museum Helveticum*
NA	*Neues Archiv der Gesellschaft für ältere deutsche Geschichte*
ND Oc.	*Notitia dignitatum . . . in partibus Occidentis*
ND Or.	*Notitia dignitatum . . . in partibus Orientis*
PBSR	*Papers of the British School at Rome*
PG	*Patrologia Graeca*
PL	*Patrologia Latina*
PLRE	*The Prosopography of the Later Roman Empire*
PPO Ill. (It., Or.)	*praefectus praetorio Illyrici (Italiae, Orientis)*
Praef. Urb.	*praefectus urbis*
RAC	*Reallexicon für Antike und Christentum*
RE	A. Pauly, G. Wissowa, and W. Kroll, *Real-Encyclopädie d. classischen Altertumswissenschaft*
REA	*Revue des Études Anciennes*
REB	*Revue des Études byzantines*
REG	*Revue des Études Grecques*
St. Patr.	*Studia Patristica*
TAPA	*Transactions of the American Philological Association*
TU	Texte und Untersuchungen
ZRG rom.	*Zeitschrift der Savigny-Stiftung für Rechtsgeschichte, romanistische Abteilung*

Introduction
Demilitarization and Christianization

THIS book is built around two related events at Constantinople in about the year AD 400: the Gainas crisis of 399–400 and the deposition of John Chrysostom in 403–4. Both were made possible by fundamental changes in Roman society since the Early Empire. The Gainas affair could happen only because the Empire had come to rely to a large extent on barbarian mercenaries. The career of Chrysostom involved situations unthinkable before the triumph of Christianity. Both events illustrate the transformation of the Ancient World.

The conspicuous role played by barbarian, particularly German, soldiers in the Late Roman state has always been recognized. It has still not been fully explained. This is not surprising since the development which made the Empire depend for defence on recruits from beyond its frontiers is a complex one, related to changes in the basic structures of Roman society. Even the simplest explanation, that the population had shrunk and that young men were simply not available for recruiting would require not only evidence that the population had decreased considerably, but also an explanation of the reduction. In any case it is likely that even if the population had shrunk, the Empire still produced enough men to fill a large army. So an explanation of changes in recruiting policy requires examination of the changes in social organization and attitudes which made the recruiting of available manpower less attractive. Political institutions, structure of landowning, concepts of citizenship and of a citizen's rights and duties are all relevant to the problems of why barbarians were recruited on so large a scale.[1] Religion is relevant too. The triumph of Christianity involved the abandonment of a civic religion which was closely integrated with secular government. Magistrates had taken a leading part in sacrifices. Priests were chosen from senators. The emperor was *pontifex maximus*, and he and the senate had the ultimate decision when problems of religious observance arose. Conflict between representatives of state and of religion was impossible, even unthinkable. This situation was transformed by Christianity. The Church had an elaborate empire-wide organization which received some support from the Empire but was quite

---

[1] See below, ch. 2.

independent of it. Moreover the Church's primary purpose was not to make the Roman state and its citizens successful but to win salvation for individual Christians. The requirements of state and Church were not totally opposed but they were far from identical.[2] From its earliest beginnings the Church had created an extraordinarily powerful sense of community and brotherhood among its members.[3] It also created division and antagonism by drawing sharp boundaries between Christians and non-Christians, and between would-be Christians who had the right beliefs and those who did not. Even disputes over the filling of ecclesiastical positions, especially bishoprics, caused passionate partisanship and conflict.

My book does not tackle the topics of demilitarization and Christianization, their causes and effects, head on. But they do provide the background to chapters dealing with narrower themes. The first chapter is a general discussion of the use of barbarians in the Roman army in the mid fourth century, and the reasons for their recruitment. The second chapter traces the consequences of the defeat of the Eastern army at Adrianople in 378. This disaster is shown to mark the beginning of the end of the famous Roman army both in East and West, even if only because it greatly accelerated developments which were already of long standing. The chapter includes a discussion of the settlements made with the Goths. It is suggested that in the agreements of 381 and 382 the Goths were not all treated in the same way, and that only some were given land to farm. Other groups received payment in kind (*annona*) like mobile units of the field-army, which is what they in effect became. Apart from this, many individuals were enrolled into regular units of the Roman army. Chapter Three distinguishes between different kinds of federate unit. The emphasis is not on contingents supplied and officered by a particular barbarian tribe, but on units of individually recruited barbarians, led by officers appointed by the Roman authorities, who need not necessarily have been fellow-tribesmen of the majority of their soldiers. Such units, it is argued, came to be the principal fighting units of the Roman army. In Chapter Four Alaric's Goths are treated as basically a regiment of that kind, rather than a migrating tribe. It is argued that they were a federate unit under a strong Tervingian leader which consolidated into what was in effect a new nation in the course of its wanderings through the provinces of the Empire.

[2] Cf. 'General observations on the fall of the Roman Empire in the West' at the end of ch. 38 of Gibbons's *The History of the Decline of the Roman Empire*, (London, 1776).
[3] W. A. Meeks, (1983) ch. 3 and elsewhere, is extremely enlightening, also Peter Brown (1987) 253–67.

The barbarized army, and especially the federate-dominated army after Adrianople, presented formidable problems of control to the civilian government. In the West the commander-in-chief became virtually the ruler of the Empire. In the East civilians remained in charge. Part II of the book describes how they managed this: a succession of outstanding civilian politicians, from Rufinus, praetorian prefect of the East 392–5, to Anthemius, prefect from 404 to 415, followed consistently a policy of keeping the army small, and solving military problems as far as possible by diplomatic means. They also displayed a strong and consistent determination to maintain the independence of the government of the East. The period saw the emergence of a confident and self-consciously Eastern aristocracy which was politically Roman, but culturally Greek. The Gainas crisis is shown to have been a reaction to the civilian policy of this group. Gainas briefly threatened both the policy and the politicians conducting it. But Gainas was destroyed, and the policy was continued to the great benefit of the Eastern Empire.

Part III centres on the preaching and fall of John Chrysostom. The sermons show how Chrysostom achieved great popularity at Constantinople. They do not throw much light on Chrysostom's part in secular affairs, but there is evidence to show that he did play an important role during the Gainas crisis. Furthermore it is reasonably clear that the secular leaders of the faction that brought him down were precisely the men who were guiding the policy of the Eastern Empire so consistently, and on the whole successfully.

Why Chrysostom incurred their determined hostility is less clear. But informed speculation is possible. There is much evidence that in the Roman Empire of the fourth century Church and secular administration had their separate spheres, comparable to sacred and non-sacred areas of the old republic.[4] Chrysostom kept within his sphere. He was not a political bishop. But the bishop's relationship with clergy and congregation inevitably made him a man of political influence. As bishop Chrysostom had a direct relationship with the population of the capital, of a kind which had previously only been enjoyed by the emperor. There would inevitably be situations like the Gainas crisis in which the potential political role of the bishop became actual. But even in normal times the position of the Church was of sufficient importance for its internal conflicts to have political significance. Altogether there was plenty of scope for friction between an active bishop of Constantinople and the men running the secular administration.

[4] A. Bouche-Leclercq (1871) 82 ff., G. Dumézil (1966, cited in English tr. by P. Knapp, 1970) 129 ff.

Tensions in Church and state were not independent of each other. The emancipation of the East, and the rise of the new capital of Constantinople provoked parallel reactions in Church and state. In the secular sphere the self-assertion of the East after the death of Theodosius I resulted in relations of extreme mutual suspicion, sometimes verging on open war, between the two halves of the Empire. In the Church provincial bishops jealous of the widening authority of the bishop of Constantinople found a champion in the bishop of Alexandria. Stresses caused by the rise of Constantinople, in the secular as well as the religious sphere, contributed to the fall of John Chrysostom.

In chapters concerned with Chrysostom, Synesius regularly figures in a supporting role as a witness, since his two pamphlets *De Regno* and *De Providentia* provide essential evidence. Both are sophisticated and elusive pieces of writing which have to be interpreted before they can be used. At the end of the book, Synesius is treated in his own right. It falls to this most untypical man to represent the bishops of provincial cities obliged to cope with the problems of this disturbed age. He certainly was obliged to deal not only with ecclesiastical business, but also with the consequences of the decay of civic institutions and the decline of the military strength of the Empire relative to that of the barbarians. Synesius saw himself playing a much more prominent role in the secular affairs of Cyrenaica than Chrysostom in those of Constantinople. It is likely that bishops of cities in frontier-provinces often found themselves in a position like his.

PART I

An Army of Mercenaries and Its Problems

I

Barbarian Officers and Generals

THE fact that the defence of the Empire came to depend very largely on troops of non-Roman, and particularly Germanic, origin is remarkable, and must seem even more remarkable if we remember that the Romans had once been warlike and militarized to an altogether exceptional degree. It is natural to ask when and why this development came about and in what ways, if any, it affected the fighting efficiency of the army, and an attempt will be made in this chapter to provide some answers.

The employment of foreign troops as part of the Roman army goes back a very long time.[1] Nevertheless there is reason to believe that the period when the barbarian troops came to be the main striking force was the period of the tetrarchy and especially the reign of Constantine. The decisive step seems to have been taken when Constantine created the mobile army with which to attack Maxentius and win the Empire for himself. For it seems that this army was recruited largely from barbarians,[2] partly from among the prisoners of war settled by the tetrarchs[3] in Gaul, partly from captives taken by himself, partly from volunteers from across the frontier. It appears that Constantine created, or at least was the first to raise in large numbers, the new *auxilia* which, to judge by their name, and by a considerable amount of mainly later evidence were recruited largely from non-citizens, and which became the main striking force of the Roman army. The Arch of Constantine commemorates the contribution to Constantine's victory of one of these units, the *Cornuti*.[4] Constantine also seems to have created in place of the praetorian guard a type of guard unit, the *schola*, which came to be officered and commanded largely, but not exclusively, by Germans.[5] Henceforth Germans of various tribal origins never ceased to play an essential

---

[1] M. Speidel, 'Ethnic units in the imperial army', *ANRW* ii. 3, 202–31, on important 3rd-cent. developments. Earlier still: H. Callies, 'Die fremden Truppen im römischen Heer des Prinzipats und die sogenannten nationalen Numeri', *Beiträge zur Geschichte des römischen Heeres, Ber. RGK* xlv (1964); M. Bang (1906). See also G. Gigli (1942).

[2] Zos. ii. 15, D. Hoffmann (1969) 130–41, 169–73, 199–201.

[3] References to settlement, G. E. M. de Ste Croix (1981) 513 ff.

[4] D. Hoffmann (1969) 131–55.

[5] Ibid. 281–5, 200–300; M. Waas (1965) 10; F. Fremersdorf, 'Christliche Leibwächter auf einem geschliffenem kölner Glasbecher', *Festschrift R. Egger* (Klagenfurt, 1952) i. 66–83.

role in the Roman armies:[6] Alamanni were prominent in the middle decades of the fourth century;[7] Franks were found in key positions during most of the century at least until the death of Theodosius in 394.[8]

Our detailed knowledge of the Late Roman officer class begins in 353/4 with the surviving part of Ammianus. It is clear that by this time German officers were numerous and in important positions. Even so the fact that German officers often Latinized their names[9] means that we are more likely to underestimate than to exaggerate their numbers. That Franks, for instance, were numerous in prominent positions and that their prominence was resented is illustrated by the story of the usurpation of Silvanus in 355. Silvanus, the *magister militum* in Gaul, was a Frank whose father Bonitus had reached the rank of general under Constantine.[10] Certain courtiers forged evidence that Silvanus intended to make himself emperor. Silvanus was convinced that if he tried to refute the accusation nobody would believe him. So he took a step, which in Ammianus' view he would never have taken otherwise, being a man 'dedicated to the empire': he had himself proclaimed emperor. Some time later he was murdered by some of his own troops who had been bribed by Constantius' general Ursicinus.[11] Two aspects of the affair are interesting. Firstly, Silvanus considered taking refuge with the free Franks outside the Empire, but decided against it, fearing that they would either kill or surrender him.[12] There was little sense of solidarity between free Franks and Franks in the service of the Empire. On the other hand there was a feeling of common interest among the Franks in the imperial service. The intrigue against Silvanus also threatened Malarich, a Frankish tribune of the *gentiles* and was seen by numerous Franks at court, including tribunes of *scholae*, as an attack on them all. So they combined to unmask it.[13]

The importance of German officers in the middle of the fourth century is also illustrated by the large number of them who rose to the highest rank of *magister militum*. Among the most prominent were Agilo under Constantius, Victor under Julian, Jovian and Valens and Arinthaeus under Valens.[14] These men had considerable

[6] A. Schenk von Stauffenberg (1948), M. Waas (1965), cf. Zos. iv. 12: Valentinian recruits Germans.

[7] K. Stroheker (1965) 130–53, 'Alamannen im römischen Dienst'.

[8] K. Stroheker, 'Zur Rolle des Heermeisters fränkischer Abstammung im späten vierten Jahrhundert', *Historia* iv (1955) 314–30.

[9] Bonitus 2 (Frank), Victor 4 (Sarmatian), Magnentius (barbarian parents). References in *PLRE* i.

[10] Amm. xv. 5. 16, 33; *PLRE* i s.v. Silvanus 2.   [11] Amm. xv. 5. 30–2.

[12] Amm. xv. 5. 16.   [13] Amm. xv. 5. 6, 9–11.

[14] References under names in *PLRE* i; also prosopography in M. Wass (1965) 79 ff.

influence on the succession to the Empire. Nevitta was evidently one of the principal assistants of Julian. As *magister equitum per Gallias* he succeeded Gemoarius, perhaps an Alaman, in 361,[15] and in the following year became *magister equitum praesentalis* in succession to Agilo, another Alaman.[16] After Julian had been killed on the Persian campaign the expeditionary force, composed of both Eastern and Western field armies, had to choose a new emperor. At the crucial meeting both armies were represented by barbarians. Nevitta and Dagalaifus were the Western spokesmen, Arintheus and Victor represented the soldiers of the East.[17] Eventually they chose Jovian, an officer of Roman origin.

Even greater power was achieved by a succession of Germans who held the rank of *magister militum* in the West during the last years of the emperor Valentinian I.[18] At that emperor's death Merobaudes, *magister peditum praesentalis*, played a central role in the proclamation as joint emperor of the dead emperor's younger son Valentinian II.[19] A little later his influence detached a large part of an army that was being transferred to help the Eastern Empire against the Goths, and kept them in Gaul to defend the provinces against possible attacks by Germans.[20] He was twice consul, and possibly designated a third time, an almost unique honour for a man not belonging to the imperial family. According to one source it was Merobaudes who by deserting Gratian made possible the usurpation of Magnus Maximus. Maximus eventually ordered him to commit suicide.[21]

A little later an even more powerful position came to be occupied by the Frank Arbogast.[22] He was the leading general of the young emperor Valentinian II, and had obtained this status after the death of his predecessor Bauto through personal influence with the troops.[23] According to John of Antioch he was actually a son of Bauto, so that he might be said to have inherited his command.[24] In 387 Valentinian II was temporarily expelled from his part of the Empire by the usurper Maximus. When Theodosius defeated Maximus,

---

[15] Amm. xxi. 8. 1. [16] Amm. xiv. 10. 8. [17] Amm. xxv. 5. 2.

[18] Perhaps Merobaudes and his immediate Western successors already enjoyed a special relationship with their troops like that documented for Stilicho, Bonifatius, Aetius, and other later generals. See below, p. 43.

[19] *PLRE* i s.v. Merobaudes 2; B. S. Roders, 'Merobaudes and Maximus in Gaul', *Historia* xxx (1981) 82–105.

[20] Amm. xxxi. 7. 4. [21] Prosper Tiro s.a. 384 = *Chron. Minor.* i. 461.

[22] *PLRE* i. 95–7 s.v. Arbogastes; B. Croke, 'Arbogast and the death of Valentinian II', *Historia* xxv (1976) 235–44.

[23] Zos. iv. 53. 1.

[24] John Ant. fr. 187 = Eunap. fr. 58. 2 ed. R. Blockley, who assumes that the fragment is ultimately derived from Eunapius via an intermediary source which added material. That John of Antioch is here to be believed is argued by A. Demandt, (1980) 609–36, esp. 633, also *RE Supp.* xii. 609.

Arbogast was one of his leading generals, and on Theodosius' instructions remained with the restored Valentinian II in the West as principal adviser, not only in military matters but in civil ones as well.[25] One suspects that Theodosius was glad to use Arbogast to control the last surviving emperor of the Valentinian dynasty, who was likely sooner or later to become a rival, either to Theodosius himself, or to his sons Arcadius and Honorius. It will be suggested that Theodosius was planning to ensure the loyalty of Arbogast by marrying his son Arcadius to Eudoxia, the sister of Arbogast—if John of Antioch is right.[26] However that may be, Theodosius' plans for Arbogast went totally wrong. Arbogast quarrelled with Valentinian II, murdered him—or drove him to suicide—and had him succeeded by Eugenius, a nonentity. This was going too far for Theodosius, who refused to recognize Eugenius and proceeded to overthrow and kill both Arbogast and his emperor.

Next in the line of over-powerful Germans was Stilicho. Stilicho had played a leading part in Theodosius' campaign against Arbogast and Eugenius. When Theodosius died soon after his victory (394), Stilicho was left as regent to Honorius, the young son of Theodosius. In relation to the young Western emperor he occupied a position similar to that previously held by Arbogast under Valentinian II, and was the virtual ruler of the West until he was executed in 408.[27]

I have surveyed the careers of Germans who decisively influenced the government of the Empire. They were only the most prominent of a large number of German and other officers of barbarian origin in high positions in these years. Of sixteen *magistri militum* who are known to have held command under Theodosius I, nine at least were not Roman by birth.[28] The high proportion of generals with foreign names implies that a similarly high proportion of officers was of non-Roman origin too. The lists of *PLRE* confirm that numbers were large even if the proportion among lower ranking officers was smaller than in high commands. That foreigners should be most strongly represented in the highest ranks is surprising. An explanation will be suggested later.[29]

[25] John Ant. fr. 187.
[26] See below, p. 24.
[27] *PLRE* i. 853–8 s.v. Stilicho.
[28] *PLRE* i. 1114, cf.A. Demandt, *RE Supp.* xii. 553–790, s.v. *magister militum*. See also O'Flynn (1983).
[29] See below, p. 23.

2

Reasons for the Recruiting of Barbarians

THE reasons why the Roman government came to rely to such a large extent on barbarians are not at all clear, even if some of the factors can be identified. In the second and third centuries the Roman army was recruited from sons of soldiers, and from inhabitants of the province in which the units were stationed.[1] Frontier areas, especially the lands along the Rhine[2] and Danube[3] were devastated in the third century, and their ability to furnish recruits was surely much reduced.[4] Loss of farmers was made good by settlement of barbarian prisoners of war on a very large scale[5]—over so long a period and so large a scale that social historians of the Later Empire still have to explain how there could have been so much empty space within the Empire. Devastation must be part of the answer, but probably not the whole.[6] The conditions of settlement varied a great deal. Settlers who had volunteered to enter the Empire peacefully,[7] and others who had entered violently, and whose settlement was not so much permitted as acquiesced in by the government, received freehold. The Visigoths who were settled in Moesia in 382 even kept the right to be ruled by their own chieftains.[8] Others, usually prisoners of war who had surrendered and were compulsorily settled, might be handed over as tenants, or even as landless agricultural workers, to landowners.[9] In either case their status was humble. They were tied to the land, and their condition could be described as a kind of slavery. In fact it has been convincingly argued that prisoners of war handed over to

[1] H. M. D. Parker and G. R. Watson (1958) 169–86; G. Forni, 'Il reclutamento delle legioni da Augusto a Diocleziano' (Milan, 1953), also in ANRW ii. 1. 339 ff.; J. C. Mann (1983).

[2] Destruction of hill-top settlements in Hunsrück in 275–6, 355, and 406–7, see K.-J. Gilles (1985), esp. 86–7.

[3] P. Lemerle (1954), V. Velkov (1962).

[4] One might add depopulation due to disease, esp. AD 165–180 and 251–260: J. F. Gilliam, 'The Plague under Marcus Aurelius', AJPh lxxxii (1961) 225–51; A. E. R. Boak (1955) 157–62; id. *Manpower Shortage and the Fall of the Roman Empire* (Ann Arbor, 1955); P. Salmon, *Population et dépopulation dans l'empire romain*, Coll. Latomus 137 (Brussels, 1974). On the effect of plague in later Europe, J. N. Biraben (1976), J. Hatcher (1977). It is doubtful whether 'plague' meant bubonic plague before Justinian.

[5] G. E. M. de Ste. Croix (1981) 511–18.   [6] Cf. ibid. 247 and notes.

[7] This was what the Visigoths (Tervingi) asked for and were promised in 376: Amm. xxxi. 3. 8, xxxi. 4. 5.

[8] See below, p. 28.   [9] Pan. Lat. iv (viii). 8. 4, 9. 1–4.

landowners as workers were the earliest rural labourers to be tied to the land as *inquilini*.[10] The barbarians handed over to landowners remained liable to conscription, indeed the provision of a source of recruits is regularly given as one of the purposes for the settlement of barbarians.[11] In the case of one class of settlers the military purpose was predominant. These were the so-called *laeti*. The status of *laeti* seems first to have been applied to provincials who had been brought back into the Empire after they had been in barbarian captivity.[12] *Laeti* were not simply distributed among landowners in need of tenants but were settled on land of a particular category (*terra laetica*)[13] which must have been a kind of public land, because the emperor had to be involved in each grant.[14] The land nevertheless seems to have remained part of a city territory, and its administration and leasing seem to have been carried out in the first place by leading decurions.[15] *Laeti* were potential soldiers, always liable to be called up.[16] Each settlement seems to have consisted of members of the same tribal grouping.[17] Clusters of settlements were subject to a *praepositus*.[18] Settlements of *laeti* are known only from Gaul, though one law referring to them is addressed to the praetorian prefect of Italy.[19] The status of a *laetus* was permanent and hereditary. Culturally they long remained barbarian enclaves.[20] *Laeti* were still found in Frankish Gaul.[21]

It is likely that settlers of similar status elsewhere were known under different names, as for instance *gentiles*.[22] Recruits from the same settlement did not necessarily serve in the same unit: they might be posted wherever recruits were required.[23] On the other hand a body of Greuthungi settled in Phrygia seem to have served as a single cavalry unit. But these Greuthungi do not appear to have served continuously. They mutinied under the leadership of Tribigild when

---

[10] O. Seeck (1901) 494–7 on *Dig.* xxx. 12.

[11] E.g. *Pan. Lat.* vii (vi). 6. 2.

[12] Earliest ref. *Pan. Lat.* iv (viii). 21. 1 and E. Demougeot (1970), (1979) 539–50.

[13] *CT* xiii. 11. 10 (399).

[14] Ibid. 'nullus ex his agris aliquid nisi ex nostra adnotatione mereatur'.

[15] *CT* xiii. 11. 10 '. . . conludio principalium vel defensorum.'

[16] *CT* vii. 20. 11 (400), *Nov. Serv.* 2 (465).

[17] *ND Oc.* xlii. 33–44; all in Gaul, cf. R. Kaiser (1973).

[18] *CT* vii. 20. 10 (369), to praetorian prefect of Italy; for examples see n. 22 below.

[19] *CT* vii. 20. 10 (369).

[20] R. MacMullen (1963*b*).

[21] R. Schmidt-Wiegand (1972) 28–30.

[22] *ND Oc.* xlii. 46–63 in Italy, perhaps the Taifali of Amm. xxxi. 4. 5. *ND Oc.* xlii. 65–70 in Gaul. Gentiles (of different type?) on African frontier: *CT* vii. 15. 1, xi. 30. 62. In the Notitia *gentiles* rank lower than *laeti*. E. Demougeot (1980–1) argues that all units entered on *laterculum minus* ranked as *gentiles*.

[23] Amm. xx. 8. 13: *laeti* recruited into *scholae*; *CT* vii. 20. 12: into legions (unless this applies to *vagi* only). But in Amm. xxi. 13. 16 *laeti* are a unit.

they had recently returned from a campaign against the Huns, and were anticipating a future of farm work. The Phrygian Greuthungi may not have been *laeti* but rather *foederati* of some kind or other.[24] There were certainly far more types of German settlement than we know about.[25]

The imperial government was concerned to maintain the distinctiveness and inferiority of these barbarians living and serving within the Empire. Even officers did not necessarily become citizens. We hear that the Gothic officer Fravitta received special permission of Theodosius I to marry a Roman wife.[26] Intermarriage between *gentiles* and Romans was prohibited. Perhaps this rule applied only to barbarians settled in the Empire.[27] Certainly the rule was maintained in the independent kingdoms founded by the federate Visigoths and Ostrogoths.[28] In spite of large-scale settlement of barbarians we hear surprisingly little of legal problems caused by the living in close proximity of citizens and non-citizens. This suggests that the status of citizen had lost a great deal of its former importance, presumably because it had been superseded for most practical purposes by the privileges of the various groups of *honestiores* as compared with the disadvantaged *humiliores*.[29]

It is likely that the law forbidding intermarriage, which is found in the Codes both of the Empire and of the Visigothic kingdom in Spain, gives an exaggerated impression of the impenetrability of the barrier between Germans and Romans.[30] The growth of barbarian bands on Roman soil suggests that it was quite possible for provincials to be accepted into a barbarian fellowship.[31] The vast

[24] On these Greuthungi see below, p. 100. There is no record of *laeti* in the East. On *foederati* in general see below, p. 32 ff.

[25] E. Demougeot (1970) and (1972), R. Günther (1972) and (1977), E. Wightman (1985) 252–6, R. MacMullen (1963*b*).

[26] Fravitta: Eunapius fr. 60 Müller = 59 Blockley, cf. Zos. iv. 56–7. Fravitta married a Roman wife with special permission, presumably as a young officer. Since he was *mag.mil. per Orientem* in 395 he presumably had long service behind him. Magnentius (Augustus 350–3) son of a *laetus* married a daughter of a senator. See *PLRE* i s.v. Fl. Magnus Magnentius, Zos. ii. 54. 1. Cf. the case of Agilo, *tribunus stabuli* of German origin, who married daughter of proconsul of Constantinople in 354. See *PLRE* i s.v. Agilo.

[27] *CT* iii. 13. 14 (*c*.370). *CJ* iv. 41. 1 (thought by O. Seeck, *Regesten* 232, to be from same law) forbidding export of oil and wine across frontier. So the law seems to have dealt with relations with foreigners, quite possibly including *laeti* or *inquilini* settled within the empire.

[28] Intermarriage forbidden in barbarian kingdoms: *Leges Visig.* iii. 1. 1, E. A. Thompson (1969) 58–9, R. Soraci (1974).

[29] *Peregrinus* status still inflicted as a penalty: *CT* vii. 5. 25 (395), iv. 6. 3 (336). On *honestiores* and *humiliores* A. H. M. Jones *LRE* 17–18, 749–50, P. Garnsey (1970) 221 to end.

[30] A. C. Murray (1983) argues from mainly Frankish and Lombard evidence that early Germanic society was not clan- and lineage-based.

[31] See below n. 62 and p. 17 and 77.

horde that crossed the frozen Rhine on the last day of 406 included a significant number of Pannonian provincials who had joined the Vandals on their migration.[32] Many prominent men in Vandal Africa had Roman names.[33] The organization of the Vandals into 'thousands' was created by Gaiseric in Africa in order to unite the various ethnic components of his people.[34]

As far as recruiting is concerned there was a tradition of very long standing that where citizen recruits were not available non-citizens might be recruited into legions, and quietly granted citizen status after enlistment.[35] No doubt this procedure could be applied to barbarians born across the frontier who were to be enlisted in regular units. It may be that if they were enlisted into 'federate' units the barbarians remained *peregrini*. There remains the question of the status of the captured barbarians settled within the empire. As surrendered enemies they were legally *dediticii*, and thus traditionally incapable of receiving citizenship.[36] If this principle was maintained into our period, nearly all the settled barbarians within the empire— not only the tribes settled by treaty—remained foreigners qualified for service in federate rather than in regular units. It is likely that this disability was quietly overlooked whenever the regular units were short of recruits. If the government had ever hoped that the settlement of barbarians might eventually make the Empire self-sufficient in recruits that aim was not achieved. Quite the reverse. Throughout the fourth century recently captured prisoners of war continued either to be enrolled straightaway into the regular army[37] or to be settled within the Empire.[38] The furnishing of recruits was regularly demanded from defeated barbarians as a condition of peace.[39] All emperors recruited beyond the frontier.[40] Above all élite units came to include a high proportion of German officers and men.[41] Up to 378

---

[32] Jerome *Ep.* 123. 6.

[33] C. Courtois (1964) 225: bishops and clergy; 255 n. 12: court officials. I suggest that some of those at least were Romans, well on the way to being accepted as Vandals.

[34] Procop. *B. Vand.* i. 5, cf. R. Wenskus (1961) 443–4; C. Courtois (1964) 216 ff.; Goths among Vandals: Possidius *V. August.* 28.

[35] J. C. Mann (1983) 51–2.

[36] J. C. Mann (1986), A. H. M. Jones (1968) 132 on Gaius i. 26. 67–8, Ulpian *Reg.* vii. 4. Magnentius was an exception, see n. 26 above.

[37] Amm. xvii. 2. 1–3, Zos. iii. 8. 1, Julian *Ep. ad Ath.* 280 cd.

[38] Amm. xix. 11. 7 (359); xvii. 8. 3–5 (358); cf. xxx. 1. 4 (378).

[39] Amm. xxviii. 5. 4 (370), xxx. 6. 1 (375), xxxi. 10. 17 (370).

[40] Amm. xx. 8. 1 (Constantius), xx. 4. 4 (Julian), Zos. iv. 12 (Valentinian).

[41] M. Waas (1965) 10. 2 out of 14 officers of *scholae* mentioned by Ammianus were certainly Romans (Valentinianus, xxv. 10. 9; Equitius 2, xxvi. 1. 4). Among other ranks there are four Romans (Gaudentius, xvi. 5. 14; Salvius and Lupicinus, xxviii. 10. 12; Sallustius, xxix. 1. 16) and four Germans (xxvii. 11. 16, xv. 5. 16; xvi. 12. 2; xxxi. 10. 3); another German (Jer. *V. Hilar.* 22). A mixed unit of Germans and Gauls (not a *schola*): Amm. xxv. 6. 13.

at least an attempt was made to have such units commanded by Romans, or by officers who though of barbarian origin had served for many years in the Roman army. After 378 it was usual for barbarian officers to command regiments made up of barbarians.[42]

The process of barbarization did not affect different kinds of unit to the same extent. It was most advanced in Gaul, in the *scholae*, the *auxilia*, and other units of the field armies. The older units, legions, cohorts, *alae*, especially in the frontier armies of the East, and perhaps in the Balkans also, are likely to have had a smaller proportion of barbarian recruits, and a higher one of Romans, no doubt largely sons of veterans,[43] but also some volunteers.[44] But the lists of the *Notitia* include a considerable number of units with barbarian names even among the *limitanei* of the East.[45] These must have been raised originally from foreigners, even if they were later kept up by local recruiting. The fact that barbarian officers with very little experience of the Roman army, or even of life within the Empire, were sometimes appointed to the position of *dux*, or commander of the *limitanei* of a province, suggests that even the frontier army included many non-Romans.[46]

But in the crack units of the field army in Gaul the great majority of the soldiers were Germans, and Germans were badly needed for the élite units in the East too. This emerges clearly from the events which led to Julian's proclamation as emperor in 360. Constantius had ordered Julian to reinforce the army on the Eastern border with some of his best troops to be drawn from the *auxilia* of the Gallic army.[47] Julian replied with the argument that these men had been recruited across the Rhine and been promised that they would not have to serve beyond the Alps. Instead of sending men from the *auxilia* Julian offered to provide recruits for Constantius' guard units (*gentiles* and *scutarii*) from *laeti*, that is, Germans settled on lands within the Empire, and from *dediticii*, German prisoners of war available for enrolment in the Roman army. Julian assumed that the East would never be self-sufficient in soldiers of first-rate quality for

[42] Amm. xxxi. 16. 80; xxv. 1. 14 Vetranius, a Roman, commands legio of Tzanni; xxv. 10. 9 Vitalianus, presumably a Roman, serves in *auxilium* of Heruli.

[43] Hereditary service: A. H. M. Jones *LRE* 614–5 n. 15. The majority of *protectores*, *praefecti legionum*, and *praepositi vexillationum* in *PLRE* i. 1121–27 have Roman names.

[44] Evagr. *HE* ii. 1 (emperor Marcian).

[45] German units in East: e.g. *ND Or.* xxvii. 25–6, 43; xxxi. 44, 48, 56, 61, 63, 65, 67; xxxii. 35–7; xxxiii. 31–2.

[46] *Duces* of foreign origin in East: Theolaifus (*comes*), Vadomarius (*dux Phoenices*), Munderichus (*dux Arabiae*), Cariobaudes (*dux Mesopotamiae*), Bacurius (*dux Palestinae*), Pusaeus (*dux Aegyptii*).

[47] Amm. xx. 4. 2–3: the Eruli, Batavi, Petulantes, Celtae, and others not named.

he offered to continue to provide Gallic *laeti* and *dediticii* for the rest of his life.[48]

If one reason why Constantius and Julian preferred to recruit Germans into their crack units was their warlike reputation, this was not the only reason. As Julian explained in his letter to Constantius, the Gauls would neither voluntarily, nor under compulsion, send recruits outside the country, since this would have left their homes without defenders to face the inevitable barbarian invasions.[49] It would therefore appear that Gauls were still thought to make good soldiers,[50] but were reluctant to be recruited into units liable to be moved out of their native province. So the Eastern army, depending for its recruiting needs in part at least on the West, took in as many Germans as it could get, particularly for the units of the imperial guard—there were very few *auxilia* in the East before the reorganization of Theodosius I.[51] It is significant that even in the East armies used the German war cry, the *baritus*.[52]

The Eastern need for recruits from the West was certainly not due to a shortage of manpower. The Later Empire, from Diocletian to the early years of Justinian, saw a steady growth of population in the Eastern provinces.[53] Manpower existed, but was either not available for conscription or considered unsuitable. As the Eastern administrative machine long remained efficient, and the growth of estates powerful enough to resist the imperial government was much slower than in the West, it can only be that Eastern recruits were not thought to make good soldiers. In many areas the peasantry of the provinces away from the frontiers had become 'demilitarized' well before the Roman conquest. Nevertheless it is clear that recruits were produced more widely in the Early than in the Late Empire,[54] when only certain regions such as Isauria and the some-time client state of Armenia had retained the habits and customs which produced good recruits.[55] So the units of the Eastern army were not easily kept up to

---

[48] xx. 8. 13.

[49] xx. 8. 15.

[50] D. Hoffmann (1969) 145 ff., argues that by 'Gauls', *laeti* are meant—not convincingly.

[51] D. Hoffmann (1969).

[52] D. Hoffmann (1969) 169. Amm. xxi. 1. 13, xxvi. 7. 17; xxxi. 7. 11; Vegetius iii. 78. Even in *Oriens* the *alae* and *cohortes* included units named after Alamans, Franks, Chamavi, Juthungi, Saxons: see above, n. 45, cf. Th. Mommsen (1910) 281–3.

[53] E. Patlagean (1977*b*) 232–5, 426–9.

[54] Synesius *De Regno* 1092: peasants not called up. Isaurians and Armenians were the exception that proves the rule. Under the early empire there had been widespread local recruitment for eastern legions: M. P. Speidel, 'Legionaires from Asia Minor', *ANRW* ii. 7. 2 730–46; J. C. Mann (1983) 41–45, 144–49.

[55] The principal internal source of recruits in the Byzantine army: A. H. M. Jones *LRE* 600 n. 120.

strength, and soldiers were precious. This was probably the principal reason for Constantius' reluctance to risk Roman casualties.[56]

The warlike qualities of the Isaurians had been displayed in brigandage for a long time before the Eastern government succeeded in harnessing them in the service of the Empire.[57] Brigandage was a problem in other parts of the Empire, notably in Gaul[58] and perhaps among the Samaritans of Palestine.[59] But as a rule the Empire was unable to exploit the fighting spirit that found expression in brigandage or banditry. It may be that the barbarian invaders, for instance Fritigern's Goths in Thrace in 376,[60] or Tribigild's Goths in Asia in 399, were better able to incorporate discontented or marginal elements of the population into their fighting forces.[61] This may explain how barbarians were frequently able to recover their fighting strength after what one might have thought a crippling defeat.[62]

The Visigoths had the institution of *commendatio* which enabled a man to recommend himself to a patron and to enter into *obsequium* towards him.[63] The man would become an armed follower of the patron, who would supply him with arms and a horse.[64] It can be argued that *commendatio* was only open to men of Gothic descent, but it is quite likely that a patron would admit any man who looked like a useful fighter, particularly if he was ready to join the Gothic Arian church. This was an age when provincials tended to look for protection to a personal patron rather than the institutions of city and Empire. According to the admittedly highly theoretical account of Salvian the society of Gaul was disintegrating and large numbers of peasants were seeking refuge among outlaws (*bagaudae*), or in the shelter of a powerful man's patronage, or among the barbarians.[65] In

---

[56] Constantius husbands his soldiers: Amm. xix. 3. 2, xxi. 13. 2, 16. 3; Libanius *Or.* lix. 88.   [57] K. Hopwood (1983).

[58] J. F. Drinkwater (1984); complete sources: B. Czuth (1965). Unrest was widespread: Armorica (Britany), the Alps, the Pyrenees.

[59] K. Holum (1982*b*), E. Patlagean (1977*b*) 299–300.

[60] Amm. xxxi. 64. 7. See also below, p. 77.

[61] Zos. v. 13. They might conceivably have been absorbed into the following of a noble. Cf. the great following, made up of *familia*, *clientes*, and *obaerati*, of Orgetorix the Helvetian, Caesar *B.G.* i. 4.

[62] Zos. v. 16–17, cf. Claudian *In Eutrop.* ii. 220–2 (Tribigild); note also the recovery of the Vandals between Hydatius 67–8 (disaster) and ibid. 90 and Procop. *B. Vand.* i. 18 (the evident recovery). For remarkable recoveries of Alaric's Goths, see below, p. 76. See also the recovery of the Ostrogoths under Totila after 541, starting with only 5000 men (*B. Got.* iii. 4. 1). Totila appealed to deserters and slaves (*B. Got.* iii. 12, 18, 23; iv. 33).

[63] *Leges Visig.* v. 3. 1 = C. *Euric* 310, ibid. 2 = C. *Euric* 311 (Saiones), ibid. 3.

[64] *Leges Visig.* v. 3. 4: the patron gives land. According to W. Kienast, (1968) 33, this is later than laws which refer to arms and other mobile gifts. On absorption of outsiders into Arab tribes see Ibn Khaldun, tr. F. Rosenthal (1958), chs. 9–11, 13.

[65] Salvian *de Gub. Dei* v. 22–4, 37–8, cf. Anon. Vales. 12. 61: 'the poor Roman imitates the Goth, while the rich Goth imitates the Roman'. Ambrose *Ep.* 10. 9 (*PL* xvi. 983): Julian

the circumstances the following of Germanic chieftains may well have had wide appeal.

By the time of the Late Empire demilitarization had certainly become a factor in the West too. Studies of recruitment for the Roman army in the Early Empire show how the civilian provinces gradually ceased to provide soldiers.[66] In addition there probably was some depopulation. This is suggested by the repeated issue of laws obliging landowners who have taken on the cultivation of abandoned land to become responsible for the taxes owed by the land.[67] On the evidence of this legislation land was being abandoned in both East[68] and the West,[69] and not only—as has been argued—by the owners responsible for the taxes, but by the cultivators as well.[70] The evidence of these laws is less conclusive than might appear at first sight. It is, for instance, by no means certain that in any particular case the abandonment was part of a long-term trend, rather than the consequence of a local and passing emergency.[71] Nevertheless the implications of this legislation are confirmed, especially in the West, by the scope for repeated settlement of barbarians in Gaul, Italy, and the Balkans.[72]

Archaeology is confirming the picture. In Gaul the destruction of rural settlements, only sometimes followed by resettlement, the going out of use of cemeteries, the settlement of armed Germans in areas that had evidently become depopulated, and the establishment of fortified hill-top settlements, cumulatively suggest a reduction of the population combined with some relocation. The gradual

Valens, exiled Arian bishop of Poetovio, ministers to Gothic soldiers (in Roman army) wearing Gothic torc and armlets. Synesius *De Prov.* 1261: 'Egyptians' (= Constantinopolitans) find it advantageous to adopt Gothic manners (σκυθίζουσιν). Priscus fr. 11. 2 p. 420 Blockley: a Greek on way to becoming a Hun? Cf. also n. 33 above on Romans who seem on the way to becoming Vandals.

[66] J. C. Mann (1983) 63–5. On the reversal of this process by 'militarization' in medieval Spain see E. Lourie (1966).

[67] e.g. *CT* v. 11. 7–12; v. 14. 30–34; vi. 2. 24.

[68] *CT* v. 11. 11 (386), 12 (391); v. 14. 30 (386), 31 (382), 33 (393); vii. 20. 3 (326); xi. 20. 5 (424), 6 (430); xii. 1. 123. 6 (391); Julian *Misopogon* 370 D (362).

[69] *CT* vii. 20. 8 (364), 11 (370); xi. 1. 10 (365); xi. 28. 12 (418). *Nov. Val.* xxxii. 5 (451), xxxiv. 3.

[70] W. Goffart (1974) 28 and 68 argues that 'deserted' land is land whose landlord registered as liable for the taxes could not be found. This certainly was a problem, e.g. *CJ* xi. 59. 1, but in the majority of the laws the government is concerned not only with taxes but also with bringing land back under cultivation.

[71] C. R. Whittaker, in M. I. Finley (1976) 137–65. G. Duby (1965) shows that in the Middle Ages abandonment after a serious recession was often temporary. P. Lemerle (1954) and V. Velkov (1962) produce evidence that even in the much invaded Balkans desertion of land was often not permanent. P. Vanangs (1979) argues that deserted land legislation aimed at countering the extension of great estates.

[72] G. E. M. de Ste Croix (1981) 509–18.

development goes back to the third century. It was most marked in the North and North-East. It was not produced by a single catastrophe.[73] While barbarian invasions and fear of barbarians are likely to have played an important part, it is probable that other social or economic factors were involved. Field surveys suggest that similar developments were taking place in Italy.[74]

But a reduction in population cannot be the whole story. Clearly even where the population was reduced there must have remained considerable manpower. Indeed the population of North Africa[75] and Britain[76] seems not to have fallen at all in the fourth century. Spain was practically untouched by war, and may conceivably have been as prosperous as Britain or North Africa, although there does seem to be evidence of urban decline from the mid fourth century.[77] There evidently was something else that prevented recruitment.

It is significant that there no longer seems to have been machinery for the mass call-up of a national army. The provision of recruits had become a tax on landowners, who were divided into *consortia* with the obligation to furnish a certain number of recruits between them. These people did not in fact organize a local conscription, but operated a kind of press-gang system, combining incentive payments with coercion, to induce a few individuals to enrol. Of the new recruits, some were unsuitable, and more extremely reluctant to serve. Even so, the duty of providing recruits was extremely unpopular with landowners, who preferred to commute the obligation into a money payment.[78] Money thus collected was used to hire

[73] Depopulation in northern Gaul: E. Wightman (1985) 243–66, also (1981). S. Walker (1981): radical changes in settlement pattern in Lyon region. W. Janssen (1976): the Franks settled only on the best land leaving the rest *empty*. Gradual migration of Franks emptied lands east of Rhine. Not even the Franks had surplus population. See also W. Janssen, in W. Janssen, D. Lohrmann (1983) 81–122: from mid-5th cent. forests on land formerly cultivated. P. Galliou (1981): breakdown of agricultural system in western Gaul.

[74] Decline in number of settlements in Southern Etruria and Molise from 3rd cent.: R. Hodges and D. Whitehouse (1983) 36–46, T. W. Potter (1979) 139–45. On Volturnus Valley: R. Hodge, J. Mitchell (1985); Biferno Valley: G. Barker, J. Lloyd, D. Webley (1987); J. Lloyd, G. Barker (1981). In Greece on the contrary, the 4th cent. saw a striking increase in occupied sites of population. J. L. Bintliff, A. M. Snodgrass (1985) 147 (Boeotia); C. N. Runnels (1983), C. N. Runnels and others (1986) 120–21 (Argolid). E. Wightman (1980) 31–2, (1981a) 34–5.

[75] C. Lepelley (1967), D. Pringle (1981) 112–13.

[76] Growing population in Britain? M. E. Jones (1979), otherwise P. J. Fowler (1978), B. Cunliffe (1978), who argue for high population for the early Roman period followed by decline.

[77] Spain: S. J. Keay (1981), P. J. Banks (1980), chs. vi–viii, thorough but unpublished.

[78] Recruiting tax: A. H. M. Jones *LRE* 615–16; branding of recruits: *CT* x. 22. 4 (398), Vegetius 2. 5. Senatorial resistance to recruiting: J. Matthews (1975) 268–9; no recruiting of Italian peasantry against Alaric: Claud. *B. Get.* 463. Inhabitants of Rome exempted: *Nov. Val.* v. 1. 2 (440); conscription ordered by emergency decree: *Nov. Val.* vi. 2. 1 (443). No conscription under Justinian: J. F. Haldon (1979) 24–7.

barbarians. It is by no means inevitable that such a system of recruiting would produce bad soldiers (after all, crews raised by the press-gang won the battle of Trafalgar[79]), but it must have been extremely difficult to raise large numbers of troops in this way.

One might think that the danger of the Empire would have produced numerous volunteers. In fact the danger was not realized widely. There was, furthermore, very little active imperial patriotism. If men worried about invaders they thought of defending their village, and not of enrolling for military operations that would take them hundreds of miles away. But without large scale spontaneous enrolment there was really no way of getting hold of the mass of the peasant population, even if manpower was available. In the 'good old days' of the Hannibalic War, when the Romans managed to call up an extraordinarily large proportion of the age groups liable to conscription, the efforts of the Roman magistrates must have been assisted by readiness and even eagerness to serve among the citizens. Citizenship meant something, and the Romans—and their allies— were militarized to an extraordinary degree.[80]

In the Later Empire military service was unpopular. Recruits had to be branded.[81] Even when provinces were threatened by barbarians there was no rush of volunteers to defend the Empire.[82] On the contrary: there was massive apathy, and we hear of a significant number of cases of discontented elements joining forces with the invaders. The Empire became more and more dependent on barbarian defenders. A relevant phenomenon was reluctance of landowners to see their tenants enrolled in the army. We have contemporary evidence for the successful efforts of the senators of Rome to prevent the conscription of their tenants at a time when Gildo, the rebellious commander in North Africa, was cutting off the food supply of Rome.[83] The ability of landowners to interfere with the government's effort to call up the peasantry was certainly much greater than under the Early Empire because a much larger proportion of land,

[79] Press-gang: S. F. Gradish (1980) 54–86.
[80] Republican levy: P. Brunt (1971) 625–34: enormous demands on man-power (K. Hopkins (1978) 32–4) surely could only have been met with local cooperation and eagerness to serve; cf. Balfour (1867) 216–92.
[81] *CT* x. 22. 4 (398), Vegetius 2. 5; see also *CT* vii. 18. 1–17 on deserters being often recent recruits.
[82] G. E. M. de Ste Croix (1981) 474–88; A. H. M. Jones *LRE* 1059–64 on defection to barbarians, indifference to the disintegration of the Roman empire, and peasant revolts. Relevant to study of the latter and of *bagaudae* is K. Hopwood (1983) 173–8, also 'Moonlighting in Isauria', unpublished.
[83] O. Seeck (1883) lxix; *CT* vii. 13. 12–14; Symm. *Ep.* vi. 58, 62, 64; and J. Matthews (1975) 268–9.

particularly in the West, was now part of large estates.[84] Moreover the weakening of the cities meant that even the independent country population attached itself for protection to the patronage of landed magnates.[85] One might ask why great landowners should be reluctant to allow tenants and dependents to serve in the army even at times of conspicuous emergency when danger threatened all classes alike. The answer may be—though it remains a conjecture—that the great men hoped to reach some arrangement with the invader which would safeguard their own interest and that of their people reasonably satisfactorily.[86] Be that as it may, it must have been very difficult indeed to carry out recruiting on a large scale in the face of obstruction by both peasantry and landowners. It is perhaps not surprising that the imperial government gave up the struggle and preferred the easier policy of enrolling barbarians,[87] who were extremely eager to enrol. It must have been tempting to make use of their keenness whenever the Empire needed to enrol a large number of recruits at a time. Often it will also have been cheaper. If the barbarians were enrolled in regular units they presumably served under the same conditions of pay and veteran provision as Romans. But the government might recruit 'federates' for the duration only, and so be able to disclaim all responsibility for their maintenance once they had done the fighting for which they had been recruited.[88]

The Late Roman military system bore some superficial resemblance to that of the Early Empire. Both systems made use of citizen and non-citizen soldiers, though under the Late Roman system the two were not rigidly separated into different units. It was no doubt hoped that non-Roman troops recruited beyond the frontier, being without homes and families in the Empire, and unable to marry Roman wives, would offer less resistance to movement orders than citizens would do. In theory—though not, as we have seen, always in practice—they should have been as mobile as the unmarried soldier of the Early Empire, and therefore particularly well suited for the arduous service

[84] Estates and remaining peasant holdings: A. H. M. Jones *LRE* 781–84, E. Wightman (1985) 263–6, A. Mocsy (1974) 299 ff., G. Alföldy (1974) 173 ff., (1979) 173–4. Moderate landowners at Milan: L. Cracco Ruggini, G. Cracco (1977) 453. Ownership unequal but stable without evidence for growth of very large estates at Hermopolis: A. K. Bowman (1985).

[85] One aspect of patronage is the regrouping of tax-payers to resist the heavy exactions, including the levy of recruits, demanded by the Empire. All factors which favoured the 'tied colonate' would also have obstructed the moving of tenants into the armed forces.

[86] Macedonian cities reached agreements with Goths: Zos. iv. 31. 5; perhaps also Nicopolis ad Istrum: Eunap. fr. 47. 1 Blockley = 50 Müller.

[87] A. H. M. Jones *LRE* 618–19; Amm. xix. 11. 7, xxxi. 1. 44; Pacatus *Pan. Lat.* xii. 32: no conscription before Maximus campaign; Claudian *B. Get.* 463: no conscription of peasants to meet Alaric in 402.

[88] On federates see below, p. 32 ff.

in field army units constantly being moved from crisis area to crisis area to meet attacks on widely separated frontiers.[89] Besides, in contrast with the Early Empire, it was among non-Roman soldiers that the more formidable fighting men were now found, and eventually at least officers of non-Roman origin were more likely to rise to the most important military commands.

How did this huge infusion of foreigners into the Roman defence forces work? It certainly helped that the Germans appear to have had little national feeling. There is very little evidence for disloyalty motivated by tribal solidarity.[90] Then the Germans will not have seemed totally foreign, as the gap between soldiers drawn from the provincial population and soldiers recruited beyond the borders was filled by men who belonged to the same German tribes as the volunteers from across the border, but who had been settled within the Empire and were becoming assimilated to the Roman way of life. One must also remember that commercial and military intercourse over many years had created a 'frontier' civilization. The frontier of the Empire was ceasing to be a cultural boundary.[91] If the majority of the men of a unit were barbarians there will have been no difficulty, and indeed considerable advantage, in having German or other barbarian officers, even if the officers did not belong to the same nation as the majority of their men.[92]

Recruiting across the frontier was presumably one aspect of the diplomatic relations with tribes and their leaders across the frontier which were being continuously maintained by the Roman authorities. The Late Roman army included many regular units named after foreign peoples. It is likely that many were first raised on the basis of a treaty between the Empire and a native people, whether a treaty to end a war or an alliance in time of peace.[93] Regimental names recall different frontiers. Assyrians, Parthians, Armenians, Sacraceni originated across the Mesopotamian frontier. Hiberi, Tzanni, and Abasgi came from the region of the Caucasus, and Sarmatians and Marcomanni from beyond the Danube.[94] Numerous

[89] They still resented transfer: Amm. xx. 4. 4.

[90] A. H. M. Jones *LRE* 621–2.

[91] Frontier civilization: metalwork on both sides of frontier: J. Werner (1950), H. Bullinger (1969), H. Kuhn (1974); linguistic evidence: B. Gerov (1959), J. P. Wild (1976). Mutual assimilation of Dacians, Romans and later Goths: R. Vulpe (1961), esp. 389, B. Scardigli (1976) 272–77, G. Diaconu (1975), I. Ionita (1975). A 'buffer zone' where some Roman money circulated and objects resembled those found on Roman side of frontier: L. Hedeager (1978), M. G. Fulford (1985), D. Protase (1964).

[92] Many Sarmatians were enrolled, but only one, Victor, rose to the top: U.-B. Dittrich (1984).

[93] Conveniently assembled in Th. Mommsen (1910) 280–83.

[94] See Index Geographicus in Seeck's edition of *ND* for individual units.

units with German names evidently originated east of the Rhine.[95] The homes of the Atecotti were in Scotland.[96]

Diplomacy across the frontier required the maintenance of close relations with tribal leaders. Awards of commissions in the Roman army surely helped to preserve good relations. Valentinian I, for instance, gave commissions and commands to Fromarius, an Alamannic king, and to Hortarius II and Bitherid who were leading Alamannic nobles (*primates*).[97] Indeed of all the not very large number of officers whose name is known to us a surprisingly high proportion were barbarian kings or nobles, who had received commissions immediately on entering.[98] In view of the social structure of Germanic tribes it is likely that chieftains would be followed into the imperial army by considerable numbers of followers. German officers and perhaps German soldiers too had very good prospects of promotion, especially if they entered the guard units (*scholae*) and became personally known to the emperor, and indeed to court-society as a whole.[99] They enjoyed the best possible start for a successful military career.

It was essential for the working of the system that the emperor should maintain close relations with leading generals. The Late Empire saw a complete separation of the civilian administration headed by the praetorian prefects and the military administration headed by the *magistri militum*.[100] The gap was widened by the fact that officers and civilian administrators normally came from different social backgrounds. The senatorial order was almost entirely civilian.[101] The same was true of the curial class of the great cities of the Empire. For instance, very few of the pupils of Libanius intended to follow a military career.[102] Officers might have risen from the ranks. More often presumably they were the sons of officers. One would also imagine that some originated among the wealthy class of the less civilized parts of the Empire, and very many were, as we have seen, of barbarian origin. The two hierarchies were united only at the very top by the person of the emperor, who headed both. For most of

---

[95] e.g. Juthungi, Alamanni, Bucinobantes, Brisigavi, Mattiaci, Tubantes.

[96] Jer. *Ep.* 69 ad Ocean.: 'Scottorum et Atecottorum ritu . . . promiscuas uxores, communes liberos habeant.'

[97] B. Stallknecht (1969) 59. *PLRE* i. s.v. Hortarius 2, Bitherid.

[98] See *PLRE* i s.v. Vadomarius (Alaman), Hormisdas (Persian), Mallobaudes (Frank), Bacurius (Iberian), Fravitta (Goth), Richomer (Frank), Arbogastes (Frank), Bauto (Frank), Modares, Pusaeus (Persian), Fraomarius (Alaman). See A. H. M. Jones *LRE* 642; D. Hoffmann (1978) 307–18.

[99] Cf. M. Waas (1965) 10. F. Fremersdorf, 'Christliche Leibwächter auf einem geschliffenen kölner Glasbecher', *Festschrift R. Egger* (Klagenfurt, 1952) 66–83.

[100] A. Demandt (1980).

[101] A. H. M. Jones *LRE* 545 ff.   [102] P. Petit (1957) 166.

the fourth century emperors alone were required to show the competence in both civil and military leadership which had been taken for granted in public figures of the Republic and Early Empire. Even so, there was a tendency for the emperor to become a purely civilian head of state permanently in residence in the capital city, who left leadership in war to professional generals.

The emperor's role as a link between the two hierarchies was helped by the fact that rulers not themselves born into the reigning imperial family almost invariably had been officers themselves, though strangely enough never officers who had risen to the top of the career as *magister militum*.[103] It is also a fact that, as if to maintain neutrality between the two hierarchies, emperors very rarely married into the senatorial nobility, or even into the family of a praetorian prefect or other high minister. On the other hand the emperor might link himself by marriage to an important general. The first case was that of Constantius II, who married a daughter of the *magister militum* Flavius Eusebius.[104] The device came to be systematically employed by Theodosius I and his sons. Theodosius arranged for his niece and adopted daughter Serena to marry Stilicho, an officer of Vandal origin obviously destined for the highest commands.[105] A nephew of the empress, Flacilla, was married to Salvina, daughter of Gildo, a Mauretanian chieftain and commander-in-chief in North Africa. Theodosius had the sons of the general Promotus brought up with his own.[106] In view of the close relationship between the family of that general and the house of Theodosius, it is perhaps not a coincidence that Arcadius, the elder son of Theodosius, in 395 married a young lady who lived in the house of one of the sons of Promotus.[107] This was Eudoxia, the orphaned daughter of Bauto and sister (according to one source) of Arbogast. Perhaps Eudoxia's marriage was the fulfilment, under unforeseen circumstances, of a scheme of Theodosius.[108]

The systematic use of marriage between generals and members of the Theodosian family was something new. It was a response to the enormous power that had come to be exercised by the commander-in-chief in the West, and this in turn was at least in part a consequence of the military crisis faced by the Empire since the disastrous battle of Adrianople in 378. Up to Adrianople it could not be maintained that the inclusion of so many non-Romans made the armies of the later Empire less effective than earlier Roman armies. Up to that disaster the imperial army seems to have done all that was asked of

[103] A. H. M. Jones *LRE* 326–9.   [104] *PLRE* i s.v. Fl. Eusebius 39.
[105] Ibid. s.v. Serena.   [106] Ibid. s.v. Nebridius 3, Salvina.   [107] Zos. v. 3. 2.
[108] Zos. loc. cit.; *PLRE* ii s.v. Aelia Eudoxia 1; John of Antioch fr. 187: sister of Arbogast.

it with traditional efficiency. It was a mercenary army, but history can provide many other examples of mercenary armies of great effectiveness. One might mention the Indian army of the British 'Raj', or the Prussian army of Frederick the Great. A. H. M. Jones has pointed out how little evidence there is that German troops of the Roman army were likely to put their German tribal loyalties before loyalty to the Emperor.[109] When young barbarians were enrolled in Roman units mixed with experienced soldiers and trained by officers and NCOs of long service, they became simply professional soldiers.

The situation was transformed in 378 because a very large part of the army was destroyed at one blow. Since it was no longer a national army the losses could not be replaced by mass conscription as they had been after Cannae. Troops had to be found in view of the barbarian threat, but the units that replaced those lost at Adrianople were neither as effective as the old units, nor in many cases as reliable.[110] It was the Eastern field army that was destroyed, and it was the army of the East that displayed the symptoms of degeneration first. But the West found it equally difficult to recover from the losses of a series of internal and external wars, and within twenty years or so the symptoms of decline were conspicuous there also. According to Vegetius Roman infantry retained its traditional efficiency until the death of the Western Emperor Gratian, who was killed by the usurper Magnus Maximus in 383. Subsequently traditional military drill was given up and the traditional armour including breastplates and helmets went out of use—perhaps because the soldiers were no longer sufficiently fit to carry the heavy weight.[111] Henceforth Roman infantry went into battle with no better protection than their barbarian opponents, and lost the great advantage in discipline and equipment which had brought them victory against numerical odds in so many engagements in the past.[112]

[109] *LRE* 621–2.

[110] A. H. M. Jones's remarks on the superiority of later Roman armies (*LRE* 1036–7) are not valid after Adrianople.

[111] Vegetius *R. Mil.* i. 20, cf. A. Ferrill (1986) 129. If Vegetius wrote soon after 378 (see T. D. Barnes 1979) the relaxation of training was earlier.

[112] E. A. Thompson (1965) 111 ff.

3

The Consequences of Adrianople
Rebuilding the Army

AFTER the heavy losses incurred at the battle of Adrianople[1] Theodosius I, the new emperor of the Eastern Empire, tried desperately to rebuild his field army. Peasants were called up and even miners.[2] Units were transferred from the eastern frontier.[3] Above all, Goths were enrolled on a very large scale, a dangerous procedure considering that they were to be used against their compatriots.[4] They were mingled with Romans in the units of the army and, if Zosimus is to be believed,[5] came to form a majority of the troops. To reduce the proportion of newly-enrolled Goths in the Balkan army some were sent to Egypt, to be replaced by individuals transferred from units of the Egyptian army.[6] Not surprisingly the new army did not prove very effective. In 380 it suffered a serious defeat, for which leakage of military information by Goths on the Roman side to the enemy was thought to be largely responsible.[7]

Laws reveal the emperor's preoccupation with conscription.[8] In addition, and especially after the defeat of 380, Theodosius made great efforts to enrol troops in the frontier zones of the Empire and across the frontier. They seem to have been organized in ethnic units.[9] Our information comes from excessively rhetorical or poetical sources, but since few units raised at this time appear in the *Notitia Dignitatum*[10] it is likely that most of them were 'federate', that is,

---

[1] D. Hoffmann (1969) 448–58; Th. Burns (1973).
[2] Themistius xiv. 181 b; Libanius ii. 251, xxiv. 16.
[3] Lib. xxiv. 38.
[4] Zos. iv. 30–31.
[5] Zosimus is strongly anti-Theodosian: iv. 28.   [6] Zos. iv. 30.   [7] Ibid. 31.
[8] CT vii. 13. 8 (29. 1. 380): slaves, tavern workers, cooks, and craftsmen not to be recruited. vii. 19. 9 (26. 4. 380): recruits to be of good character. vii. 13. 10 (5. 9. 381): self-mutilated must serve. vii. 13. 11 (15. 5. 382): penalty for offering another's slave. vii. 22. 9 (14. 5. 380), 10 (8. 7. 380): sons of soldiers compelled to serve, cf. xii. 1. 83 (14. 5. 380). vii. 18. 3 (29. 4. 380), 5 (16. 1. 381), 6 (2. 4. 382), 7 (12. 7. 383): deserters hidden on great estates.
[9] Them. xvi. 207 (383): Celts, Assyrians, Libyans, Iberians; xxxiv. 20: in addition to troops of East and West soldiers from Tigris and Armenia; xv. 189 d, xviii. 219 b: Armenians, Iberians. Claudian's descriptions of the army of Theodosius (after 394) also suggest that it was composed of a mass of different national or tribal units. *In Ruf.* ii. 108 ff., *iii Cons. Hon.* 68 ff., *B. Gild.* i. 243 ff., *Cons. Stil.* i. 155 ff.
[10] D. Hoffmann (1969) 467–8.

contingents from 'allied' tribes in or outside the Empire, sometimes serving under their own chieftains.[11]

With the reinforced army and with the very active cooperation of the Western emperor Gratian operating from Illyricum, Theodosius managed to keep the Goths in check, but was far from being able to impose his will on them. Gratian first came to an agreement with the Goths under Alatheus and Saphrac and their Alan allies.[12] The miserable sources scarcely allow us to reconstruct the terms. It has often been assumed that they were simply settled on land.[13] But this is not necessary.[14] It may be that all, or some, were simply provided with quarters and pay and treated as part of the field-army.[15] The fact that these barbarians were accompanied by families need not have prevented them from being treated like soldiers on active service. Regular soldiers too were at the time accompanied by significant numbers of camp followers.[16] It may be that some of the men of Alatheus and Safrac were recruited individually into cavalry units on the frontiers.[17] There is no agreement about their location under the treaty. One suggestion is the valley of the Dravus near Poetovio,[18] another the province of Savia.[19] Saproni has pointed out that the absence of Germanic finds between the rivers Drave and Save suggests that the Goths were not settled in this area but in groups as *limitanei* on the *limes* of the three Pannonian provinces.[20] If the bulk of these Goths were settled (or stationed) near the *limes*, with some

[11] On different types of federates see below, pp. 34–9.

[12] This is the standard view, not conclusively supported by the sources; it still seems the most satisfactory reconciliation of Zos. v. 33 and Jordanes *Getica* xxvii (139)–xxviii (145), each of which has serious confusions. The argument is too long for a footnote. When Theodosius marched against Maximus large numbers of Goths, Huns, and Alans joined his army on the march, seemingly in Pannonia. Since the Moesian federates surely formed part of his army from the start, these were presumably the federates stationed in Pannonia since the agreement with Gratian (Pacatus *Pan. Lat.* xii. 32). Them. xv. 283 (Downey) of Jan. 381 envisages campaigns by *both* emperors against Goths in the spring. This does not exclude the possibility that Gratian had already made peace with one group of more remote Goths.

[13] e.g. H. Wolfram (1979) 155–6.

[14] E. Demougeot (1979) II i. 185–90 ascribes the recruiting of settled barbarians into frontier squadrons of cavalry to Stilicho after 400.

[15] Jordanes *Get.* 141: 'pacemque, victualia illis concedens, cum ipsis inito foedere fecit'. Amm. xxxi. 6–1 shows that the Gothic nobles Sueridus and Colias together with their followers (*populis suis*) were stationed in this way near Adrianople in winter quarters. Cf. also the band attacked by regulars under Gerontius: Zos. iv. 40. 1. Is SHA *Firmus, Saturninus, Proculus* and *Bonosus* 15.6 a satire on the awarding of *annona* to barbarian tribes as if they were military units? 'ut optimates Gothicas apud Perinthum conlocares decretis salariis, non ut singulae acciperent, sed ut simul unum convivium haberent.'

[16] *CT* vii. 1. 10 (367). These seem to have lived inside camps: C. M. Daniels (1979).

[17] *ND Oc.* xxxii. 22–38, xxxiii. 24–45, powerful forces—or into the guard of the empress Justina, who was prevented by Ambrose from offering them a church for Arian services: Ambrose *Ep.* 20.1.

[18] A. Mocsy (1974) 341.

[19] J. W. Eadie (1982) 27.   [20] S. Soproni (1985).

individuals recruited into existing frontier units, that might explain how Pannonia II and Valeria managed to maintain so many cavalry formations around AD 400.[21] That the mass of the Goths were stationed in one area rather than dispersed among the forts of the very long frontier would help to explain the volatile and mobile role which the Gothic and Alan tribesmen of Pannonia, which some scholars have identified with the band of Saphrax and Alatheus,[22] were to play in the following decades.[23] If the theory is true the 'settled' barbarians of Pannonia retained the mobility and cohesion of a mobile army.

About a year later, 3 October 382, the general Saturninus made a treaty with the Visigoths who had been led by Fritigern,[24] which ended the war by compromise. The settlement starts a new epoch in the history of the Empire. For good and ill it set a precedent which had many subsequent imitators. Unfortunately the sources are extremely unsatisfactory,[25] and it is impossible to reconstruct the agreement with any degree of certainty. It is unclear whether all the Goths were treated the same or whether separate arrangements were made for different sections of them. The latter is more likely. Themistius leaves no room to doubt that many Goths were settled as farmers.[26] We know that in the last phase of the frontier in Tripolitania and Numidia-Mauretania frontier defence seems to have been in the hands of local tribesmen commanded by local chiefs, given the imperial rank of *tribunus* or *praefectus* with their headquarters in a fort or *centenarium*.[27] It is quite likely that Goths were settled in the frontier region under their own chieftains in the same way and with the same purpose. On the other hand we are also

---

[21] See n. 6 above. E. Demougeot (1979).

[22] G. Alföldy (1974) 341–5; L. Varady (1969) 31–3, 36–9; H. Wolfram (1979) 154–5, 310–11.

[23] Campaigns for the Empire in 388, 393, and perhaps 402, separated by periods of marauding in Pannonia.

[24] The date: *Chron. Minor* i. 243 'universa genus Gothorum cum rege suo in Romaniam se tradiderunt die V non. Oct.' The chronicle does not name the king. Orosius vii. 34. 7, Zos. iv. 34, Jordanes *Get.* 142 link the treaty with Goths with Athanaric, which is certainly wrong as he had died on 25 January 381 (*Chron. Minor* i. 243). Perhaps some (now lost) official version had deliberately confused the surrender of Athanaric with the treaty in which the Empire made great concessions, in order to make the agreement seem less humiliating for the Empire. Them. *Or.* xvi. 256. 7, spoken soon after the agreement, implies that there was no supreme leader of the Goths, referring to ἔξαρχοι καὶ κορυφαῖοι who swore the treaty. In subsequent years the Goths had no king.

[25] Them. xvi. 211, xxxiv. 22; cf. also Pacatus *Pan. Lat.* xii. 22. 3, 32. 3–4; Synesius *De Regno* 19–21; Jordanes *Get.* 145; Procop. *BGot.* iv. 5. 13. On the agreement see H. Wolfram (1979) 156–7, E. Demougeot (1974). On agreements with Goths see M. Cesa, *Studi Urbinati* LVII (1984), 63–99.

[26] Goths as farmers: Them. *Or.* xvi. 11. 27, xxxiv. 227 ff., Pacatus *Pan. Lat.* xii. 22. 3, Synesius *De Regno* 29 (1093 B).

[27] Tripolitania: R. G. Goodchild *JRS* xl (1950) 30–38, P. Trousset (1974), August. *Ep.* 46–7. Numidia-Mauretania: J. F. Matthews (1976).

told that Goths shared the same roof with Roman ὁμωροφίους.[28]
I would suggest that these Goths were not settled as farmers at all but
billeted as actual or potential soldiers. Significantly they are said
to have shared the homes not only of Thracians but also of
Macedonians. They were therefore not all stationed in the frontier
zone. It is likely that the Goths who shared the homes of Thracians
and Macedonians were treated as part of the field army, on conditions
similar to those given to at least some of the Pannonian Goths in 382,
and repeatedly offered to Alaric's Goths in subsequent years.

The settled Goths are thought to have been given land to farm in
Thrace, that is, in the province of Moesia Secunda between the
Danube and the mountains, an area in which the Goths seem to have
taken roots during the previous campaigning. In 378 they had
established permanent 'garrisons' around Nicopolis ad Istrum and
Beroea, that is, on both sides of the Balkan chain.[29] In 379 or 380
Nicopolis was attacked by the Goths, and possibly came to an
agreement with them.[30] Goths were still found near Nicopolis more
than 150 years later.[31]

The Goths agreed to provide troops for the Roman army. These
certainly included two 'regular' units, the Visi and the Teruingi.[32] In
addition they provided federate units, led by Gothic officers for
particular campaigns.[33] There can be no doubt that many Goths
enlisted as individuals,[34] humble Goths in the ranks, noble Goths as
officers with excellent prospects of promotion.[35] It can be assumed
that the Gothic leaders who accepted this agreement[36] continued to
have jurisdiction over their settled or billeted tribesmen. But it was

---

[28] Synesius *De Regno* 15, Them. xxxiv. 24. 228.
[29] Amm. xxxi. 11. 2. Valens had intended to give them land in Thrace (Amm. xxxi. 4. 5).
[30] Eunapius fr. 47 Blockley; cf. Zos. iv. 31. 5: Macedonian cities pay money to Goths.
[31] Jordanes *Get.* 267.
[32] *ND Or.* v. 61, vi. 61. E. Demougeot (1979) 154 suggests that the Visi were provided by
Goths that had been Fritigern's, the Tervingi by those of Athanaric.
[33] No doubt a young Gothic noble could join the imperial army with a unit he had raised
among settled Goths, like young Theodoric in 471: 'ascitis centis ex satellitibus patris et ex
populo amatores sibi clientes' (Jordanes *Get.* 282). But officers were not necessarily appointed
by the tribesmen see below, pp. 54 and 100.
[34] So presumably the Goths serving under Roman officers massacred in the East on orders of
Julius the *mag. mil. per Orientem* in 378 (Amm. xxxi. 16. 8). Zos. iv. 26 makes these Goths
young hostages, but Ammianus is to be believed. Later Gainas' Goths too (see below, p. ooo)
presumably enlisted individually, as did Goths mingled with Romans in regular units: Zos. iv. 31.
[35] See *PLRE* i s.v. Fravitta, Gainas, Modares, Munderichus, Tribigild.
[36] *Nothing* is known of the government of the settled Goths, but the facts that their sense of
tribal identity survived so strongly, that most of them did not receive citizenship, and that
Gothic units were led by Gothic nobles all suggest that they continued to be ruled by their own
leaders in accordance with their old customs—as far as still relevant. Survival of Gothic
customs: Synesius *De Regno* 1091. Huns settled with their tribal leaders, Eunapius fr. 60. 1
Blockley = 61 Müller.

hoped that the Goths would be assimilated in the same way as the Galatians, the Celtic invaders of Asia Minor, had been assimilated long since.[37] Meanwhile the Goths were not given *connubium*, the right to enter into legal marriage with a Roman citizen.[38]

After the treaty the Tervingi and Romans were at peace. In 386 a Gothic group (Greuthungi) under Odotheus crossed the Danube in order to enter the Empire. They were promptly defeated by the general Promotus, who transported the survivors to Phrygia, where they were settled on land, to provide men for a cavalry unit (*ala*). These probably were the people who were to mutiny under Tribigild and to cause a crisis in the affairs of the Eastern Empire in 398.[39]

In 387 Theodosius felt sufficiently confident to attempt to overthrow Magnus Maximus who had proclaimed himself Augustus in the West in 383, had killed Gratian, and subsequently in 387 expelled Valentinian II from Italy. Theodosius had waited several years before deciding that Maximus was not to be tolerated.[40] No wonder, for to attack Maximus required war against Western armies which had not suffered the disaster at Adrianople. Furthermore good recruits had always been easier to find in the Western provinces of the Empire. It was therefore an act of considerable boldness for the emperor of the East to challenge the Western army. Once again he seems to have relied largely on federates. In the years leading up to the campaign Theodosius seems to have created comparatively few new regular units, perhaps six new *auxilia*.[41] But his expeditionary force was remarkable for the number of its national units; Goths, Huns, Alans, Iberians, and Isaurians are mentioned.[42]

We do not know to what extent tribal contingents were officered by tribal chieftains in the campaigns against Maximus. In the later campaigns against Eugenius it looks as if blocks of units provided by a particular tribe were commanded by a man of the same tribal origin, but a professional officer, not a tribal chieftain. At any rate Gainas, Saul, and Bacurius, the three commanders of federate troops,[43] were respectively a Goth, an Alan, and an Armenian, and their origins correspond to each of the three main providers of federates, the Thracian Tervingi, the Goths and Alans stationed in Pannonia, and the

[37] Them. xvi. 211–12.

[38] *CT* iii. 14, Eunapius fr. 59 Blockley = 60 Müller.

[39] Zos. v. 13 and below, p. 100. The earliest reference to *Ostrogoths* is Claudian *In Eutrop.* ii. 153.

[40] J. Matthews (1975) 223–5.

[41] D. Hoffmann (1969) 467.

[42] Pacatus *Pan. Lat.* xii. 32. 3–4, 33. 4–5; Ambrose *Ep.* 40. 22.

[43] Zos. iv. 57; for biographies see *PLRE* i. Saul is probably identical with the Saul in *PLRE* ii. 981 who commanded the Romans at the start of the battle of Pollentia (402).

Armenians, who were the principal source of federates in the East.[44] It is surely likely that each officer commanded his kinsmen, with Gainas occupying the most senior position, which might be compared to the later office of *comes foederatorum*.[45]

The campaign was successful. Maximus was crushed. His army was taken over by Theodosius, who now at last had under his command a sufficiently large number of soldiers to be in a position to rebuild the regular army of the Eastern Empire. He did this by incorporating a considerable number of units of the Western field army into that of the East. It is this new army essentially that is described in the chapters of the *Notitia* listing the units of the two praesental armies of the Eastern emperor.[46]

[44] Confirmed for Gainas and Saul by Eunapius fr. 60 Blockley = John of Antioch fr. 187. See also D. Hoffman (1974) esp. 396–7: the two praesental armies were administrative, not tactical, organizations. Otherwise A. H. M. Jones *LRE* iii. 347.

[45] A. H. M. Jones *LRE* 663–6, J. Haldon (1984) 100. References to two *comites foederatorum* in 5th cent., Areobindus (Malalas 364, cf. *PLRE* ii s.v. Areobindus), Patriciolus (Theophanes a.m. 6005, cf. *PLRE* ii. 837), need not be anachronistic.

[46] D. Hoffmann (1969) 490–516.

4
Regulars, Federates, and *Bucellarii*

IN the previous chapters repeated mention has been made of federate troops. Federates have been distinguished both explicitly and implicitly from regular soldiers. The difference between these categories of troops has not, however, been defined. In fact there is no incident for which the evidence is full enough to provide a clear picture of the conditions of service of the various categories of troops involved. In order to get a more complete picture of late Roman federates it is necessary to take evidence from a succession of campaigns even if that involves referring to events which are dealt with in greater detail in later sections of this book.

In accounts of campaigns after 378, as for instance Theodosius' expedition against the usurper Maximus in 388,[1] or against Eugenius in 393,[2] the Eastern army is divided into units of two kinds, Romans and barbarians. This distinction appears in accounts of every campaign for which we have literary evidence.[3] The division does not mean that some units were composed of Roman citizens while the others were made up of barbarians. Roman units too included a good proportion of soldiers of non-Roman origin.[4] The difference appears to be one between regular units and units that were not part of the regular army. The distinction is made so consistently that it must correspond to a formal division within Roman army units.[5] Late Roman campaigning armies must have been made of regular units together with auxiliaries, entirely or almost entirely recruited from barbarians, that did not count as regular units.

There has survived a survey of the Late Roman army, the famous *Notitia Dignitatum*.[6] This seems to represent the disposition of the

---

[1] Tribal units: Ambrose *Ep.* 40. 22, Pacatus *Pan. Lat.* xii. 39. 2; barbarians in Roman units: Zos. iv. 31, 45. 3.

[2] Zos. iv. 57; John Ant. fr. 187 (*FHG* iv. 609).

[3] Gainas in 396: Theodoret *HE* v. 32. 1; Socr. vi. 6 (text uncertain); cf. Soz. viii. 4. 1. Tribigild revolt in 398: Zos. v. 13. 2; 17. 1; 18. 10.

[4] See D. Hoffmann (1969) 81–3 on evidence of Concordia sarcophagi; ibid. 137 ff. on the Germans recruited into *auxilia* in contrast with citizens into legions; ibid. 299 on Germans in the *scholae*. But after 378 Germans were recruited into all kinds of Roman units: Zos. iv. 31. A unit of Germans and Gauls on Julian's Persian expedition: Amm. xxv. 6. 13. Captured Lentienses mingled with Roman recruits: Amm. xxxi. 10. 18. Goths mingled with Romans on Maximus' campaign: Zos. iv. 45.

[5] Most clearly in the narrative of the fall of Stilicho: Zos. v. 31. 33; 33–5.

[6] O. Seeck (1876), G. Clemente (1968).

regiments of the Eastern empire around 394, while the Western lists appear to have been brought up to date until around 420.[7] The *Notitia* distinguishes between different classes of units, but it shows no sign of a distinction between regular units and foreign irregulars. True, there is an important class of crack infantry units described as *auxilia palatina*, whose title suggests that they were originally recruited from barbarians, and which—as we have seen—never ceased to include a high proportion of men of barbarian origin.[8] But the soldiers, or at least the officers serving in these units, appear to have become Roman citizens. At any rate a majority of them seem to have borne the name (or title) of Flavius.[9] It is extremely unlikely that these regular units could have been described simply as barbarians or that they were classified as federates. On the other hand campaigning armies regularly appear to have included units which are not listed in the *Notitia*. The tribal units mentioned in the literary sources seem to have been omitted.[10] Most strikingly the Goths who figure so prominently in the narrative of Theodosius' campaign against Eugenius, in which they are said to have lost 10,000 dead,[11] are represented in the *Notitia* by no more than two regiments,[12] that is, at most 2,000 men.[13] It is likely that the bulk of the Goths were enrolled in barbarian regiments which are not shown in the *Notitia*. Presumably they were to be sent home and disbanded after the campaign.

Another indication that the lists are incomplete is that the Western field army has been given very few cavalry units.[14] The proportion of cavalry in the Western field armies is likely to have been as high as in the East, that is, approximately one third. So presumably on campaign the army was accompanied by a considerable number of cavalry units which are not mentioned in the *Notitia*. A high proportion of cavalry is likely to have been recruited from barbarians.[15]

[7] On this much discussed question: A. H. M. Jones *LRE* iii. 347–80, also J.-C. Mann (1976), J. H. Ward (1974), E. Demougeot (1975).

[8] D. Hoffmann (1969) 130–73.

[9] D. Hoffmann (1969) 76–78 (sarcophagus inscriptions from Concordia). Mocsy (1964) suggests that the few privates with the Flavius title inherited it from fathers who were officers. On the Flavius title see Alan Cameron, R. S. Bagnall, K. A. Worp (1987) 36–40.

[10] e.g. Armenians and Iberians: Them. *Or.* xvi. 207 a of AD 383, xv. 189 d of 381, and xviii. 219 of 384. Also in Stilicho's army in 395: see D. Hoffmann (1969) ii. 191 n. 268.

[11] Jordanes *Get.* 145: 20,000 Goths; Orosius vii. 35: 10,000 dead; cf. Zos. iv. 58. Socr. v. 25: volunteers from across the Danube, presumably individually recruited.

[12] *ND Or.* v. 20: Visi, Teruingi.

[13] A. H. M. Jones *LRE* 680–2.

[14] D. Hoffmann (1969) 193 ff.

[15] Cavalry could only be recruited in certain regions of the empire, especially in the Balkans and North Africa, also from barbarians across the border, e.g. the *comites* of Amm. xviii. 9. 4, cf. D. Hoffmann (1969) 243 ff.

In 398–9 in the East the barbarians of Tribigild[16] and Gainas[17] certainly included a high proportion of cavalry. Against Radagaisus in 404–6 Stilicho employed many Huns and Alans as allied cavalry, in addition to 30 units of regular Roman troops.[18] But if allied cavalry has been omitted, the reason is likely to be that allied units (*foederati*) in general did not qualify for inclusion in the *Notitia*.

Omission of *foederati* units would be quite natural if they were not part of the permanent establishment but had only been enrolled for a particular campaign. It appears to be a fact that at this period the standing army was not large enough to deal with emergencies as they arose, so that major wars like Stilicho's operations against Alaric in 397,[19] or 401–2,[20] or against Radagaisus in 405–6,[21] were preceded by desperate recruiting campaigns. We also know that Stilicho made agreements with Alaric with a view to having Alaric's Goths as allies in campaigns which he was planning against the government of the Eastern Empire[22] and against the usurper Constantine in Gaul.[23] The employment of barbarian allies for the duration had obvious financial advantages. It enabled the government to manage with a much smaller permanent army, as the Eastern government at any rate seems to have done[24]—and to save the cost of the retirement benefit which was owed to regulars after twenty or more years of service.[25]

That allied peoples beyond the frontiers or client kings provided units to assist the imperial army for the duration of a campaign goes back to the early days of the Roman Empire.[26] So the army which Vespasian led to suppress the Jewish revolt included 15,000 men supplied by Eastern client kings.[27] The armies of client kings eventually ended up as part of the imperial army when their kingdom was incorporated.[28] But the same kind of help continued to be required from barbarian rulers beyond the frontier in treaty relations with the Empire.[29] Constantine, for instance, made a treaty with the Goths which put them under an obligation to provide troops in

---

[16] Zos. v. 15. 5; 16. 1.   [17] Synesius *De Prov.* ii. 1 (1260 BC).

[18] Zos. v. 26.

[19] Claud. *IV Cons. Hon.* 485 ff. of AD 398, cf. Alan Cameron (1970) 375. Some German offers of recruits rejected: *I. Cons. Stil.* 234–5. Earlier the large new army which Theodosius led against Eugenius was reinforced with numerous federates recruited on the march: Socr. v. 25.

[20] *B. Get.* 401–3, 463–6, cf. 105–6.

[21] *CT* vii. 13. 16–17 (406); Hun and Alan federates: Zos. v. 26.

[22] Zos. v. 27, 29.

[23] Zos. v. 31.

[24] At the expense of regular subsidies to barbarians, and of having to leave one frontier undefended when campaigning on another, e.g. B. Croke (1977) 347–67. See also the inadequate defence of Mesopotamia in early 6th cent.: Josh. Styl. *Chron.* 53, 81.

[25] A. H. M. Jones *LRE* 635–6.   [26] H. Callies (1964).

[27] Josephus *BJ* iii. 4. 2, cf. ii. 18. 9 and E. N. Luttwak (1976) 27.

[28] D. B. Saddington (1982), D. L. Kennedy (1977).   [29] G. Wirth (1967).

return for subsidies.[30] Constantius took allied units on campaign.[31] Julian did not believe in the employment of allies on principle, but he nevertheless ordered the king of Armenia to get ready an army to support the Persian expedition.[32] Such support continued to be sought and given after 378. For instance, a force of Uldin king of the Huns played an important part in the defeat of Radagaisus in 406.[33]

It was an innovation—and a disastrous one—that units were now also being provided by allies who were permanently stationed within the borders of the empire, whether by agreement, or because the empire was no longer strong enough to keep them out.[34] It is often assumed that a treaty involving a land settlement was the only kind desired by the Germans. In fact this does not seem to have been so. We have already come across cases where bands of barbarians appear to have been given simply money or supplies. Ammianus tells us of small bodies of Goths under Sueridus and Colias who were living in the neighbourhood of Adrianople and received an order from the emperor to move elsewhere. Their response was to demand *viaticum* just as if they had been a unit of field army troops on the move— which is what in fact they were, even if they are likely to have been more heavily encumbered with family. Arrangements of this kind are likely to have been made with smaller and younger bands of warriors.[35]

It has been persuasively argued that the treaty made by Gratian with Alatheus and Saphrax in 380 was of the same kind, that they were simply provided with hospitality like mobile army units.[36]

Similar status may have been enjoyed by Germans stationed outside Tomi in the province of Scythia who came into conflict with the regular garrison under the command of Gerontius and who were all but wiped out. These Germans were in receipt of imperial subsidies both in money and supplies.[37] Again one wonders whether the Huns of Thrace, whom Theodosius raised together with their chieftains to take part in the expedition against Eugenius, were

---

[30] Constantine's treaty with the Tervingi (c. 330): Anon. Vales. 6. 31. Them. *Or.* x. 205. 11. 11 ff. They were paid to maintain troops which they supplied when requested by the Empire— in 348 (Lib. *Or.* lix. 89); in 360 (Amm. xx. 8. 1); in 363 (Amm. xxiii. 2. 7); for Procopius (Amm. xxvi. 10. 3).

[31] Amm. xvii. 13. 19.   [32] Amm. xxiii. 2. 1.

[33] Oros. vii. 37. 12; Marcell. Com. s.a. 406, cf. *LRE* iii. 38 n. 61; R. Grosse (1920) 80–1.

[34] Cf. *LRE* 199–200. The innovation must have seemed less drastic because some tribes outside the frontier did receive *annona* as if they were imperial troops, *gentes annonariae* (*Nov. Theod.* 24). Settled barbarian peoples received the same kind of pay, in return for the same kind of assistance, e.g. Procop. vii. 33. 13 (Eruli).

[35] Goths of Sueridus and Colias: Amm. xxxi. 6. 1 (377). A very similar band attacked by regulars under Gerontius 4: Zos. iv. 40. 1 (384/7).

[36] See above, p. 27–8.   [37] Zos. iv. 40.

tribesmen maintained and rewarded for use as mercenaries rather than peasants settled on land.[38] But by far the most conspicuous example of this mobile type of federate band were the Goths of Alaric—or so it will be argued in a later chapter.[39]

But often the barbarian or 'federate' units mentioned in the sources do not appear to have been provided by the rulers, or indeed any collective organization, of a barbarian people. Such federates appear to be simply units composed of individually enlisted mercenaries of barbarian origin. To these units Procopius' later definition of federates seems to apply, namely that they were men who had entered the empire (τὴν πολιτείαν) not as slaves (i.e. as *dediticii*) but on terms of complete equality.[40] In our period they included a high proportion of Goths[41] because a large number of Goths were available, eager to be enrolled both within the Empire and on the far side of the Danube, but they may well have included others as well. A fragment of Olympiodorus which tells us that the title of 'federates' was first given to mixed units in the reign of Honorius[42] dates the origin of the new type of federate unit. Unfortunately our sources, which are very inadequate for this period, do not specify individual units of this type, in the way Procopius describes certain units in the army of Justinian as federates.[43] But if we cannot identify units we have numerous references to barbarian troops that are contrasted with Roman troops and do not appear to have links with any organized body of tribesmen, whether within the empire or outside it. What cohesion such bodies of men possessed appears to be the result of their serving under the same commander in the Roman army.

Barbarian contingents of this kind played a key role in two important episodes, the fall of Stilicho and the Gainas revolt. In the case of Stilicho, it is clear that the barbarian units were recognizably a distinct division of his army, with distinct leaders, and political attitudes different from those of Roman units. Numerically they were of a strength comparable with but not overwhelmingly superior to that of the Roman units.[44] Their families were quartered in a number of cities, and evidently identifiable as families of federate soldiers.[45] Their total strength is given as 30,000. After the execution of Stilicho and the massacre of their families these men joined Alaric's Goths. They evidently had nowhere else to go to.[46]

---

[38] John Ant. fr. 187 = Eunapius fr. 60 Blockley; Huns were after all nomads.
[39] See below, pp. 48 ff.　　　　　　　　　　　　　[40] Procop. iii. 11. 3.
[41] Malchus fr. 11 Müller (= 15 Blockley): federates synonymous with Goths.
[42] Olympiodorus fr. 7. 4 Blockley.
[43] Procop. iii. 11. 5–6; other refs.: A. H. M. Jones *LRE* 664–6. J. F. Haldon (1979); A. Müller (1912), esp. 114–16; J. Teall (1965).
[44] Zos. v. 33.　　　　　[45] Zos. v. 34. 2; 35. 5.　　　　　[46] Zos. v. 35. 6.

Gainas' forces are consistently described as barbarians and contrasted with the Roman forces of Leo.[47] Unlike the force of the mutinous Goth Tribigild, which was recruited from Greuthungi settled in Phrygia,[48] Gainas' Goths appear to have been recruited among fellow Goths from the east of the Danube outside the Empire.[49] But there is no suggestion that they were supplied under treaty by a local ruler. The territory was under the government of Uldin king of the Huns. It is likely that the Goths presented themselves individually, having their families with them[50] at Gainas' instigation, and were enrolled by him under officers that he appointed. They were numerous, since the 7,000 reported killed inside Constantinople are said to have been only a fifth of the whole force.[51]

In the case of both barbarian armies it is clear that the commander-in-chief himself took a considerable part in recruiting. Gainas is said to have invited Goths into the Empire to enrol.[52] Stilicho preceded the expedition to Greece against Alaric, and the defence of Italy against Alaric's first invasion, with expeditions to the northern frontier which culminated in large-scale recruiting of barbarians into the Roman army.[53] We owe our information to poems of Claudian, and Claudian's account of recruiting in 396, vague as it is, would fit recruitment into Roman units rather than into barbarian units.[54] There is, however, no reason why both kinds of recruiting should not have gone on at the same time. Certainly Stilicho must have recruited cavalry. The *Notitia* includes a large number of infantry units raised by Honorius,[55] but only two units of cavalry.[56] Presumably the bulk of the cavalry units were enrolled as federates. Not all the recruiting will have been done by Stilicho personally. Outstanding among his barbarian officers was Sarus sometimes

---

[47] Zos. v. 17. 1; 18. 10; 19. 1.

[48] Claud. *In Eutrop.* ii. 196; Zos. iv. 38–9, *Chron. Minor* 1, p. 244 (Mommsen), cf. G. Albert (1984) 89–90.

[49] Gainas leads men back to their (or only his) homeland: Zos. v. 21. 9. Gainas recruits: Socr. vi. 6: Soz. viii. 8. 1. Albert (1954) 111–12 argues that this was within the Empire.

[50] Volunteers walk to Constantinople to enrol: Procop. iv. 16. 13, *HA* 6 (Justin and Justinian). Mounted Goths demand to be enrolled: Synesius *De Regno* 1097 B. Gothic soldiers certainly acquired families, Synesius *De Prov.* ii. 1 (1261).

[51] Generals were deprived of the right to issue *probatoria* by Zeno. See A. H. M. Jones *LRE* 668 on *CJ* xii. 35. 17 of AD 472.

[52] See above, n. 49.

[53] See above, nn. 19–20.

[54] Claud. IV *Cons. Hon.* 485 'proiecta pelle Gelonus militat . . . in Latios ritus transistis Alani'. The recruiting of 401, *B. Get.* 400–3, has no allusions to romanization, and the Alans are described as *externa auxilia*, *B. Get.* 580–1, cf. also Symmachus *Ep.* vii. 13–14.

[55] See D. Hoffmann (1969) 358–67, summed up p. 365: 15 units before 398; 10, possibly 14, after 398, and in Hoffmann's view, but not necessarily, before 406. The chronology remains uncertain.

[56] *ND Oc.* vi. 59, 60, not counting cavalry units stationed in Africa.

described as 'king',[57] sometimes as *dux* of the Goths,[58] who had a large force which stood in a special relationship to him personally.[59]

An officer did not have to be commander-in-chief to build a federate force with a strong sense of loyalty to himself, or at least to obtain the leadership of a coherent body of men. Tribigild, the Goth who led a force of mutinous Greuthungi through south-western Asia Minor in 399, is a case in point. His official position seems to have been commander of all the barbarian troops (federates) stationed in Phrygia, with the rank of *comes militaris*.[60] These included a number of Greuthungi with wives and families settled on land near Nacoleia.[61] They were almost certainly survivors of a band of barbarians that had been defeated by Promotus when attempting to cross into the Empire in 386.[62] Tribigild was a kinsman of Gainas, and therefore does not appear to have been one of the Greuthungi himself.[63] At any rate he did not live in Phrygia but in Constantinople. It is not at all clear what factors other than his rank as their commander induced the Greuthungi to trust him to the extent of following him into mutiny and rebellion. By far the most likely explanation is that the Goths had taken part in Eutropius' campaign against the Huns, and that Tribigild had led them.[64] If that was so, the common motive of leader and men was a grievance over inadequate rewards for their contribution to victory. If at the start Tribigild's band was mainly made up of Greuthungi, it certainly did not remain limited to members of that tribe. It grew and gathered strength by absorbing large numbers of slaves and perhaps other provincials.[65] Tribigild died soon after he had submitted to the command of Gainas.[66] and it is likely that his force joined up with that of Gainas in Thrace and was destroyed together with it.[67]

Sarus, mentioned earlier, was another Gothic officer to make progress towards creating a private army without, however, succeeding in the end. Sarus was of noble birth and heroic qualities and character.[68] He commanded a large force under Stilicho in the battle against Radagaisus.[69] At the time of Stilicho's death he had a powerful

---

[57] Marcell. Comes s.a. 406; Jordanes *Get.* 321.   [58] Oros. vii. 37. 12.

[59] See below, p. 100.

[60] Zos. v. 13. 2, Socr. vi. 6. 5, Philos. xi. 8.

[61] Philos. xi. 8. They served as cavalry: Claud. *In Eutrop.* ii. 176 'Geticae dux improbus alae'. Gainas' force too included much cavalry: Synesius *De Prov.*, 2. 1 (1260).

[62] See Zos. iv. 38.

[63] Socr. vi. 6, Soz. vii. 4. 2. G. Albert (1984) n. 20 argues that Tribigild must have been one of the Greuthungi: otherwise he would have lacked authority to lead the revolt. I would argue that his authority came not from being a fellow tribesman but from his Roman rank.

[64] G. Albert (1984).   [65] Zos. v. 13.   [66] Philost. xi. 8.

[67] Zos. v. 18. 9.   [68] *PLRE* ii. 978 s.v. Sarus.

[69] Oros. vii. 37. 12, Marcell. Com. s.a. 406.

following of barbarians. With more luck he might have become another Stilicho—or another Alaric.[70] In the event his following became reduced to 200–300 and less.[71] He was eventually executed by Athaulfus, with whom he had conducted a deadly feud. Jones has suggested that Sarus and his followers were a splinter group of Alaric's Goths who had deserted their leader after the battle of Verona.[72] It is just as likely that Sarus had assembled his men himself. But he seems to have been a dangerous rival for the leadership of Alaric's Goths. At any rate when Athaulfus was murdered, he was briefly succeeded by Sarus' brother Segericus.[73]

The ease with which men of different tribal origins fused into a coherent war band must have a basis in elements of culture shared by all these peoples, who had after all lived for a century or more next to each other and close to the border of the Empire.[74] Leaders will have had close dealings with the Romans for generations. Many will have served in the Roman army, learnt Latin, and become familiar with fighting alongside men of a whole range of tribal backgrounds.[75] Over generations many barbarians outside the Empire will have become quite used to Roman discipline and organization.

It is likely that the factors which made possible the cohesion of federate units of mixed origin did the same for the wandering German bands making their plundering way through the provinces of the Empire. Few of these collections of warriors accompanied by families were tribally homogeneous. Radagaisus' horde is said to have combined Goths and Celts.[76] Athaulfus led a force of Goths and Huns from Pannonia to join Alaric in Italy.[77] The Vandals invading Africa included Alans and Goths.[78] The Lombard army which invaded Italy in 568 was made up of Gepids, Huns, Sarmatians, Suebi, and provincial Romans, as well as Lombards.[79] In the case of

---

[70] If he had not suffered a setback in Gaul in 407, Zos. vi. 2. 4–5; or if he had been appointed successor to Stilicho in 408, Zos. v. 36. 2.

[71] Zos. vi. 13. 2, Olympiodorus fr. 6 Blockley.

[72] *LRE* 186, 200.

[73] *PLRE* ii s.v. Segericus.

[74] Th. S. Burns (1984) 11–12; evidence from metalwork: J. Werner (1950).

[75] There is little written evidence that barbarian officers or soldiers returned home after military service: A. H. M. Jones *LRE* 621–2, Amm. xxxi. 16. 3. It must have been quite common. Some chieftains were perfectly familiar with Roman ways, e.g. the Alamann king Vadomarius (*PLRE* i. 928, A. H. M. Jones *LRE* iii. 62). Alaric was on close terms with Jovius 3, praetorian prefect of Illyricum in 407 (Zos. v. 48. 2, *PLRE* ii. 623), and Joannes 2 (PPO Italiae 412–13, 422?). See *PLRE* i. 459. Evidence for return of soldiers to their German homes may be provided by buckles and other metalware manufactured in *limes* area found in burials in inner Germany. See S. Hawkes (1961), J. Ypas (1969), H. W. Böhme (1974), M. Todd (1977) 42–3.

[76] Zos. v. 26. 3. On the tribally mixed nature of migrating barbarians see R. Wenskus (1961) 440 ff.

[77] Zos. v. 37. 1.   [78] Procop. iii. 5. 19–20.

[79] Paul the Deacon ii. 26, cf. R. Wenskus (1961) 492–4.

the Lombards it has been suggested that the relationship between some important leaders and their followers had been shaped by common service in the Roman army. There certainly can be no doubt that the Lombard organization of Italy was strongly influenced by the ranks and structures of the Roman army.[80] In our period the most striking example of a coherent band, in fact a potential nation, being built up out of a combination of Roman military institutions and German tribal traditions is provided by the rise of Alaric's Visigoths.[81]

It might be argued that of all Late Roman military institutions the most influential was the *annona*, the organization which made possible the levy and distribution of vast quantities of corn to feed large numbers of troops or civil servants.[82] It was above all the prospect of drawing *annona* that drew Germans into the Empire and persuaded people who had been settled farmers to renounce sedentary existence for an indefinite period and to become reconciled to the mobility and homelessness of professional soldiers. There is good evidence that before entering the Empire many Goths were peasants settled in villages in the south of Russia.[83] Presumably their leaders still held the ideals ascribed to Germans by Tacitus: 'You will find it harder to persuade a German to plough land and to await its annual produce with patience than to challenge a foe and earn the price of wounds. He thinks it spiritless and slack to gain by sweat what he can buy with blood'.[84] The *annona* enabled a vastly greater number of Germans to earn their livelihood in this more honourable manner.

The extensive employment of federates raises another question. The units recorded in the lists of the *Notitia* amount to a very large army. A. H. M. Jones has calculated that the Eastern army comprised 157 units of *comitatenses*, amounting to around 104,000 men, with an additional 248,000 *limitanei*. The Western field armies contained 169 units with a total strength of about 130,000, with besides around 136,000 serving in the frontier army.[85] With regular armies of such size what need was there of federates? A partial explanation is that Jones's estimates (which are based on the assumption that the army was composed of legions of 1000, other units of 500, and legions of *limitanei* in the East as large as 3000) are too high because the units of

[80] T. S. Brown (1984) 71 n. 17 citing D. Bertolini (1968), P. S. Leicht (1923). G. P. Bognetti (1966–8) iii. 146, 439–75.

[81] See below, p. 48 ff.

[82] A. H. M. Jones *LRE* 448–60.

[83] E. A. Thompson (1966) 27.

[84] *Germ.* 14, tr. H. Mattingly.　　　　　[85] *LRE* 682.

the Late Roman army were in fact considerably smaller.[86] Besides, paper strengths may well have been a long way above actual strength. There is the additional consideration that the Eastern field army lists basically represent the 'new model' army organized by Theodosius I after the defeat of Maximus.[87] At that moment regulars will have been at a maximum strength—which was not, however, strong enough to persuade Theodosius that he could set out against Eugenius without enrolling in addition large numbers of federates.[88] In any case the regular strength was not kept up. One of the most striking circumstances of the Tribigild-Gainas troubles in 399 was the weakness of the Eastern regular forces.[89]

The Western field armies too may give a misleading impression of normal field army strength. They seem to represent the state of 413 when after the overthrow of Stilicho and the desertion of most of the German federates, and the disasters of Alaric's invasion of Italy, the *magister militum* Constantius made an attempt to rebuild the field armies by enrolling large numbers of frontier troops.[90] Earlier, even under Stilicho, the Western field armies were not strong enough to cope with more than one crisis at a time. There was only one field army able to challenge a major invasion: Stilicho's in Italy. In 406 the Rhine frontier was defended not by Romans but by allied Franks east of the river. It was by defeating these allies that the Vandals and Alans opened the way for their invasion of Gaul across the frozen Rhine on the last day of 406.[91]

The *Notitia* lists army units for both Eastern and Western Illyricum. The separate lists must be later than the division of Illyricum, which in all likelihood was made in 396. On the other hand, it seems that many of the units have been stationed in Illyricum for a long time: they are not a recent creation.[92] So to judge by the lists of the *Notitia* Alaric's invasion of Greece should have been opposed by 26 regiments of the field army. Accounts of the campaign suggest that before the arrival of Stilicho in 397 Alaric met with very little resistance.[93] One conclusion is inevitable: the *Notitia* is misleading. Either the so-called field army units were very much smaller than has

---

[86] S. Soproni (1985), R. P. Duncan Jones (1978), R. MacMullen (1980), C. M. Daniels (1979). Smaller forts: J. Schwartz (1951) 91, E. Birley (1961) 6, P. A. Holder (1982) 98; D. A. Welsby (1982) 79–90. It also seems to be the case that lists of units are not contemporary. The Spanish field army represents arrangements to deal with the invasion of 409. Other units represent an earlier state of affairs, see J. Acre (1980). Simple addition is bound to produce too large a total.

[87] D. Hoffmann (1969) 490 ff.   [88] See above, p. 30–1, 54–5.

[89] On Tribigild and Gainas see below, p. ooo.

[90] E. Demougeot (1979) ii. 2, 473.

[91] Greg. Tour. *H. Franc.* ii. 9; ii. 2. 9, cf. E. Demougeot (1951) 382–3.

[92] E. Demougeot (1979) 431–2, D. Hoffmann (1969) 19–21.

[93] Zos. v. 4–7. Claud. *In Ruf.* ii. 36 f.

been assumed for instance by A. H. M. Jones, or they were dispersed as garrisons in numerous cities of the diocese. In either case they were quite incapable of being used as a field army.

If the Western field army as described in the *distributio* was the field army as reconstructed by Honorius' *magister militum* and, briefly, colleague Constantius,[94] it does not appear to have effectively outlived its creator.[95] In subsequent campaigns federates played a more prominent part than ever.[96] Federates were evidently much easier to enrol, needed little or no training, and if the corn raised in taxation was used to maintain federates and their families it was not available for regulars. So the famous Roman army was replaced by one composed largely of federates of various kinds.

In spite of their indispensability, federates were economically in a weak position, since they served the Empire without a guarantee of permanent employment. There was a possibility of their units becoming part of the regular army,[97] or they might be used to bring regular units up to strength.[98] But their future must have depended very largely on the support of the general who had enrolled them. The way in which the troops depended for rewards of service on their general, and the pressure which they consequently exerted on him was well understood by Augustine when he wrote to Bonifatius, *comes Africae* and a general with his own following of federates, urging him to set a limit to the acquisitiveness of his troops. Tacitus' comment on the problem facing a Germanic chieftain still applied. 'You cannot maintain a large body of companions except by violence and war. The companions are prodigal in their demands on the generosity of their chief, one asking for a war horse, another a bloody and victorious spear.'[99] Close bonds were formed between commander and men, with the troops anxious that their general should keep, or if possible increase his rank in the imperial service, and thus enhance his ability to look after their interests.[100] In consequence a commander

[94] See *PLRE* s.v. Constantius.

[95] This dating of the field army is in E. Demougeot (1975).

[96] See the role played by Huns in the military operations of Aetius: Prosp. Tiro s.a. 425, *Chron. Gall.* 452 no. 100; Prosp. Tiro s.a. 432, *Chron. Gall.* 452 no. 112 (s.a. 433), no. 115 (s.a. 434), Prosp. Tiro s.a. 435. Other examples of use of federates of various kinds against opponents of Empire: J. Matthews (1975) 315, 330, 337.

[97] A. H. M. Jones *LRE* iii. 38 n. 62 on Orosius vii. 40. 7; perhaps also the post-Theodosian Western *auxilia* named after barbarian tribes, Atecotti, Marcomanni, Brisigavi, Mauri, cf. *LRE* iii. 355.

[98] D. Hoffmann (1969) 503 suggests that in 388 Theodosius filled up the new *auxilia* for the two praesental armies with men from his own federate contingents or from surrendered contingents of Maximus.

[99] August. *Ep.* 220. 6: he clearly had a following even though the word *bucellarii* is not used. Tac. *Germ.* 14, tr. H. Mattingly.

[100] Hence the barbarians' eagerness for Roman commands, Zos. v. 13. 1, 17. 4 (Gainas);

like Stilicho or Gainas, or Bonifatius or Aetius could be deposed against his will only by assassination or battle. This, rather than the command structure of the Western army, is the basic reason why the *magister militum* in the West became the virtual ruler of the Empire.

It is in the context of the individual recruitment of *foederati* that I would explain the development of the institution of *bucellarii*.[101] *Bucellarius*, 'biscuit eater', is a nickname for what seems to be a private soldier of a military or civilian magnate which by the sixth century had become almost a technical term. The evidence about *bucellarii* is mostly late: fragments of the Code of Euric who ruled Visigothic Gaul 466–85,[102] Procopius' *Histories of the Wars of Justinian*,[103] and papyri of the sixth century or later.[104] Even in the sixth century *bucellarii* was only one of a number of names given to retainers of this type.[105] It is clear that when studying this institution we must not restrict our attention to military retainers who are explicitly described as *bucellarii*.

In the early fifth century the calling of these men by their nickname had evidently not yet become predominant,[106] but there is evidence that the institution existed and that the nickname was already sometimes applied to it. Magnates who appear to have had *bucellarii*-like bodyguards in our period are Stilicho,[107] Rufinus the praetorian prefect of the East,[108] Bonifatius,[109] and Aetius.[110] It is likely that other

Claud. *In Eutrop.* ii. 178 ff.; ibid. 317–21 gifts and title of *magister militum* rejected (Tribigild); Zos. v. 5. 4, Claud. *B. Get.* 535 ff.; Zos. v. 31, 48. 3 (Alaric).

[101] H. -J. Diesner (1972).

[102] K. Zeumer, *Leges Visigothorum, MGH legum sectio 1* (Hanover and Leipzig, 1902). 18–19 = *Code of Euric* fr. 310. E. A. Thompson (1969) 187–8; D. Claude (1971) 46 ff.

[103] See refs. in A. H. M. Jones *LRE* iii. 206–7. Ch. A. Lécrivain, 'Les soldats privés au Bas-Empire', *Mél Éc. Fr. Rome* x (1980) 267–83. J. F. Haldon (1984), 101 ff.

[104] J. Maspero, *Organisation militaire de l'Égypte byzantine* (Paris, 1912) 66 ff.; J. Gascou (1976).

[105] See H. -J. Diesner (1972) 322–3: among them *amici, armigeri, comites, satellites,* δορυφόροι (officers), ὑπασπισταί, ὀπαδοί, ἐπομένοι.

[106] The earliest reference to an individual described as a *bucellarius* is in 455—in texts which are considerably later still. See note 110 below.

[107] Zos. v. 34 (Huns). He was without them when he entered the consulate at Rome: Claud. *Cons. Stil.* iii. 220–3.

[108] Claud. *In Ruf.* ii. 76, so also John the Cappadocian praetorian prefect of Justinian: Procop. *B. Pers.* 1. 25.

[109] August. *Ep.* 220. 6 'quod multi homines tibi cohaerent ad tuendam tuam potentiam vel salutem', cf. H. -J. Diesner (1972) 340–1. Note that Bonifatius' power could be inherited by his son-in-law Sebastianus 3 (Hydatius 99); Aetius married Boniface's widow for her property (John Ant. fr. 201. 31 = Priscus fr. 30 Blockley), perhaps also for her late husband's *bucellarii*.

[110] Optila (*PLRE* ii. 810) killer of Valentinian III in 455, *bucellarius Aetii* (*Addit. ad Prosp. Haun.* 572 s.a. 455 and Greg. Tour. *H. Franc.* ii. 8) is the earliest individual to be described as a *bucellarius*. In Marcell. Comes s.a. 455 and Jordanes *Rom.* 334 he and his partner Thraustila are *Aetii satellites*. Priscus fr. 64 Blockley: domestic force of barbarians of Ricimer.

generals, for instance Gainas,[111] had them too. The earliest use of the word *bucellarii* occurs in the title of the *comites catafractarii bucellarii iuniores*, the most senior of the cavalry regiments under the *magister militum per Orientem*, an élite regular unit of the Eastern army.[112] If the word already had its later meaning one might conjecture that this unit was intended to enjoy a specially close relationship with the commander-in-chief. A fragment of Olympiodorus informs us that in the time of Honorius the name *bucellarius* was used not only with reference to Roman soldiers but also to some that were Goths.[113] Since the later *bucellarii* were most often of barbarian origin it is a fair inference that the fragment of Olympiodorus refers to *bucellarii* in the later sense, that is, a body of soldiers enjoying so close a relationship with their commander that they appear to be members of a private force rather than of the imperial army. If this is right we have evidence for the existence in our period not only of the institution of the later bucellariate but also of its name.

The institution has been explained as an example of German influence, the adoption on the part of powerful Romans of a following of armed companions of the kind described by Tacitus in his account of the household of a German noble.[114] *Bucellarii* have also been seen as evidence of developing 'feudalization', that is the usurpation of prerogatives of the state by powerful landed magnates.[115] There is something in these explanations. There can be no argument that the resemblance of the bucellariate to a German noble's armed following helped its introduction at a time when so many officers were Germans.

Similarly there can be no doubt that the *bucellarii* of great landowners like the Apions obviously strengthened the landowners relatively to the agents of the imperial government.[116] Nevertheless neither 'German influence' nor 'feudalization' accounts for the admittedly scanty evidence we have about the origin of the

---

[111] Synesius *De Regno* 15 (*PG* lxvi. 1094 B) ὀπαδοί, cf. G. Albert (1984) 56, 117–19, who does not distinguish sufficiently between mixed federate units and the personal retainers that were the core of them.

[112] *ND Or.* vii. 25, cf. D. Hoffmann (1969) 273–4.

[113] Fr. 7. 4 Blockley. Olympiodorus evidently used the term *bucellarius* for a particular kind of soldier (presumably in the sense in which it was used later), and seems to have explained it, fr. 12. Both fragments seem to come from a narrative later than that of the fall of Stilicho, and before that of Alaric's creation of a puppet emperor (fr. 14). The only armed following mentioned in the corresponding section of Zosimus (based on Olympiodorus) is that of Sarus (v. 36), but of course most of Olympiodorus' narrative has been lost.

[114] *Germ.* 13, but *bucellarii* (at least their other ranks) were dependents rather than companions of their chief.

[115] E. Patlagean (1977*b*) 289–90.

[116] *Nov. Theod.* xv. 2 (AD 444): following of Valerian decurion of Emesa; *CJ* ix. 12.10 (468): the East generally; on *bucellarii* of Apions in Egypt see below, p. 45–6.

institution. That the armed retainers were known by a Latin name
even in a Germanic kingdom[117] shows that this precise type of
following must be of Roman origin. As we have seen, both
Olympiodorus and the *Notitia* suggest that the name *bucellarii* was
first applied to soldiers. This makes it likely that the institution
started in the imperial army rather than on great estates. This
deduction is confirmed by the fact that elsewhere than in Egypt the
great public figures known to have had armed followings acquired
them as a consequence of their being, or having been, military
commanders, and not simply men of great landed wealth.[118] The
exception, Rufinus, the praetorian prefect of the East, AD 392–5, who
is actually the earliest known case of a Roman official with an armed
following, was of course a civilian.[119] But his following was
not an expression of local landed power—after all Rufinus was in
Constantinople while his ancestral property was in Gaul. It was a
bodyguard[120] for the man who was ruling the East while the emperor
Theodosius was campaigning against a usurper in the West.

Bucellarii did become a threat to the imperial administration,[121] but
this does not mean that they originated as bodies of private retainers.
On the contrary, the sixth-century papyrus evidence as interpreted
by J. Gascou suggests that the *bucellarii* of the Apion family and
other great houses of Egypt still belonged to the imperial army.[122]
The *bucellarii* of the Apions were part of their household and were
maintained by them. But it seems that they were enrolled on instructions of the government,[123] and that their payment was *annona* and
therefore presumably counted against the estate's tax bill.[124] They
were employed for local police duties like keeping order in the hippodrome, also for tax-collecting. In military emergencies the *bucellarii*
of various houses were concentrated and put at the disposal of the
duke of the Thebaid.[125] This arrangement might be called 'privatization'

---

[117] *Code of Euric* 310. 1 and 3, cf. 286. 1 f., 307. 1 ff.

[118] See notes 107–111 above, also Aspar (Malalas 371) and Belisarius, Procop. *B. Got.* iii. 1.
18–20. We know nothing of the background of Valerian of Emesa (note 116 above).

[119] Claud. *In Ruf.* ii. 76; they were Huns: *Chron. Minor.* i. 650. 34.

[120] Not mentioned in account of assassination: ibid. 400 ff.   [121] *CJ* xii. 10, cf. 468.

[122] (1976) 143–56. For a soldier to be made *bucellarius* was an honour, Procop. *B. Got.*
iv. 29. 28, but surely did not take him out of the army. *Bucellarii* were sworn to the emperor as
well as their patron, Procop. *B. Vand.* ii. 18. 6.

[123] J. Gascou (1976) 146–7 on *P. Oxy.* 156; *bucellarii* receive *annona*, *P. Oxy.* 2046, cf.
A. H. M. Jones *LRE* iii. 191 n. 44, also *P. Oxy.* 2196, cf. A. C. Johnson, L. C. West (1949)
227–9.

[124] J. Gascou (1976) 146–7 on *P. Oxy.* 156 and *P. Wilk. Chrest.* 147. It is difficult to believe
that Belisarius undertook to pay his 7000 *bucellarii* (Procop. *B. Got.* iii. 1. 18–20) for the rest of
their lives. More likely they received basic *annona* out of taxation and only some extras from
their patron. Procop. *HA* 24: *bucellarii* suffered from cuts in government expenditure.

[125] J. Gascou (1976) 150; cf.Procop. *B. Vand.* ii. 18. 6–7 (491. 19): Germanus takes over

of part of the administration of the defence forces.[126] The head of the house and therefore the patron of the *bucellarii* might not be an office holder himself. On one occasion it was a woman. But the Apion family produced many holders of high imperial office,[127] and there is no reason why the family's force of armed retainers might not have originated when one of the Apions held a high military command. The relationship between a *bucellarius* and his 'lord' was one of patron and client.[128] It would therefore not have been limited to the duration of a particular period of office-holding, or even the lifetime of a single generation of 'patron' or *bucellarius*, but would continue from father to son or other heir[129] unless it was deliberately ended by the parties concerned[130] or by the imperial government.[131]

One might ask why the government helped to build up this potentially dangerous institution. The government's policy can be quite plausibly explained as a response to recruiting problems of the late fourth century and after. As we have seen, this was a time when the army had to be expanded in a hurry before major campaigns, and when the commander-in-chief himself led expeditions to the frontier for recruiting purposes before risking confrontation with a major foe. This was the time when at a lower level a leader like Sarus the Goth might build up a band of dependent federates. These men must have faced a serious problem if, as I have argued, they recruited for campaigns rather than for a lifetime of military service: they could not offer their men a certain future. Now the institution of the bucellariate, because it established a formal relationship of patron and client between commander and men, gave the latter the assurance that it would be a powerful man's·responsibility to provide for them, without imposing an expensive obligation on the state. I am not suggesting that when Stilicho, for instance, recruited Germans they all became his *bucellarii* but that perhaps the most valuable and most influential among them did. In this way Gainas, or Stilicho, or Bonifatius, or Aetius (the only one of the four whose followers are

δορυφόρος (i.e. *bucellarius*) of another; see also *B. Got.* iii. 39 (447. 12), iv. 26 (598. 14): other men's *bucellarii* (ἑπόμενοι) led to Narses.

[126] Cf. R. Rémondon (1974) 27–8 on 'privatization' of army in 6th-cent. Egypt.

[127] *PLRE* ii. s.v. Apion 1–2, Strategius 8.

[128] *Leges Visigothorum* 216, cf. 217. 10: 'qui in patrocinio est' = *bucellarius*, cf. also Claud. *In Ruf.* ii. 46 'clientum agmina'.

[129] Procop. *B. Got.* ii. 7. 26 (176. 22): nephew leads 400 of uncle's *bucellarii* (ἑπόμενοι) while uncle is *mag. mil.* in Armenia; ibid. iv. 26 (598. 14): John, nephew of Vitalian, leads his own and father-in-law's 'followers'.

[130] *Bucellarius* can transfer to another patron, *Leges Visigothorum* 18 fr. 310. Procop. *B. Got.* iii. 39. 17: *bucellarii* of other commanders join Germanus.

[131] By a law like *CJ* xii. 10 of 468 (see below) or by redistributing *bucellarii* of a disgraced commander (e.g. Procop. *HA* iv. 17), or by taking them over himself, John Ant. fr. 201. 4–5.

actually described as *bucellarii*) would provide themselves with a core of loyal and reliable men around whom they could build up a much larger military following.[132]

In 468 the emperor Leo seems to have made an attempt to put an end to the keeping of *bucellarii* by individuals in cities and estates.[133] It may be significant that four years later the same emperor forbade all generals to enlist soldiers without enrolment papers (*probatoriae*) originating from the emperor.[134] It looks as if Leo was trying to suppress private military power as represented by *bucellarii* and realized that the source of the problem was the free recruiting by *magistri militum* and *duces*. Leo's laws remained in force. The law of 468 was even repeated by Justinian,[135] but it evidently was not interpreted in such a way as to make *bucellarii* as such illegal: as we have seen, they played a perfectly open and even essential part in Justinian's campaigning armies and in the military organization of Egypt. One might suggest that what was illegal was the continued employment of *armed bucellarii* by officers who had returned to civil life, or by their heirs or by great private landowners who imitated the 'privatized' bodyguards of officials.[136]

---

[132] According to R. Rémondon (1961), esp. 88, the emergence of *bucellarii* in 6th century Egypt coincided with the raising of mobile units of mainly barbarian *federati*.

[133] *CJ* ix. 12. 40.

[134] *CJ* xii. 35. 17 of 472. Both laws are likely to be associated with Leo's conflict with Aspar's private military power.

[135] *Nov. Just.* xxx. 7.

[136] R. Rémondon (1974) 25 against I. F. Fikhman (1970) shows how in 6th cent. Egypt *bucellarii* were raised by progressively lower officials, and finally also by mere owners of estates. The *bucellarii* of Titus (*PLRE* ii s.v. Titus 1) were his own employees, not the emperor's: *Vita S. Danielis Stylitae* 60–1.

5

The Visigoths[1] and Alaric's Goths

IN the ensuing decades a decisive part in the affairs of the Empire was played by the Goths. We have seen that Theodosius made a treaty with them in 383. The details are by no means clear, but it is certain that it provided for the settlement of at least a considerable part of the tribe in Thrace. It was hoped that they would eventually be assimilated to neighbouring citizens of the Empire, and Theodosius tried to further this process by entertaining Gothic nobles, presumably leaders of federate units, at his court.[2] Clearly many Goths were not assimilated. In fact the procession of Alaric's Goths through the provinces of the Western empire proved that they had very considerable ability to assimilate other Germans, and perhaps even Roman provincials to their own ways, or at least to get them to identify with Visigoths.[3]

It has been argued that Valens' campaign of 367–9 had left them with a feeling of extreme bitterness,[4] and that in this spirit they swore the oath reported by Eunapius that once inside the Empire they would do their utmost to damage the Romans and to gain control of their land.[5] In E. A. Thompson's reconstruction of the Gothic invasion this spirit of resentment, aggravated by the terrible exploitation suffered by the Goths immediately after entering the Empire, continued to motivate the mass of the tribesmen for decades, and to fill them with deep antagonism towards all things Roman. So lasting accommodation between Goths and Romans was difficult to achieve. For while the

[1] I have used 'Visigoths' to describe the Gothic nation admitted by Valens, as has become conventional. In fact the idea of the division of all the Goths into the two groups of Visigoths and Ostrogoths is probably a 5th cent. development. Ammianus calls the Goths of Athanaric and Fritigern 'Teruingi', those of Ermenerichus 'Greuthungi' (xxx. 3. 1–5). SHA *Claudius* 6 mentions Greuthungi, Austrogothi, Teruingi, Visi, as if they were all separate tribes. So also seemingly Claud. *In Eutrop.* ii. 153, Sid. Ap. *Carm.* ii. 377, *Ep.* vii. 9.

[2] Zos. iv. 56, cf. Eunapius fr. 59 Blockley: described as leaders of tribes. They were accompanied by fellow tribesmen described as 'soldiers' (Zos. iv. 56. 3), presumably members of the federate units they commanded. Fravitta received a Roman wife and presumably citizenship. The killing of Eriulf seems to have happened just before the Eugenius campaign.

[3] Gothic assimilation of non-Goths even before entry into empire is shown by list of 26 'Gothic' martyrs of AD 370 (H. Achelis (1900) 323), the majority of whose names are said to be non-Gothic, i.e. Phrygian, Cappadocian, Syrian, and in a few cases Roman: R. Löwe (1923), cited by E. A. Thompson (1966) 84. On 'Gothicizing' by Romans see above, p. 14 n. 32–4; on mixed character of invading barbarian hordes see above, p. 17 n. 65.

[4] E. A. Thompson (1966) 24, (1982) 39.

[5] Eunapius fr. 60 Müller = 59 Blockley. Is this oath not likely to be anti-Gothic propaganda, like that (not it would seem the same) ascribed to Alaric in Claudian *B. Get.* 81?

Gothic optimates had much to gain by reaching agreement with the authorities of the Empire, their followers would not let them.[6]

In the following account the motivation of the constant renewal of hostilities between Goths and Romans will be seen in a different light. The behaviour of the Goths will not be explained in terms of national or tribal consciousness resulting in conflict between leaders and led within the tribe. Instead it will be argued that the fundamental problem of Gothic groups was that of maintaining the physical survival and psychological cohesion of a war band of Gothic tribal 'ideology', whose origin was only partly Gothic,[7] and whose composition was consequently unstable. This view of the Goths obviously owes a great deal to the work of R. Wenskus on various migratory groups during the Dark Ages as well as to H. Wolfram's more specialized writings on the Goths.[8] Accordingly Alaric's Goths will be shown not so much as a tribal nation in process of migration but as a tribal nation being transformed and reconstituted in the course and as a result of its wanderings.

In this process the conversion of the Goths to Christianity would seem to have played an essential role. The official conversion of the Goths was in all likelihood a concession to facilitate this entry into the Empire.[9] In the circumstances it was natural that they should adopt the Arian form of Christianity which was the religion of the emperor Valens who received them. But the fact that they stuck to Arianism when the Romans around them abandoned it suggests that Christianity fulfilled a further social need. Conversion to Christianity had been an act of assimilation to the civilization of the world they were entering. On the other hand adherence to a form of Christianity which came to be rejected, and even persecuted, by the Roman government ensured that the Goths would remain separate from the Roman provincials whom they were bound to resemble more and more the longer they lived within the Empire. As a group their survival depended on their military effectiveness, and this in turn depended on their cohesion and shared sense of solidarity. As the proportion of genuine Goths shrank, and tribal institutions became irrelevant, group consciousness must have become extremely difficult to maintain. Orthodox Christianity would have been a powerful factor working to integrate the Goths into the society of the Empire.

---

[6] See E. A. Thompson (1963*b*), (1982) 38–52, (1966), which remain indispensable as well as enjoyable reading on the Goths.

[7] On the mixed character of Vandals see above p. 14 n. 32.

[8] R. Wenskus (1961), H. Wolfram (1979), (1983).

[9] Convincingly argued by Peter Heather (1986) against E. A. Thompson (1966) 78–110 on the basis of contradictory sources, Zos. vi. 37, Oros. vii. 33. 19, Socr. iv. 33.

After all, even the Arianism adhered to by the Goths was altogether the product of the Christian culture of the Empire. There was nothing specifically Gothic about its doctrines. Its creed was that which had been declared orthodox by the Council of Rimini (Ariminum) in 359 under the pressure of the Arian emperor Constantius.[10] The one small body of Gothic Arian theological writings to survive seems to be practically indistinguishable from orthodox theology.[11] So what kept Gothic Christians separate was first the fact that as Arians they could not be integrated into orthodox ecclesiastical organization, and secondly that their services or at least their scriptures were in Gothic.[12] How long, and how exclusively, Gothic was used in services among the Goths, indeed to what extent and for how long they continued to use their language among themselves, are questions not easy to answer. Certainly Latin must have made rapid progress in daily life. In the circumstances the fact that the Goths gave their allegiance to a sectarian and condemned form of Christianity will have played an important part in keeping them separate from their neighbours and must have helped to give a new and more relevant content to their traditional sense of ethnic identity.[13] In the Visigothic kingdom of Spain the conversion of the Goths to Catholicism was rapidly followed by the final fusion of Goths and Romans.[14]

What makes their sense of shared identity more remarkable is the fact that at the time they entered the Empire the Goths were far from unified. They were a confederation rather than a single nation, even if the appointment of a national king seems not to have been a temporary arrangement in emergency.[15] Once inside the Empire the Goths tended to split into small marauding groups. At the time of the treaty with Theodosius, Fritigern, who had led them into the Empire, was dead, and the terms were sworn by several leaders.[16] It is by no means certain that the Goths settled in Thrace ever had institutions of government uniting all of them. It is almost certain that in 383 a large number of Goths were still living outside the Empire altogether, in their old homes across the Danube.[17]

---

[10] See K. Schäferdiek (1979a).

[11] E. A. Thompson (1966) 119 ff. on the writings of bishop Maximinus (in Latin).

[12] Ibid. 144 ff. on the later history of Ulfila's text.

[13] Gregory Nazianzen's ironical οὓς ἡ τριὰς λυομένη συνέστησε (*Or.* xxxiii. *PG* xxxvi. 215) is literally true.

[14] E. A. Thompson (1969) 108. Settled in Gaul, Visigoths called Catholics 'Romans': Greg. Tour. *Gloria Mart.* 24.

[15] E. A. Thompson (1966) 45.

[16] Them. *Or.* xvi. 210 b τοὺς ἐξάρχους καὶ κορυφαίους.

[17] H. Wolfram (1979) 158–9 (Gaatha), otherwise E. A. Thompson (1966) 159–60; H. Wolfram (1979) 202–3 (Radagaisus).

Goths settled in Thrace or Moesia are not mentioned for more than half a century in historical sources.[18] Meanwhile the history of the Goths in the Empire concerns Alaric's Goths. Admittedly the settled Goths and Alaric's Goths have usually been identified. But this—at least so it will be argued here—is arbitrary.[19] It will be suggested that while the core of Alaric's great war band certainly consisted of men who had entered the Empire by agreement with Valens in 376—or their children—and they evidently thought of themselves as the men who had won the battle of Adrianople,[20] the mass of Alaric's followers, whether Visigothic or of some other tribal origin, became attached to his group only in the course of its wanderings. There is no evidence moreover that the Goths who had been given land—and, as we have seen, not all were given land[21]—abandoned this *en masse* to follow Alaric.

Alaric, who was to lead his followers to the sack of Rome itself, is first mentioned in connection with an obscure guerrilla campaign fought in Macedonia between 388 and 391, the years of the emperor Theodosius' Italian campaign to overthrow Maximus, the usurper ruling the West.[22] No sooner had Theodosius set out on this campaign than he was informed that certain barbarians mixed in with Roman units (i.e. regulars not federates)[23] were in the pay of the usurper and ready to betray the army. When this became known the barbarians fled into the marshes of Macedonia presumably around the mouth of the Axios (Vardar) near Thessaloniki[24] and had to be hunted down in a laborious guerrilla campaign. They were not, however, wiped out. While Theodosius was in Italy they recovered and engaged in regular raiding of Macedonia and Thessaly.[25] When Theodosius returned in 391 the situation had deteriorated.

A serious campaign was required in autumn and winter 391–2. Even before Theodosius had returned to Constantinople, he had to fight the barbarians in the marshes. By now these had grown so confident that they advanced to meet him, and actually managed to hold him up on the Hebrus (Maritsa).[26] Subsequently Theodosius won some success. But after his army had been surprised at night and badly mauled he handed over campaigning to Promotus,

[18] Is it not possible that the Goths of Theoderic Strabo were descended from Goths left behind in Thrace or Moesia?

[19] Cf. below, p. 78–80. [20] Claudian *B. Get.* 489, 611. [21]Cf. above, p. 27–9.

[22] Zos. iv. 45. 2 and 48. 1.

[23] Zos. iv. 45; 'mixed' units: Amm. xxv. 6. 13, xxxi. 10. 18.

[24] Zos. iv. 45: marshes and shrubby country; 48: marshes and forests around lakes.

[25] Zos. iv. 48, Eunapius fr. 58 = 55 Blockley.

[26] Claudian VI *Cons. Hon.* 107–8, cf. *B. Get.* 524 plural: 'Augustos' rhetorical? But *Thracum venientem e finibus* suggests that the engagement happened when Theodosius was *leaving* Thrace for Italy, i.e. in summer 388.

until that general too was caught in ambush and killed.[27] Meanwhile the mutineers had been joined by other barbarians—at least that is the conclusion to which we are driven if we add the evidence of Claudian to that of Zosimus.[28] Bastarnians were attacking across the Danube.[29] Alans too are mentioned. There had probably also been considerable reinforcement of Goths from the tribal settlement in Moesia not very far away. At any rate the imperial forces no longer had to deal simply with guerrillas exploiting the difficult terrain of marshlands, but with a large army accompanied by a characteristic Gothic waggon train.[30] The mutiny had snowballed. A warrior band of mixed origin had consolidated.

After the death in action of Promotus the imperial forces were under the command of Stilicho, perhaps as *magister militum per Thracias*.[31] According to Claudian, Stilicho succeeded in shutting up a large force of barbarians in a narrow valley, and was about to launch the final attack when he received orders to wait.[32] The great attack never took place though Stilicho did manage to scatter a recently arrived detachment of Huns—or so Claudian claims.[33] The war was ended by a treaty negotiated by Rufinus, the praetorian prefect of the East. Presumably the barbarians returned to the status of *foederati*.

Claudian, and indeed Zosimus too,[34] claim that Rufinus had been conspiring with the barbarians all the time, and that the praetorian prefect had actually instructed the barbarians to ambush Promotus.[35] In fact it is likely that Rufinus was simply continuing to implement the policy which Theodosius and Saturninus had launched through their treaty with the Goths in 382.[36] Finding themselves unable to crush a barbarian band in the traditional Roman manner, they allowed them to remain on imperial territory on agreed conditions.

The episode thus illustrates a recurring feature of the military history of this period: the Roman authorities found it almost impossible to use the army to put down mutinies of federate troops decisively. Various reasons can be suggested. The federates were thoroughly familiar with Roman tactics. Many of their officers had long experience of the Roman army. They could draw on reinforcements from foot-loose barbarians inside the Empire, as well as from outside its frontiers,

---

[27] Zos. iv. 48–51.   [28] Claud. *Cons. Stil.* i. 94–115.

[29] On the question whether reference to Bastarnae and others is precise, or literary and anachronistic, see H. Wolfram (1979) 162 n. 128.

[30] Claud. *Cons. Stil.* i. 94; 140–1 shows that the campaign described earlier took place before the death of Theodosius I. *In Ruf.* i. 308–22.

[31] *CT* vii. 4. 18 and 9. 3 of July 393.

[32] Claud. *In Ruf.* i. 320, *Cons. Stil.* i. 106–115.

[33] *In Ruf.* i. 349–50.   [34] Zos. iv. 51.

[35] *In Ruf.* i. 309–10, cf. Alan Cameron (1970) 71.

[36] See above, p. 28.

so that a roving band would become more powerful the longer it was at large. The Roman government faced so many difficulties at the same time that it was rarely able to concentrate all its forces on one group of marauders—although just in 392–3 this would have been possible. But when all these factors have been taken into account one still wonders whether the indecisive outcome of, for instance, no less than five head-on confrontations between Stilicho and Alaric,[37] does not suggest the existence of a sense of solidarity which prevented barbarians in the armies of the Empire from fighting to the death against fellow-tribesmen, who might even once have been fellow-soldiers. In such encounters Goths fought on both sides. But tribal divisions did not form strong barriers. The tribes that supplied large numbers of soldiers, Visigoths, Greuthungi, Sarmatians, Taifali, Vandals, Gepids, had all been close neighbours in what are now Rumania and Southern Russia.[38] They all shared more or less the same sub-Roman frontier civilization which makes them so very difficult to distinguish from each other archaeologically.[39] Nearly all shared the Arian form of Christianity whose organized worship among Romans was harassed by imperial legislation. So barbarians in and out of Roman service had a good deal in common, and this is a more likely explanation of the failure of Roman armies to destroy the marauding bands than, for instance, the value of defeated barbarians as potential recruits.[40] There does not seem to have been any shortage of barbarian warriors. But whatever its cause, the inability of the authority to destroy barbarian bands had the result that if some large body of federates broke loose and vented its resentment on civilian areas within reach, the authorities were helpless;[41] at least they were never strong enough to impose terms which would make repetition of such behaviour impossible. Being unable to defend civilians the Empire lost the principal justification for its existence. No wonder the authorities got no spontaneous support among the plundered, though tax-paying, citizens.

If Stilicho had not been able to win a decisive victory in 393, the campaign did not harm his career, quite the reverse. In the following year when Theodosius took an army to the West to overthrow Eugenius, Stilicho was second-in-command under Timasius, and when Theodosius lay dying in 394, he appointed Stilicho guardian of

[37] AD 392/3, 395, 397, 402 (twice).
[38] E. A. Thompson (1966) ii (map).
[39] Frontier civilization: Th. Burns (1984) 11–13, J. Werner (1950).
[40] Suggested by H. Wolfram (1979) 161; cf. reluctance of Goths to fight Goths in Malchus fr. 18. 2 Blockley.
[41] The only consistent advantage enjoyed by the Empire was its ability to organize corn supplies, something the barbarians were unable to do when plunder was insufficient, cf. below.

his son Honorius, the emperor in the West.[42] The Thracian campaigns of 388 and 392–3 also brought Alaric into prominence for the first time. He was possibly one of the leaders, perhaps even the leader, of the Goths fighting imperial forces in the Macedonian marshes. He certainly succeeded in winning a notable victory over Theodosius himself.[43] Presumably he was one of the men who made the treaty with Rufinus, and was henceforth—as he may conceivably have already been before the mutiny—a *foederatus*. As had happened in the case of Stilicho, the military qualities displayed by Alaric in the Thracian campaign—though on the wrong side—were recognized. In the army sent against Eugenius he led a force of Gothic federates. He did not command them simply as a Gothic chieftain, but because he had been put in command by Theodosius.[44] At this time Theodosius was cultivating Gothic leaders by entertaining them at court. It was after one of these banquets that Fravitta killed his fellow guest Eriulf.[45] The purpose of the emperor's hospitality just before a major campaign was presumably to make sure of the loyalty of federate officers. We are not told that Alaric was one of the chieftains entertained, but he could well have been. Alaric was not the senior Gothic officer: that was Gainas.[46] It is likely that Alaric's soldiers included many who had fought under him in the marshes. The story of Alaric's Goths had begun.

The army that Theodosius sent against Eugenius and his *magister militum* Arbogast was much more powerful, or at least better organized, than the one that had overthrown Maximus. A large part of the defeated army of Maximus had been integrated into the Eastern army.[47] A considerable number of new regular formations had been raised, including at least twelve *auxilia*. Out of these units, old and new, Theodosius built up the two praesental armies recorded in the *Notitia Dignitatum*.[48] Many recruits for the new regular units are likely to have come from federate units which had fought against (or for) Maximus. They included a high proportion of Goths; for when Gainas returned to the East after the death of Theodosius his force was largely Gothic.[49] But Theodosius' army was not composed of

---

[42] Zos. iv. 59. 1, Oros. vii. 37. 1.

[43] Claud. *B. Get.* 524; VI *Cons. Hon.* 107–8. Was it perhaps the night attack of Zos. iv. 49? But see p. 51 n. 26.

[44] Zos. v. 5. 4.   [45] Eunapius fr. 59 Blockley, dated with ref. to Zos. iv. 56.

[46] Zos. v. 57, Eunapius fr. 60 Blockley.   [47] D. Hoffmann (1969) 470.

[48] D. Hoffmann (1974) 396–7 points out that the *Notitia* organization applied to the standing army in peace, but not its command on campaign. Zos. iv. 57 shows that on the Eugenius campaign division was not into three field armies but into one regular force and three federate contingents. The army did, however, march in three divisions: Pacatus *Pan. Lat.* xii. 32. 3. In peace the two praesental armies survived in 473–4 (Malchus fr. 2).

[49] See below, p. 102.

regular units only; there were federates as well. According to the not very reliable Jordanes these included no fewer than 20,000 Goths.[50] Of these, Alaric's men were presumably only a part. For instance a large number of volunteers from across the Danube is said to have joined Theodosius on the march.[51] No doubt the Goths settled in Moesia provided others. As was a Roman tradition, the federates were made to bear the brunt of the battle and casualties: as many as 10,000 Goths are reported to have died on the victorious side.[52] But Theodosius won the battle and the war. The usurper and his commander-in-chief were killed. Theodosius' army had done its duty once more.

Subsequent events saw the emergence of Alaric's Goths into the full light of history. The circumstances were these. Theodosius died in January 395, and Stilicho was left in charge of the West as guardian of young Honorius. Stilicho kept the bulk of the Eastern field army with him but returned what are said to have been weak and worn out units to the East.[53] The East certainly needed troops. There had been another invasion across the Danube when the river was frozen over. This time the invaders seem to have been Huns, who were particularly restless at this time: in the following summer they passed through the Caspian Gates to overrun wide areas in the East.[54] Widespread traces of devastation in the Balkans have been assigned to this period.[55] According to Claudian 'Europe to the frontiers of fertile Dalmatia' was plundered by Celtic (i.e. Gothic) bands, and all the land between the Black Sea and the Adriatic suffered devastation. It may be that the Goths and Alan federates in Pannonia had exploited the imperial army's preoccupation with the Eugenius war to break loose and to plunder their neighbours.[56] But there is no doubt that the enemy that mattered most were the Goths led by Alaric. They were the enemy against whom Stilicho led a large part of the combined field armies of East and West. In Claudian's view Stilicho would have destroyed this enemy if he had not once more been frustrated by Rufinus, prefect of the East, who negotiated an agreement with the Goths before Stilicho and his army had arrived.[57]

After Theodosius' victory over Eugenius, Alaric and his Goths had been sent back to the East, while the bulk of the army, including

---

[50] Jordanes *Get.* 145.　　　　　　[51] Socr. v. 25.

[52] Oros. vii. 35, cf. Tac. *Agr.* 35. 2.　　[53] Zos. v. 4.

[54] Claud. *In Ruf.* ii. 26 ff.; Philostorg. xi. 8, Jerome *Ep.* lx, lxxvii. 8 cf. H. Wolfram (1979) 164.

[55] J. Wilkes (1969) 419.

[56] *In Ruf.* ii. 36–8: Stilicho restores peace to Pannonia. Plundering by the returning Goths under Alaric has also been suggested as a cause of devastation, H. Wolfram (1979) 163 n. 130.

[57] *In Ruf.* ii. 75.

Gainas, the supreme commander of Gothic federates, had remained with Stilicho in the West. Although Alaric's services had been rewarded with a Roman dignity, perhaps the rank of *comes militaris*,[58] he was not satisfied. One reason for dissatisfaction was that he wanted to have regulars as well as federates under his command.[59] This was a demand regularly made by leaders of federates,[60] presumably because it represented higher prestige and a more secure position in the imperial hierarchy. It put the barbarian leader in a stronger position to demand supplies and other rewards for his followers. According to Zosimus it was anger at not being given Roman troops that motivated Alaric's rebellion and his invasion of Macedonia and Thessaly.[61] One might conjecture that resentment at the way the Goths had been made use of in battle, and fear that their return to the East was a preliminary to disbandment, or at least a cutting off of supplies, also played a part. It must also be remembered that the Goths were sent back after the death of Theodosius on 17 January 395, that is, in mid-winter when supplies would have been difficult to obtain, even if stocks had not been consumed in summer by Theodosius' great army on the way to Italy.

Thus it is easy to understand why the returning Goths should have first turned to plunder the countryside through which they were passing, and then entered into full mutiny. The standard view is that Alaric and his men were not content just to mutiny, but that they appealed to their fellow tribesmen settled in Moesia to leave their farms, and to join them in an attack on neighbouring provinces. As the settled Goths left their settlements, Alaric extended his authority from that of the leader of a mutinous regiment to that of the ruler of a migrating people. Alternative motives for the resumption of migration have been suggested: either that the Goths were eager to find a safer home because the lands near the Danube had proved excessively vulnerable to attack by Huns[62] or that they were seeking freedom from Roman rule.[63] According to either view the great mass of Teruingi, men, women, and children, now abandoned Moesia, leaving behind only what were to be called the 'Lesser Goths'.[64] The migration of Visigoths was resumed. But is this correct?

The evidence is unfortunately exceedingly scanty. The fullest account of the crucial rising is that of Zosimus, unsatisfactory as it is. His story is only a précis of the lost narrative of Eunapius, and already Eunapius' version seems to have fused two campaigns, Alaric's

[58] Socr. vii. 10. [59] Zos. v. 5.
[60] Cf. Malchus fr. 2. 24, fr. 18. 4; cf. also below, pp. 71, 82, and 101.
[61] Zos. v. 5. [62] H. Wolfram (1979) 163.
[63] L. Schmidt (1941) 423. [64] Ibid. 425; cf. below, p. 80.

invasion of Thessaly in 395 and his invasion of Greece in 396, into a single episode.[65] Furthermore, the account is so distorted by its bias against Rufinus that it is closer to invective than history. Unfortunately, Claudian, the other principal source, shows the same bias. Both are more concerned to accuse Rufinus of treasonable cooperation with the barbarians that to reveal what really happened. So the background to most of the recorded events remains extremely obscure.

As we have seen, the way Socrates and Zosimus describe the rebellion of Alaric in 395 makes it look like a straightforward mutiny of part of the Gothic federates of the Roman army. It is likely enough that they were joined by others when they were returning through the Balkans plundering as they went. In those disturbed times strength lay in numbers, and groups of barbarians tended to snowball, at least as long as they were successful. It is thus probable that Alaric's Goths attracted reinforcements from the federates in Pannonia and, in greater numbers, from their kinsmen settled in Moesia.[66] When the band eventually camped outside Constantinople they had become a formidable force.[67] But there is not a shadow of evidence that there had been a mass uprising of Goths settled on land. In fact the subsequent behaviour of Alaric's Goths was not that of men whom fear had induced to leave their farms and who were above all concerned to get back on to the land, somewhere safe from the Huns. After all, even if the Empire was not as formidable as it had once been, yet to make war on it must still have seemed an extremely unsafe thing to do. Moreover, in the negotiations between the Goths and Rufinus,[68] as in subsequent negotiations entered into by the Goths,[69] demand for farmland seems to have enjoyed a low priority. What does appear to have been the principal objective of the Goths was to put pressure on the government to concede more favourable conditions of maintenance for themselves as federates.[70]

The climax of Alaric's military operations in winter 395 was the plundering and devastation of farms in the immediate neighbourhood of Constantinople. Rufinus came out of the city dressed in furs like a barbarian and talked to their leaders, who presumably included

---

[65] Zos. v. 5. See Alan Cameron (1970) 474–7. For a comparable, probably Eunapius-derived, error see Zos. v. 26. It is known that Eunapius produced a second edition expurgating anti-Christian passages (Photius *Bibl.* 77). Could these deletions have confused the ecclesiastical historians, John of Antioch and Zosimus, when they used Eunapius as their principal source?

[66] Zos. v. 5. 4 ἄλλως σύγκλυδας. On Pannonian federates see above, p. 27–8.

[67] Claud. *In Ruf.* ii. 54.

[68] On these E. Demougeot (1951) 148.

[69] See below, pp. 59–60 and 63 ff.

[70] Cf. the behaviour of Theoderic Strabo, Malchus fr. 2. 22 Blockley.

Alaric.[71] Since the Eastern field army was still in the West, Rufinus' position was very weak, but he persuaded the Goths to withdraw, and, as his emperor Arcadius' subsequent orders to Stilicho showed, he seems to have thought that peace, or at least a truce, had been established between the Goths and the Empire. We are not told what the terms were. Rufinus presumably offered the Goths billets (*hospitalitas*) and subsidies.[72] There is certainly no suggestion that he offered them land. At any rate in spring 395 when Stilicho arrived with the combined armies of West and East they were in Thessaly seemingly at peace with the Eastern Empire. Claudian suggests that they were still devastating the countryside, but he may be referring to activities that had already ceased, or alternatively exaggerating into incendiarism what the Goths considered peaceful foraging. When Stilicho arrived, the Goths had concentrated their forces in a single plain and built a formidable camp with moat and double palisade, surrounded by a continuous circle of waggons.[73] When Stilicho was about to launch the assault, he received a letter from Arcadius forbidding him to do so. Instead he was to return to the Eastern government the units of the Eastern field army which had been in the West since the Eugenius campaign. Stilicho complied. It may be that he obeyed only because he could not control his huge army.[74] But the Eastern government would hardly have given the order unless it considered that hostilities with the Goths had already come to an end. The return of an important part of the army is likely to have been combined with a redistribution of military responsibilities. It has been shown that at the time of the death of Theodosius the whole of Illyricum was under the Eastern government.[75] Yet in 399, and probably even in 397, Illyricum was governed by the Western praetorian prefect Theodorus, while the eastern Balkans were governed by the Eastern prefect Anatolius.[76] The likeliest date for the division of Illyricum is surely that of the division of the army, and the occasion an agreement between Stilicho and Rufinus or, after the murder of Rufinus, between Stilicho and the eunuch Eutropius. The arrangement may have seemed common sense in 395/6. In the long term it satisfied neither party.

The Goths did not stay at peace. Soon after Stilicho's withdrawal we find them in Greece and the Peloponnese living off the country-

---

[71] *In Ruf.* ii. 73 ff.

[72] Cf. offer made to Theoderic Strabo, Malchus fr. 2; 18. 4. Zos. v. 5. 4: Alaric said to have campaigned on instruction from Rufinus.

[73] *In Ruf.* ii. 124 ff.   [74] Ibid. 169 ff.; cf. Alan Cameron (1970) 159–68.

[75] D. Hoffmann (1969–70) ii. 207–15.

[76] Ibid. 214 on Claudian *Pan. Manl. Theod.* 198–205; *CT* xi. 14. 3, cf. *PLRE* ii. 83 s.v. Anatolius I.

side and devastating it.[77] We are not told why the Goths broke loose once more. Of course federates tended to do this with very little provocation. The most common cause was that the imperial government had paid them insufficiently high subsidies. In the present situation the murder of Rufinus, who had reached agreement with the Goths, by Gainas with the evident support of the civil authorities at Constantinople may well have produced a sense of insecurity among the Goths.[78] This would have been particularly strong if Gainas and Alaric had been rivals while serving in the army, for Gainas had now become one of the principal figures in the East.[79] On this and subsequent occasions it is difficult to explain Alaric's behaviour on the assumption that he was the chosen leader of a nation of peasants in search of secure farmland. It is much easier to account for it if Alaric was a leader of mercenaries who sought to extort the highest possible pay for his men, and a command of prestige and high remuneration for himself. The pay of a Roman *magister militum* must have been beyond the dreams of avarice for a Goth. At any rate this is precisely what he eventually achieved.

Alaric invaded Greece, his forces by now including a strong body of cavalry.[80] In 397, two years later, Stilicho intervened once more.[81] He won some kind of victory over Alaric but not one that was decisive.[82] Alaric withdrew into Epirus, taking his plunder and seizing more from his new environment.[83] It was the Eastern government, at the time dominated by Eutropius,[84] that pacified him for the time being by giving him the command of its forces in Illyricum, with the title presumably of *magister militum*. This post put at his disposal the armament factories of the Illyrican diocese and entitled him to demand levies of iron from its cities.[85] He is even said to have exercised jurisdiction.[86] His Roman office was, however, a purely

[77] Zos. v. 5. 5; Claud. *In Ruf.* ii. 186 ff.

[78] *In Ruf.* ii. 366 ff.; cf. G. Albert (1984) 104–5.

[79] Alan Cameron (1970) 146–7 and below, p. 000.

[80] Sources for campaign: *PLRE* ii. 44 s.v. Alaricus I. Alaric's cavalry in Greece and later: Claudian *BG* 192–3; 216–18; *VI Cons. Hon.* 283. At Adrianople the Teruingi, the parent body of Alaric's Goths, had fought on foot. Cavalry was provided by the Greuthungi and Alans of Alatheus and Saphrax: Amm. xxx. 3. 1–3, xxxi. 12. 12; 12. 17.

[81] Why the delay? Perhaps he was short of troops after giving up the Eastern units, cf. above, p. 58. Perhaps he relied on Gainas.

[82] Claud. *IV Cons. Hon.* 459 ff.; *In Ruf.* ii praef. 9–15; *Cons. Stil.* 1. 185–6; *B. Get.* 513–17, 564; Socr. vii. 10.

[83] *In Ruf.* praef. 1–12, *IV Cons. Hon.* 473, *Cons. Stil.* 1. 184, Zos. v. 26. 1.

[84] See below, p. 93 ff.

[85] *B. Get.* 535–9, cf. 496–7. The armament factories of Illyricum were at Thessalonica, Naissus, Ratiaria, and Horreum Margi (*ND Or.* xi. 35–9). Were these the cities where the Goths were stationed?

[86] *In Eutrop.* ii. 214–18 (of Aug. 399).

military one since one Anatolius I is known to have headed the civilian administration as praetorian prefect of Illyricum between 397 and 399.[87]

Meanwhile Alaric's men and their wives[88] are said to have lived in cities, served by the slaves they had captured in Greece.[89] In other words, there was no attempt to settle Alaric's Goths on the land. They remained an army, quartered like other field army units in cities, and ready to go into action at any moment. In this their position was quite different from that of the settled Greuthungi of Tribigild in Asia Minor[90] who were expected to live by farming. Alaric's Goths must have received *annona* and perhaps pay.[91] If the Goths were stationed where their weapons were being produced their billets were in Naissus, Ratiaria, and Horreum Margi in Moesia Secunda.[92] Certainly his invasion of the Western Empire late in 401 was launched from this area, for they entered Pannonia near Sirmium.[93]

What we know about the quartering of the Goths is pitifully little, and yet it is more than we know about their circumstances during other stages of their wanderings. To supplement it we have a few details about those who were stationed in Aquitaine in support of the usurper Attalus in 414. At that time Goths were assigned to the well-to-do houses of Bordeaux as 'guests'. Later when the Goths abandoned Bordeaux with much pillaging these 'guests' protected the houses of their former hosts.[94] I think that we can assume that this kind of *hospitalitas* was how the Goths were generally accommodated when not actively campaigning.[95] Furthermore, there is very little evidence that for many years they demanded any more permanent arrangement which would involve farming their own land.

But even if Alaric's Goths were not in a hurry to settle down as farmers, they did not remain permanently satisfied with their status in eastern Illyricum, for late in autumn 401 Alaric invaded Italy.[96] The circumstances are obscure. The later Gothic version is that the Eastern government stopped its subsidies, and this compelled the Goths to seek food wherever it might be found.[97] It may be that the govern-

---

[87] *CT* xi. 14. 3; xvi. 8. 12; iv. 12. 7; vi. 28. 6, June 397–November 399.
[88] Cf. wives of Stilicho's federates: Zos. v. 35. 5.
[89] *In Eutrop.* ii. 196–201.　　　　　　[90] *In Eutrop.* ii. 196 ff.
[91] J. W. Eadie (1982) 34. Around Sirmium and in frontier forts coins end in the reign of Arcadius.
[92] See n. 85 above.　　　　　　[93] Jordanes *Get.* 147.
[94] Paulinus of Pella *Eucharisticus* 285 ff.
[95] On *hospitalitas* of this kind see W. Goffart (1980) 418–584, E. Demougeot (1956) 25–49.
[96] *Chron. Minor* i. 299, Claud. *B. Get.* 151–3 (in Italy one winter before the battle of Pollentia).
[97] Jordanes *Get.* 146.

ment at Constantinople, led by the *comes* John, encouraged Alaric to attack the West in the same way as later Eastern politicians were to encourage Theoderic, nephew of Valamer,[98] but if this is the case it is surprising that Claudian's poems, written soon after the invasion, do not attack the perfidy of the Eastern government. Surely they would have done if it had been known that the Eastern government had openly set in motion the dangerous barbarian invasions of Italy.[99]

If the Eastern government did not instigate Alaric's attack on the West, and Stilicho made no attempt to pin responsibility for the invasion on the ministers at Constantinople, it is nevertheless likely that an act of the Eastern government was the ultimate cause of Alaric's move. According to Jordanes the Eastern government had stopped the customary gifts (*dona*),[100] that is, the Goths' pay (*annona*) as federates. That Alaric and his Goths began military operations from dissatisfaction with the supplies provided for them is likely enough. Supplies were usually at the centre of conflicts between federates and the imperial government.[101] It is possible to construct a scenario to account for a cut in provisions for Alaric's Goths in late 401. In autumn 400 Thrace had been devastated by the Goths of Gainas.[102] In 401 it was plundered by 'runaway slaves and deserters claiming that they were Huns',[103] a combination recalling the followers of Tribigild in Asia two years earlier.[104] These marauders were eventually destroyed by Fravitta and his regular army, but the warfare must have produced a shortage of corn in the area. If Fravitta's recently victorious regulars were given precedence, Alaric's men will have gone short. The presence of Fravitta's army would have made warlike protestation against the Eastern empire unattractive. Italy on the other hand was undefended, since Stilicho and his field army were dealing with what appears to have been a large-scale invasion of Rhaetia.[105] So Alaric chose the easier option and invaded

---

[98] See below, p. 82.

[99] Claud. *B. Get.* 566–8 blames discord between the two courts for survival of Alaric. The East is not blamed for the invasion. That both emperors were consul in 402, that coins (not precisely dated) celebrate concord of East and West, the prominence of both emperors on the base of Arcadius' column, as well as the fact that Stilicho's claim to the regency of the East was omitted from Claud. *VI Cons. Hon.* all suggest that the invasion coincided with an attempt at reconciliation.   [100] Jordanes *Get.* 146, also below 106 n. 20.

[101] Cf. Malchus fr. 18. 1 Blockley = 10 Müller, 18. 4 Blockley = 11 Müller, etc.

[102] See below, p. 83.

[103] Zos. v. 22. Alan Cameron and others (1990) suggests that Uldin's Huns, *federates* after their defeat of Gainas (Zos. v. 22), threatened the Goths in Illyricum and induced them to leave for Italy. This could have been a factor.

[104] See below, p. 101.

[105] Claud. *B. Get.* 279–80, 363–5. The enemies were Vandals (ibid. 415), who were on the move from their previous territory in SE Europe and building up the huge band that was to break the Rhine frontier in December 406.

Italy, which also promised vastly more booty than the recently plundered European provinces of the Eastern empire. A possible sequence of events is that Alaric first offered to sell the services of his force to the Western Government, and launched the invasion after his offer had been refused.[106]

The decision to invade Italy was a momentous one. It is not surprising that it should have been remembered in Gothic tradition: indeed it is the first of Alaric's feats to have been so remembered. According to Jordanes the invasion was preceded by the election of Alaric to be king of his people. Jordanes' account of this phase of Gothic history is demonstrably unreliable[107] and it may well be that the Visigothic monarchy was created a few years later.[108] However this may be, there can surely be no doubt that the invasion of Italy represented a 'quantum leap' in the progress of Alaric and his band. No longer simply the leader of a force of seditious mercenaries basically concerned to improve their own conditions of service, Alaric had now achieved the stature and power of a tribal leader. Alaric's kingship inaugurated a new epoch in his warriors' view of themselves as well as of him, a view which was accepted by the Romans only later.[109]

To judge by admittedly very inadequate source evidence Alaric did not meet with resistance before entering Italy.[110] The substantial frontier forces listed in the *Notitia*[111] were either no longer (or not yet) in position,[112] or did not consider it their duty to confront a major invasion. When Alaric's force arrived in Italy it seemed like a

---

[106] *B. Get.* 568: 'et alternae periuria venditat aulae' suggests that Alaric made an offer to the West before the invasion—at least we hear of no earlier attempt by Alaric to 'sell his perjuries' to the Western court.

[107] Jordanes *Get.* 153–4, 159, 160.

[108] See *PLRE* ii s.v. Alaricus for titles given to Alaric by classical authors. Prudentius *Contra Symmachum* ii. 695: 'tyrannus'. It is significant that he is not called 'King' by Olympiodorus, or by Sozomen and Socrates, who probably derive from Olympiodorus. He is a king in Orosius (finished c.418) and in Augstine's *Retractatio* ii. 43. 1 (c.427), but not in *De Civitate Dei*, where there is only one direct reference to him (i. 2). Judging by Ammianus, Romans had a view as to what position among barbarians constituted kingship. Athanaric was a king or 'judge' of the Teruingi (xxx. 7. 7; xxxi. 3. 4); Ermenerichus was king of the Greuthungi, as was his successor (xxxi. 3. 3, 4. 12). But neither Alavius nor Fritigern who led the Teruingi within the empire is described as king.

[109] Cf. reluctance to recognize the kingship of Theoderic Triarius and Theoderic Valamer; Malchus fr. 2: Leo recognizes Triarius as sole αὐτοκράτωρ of Goths (in Thrace?), but not as king. In Malchus Theoderic Valamer is not described as 'king' either, though *he* surely was.

[110] Roman defeat on Timavus: Claud. *B. Get.* 562.

[111] *ND Oc.* xxxii. 22–39, E. Demougeot (1979) 106.

[112] Finds of coins end in this frontier region in the reign of Arcadius, perhaps soon after the death of Theodosius I. Was this because troops had been withdrawn or only because payment of *stipendium* in money had been given up? (So A. H. M. Jones (*LRE*) 443.) It seems that after 396 the empire no longer issued silver currency: J. W. E. Pearce, *Roman Imperial Coinage* ix. xxvi ff.

conquering army. At least Claudian maintains that Alaric's objective was nothing less than the conquest of Italy.[113] But his demands in the course of subsequent invasions, when he was in an even stronger position, make it unlikely that conquest was his objective. The problem is that for the history of this invasion we depend largely on the evidence of Claudian's *De Bello Getico* and *De Sexto Consulatu Honorii*, and, as Alan Cameron has seen, Claudian has not told the whole story.[114] On the contrary, he seems to have been as anxious to obscure as to reveal. For although Stilicho did succeed in checking Alaric's invasion of Italy he evidently did not win decisive victories of the traditional Roman kind. The battle of Pollentia at Easter 402 could be claimed as a victory, as the Romans captured Alaric's camp, containing his and his men's families and much treasure.[115] But the battle left Alaric strong enough to advance across the Po in the direction of Rome.[116] Then negotiations ensued, Stilicho presumably using the Goths' dependents as a bargaining counter. Firm terms were agreed,[117] though Claudian is careful not to give details, presumably because the Romans made significant concessions. Subsequently Alaric withdrew by slow stages[118] across the Po and towards Venetia, probably carrying out an agreement to leave Italy. But then, in circumstances that remain obscure, agreement broke down and hostilities were resumed.[119] In summer 402[120] another battle was fought, this time outside Verona. Alaric suffered a serious defeat. He decided to abandon Italy and to march through Rhaetia into Gaul.[121] When this operation was defeated by Stilicho Alaric was abandoned by considerable parts of his force, particularly cavalry.[122] The last we hear of him is that he was retreating with the remnants of his band followed by Stilicho.[123] He must have retreated towards the Balkans. Claudian says nothing about this although at the time of his poem on

[113] Claud. *B. Get.* 530; *IV Cons. Hon.* 183; Jordanes *Get.* 152–3: Alaric asked for Goths to be allowed to live in Italy so that one might think them one people with Romans. But Jordanes' account is confused, possibly because it telescopes pieces of information about incidents widely separated in time, e.g. he has Gaiseric king of the Vandals in 401—and in Gaul.

[114] Alan Cameron (1970) 80 ff.

[115] *B. Get.* 624 ff.; *VI Cons. Hon.* 297–8, cf. 130.

[116] *VI Cons Hon.* 285 ff., cf. *B. Get.* 90–103, *VI Cons. Hon.* 211–12.

[117] Treaty: *VI Cons. Hon.* 210. That it involved the abandonment of Italy by the Goths: *B. Get.* 144; *VI Cons. Hon.* 130. *B. Get.* 646–8 surely implies that the invasion is over.

[118] Hindered by floods: *VI Cons. Hon.* 193 ff.

[119] Ibid. 210.

[120] On the date I am persuaded by N. H. Baynes (1955a) 326–30 against T. D. Barnes (1976) 373–6. Stilicho was at Rome after Pollentia and before Verona (*VI Cons. Hon.* 123–4). This need not mean that Alaric had left Italy. One can imagine a variety of urgent reasons why Stilicho should have come to Rome presumably to negotiate with senators and senate, even though Alaric was still in Italy, or even precisely because he was still in Italy.

[121] *VI Cons. Hon.* 230 ff.

[122] Ibid. 251 ff.; cf. p. ooo below.   [123] Ibid. 320–24.

the sixth consulate of Honorius (early in 404?) he must have known what had happened. It is likely that once again an agreement involving compromises had been reached. Perhaps the Romans gave hostages[124] as well as the Goths. Perhaps they agreed to provide *annona* in return for the Goths stationing themselves in the barbarous regions bordering on Dalmatia and Pannonia,[125] perhaps in Savia or Pannonia II,[126] as at least a potential army ready to be used by—or against—the conqueror; a large band of federates differing from other such groups only in the extent of their independence. Certainly it was as federates that Stilicho in due course proposed to use them against the Eastern emperor.

During 404 relations between East and West again fell to a very low ebb.[127] When Arcadius sent images of the empress Eudoxia together with his own into the provinces around New Year 404 the Western government took umbrage.[128] About the same time there was a barbarian invasion of Eastern Illyricum of which the East did not formally notify the West.[129] Some time later we find Stilicho making an alliance with Alaric to seize the Illyrican provinces under Eastern administration.[130] He appointed one Jovius to be praetorian prefect with instructions to cooperate with Alaric in an invasion of Eastern Illyricum.[131] What was the cause of the renewed conflict? One possible explanation involves political manoeuvres of the *comes* John who was at that time *comes sacrarum largitionum*, and very influential in the East.[132] John was accused of working for conflict with the West, and was held to be indirectly responsible for the death of the general Fravitta, who had favoured a policy of concord between the emperors. The date of this affair is uncertain but it may be that it happened in 403–4.[133] In that case the dispute is likely to have been over the policy the East should adopt towards Alaric's return to its half of Illyricum.

As we have seen, Alaric had withdrawn from Italy into the territory between the empires.[134] Sometime after,[135] according to Honorius'

---

[124] Merobaudes iv. 42–6, 'Latio faces removit' (Aetius as hostage with Goths), fits 402 better than 405.   [125] Soz. viii. 25. 3–4, ix. 4. 2–4.

[126] Around Savia? (L. Schmidt (1941) 441; Moesia I (P. Heather (1986) 200). It is more likely that before marching into Epirus the Goths were in a Western province, e.g. Pannonia II. Cf. below, p. 65. Honorius *Ep.* 38 (*CSEL* xxxv. 85).

[127] No hostility yet in Claud. *VI Cons. Hon.* of early 404. But Stilicho did not recognize Eastern consuls of either 404 or 405: Alan Cameron (1988*b*) 32.

[128] Honorius *Ep.* 38 (*CSEL* xxxv. 85).

[129] Ibid. 'excidium pereuntis Illyrici'. *Ep.* 38 is of summer 405. The destruction of Illyricum was earlier, perhaps autumn 403: W. Liebeschuetz (1985*a*) 29.

[130] Zos. v. 26; Soz. viii. 25, repeated 17. 4.

[131] Soz. viii. 25, cf. *PLRE* ii s.v. Iovius 3.

[132] Pall. *Dial.* 19, Synesius *Ep.* 110, cf. *PLRE* ii s.v. Ioannes 2.

[133] Eunapius fr. 71. 3 Blockley = 85 Müller. On this see below, p. 123–5.

[134] See above, n. 126.   [135] See above, n. 129.

letter, Illyricum and more specifically eastern Illyricum, was devastated.[136] We know of no band of barbarians in this area other than
Alaric's Goths, and the next we hear of Alaric's Goths is that they are
in Epirus, 'the lands inhabited by Molossians, and Thesprotians as far
north as Epidamnus'.[137] According to Zosimus and Sozomen the
Goths had moved into Epirus by agreement with Stilicho.[138] So it
might have seemed from the point of view of the East, but Honorius
suggests that the Goths had moved back into Eastern territory spon-
taneously, certainly without his knowledge.[139] It would not be surprising if they had decided to return to the area where their strength
had grown so much before they had set out to invade Italy.

This theory of the movement of Goths has the advantage of providing an explanation of Stilicho's alliance with Alaric. The Goths
had withdrawn into Eastern territory where they were out of Stilicho's
reach. The Eastern government, far from making an attempt to control them, simply ignored their presence. In the circumstances they
represented a potential menace to Italy. Stilicho's counter was to
make a treaty with the Goths—as he was almost bound to do sooner
or later. But as they were on Eastern territory the agreement involved
an infringement of the rights of the East. The position of Alaric in
Eastern Illyricum in alliance with Stilicho was comparable to that of
Gildo in North Africa after he had transferred his allegiance from the
Western court to that of the East.[140] No wonder that something close
to a state of war arose between East and West. The East will have
been eager to regain control of the territory as soon as possible,
Stilicho to make sure that the warlike energies of Alaric's Goths
continued to be directed towards Eastern objectives. If the Goths
could become thoroughly involved in a campaign against armies of
the East, Italy would be safe from them.

In the end the campaign had to be postponed because in 405
Radagaisus, the Gothic leader of another vast war band made up of
Germans and 'Celts' entered the empire and invaded Italy.[141] The

[136] 'Etiam super excidio pereuntis Illyrici pio apud vos prodiderimus affectu esse nobis
dolori, cur ista nos detrimenta rei publicae nolueritis agnoscere et aliis potius indicibus quam
pietatis vestrae litteris fuerint nuntiata.'

[137] Zos. v. 26. The dating of this second Gothic occupation of Epirus is difficult because Zos.
v. 26 telescopes events of 397/8 and of 404, while Soz. viii. 25 and ix. 4 put the same events in
404 and 407/8. In favour of dating Alaric's arrival in Epirus to 404 rather than 407/8 is that
the senate in 408 Stilicho said that Alaric had been in Epirus 'a long time' (Zos. v. 29). This
would fit 404 rather than 407.

[138] Zos. v. 26, 29; Soz. viii. 25.

[139] Honorius' complaint is that Arcadius had not informed him about events in Illyricum.

[140] See below, p. 98.

[141] *PLRE* ii. 934, J. Matthews (1975) 274 n. 5: date of invasions 405–6, execution of
Radagaisus 23. 8. 406. *Additamenta ad Prosp. Havn.* (marg.) ad a. 405.

situation was extremely dangerous, but Stilicho managed to bring him to battle and to destroy his force. Stilicho's army included 30 units of regulars,[142] as well as Gothic federates led by Sarus and Huns from across the Danube under their king Huldin.[143] Alaric took no part. In Epirus he was well out of the way of the invading horde. After the defeat of Radagaisus preparations for the attack on the East were resumed. Stilicho would join Alaric in Illyricum, and together they would seize the eastern half of that region for the Western Empire.[144] Alaric's role was still essentially that of a leader of federates.

Once again fate intervened. On the last day of 406 the Rhine frontier was broken by a huge and mixed horde of barbarians.[145] Gaul was being overrun. Strangely enough it was not the catastrophic invasion which induced Stilicho to put off operations against the East. What moved him was the reaction of the threatened provincials. Constantine III, a usurper set up by the army in Britain, crossed over into Gaul, presumably to organize defence, and won the support of the Gallic army.[146] As during the crisis of the third century, Gaul had lost confidence in the willingness of the imperial government in Italy to defend the western provinces and set up an emperor of its own.[147] Constantine III gained control of the whole of Gaul and made Arles his capital. It was Constantine's success that induced Honorius to prohibit Stilicho from proceeding against the East, and Stilicho to obey.[148]

Even now the eastern operation was postponed rather than cancelled. Alaric was left in Epirus during the whole of 407.[149] Stilicho remained in Italy and sent Sarus with a force of federates into Gaul to fight, not the invading Germans, but Constantine III. Sarus was unsuccessful. On his retreat across the Alps he encountered Bagaudae who compelled him to surrender his booty.[150] In 408, more than a year after the barbarians had crossed the Rhine, Alaric left Epirus and pitched camp at Emona, on the route from Pannonia into Italy[151] and actually within the diocese of Italy.[152] He was now in a position to back his demands for money with threats of instant invasion. It is likely that this was the reason for his move, but it is possible that he had been formally recalled by Stilicho. After the defeat suffered by Sarus Stilicho must have been in need of an army to send to Gaul. At any

---

[142] Zos. v. 26.   [143] Oros. vii. 37.   [144] Zos. vi. 27.
[145] Rhine frontier broken: last day of 406. Constantine comes into Gaul: 407. See *PLRE* ii. 316 s.v. Constantinus 21.
[146] Zos. vi. 2–3.   [147] J. F. Drinkwater (1983) 225 ff.
[148] Zos. v. 27.   [149] He left in 408, more than a year later: Zos. v. 25.
[150] Zos. vi. 2.   [151] Zos. v. 29, cf. R. Egger (1948) 57 ff.
[152] J. Matthews (1975) 47 n. 1.

rate, Alaric now demanded to be paid, not only for the period spent in Epirus, but also for the return march to Emona.[153] He demanded no less than 4000 lb. of gold,[154] enough to keep 72,000 men for a year,[155] or twice the cost of the praetorian games produced by Symmachus in the name of his son.[156] Alaric and his men were bargaining just like mercenaries enrolled for a specified campaign. For the operations in Epirus the Empire must have guaranteed food supplies, but evidently had not provided pay. Presumably portable reward was anticipated in the shape of booty. Since there had been no campaign and no booty the federates demanded compensation. They pitched their demands high because their employer was in difficulties, but the demands remained within the category of payment for services. After receiving their payment the Goths would remain in the employment of the Empire. It was Stilicho's intention that Alaric should proceed to Gaul with part of his own Gothic forces, as well as regular Roman units and officers, to lead an offensive against Constantine the usurper.[157] He had great difficulty in persuading the senate to vote the payment. It is likely that the 'deal' was seen as a betrayal by many influential Romans[158] and that it formed a motive for the conspiracy which not long after brought about the destruction of Stilicho and his civilian supporters.[159]

Even now although Gaul was in uproar, and Alaric at the gates of Italy, Stilicho had not given up his plan of launching operations against the East eventually. Indeed the death of Arcadius on 1 May 408 revived his hope of becoming regent for a child emperor in the East, the six-year-old Theodosius II.[160] When his power collapsed in August 408 Stilicho was hoping to proceed to the East himself with four regiments of regulars, while Alaric with part of his Goths, and some Roman troops, was to campaign in Gaul against the usurper Constantine. It is difficult to understand Stilicho's obsession with control of Illyricum and the East. Perhaps he and his advisers were motivated by an emotional attachment to the unity of the Empire. There certainly is no evidence that he regarded the Balkans as an indispensable recruiting area. When he needed troops he seems to have looked for Germans.[161] Again, one wonders why Stilicho was so much more concerned with the usurper than with the German invaders whom the usurper was resisting. But as far as Alaric is

[153] Zos. v. 29.   [154] Zos. v. 29.

[155] H. Wolfram (1979) 183.

[156] J. Matthews (1975) 277 on Olympiod. fr. 44.

[157] Zos. v. 31; perhaps Jordanes *Get.* 153 is a garbled memory.   [158] Zos. v. 29.

[159] v. 32–4; 30. 1: peace achieved, presumably the gold had been paid.

[160] Zos. v. 31; on Stilicho and the regency see A. Cameron (1970) 37–45.

[161] See above, p. 34; cf. Olympiod. fr. 5. 2 Blockley.

concerned Stilicho's attitude is clear. He regarded him and his men as
an unreliable and dangerous, but also potentially useful, mercenary
force. Moreover the Goths seem to have seen themselves in the same
light. They ruthlessly exploited the difficulties of the Empire to extort
pay for themselves. But they were also willing to move from province
to province, from one campaign in the Empire's service to the next.

This attitude survived the coup d'état which overthrew Stilicho and
finally put an end to his plans. The catastrophe of Stilicho affected
Alaric and his Goths in two ways. First, it meant that the government
of Rome was now in the hands of men determined—rather too late in
the day—to reverse the growth of barbarian power in the Western
Empire.[162] Secondly, Alaric's army had been reinforced by a very
large number of what had been Stilicho's federates, bitterly hostile to
everything Roman, because their wives and children had been
massacred.[163] Thus Alaric's army was greatly strengthened, while the
forces of the Western government were disastrously weakened.
Alaric must have been tempted to make war and to extort land for
settlement—if land was what he had really wanted. But in fact Alaric
was content to preserve the truce which he had made with Stilicho.
He only asked for additional money. If he got that, and if there was
an exchange of hostages, he would move his army out of Noricum
(from where he was threatening Italy) into Pannonia.[164] It has been
suggested that this meant that Alaric asked to be assigned land which
his men might farm. But this is not necessarily so. Zosimus' words
need not imply that Alaric demanded anything more permanent than
the status which he and his men had enjoyed first in Eastern
Illyricum, later in Pannonia, and after that in Epirus: that is, a claim
to billets and to supplies derived from the regular taxes in kind of the
province—and possibly a special issue of corn to tide them over to
the next harvest.[165]

It is true that Orosius writing around 416 implies something more
when he claims that 'Alaric and the whole Gothic people were
humbly seeking fair terms and somewhere to live (*sedes*)'.[166] But this
statement should not be accepted without qualification. It is part of a
highly tendentious passage. Orosius is extremely apologetic as far as
Alaric is concerned. He was after all writing not so much a history as
a defence of Christianity, which had recently become the new state
religion of the Roman Empire and had signally failed to prevent the

[162] Zos. v. 32 (Olympius), 35 (his friends); cf. J. Matthews (1975) 284–6.

[163] Zos. v. 35. 6: 30,000 men.

[164] Zos. v. 36. I see no evidence that Alaric asked to rule the provinces in which the Goths
would live, as suggested by A. H. M. Jones *LRE* 201.

[165] Cf. Malchus fr. 20 p. 438. 54–8, 440. 96.

[166] Oros. vii. 38.

sack of Rome.[167] To explain why the God of the Christians had allowed Alaric to sack Rome Orosius insists that Alaric too was a Christian, if a heretical one, that his cause had been just, and that he used his victory with moderation. The portrait of Alaric is likely to be just as distorted as that of the villainous Stilicho which is a foil to it. This does not of course disprove that Alaric asked for *sedes*, whatever the precise meaning of this might be, but it does weaken the value of Orosius' evidence.

It should also be borne in mind that Orosius' statement does not refer to any particular point of time. It is possible that he had attributed to Alaric in his negotiations with Stilicho a negotiating position which in fact the Goths were only to take up at a considerably later stage of their campaigning within the Empire. But whether this is so or not, it remains the case that, with the exception of this imprecise and rhetorical passage of Orosius, the other sources do not suggest that a demand for land to farm was an important issue in the negotiations between the Goths and the Empire.

When Alaric's seemingly very moderate demands were turned down he prepared for war, calling for massive reinforcements in the form of an army of Goths and Huns to be led from Pannonia by Athaulfus, his brother-in-law.[168] Evidence is poor, but Athaulfus' army may well have been a roaming force of warriors very similar to that of Radagaisus or Alaric's own.[169] After it had been reinforced by Athaulfus[170] Alaric's army must have been a very large one, and the people who had been with him since his invasion of Thrace and Greece in 394/5 will have become quite a small proportion of it. But presumably Goths predominated among the newcomers as they had done in the original force. Alaric launched his invasion of Italy before Athaulfus had joined him. Even so, there was practically no resistance.[171] Rome was besieged during the winter of 408/9, and the imperial army could do nothing about it. Alaric was being joined by large numbers of slaves until his force is said to have amounted to 40,000.[172] He dictated the terms on which he would allow food into the city: 5000 lb. of gold, 30,000 lb. of silver, large quantities of clothing and spices.[173] He also demanded hostages.[174] If these were granted he would not only make peace, but also a defensive alliance (ὁμαιχμίαν) and march with the Romans against any of their enemies.

---

[167] On Orosius see S. Teillet (1984) 112–60.

[168] Zos. v. 37.

[169] H. Wolfram (1979) 200–2 suggests that he was a successor of Alatheus and Saphrax in the leadership of the Gothic, Hun and Alan federates.

[170] Zos. v. 45.

[171] v. 37.   [172] v. 42.   [173] v. 41.

[174] v. 42.

The money was paid, but peace was not achieved.[175] The reason given by Zosimus is that the emperor refused to hand over hostages to Alaric.[176] If Zosimus is right, land for settlement did not figure in the negotiations. We cannot, however, be sure of this, as Zosimus is merely summarizing the now lost, but probably reliable, account of Olympiodorus, and Zosimus' summarizing is—as we have seen—liable to be careless.

There was another bout of negotiations in 409. Imperial reinforcements from Dalmatia were wiped out in an ambush[177] and the senate was becoming anxious for a negotiated settlement.[178] Alaric demanded annual payments in corn and gold, and that he and all his men should be allowed to live (οἰκεῖν) in the two Venetian provinces, in Noricum, and in Dalmatia. It was also hinted that Alaric might be content with less if he was given the command of both Roman and Gothic forces, that is, if he was once more given a position similar to that which had been his in Epirus by agreement with Eutropius, and later in Western Illyricum by agreement with Stilicho. Again it looks as if what was being discussed was the stationing of an army and not the settlement of peasants. This time the negotiations failed because the emperor, while ready to grant all concessions which involved finance, refused to confer on Alaric the rank of general.[179] After this the emperor strengthened his position by enrolling 10,000 Hun federates,[180] and Alaric reduced his terms. He dropped the demand to be made a general and he no longer required all the provinces previously demanded for habitation, πρὸς οἴκησιν.

He would be content with the two Norican provinces, situated as they were on the Danube frontier of the Empire and exposed to continual barbarian attack. The Goths would be content with as much corn annually as the emperor thought suitable, and would drop the demand for gold. He also once more proposed a formal military alliance with the Empire.[181] This looks like a demand that the Goths should be recognized as an independent but allied army stationed in the Empire. There is no explicit reference to settlement on land. 'Dwell' and 'habitation' (οἰκεῖν, οἴκησις)[182] need not imply 'settlement'. Indeed, the fact that the Goths asked for corn annually suggests that farming was not envisaged: if it had been, they would have been able to grow their own. But if, as intended, the Gothic men would march or ride off on campaigns as soon as the emperor needed them, they would be unable to cultivate fields and would thus require

---

[175] v. 42.   [176] v. 44.   [177] v. 45.

[178] v. 44. 1; 45. 5.   [179] v. 48–49.

[180] v. 50.   [181] v. 50.

[182] Zos. v. 50. 31, Olympiod. fr. 8. 1 Blockley = Soz. ix. 7.

government supplied corn (*annona*) like regular units of the Roman army. Gold they could win for themselves by plundering.

These terms were rejected by Honorius and his advisers on the grounds that they had sworn an oath never to make peace with Alaric.[183] The Roman authorities were following the ancient, but no longer appropriate principle of refusing to negotiate with an armed enemy in Italy. In this situation Alaric gave up hope of coming to terms with Honorius, but since the Goths needed to come to terms with somebody, he proceeded to create a more compliant emperor. He got the war-weary senate to elect Attalus, the prefect of the city. The new emperor and his ministers must have come to some sort of arrangement with the Goths. Attalus gave Alaric the position of *magister militum*,[184] Athaulfus of *comes domesticorum equitum*. Alaric confirmed his agreement by an oath.[185] We are not told what the rank-and-file Goths received, perhaps corn and gold. Their return was to campaign to win Northern Italy for Attalus.[186] They remained what they had always been, an army. As such the Goths expected to be called upon to participate in an expedition which Attalus was going to send to Africa. Attalus did not trust the Goths sufficiently and refused to use them for this mission. As a result the expedition failed, and not very long after Alaric formally deposed Attalus[187] and resumed negotiations with Honorius.

When we look back over the successive negotiations between Alaric and Roman authorities it is clear that the problem of finding farms in sufficiently large numbers to satisfy the Goths is not mentioned as an issue that caused negotiations to break down: it is in fact not mentioned at all. Problems of finance and the provision of gold and supplies did arise, but appear to have been solvable.[188] The fatal difficulties lay elsewhere. One primary issue was evidently whether Alaric might be given a command that would include Roman regulars as well as his own Goths.[189] Even more troubling to the Roman authorities was the question whether in the circumstances it was right to make a treaty with Alaric at all.[190] It was a matter of traditional pride and self-respect. The dilemma might be formulated as reluctance to formally recognize the roaming army of Alaric as independent allies, (*foederati* in the traditional sense) and the insistence that they should be treated as surrendered enemies (*dediticii*).[191]

---

[183] Zos. v. 49, 51.
[184] Zos. vi. 7. 2; Soz. ix. 8. 2.
[185] Zos. vi. 10. [186] Zos. vi. 9–10.
[187] Zos. vi. 7. 5, 9. 2–3; Olympiod. fr. 13.
[188] e.g. Zos. v. 45, 48. [189] v. 48. [190] v. 29.
[191] On *dediticii* Amm xx. 8. 13, *CT* vii. 13. 16 (406).

It would seem, therefore, that the issues facing the officials of Honorius after 395 were quite different from those which had faced Valens in 375 or Theodosius in 383. Valens and Theodosius had to find land for an uprooted peasant nation pressing to be resettled on farms. The officials of Honorius were asked to recognize and give the status of independent allies (*foederati*) to an army permanently billeted within the borders of the Empire, and at least as ready to fight against the emperor as for him. It was because the agreements proposed by Alaric would have left the Goths with their independence and mobility as well as their arms, that the government found it so difficult to reach lasting accommodation with them.

The climax of the Goths' campaigning in Italy was the capture and sack of Rome in 410.[192] Then and during the following three or four years no Roman army could seriously interfere with their operations. One would imagine that if they had been determined to seize a permanent home they could have done so. But their campaigning seems to have been extraordinarily aimless. Shortly before his death Alaric tried to move his Goths into Sicily and from there into Africa. It may be that he wanted to conquer the provinces and settle his men there in the way the Vandals were to do some years later. Alternatively, he might simply have intended to punish Heraclianus III, the *comes Africae*, who had been a vigorous opponent of himself and of Attalus, his puppet emperor.[193] We shall never know what the operation was intended to achieve, since it failed with a number of ships and the men on them foundering in a storm.[194]

In detail the history of these years is obscure, as the great narrative history of Olympiodorus has survived only in fragments.[195] Certain elements in the situation are clear enough. The Goths did not encounter any regular force powerful enough to defeat them decisively in the field. On the other hand they were never themselves in a position to dictate terms. Their recurring weakness was inability to provide sufficient food for themselves by plundering.[196] Repeatedly they were forced to try to reach agreement with Roman authorities, because only the Roman authorities had at their disposal the administrative machinery needed to bring adequate supplies to the Goths. So when Athaulfus, the successor of Alaric, had plundered large areas of Italy[197] and the government of Honorius still would not negotiate, he allied

---

[192] See refs in *PLRE* ii. 485 s.v. Alaricus I.
[193] Zos. vi. 7. 11–12.
[194] Jord. *Get.* 156–7; Oros. vii. 43. 2; Olympiod. fr. 15.
[195] E. Demougeot (1979) 460–72.
[196] e.g. Olympiod. fr. 22. 1–2 Blockley; ibid. 26. 2; Oros. vii. 43. 1.
[197] Jordanes *Get.* 159, *CT* xi. 28. 7 (May 412) by implication.

himself with the usurper Jovinus (*c.* 412) and entered Gaul.[198] Disillusioned with Jovinus he negotiated with Honorius' representative Dardanus, the praetorian prefect of the Gauls.[199] In 412/3 the Goths became federates in the service of the government of Honorius and were assigned *hospitalitas* in Aquitaine.[200] When the government either could not, or would not, provide all the corn it had promised the federates rebelled.[201] An attempt to end dispute by means of the marriage, accompanied by impressive ceremonies, of Athaulfus with Galla Placidia, a daughter of Theodosius I, was unsuccessful in the long run (January 414).[202] Full war was resumed. Blockade was the most successful weapon on the Roman side.[203] The Goths were forced to leave Gaul and enter Spain.[204] They roamed through Spain as they had recently done through Italy. An attempt to cross into Africa failed.[205] Eventually they tried to return to Gaul across the Pyrenees but found that the imperial army blocked the routes.[206] The Goths were once again desperately short of corn.[207] Negotiations had a chance and succeeded. A balanced agreement was reached. The Goths were to receive 600,000 *modii* of corn,[208] enough to feed 15,000. In return they gave hostages, agreed to liberate Gallia Placida, by now the widow of Athaulfus who had been taken prisoner during the sack of Rome in 410,[209] and to campaign on behalf of the empire once more in order to free Spain from Vandal and other invaders.[210] In other words the Goths agreed once more to take service as federates. But the agreement probably contained another highly significant provision: the Goths were promised that after the coming series of campaigns they would be given land to farm in Gaul.[211] In the long

---

[198] Prosper Tiro *Epit. Chron.* 1246 a 412 (*Chron. Minor.* i. 466), *Chron. Gall.* 67 a 411 (*Chron. Minor.* i. 654).

[199] Olympiod. fr. 20. 1 Blockley, *Chron. Gall.* 69 s.a. 411 (*Chron. Minor.* i. 654).

[200] Paulinus of Pella *Eucharisticus* 285 ff. suggests that the hospitality in Aquitaine had already been arranged by Jovinus and Attalus before the agreement with Honorius. But see also Prosper Tiro 1254 s.a. 414; Paulinus of Pella *Eucharisticus* 294–301.

[201] Olympiod. fr. 22. 1–2 (AD 413?).

[202] Olympiod. fr. 24; Oros. vii. 40. 2; 43. 2; Hydatius 57 s.a. 414.

[203] Famine: *Chron. Gall.* 72.

[204] Oros. vii. 43. 1; Paulinus of Pella *Eucharisticus* 311 ff.; Rutil. Namat. *De Red.* 1. 496; Jordanes *Get.* 163.   [205] Oros. vii. 43. 11–12 (storm and shipwreck).

[206] Jordanes *Get.* 164–5.   [207] Olympiod. fr. 29. 1.

[208] Olympiod. fr. 30. According to A. H. M. Jones *LRE* iii. 39 n. 65 a year's ration for 13,000–15,000. For basis of calculation see ibid. 191 n. 44, 217 n. 23. M. Rouche (1971) estimates 20,000 warriors and following. In 503 and 505 Roman armies campaigning in Mesopotamia drew respectively 630,000 and 850,000 *modii*. A. H. M. Jones *LRE* 231–2 estimates armies at 16,500 and 20,000 respectively.

[209] Olympiod. fr. 30, Oros. vii. 43 on Galla Placidia, cf. *PLRE* ii s.v. Aelia Galla Placidia 4.

[210] Jordanes *Get.* 165–6.

[211] Olympiod. fr. 26. 2 = Philostorgius 12. 4–5 χώρας εἰς γεωργίαν ἀποκληροσάμενον—only a promise, as the next two years were spent in Spain fighting the Vandals: *Chron. Gall.* 562, Hydatius 63, 67, 68.

sequence of summaries of negotiations between Goths and Romans this is the first time that the provision of land for farming by the Goths is explicitly mentioned. After more than twenty years as an army the band that had been Alaric's Goths were about to undergo metamorphosis into a settled peasant people.

After two years of highly successful fighting, and before they had had the opportunity to defeat the Asding Vandals and the Suebi, the Goths were recalled to Gaul by the imperial general Constantius.[212] It may be that Constantius required the presence of the Goths in Aquitanica II in order to protect the landowners against the unrest spreading from Armorica.[213] Alternatively he may have thought that settlement of the Goths was the only way to restore stability to the Western provinces, and decided to settle them in an area which had good land whose owners had been badly shaken by the invasions of the previous ten years and were too demoralized to resist a command to share their land.[214]

In fact the sacrifice demanded from the Aquitanian landowners seems to have been heavy. The principle on which the Goths were assigned land was related to the rules in accordance with which they had previously been billeted.[215] A soldier was entitled to use a third of the house in which he was quartered. Division in the proportion of one to two was also employed in the land settlement, except that in this case the 'guest' received two thirds of the estate while it was the previous owner who had to be content with one third.[216] W. Goffart has shown that in detail the laws of military hospitality found in the Roman Codes are quite inappropriate to a situation like that of the Goths in Aquitaine, and that they do not in fact provide any guidance to what arrangements were actually made in 418.[217] But his conclusion that what was divided in Aquitaine was not land but revenue is unconvincing.[218] Admittedly the chronicles are ambiguous, since they do not actually state that the Goths were given land for the purpose of farming it.[219] But the Visigothic laws have to be interpreted very

[212] *Chron. Gall.* 565, Hydatius 70.

[213] E. A. Thompson (1956).

[214] R. W. Mathisen (1984).

[215] In each case the arrangement is described as *hospitalitas* and the recipient as a 'guest' (*hospes*).

[216] For detail and references to sources see A. H. M. Jones *LRE* 249–53.

[217] W. Goffart (1980) 40–55.

[218] 118 ff. See the excellent discussion of Goffart's theories by S. J. B. Barnish (1986).

[219] Hydatius 69 (*Chron. Minor.* ii. 19) 'sedes in Aquitanica a Tolosa usque ad Oceanum acceperunt a mare Terrenum et fluvio Rodano per Ligerem fluvium usque Oceanum possident.' Isidorus *Chron.* 22 (*Chron. Minor.* ii 276) 'data ei ab imperatore . . . secunda Aquitania cum quibusdam civitatibus confinium provinciarum usque ad Oceanum.' Prosper Tiro *Chron.* 1271 (*Chron. Minor.* i. 469) 'data ad inhabitandum secunda Aquitanica et quibusdam civitatibus confinium provinciarum.'

unnaturally in order to get them to support Goffart's case. Their natural meaning is that the Goths received a share of the land itself.[220] In any case the behaviour of the Goths was transformed in a way that suggests that their means of subsistence had been fundamentally changed. From 418 until the destruction of the Visigothic kingdom in Gaul by the Franks in 507 the Goths behaved like a warlike but settled agricultural people. Their days as a wandering army were over.[221]

The Goths were settled in Aquitaine twenty-three years after Alaric's band began their campaigning through the Western provinces in 395. Is it a coincidence that this is almost the period of military service after which Roman veterans retired from the army?[222] By 418 all the veterans of Alaric will have been growing too old for active service.

Why did it take so long? The delay is difficult to explain. After all, the Romans had a tradition of settling barbarians in large numbers within the Empire. Furthermore, in the first decade or so of their wanderings Alaric's band would seem to have had opportunities of settling in Epirus, or later in Pannonia, if this had been their aim. It might be argued that what they wanted, and what was so long refused them, was settlement combined with independence from Roman civil administration. But then the fact that the Roman authorities maintained a separate legal status for barbarian military settlers, and did not permit intermarriage between them and Roman citizens, showed that the objectives of the Roman authorities and of Gothic nationalism were by no means irreconcilable. The most likely reason why Alaric's Goths 'wandered' for so many years, is that they did not want to settle, that they had the outlook not of an uprooted peasant nation, but of a professional army. If my argument is right that is precisely what they were. The Goths with Alaric at the start were a band of young men, mainly of Visigothic origin, who followed him in the hope of adventure and fortune, first into the service of the Empire, but also if necessary against the Empire, confident that they could name their own price for military support. As a result of his success Alaric was reinforced by individuals and groups of varying size and tribal origin.

Alaric's band grew or shrank in proportion to his success. He is said to have been joined by 30,000 former federates of Stilicho.[223]

---

[220] It is hard to believe that revenue is alluded to in *C. Euric* 277 'Antiquos vero *terminos* sic stare iubemus', or *L. Visig.* 10. 1. 8 'Divisio inter Gotum et Romanum facta de portione terrarum sive silvarum nulla ratione turbetur'.

[221] E. A. Thompson (1982) 50–2.

[222] H. M. D. Parker (1958) 212–14.

[223] Zos. v. 35. 6.

Later when his band had been joined by numerous fugitive slaves from Rome itself,[224] as well as the large force of Goths and Huns led by Athaulfus his brother-in-law, it is said to have reached a total of 40,000.[225] On the other hand his army was reduced by defections on a large scale after the defeats at Pollentia[226] and Verona.[227] If Claudian's language can be pressed the men who left Alaric after Pollentia and Verona were allies [228] or dependents[229] of some kind or other rather than Goths, though he was weakened by the desertion of some of his own people as well.[230] We are told about further major losses suffered by the war band at sea in the course of unsuccessful attempts to cross into Sicily (AD 410) and from Spain into North Africa (AD 415).[231] Hunger suffered by the Goths at different times in Gaul and in Spain must have produced defections and casualties. So the army that was settled in 418 can have included only a small proportion of the men who had set out in 395.

In many ways they had become a new people. Time, danger jointly faced, and leadership made a nation of them. H. Wolfram has called this process 'ethnogenesis'.[232] This useful term does, however, have some misleading implications. Alaric's band possessed a sense of ethnic unity from the beginning. The group was always thought of as Goths and as descendants of the tribe that had been led into the Empire by Fritigern in 376.[233] The tradition of a common origin, which for many individuals must have been a myth,[234] was confirmed by the preservation of Gothic as the national language[235] and, thanks to Ulfila's translation, as the language of the Bible.[236] Presumably this same Gothic nationhood was particularly powerful among the nobles, who were able to assimilate large numbers of outsiders of the most varied origins into their personal followings, and thus into the war band as a whole.

[224] Zos. v. 42.   [225] Soz. ix. 8. 2; Zos. v. 37. 1; 42.
[226] Claud. *B. Get.* 87–9; *VI Cons. Hon.* 129–30.   [227] *VI Cons. Hon.* 314–15.
[228] *VI Cons. Hon.* 129 'tot amissis sociis'; 309 'socius suspectior hoste'.
[229] Ibid. 314–15 'nullusne clientum permanet?'
[230] *B. Get.* 98–9 'desertus ab omni gente sua'. He seems to have lost above all cavalry; 253 'cunei totaeque palam discedere turmae'.
[231] Sicily: Olympiod. fr. 16 Blockley = 15 Müller; Oros. vii. 43. 2; Jordanes *Get.* 156–8. N. Africa: Oros. vii. 43. 11–12.
[232] H. Wolfram (1979) 191.   [233] Claud. *B. Get.* 166 ff.
[234] J. Jarnut (1982) 26–7 on the importance of myth of common origin in holding together bands of migration period, also G. A. Loud (1982) on myth of Norman *gens*. The Normans were extremely mixed, but 'because the individuality of each *gens*, and the hereditary concept of the *gens* was part of the medieval thought-world . . . it was easy to accept, and because it was accepted became reality'.
[235] How long did Goths preserve their language? H. Wolfram (1979) 258 refers to W. Kienast (1968) 44 ff., D. Claude (1970) 42. On Gothic place-names in Gaul and their problems: H. Wolfram (1979) 282 ff. M. Rouche (1971) 554–8.
[236] E. A. Thompson (1966) 144–55.

The ability of Alaric's Goths to absorb outsiders and to replace even heavy losses with recruits from other German tribes, and probably even Roman provincials,[237] was certainly aided by the marked adaptability acquired by the Goths and neighbouring German peoples during the years when they lived outside the frontier but subject to strong cultural influence of the empire.[238] Trade over a long period, and during the fourth-century recruitment of barbarians into the Roman army[239] had narrowed the cultural gap between the different barbarian tribes and between them and the Romans. Clearly the Romanization of the Goths and others intensified while they wandered through the Empire, and the institutions which were created to unite the various elements of the warrior band contained a strong Roman element.[240] It is certain that customs and institutions of the Visigoths settled in Aquitaine in 416 were far removed from those of the Goths when they abandoned their homes in Rumania and the Ukraine in 375. The model of the Goths presented has differed from the generally accepted view, but it is one which has many historical analogies. To cite J. M. Wallace-Hadrill, 'warbands are tribes in the making'.[241] The existence of the Normans, for instance, as a separate people, distinct from Danes and Norwegians, not to mention Franks, dates from Rollo's settlement in Normandy. The Normans were in fact extremely mixed, but the myth of their common descent helped to make them into the formidable people that they became.[242] It has recently been argued that the Ottoman Turks similarly grew out of multiconfessional polyglot war bands, composed of an unlikely mixture of Turkish pastoralists and Byzantine peasants which crystallized around Osman, a great warrior and leader who played a role like that which I have suggested for Alaric. The resulting powerful group acquired a tribal myth of common descent. What had in fact brought the different elements together was shared interest and mutual advantage and service.[243]

[237] On slaves, miners, and others who joined the Visigoths after 376 see G. E. M. de Ste. Croix (1981) 479–81, and esp. Amm. xxxi. 6. 4–7; 7. 7; 15. 2.

[238] B. Scardigli (1976), esp. 272–7.

[239] The evidence of the influence of military service in the Roman or rather Byzantine army on Germans is especially well documented in the case of the Lombards. G. P. Bognetti (1966–8), P. S. Leicht (1923), T. S. Brown (1984) 71.

[240] Early Roman influence shown in the Gothic language: H. Wolfram (1979) 131–4. Very strong Roman component in the Code of Euric (AD 475): K. Zeumer (1898–1901), Th. Melicher (1930), E, Wohlhaupter (1948).

[241] J. M. Wallace-Hadrill (1971) 11. Ariovistus' force was a war-band made up of units of different tribal origins (accompanied by wives): Caesar *BG* i. 51. They might well have become a nation if they had been able to consolidate their hegemony in Gaul, cf. *BG* i. 31.

[242] G. A. Loud (1982).

[243] R. P. Lindner (1983) 32 ff.

Most strikingly Ibn Khaldun, the Arab political theorist, has written a sociology of 'ethnogenesis' among the tribes with whom he was most familiar:[244]

It is clear that a person of a certain descent may become attached to a people of another descent, either because he feels well disposed towards them, or because there exists an old alliance or client relationship, or yet because he has to flee from his own people by reason of some crime he has committed. Such a person comes to be known as having the same descent as those to whom he has attached himself and is counted as one of them with respect to the things that result from common descent such as affection, the rights and obligations concerning talion and blood money, and so on. When the things which result from common descent are there, it is as if common descent itself were there, because the only meaning of belonging to one or another group is that one is subject to its laws.

I would suggest that Ibn Khaldun's generalizations can be applied almost unaltered to the ethnogenesis of Alaric's Goths.

Earlier I have argued that when Alaric's avalanche began to make its way across the Roman Empire the bulk of the Visigoths settled in Moesia remained where they were. The commonly accepted view is, of course, that the settled Goths elected Alaric their leader, and then left the lands assigned to them to follow where he would lead. This cannot be disproved, but it is supported by very little positive evidence. The Goths themselves did not have any definite traditions to that effect. The fact that the two surviving representatives of the Gothic tradition, the *History* of Jordanes and the *Chronicle* of Isidore, have different versions of the 'election' of Alaric suggests that there was no agreed tradition at all. According to Isidore, Alaric was 'elected' and started his rebellion against Rome in the fourth year of Theodosius, AD 382.[245] We have seen that the rebellion of Alaric cannot have started before 394/5. In Jordanes' *History* the crucial election happened in the year of the consulship of Stilicho and Aurelian, i.e. 400.

Jordanes writes that under the sons of Theodosius the Goths were deprived of their customary gifts. In addition they feared that their military qualities would be undermined by lasting peace. So they appointed Alaric king over them. When Alaric had been made king, he debated the matter with his men and persuaded them to seek a

---

[244] Ibn Khaldun, ed. F. Rosenthal (1958) 267.

[245] Isidor. *Chron.* 12, implying that the treaty of 383 had been agreed by Alaric for the Goths. According to Themistius no single leader signed the treaty on the Goths' side. How to explain the tradition? Perhaps Alaric was thought to have been successor of Athanaric who died in 381, and whose importance at the time of his death was greatly exaggerated in the East. See above, p. 28 n. 24.

kingdom by their own assertions rather than to serve others in idleness. In the consulship of Stilicho and Aurelian he raised an army and entered Italy.[246]

Jordanes' account does not explain how Alaric came to have been in charge of a very powerful force as early as 395, and it is obviously unreliable in detail. But perhaps it need not be rejected completely. It is likely enough that so bold an enterprise as the invasion of Italy should have been preceded by some formal act of consolidation of Alaric's force. It is probable that, before changing from the role of a general of the Empire to that of invader of the Empire, Alaric should have consulted his men, and assured himself of their wholehearted support. It is likely enough, therefore, that he was, at this point elected leader, although we cannot be certain what title was used to describe the leadership.[247] But if there was an election in 400 it was held by Visigoths and other federates stationed in Epirus under Alaric's command. It was not an election by Goths settled in Moesia.

It is argued in favour of the view that Alaric led the Goths out of Moesia, that there is no evidence of the presence of Visigoths in Moesia after the 380s. This argument from silence is not a strong one. Our literary sources tell us very little indeed about who inhabited Moesia in the fifth century AD. The absence of archaeological evidence is not surprising as barbarian tribes are not easy to identify archaeologically, and Moesia was repeatedly invaded by a variety of people. Finally, it is by no means certain that there is no literary evidence. A well-known passage of Jordanes describes the 'Lesser Goths', a 'great people whose priest and primate (*primas*) was Vulfilla (Ulfilas), who is said to have taught them to write. And today they are in Moesia, inhabiting the Nicopolitan region as far as the base of Mount Haemus. They are numerous, but poor and unwarlike, rich in nothing save flocks'.[248] Now it is usually assumed that these Goths were descendants of the Christian Goths who had been expelled from Gothia during a persecution of Christians in the 340s and had settled inside the Empire.[249] It is argued that these people kept separate from the great mass of Goths who were admitted into the Empire in 376 and stayed behind when the mass left. But it is not necessary to assume that the 'Lesser Goths' had always been separate. After all Ulfilas was primate not only of the people who had entered the Roman Empire together with him. On the contrary, he appears to have been the religious head of all Goths, including the Gothic

---

[246] Jordanes *Get.* 146–7, cf. above n. 61.
[247] Evidence on Alaric's title: *PLRE* ii. 43, cf. above, p. 62.
[248] Jordanes *Get.* 267.
[249] e.g. by E. A. Thompson (1966) 103.

mercenaries in Constantinople, a position which was later inherited by his secretary Selenas.[250] At least as likely as the view that the numerous 'Lesser Goths' were the descendants of the handful of refugees that accompanied Ulfilas into the Empire is that they are the descendants of the Goths who remained settled in Moesia when the young and enterprising men of their race joined Alaric's band of adventurers. Presumably they were forced into the more remote and mountainous parts of Moesia by successive waves of invaders of that exposed province. The title Lesser Goths will have been given them to contrast them with their more formidable kinsmen who established kingdoms in Gaul, Spain, and Italy.

A passage of Isidore is sometimes used to support the view that the 'Lesser Goths' were the descendants of earlier Christian immigrants who had refused to join the mass of fellow Goths who entered the Empire in 376 when they turned against the Romans. This passage describes Catholic Goths who had been admitted into the Empire during a persecution in Gothia and who resolutely refused to join the Goths of Fritigern when they turned against the Roman Empire. These Catholic Goths retreated into the mountains and remained loyal to the Romans.[251] But the fact that these pro-Roman Goths were Catholic makes it unlikely that they can be identified with the 'Lesser Goths', who evidently regarded Ulfila as their founder. For Ulfila had undoubtedly been an Arian and spiritual leader of Arian Goths at Constantinople no less than in the Danube province. Goths whose political allegiance was determined by the fact that they were Catholics must have been a different group from Ulfila's Goths.

The history of Alaric's Goths was to have parallels in that of the Gothic bands of Theoderic Strabo, son of Triarius and of Theoderic, nephew of Valamer, in the fifth century. The origins of the band of Theoderic Strabo are obscure. They are first mentioned around 459.[252] The original force may have been recruited from Goths settled in Thrace. At any rate the group never moved very far from Thrace, quite possibly because at least some of its members owned land there. But the bulk of them evidently did not, or not nearly enough to satisfy them, for in 471 Theoderic asked the emperor to be allowed to possess or exploit (νέμεσθαι) Thrace,[253] and some years later most of Theoderic Strabo's men had come to depend simply on the pay and resources provided by their general.[254] The size of the group seems to

---

[250] On Selenas: K. Schäferdiek (1977) 505, Socr. v. 23, Soz. vii. 17. Alaric's band had its own bishop: Sigesarius, Soz. ix. 9. 1, Olympiod. fr. 26.

[251] Isidor. *Chron.* 10 (*Chron. Minor.* ii. 271).

[252] Jordanes *Get.* 270.

[253] Malchus fr. 2 Blockley.

[254] Malchus fr. 18 Blockley = 14 Müller.

have fluctuated. At any rate by 480/1 it is said to have grown to 30,000 warriors.[255] But in 481 Strabo died. Rehitah his son took over the leadership after killing rivals in the family. He proved incompetent. When in 484 he was assassinated by Theoderic, nephew of Valamer,[256] his army disintegrated. At any rate this once great band of Goths now disappears from history.[257] The most likely explanation is that the men and their families joined the highly charismatic Theoderic, nephew of Valamer, and became part of the consolidating Ostrogothic people which he eventually led to Italy.

The origins of Theoderic Valamer's band[258] are better documented than those of Theoderic Strabo's. Theoderic's father Theodemer was one of three brothers who were ruling over a group of Goths 'settled' in Pannonia.[259] The fact that they were settled did not mean that they lived entirely, or even mainly, on the produce of the land they farmed. They had the status of *foederati*,[260] received imperial subsidies, and made up for what they felt to be the inadequacy of this imperial pay by plundering their neighbours.[261] They also captured *coloni*, perhaps to work on the land for them.[262] They were, moreover, anything but rooted in the territory they occupied, and they did not behave like people for whom the condition of settled farmers was the normal state to which they were always seeking to return. In 473 these Goths abandoned Pannonia. Perhaps famine was one of the motives, but it also appears that a peaceful stable existence was simply not congenial.[263]

Videmer, one of the two surviving brothers, went west, and ultimately his son and followers joined the Visigoths in Gaul.[264] Theodemer, the other, attacked the Eastern Empire.[265] By plundering after the manner of Alaric, capturing Naissus, and threatening Thessalonica Theodemer and his son Theoderic compelled the emperor Zeno to assign them and their people 'places to inhabit' in Macedonia, that is, Cyrrhus, Pella, Europus, Methone, Beroea, Pydna, and Dium. These places remained their base for three years.[266] Only the names of

[255] John Ant. fr. 211. 4–5.
[256] John Ant. fr. 214. 3.
[257] Cf. above, p. 39, on the dispersal of Sarus' band after he lost his booty to the Bagaudae.
[258] See *PLRE* ii s.v. Fl. Theodoricus 7.
[259] Jordanes *Get.* 268; they had 'received' the land from the emperor Marcian: *Get.* 264.
[260] Treaties and subsidies: *Get.* 270–1.
[261] *Get.* 272.
[262] Eugippius *V. S. Severini* 5.
[263] Jordanes *Get.* 283: 'As the plunder taken from neighbouring tribes got less the Goths began to be short of food and clothing, and peace became distasteful to men for whom war had long furnished the necessities of life.'
[264] *Get.* 284, *PLRE* ii s.v. Videmer 1 and Videmer 2.
[265] On Theodemer (Thiudmer) see *PLRE* ii s.v. Theodemer 2.
[266] Jordanes *Get.* 287–8.

cities are mentioned. It is not said that the Goths were assigned farms or even the revenues of farms. It is at least as likely that they lived in the cities and drew *annona* from the cities' tax payments. Shortly afterwards Theodemer died and was succeeded by his son Theoderic. In subsequent years Theoderic's band were mostly on campaign, sometimes for and sometimes against the Empire—just like Alaric and his Goths. In 475–6 they assisted Zeno against the usurper Basiliscus.[267] Theoderic was rewarded with the rank of *magister militum*.[268] At this time Novae on the Danube was their centre of operations, and was to remain so, at least intermittently, for twelve years.[269] But this does not mean that it became their home. They were constantly on the move,[270] taking their families and belongings with them on their operations[271] and, sometimes at least, carrying corn to sow, or have sowed for them, at some temporary base area.[272] In 479 they were in Macedonia, and Zeno proposed that they should settle in Pataulia, in the province of Dardania between Stobi and Serdica. Theoderic instead took his men into Epidamnus (Dyrrhachium) in Epirus. They were again offered settlement in Dardania, but nothing came of it.[273] In 483 Theoderic made peace with the emperor and for the time being he and his followers 'held' parts of Dacia Ripensis and Moesia Inferior, the Danube frontier area in which Novae was situated too.[274] The ultimate solution was of course that Theoderic and his people left the Eastern Empire, moved into Italy, and after a long war finally settled there. It is clear that neither the cities of Macedonia nor the territory around Novae nor the province of Dardania were ever thought of as more than a temporary station for Theoderic's Goths. There is no evidence that they ever tried to set up and defend a homeland of the kind they had had in Pannonia in any of these places.[275]

---

[267] Anon. Vales. 9. 42, Ennod. *Pan.* 12.

[268] Malchus fr. 18 pp. 125, 129 Müller = 20 pp. 436, 444 Blockley.

[269] Anon. Val. 9. 42 (AD 476); Marcell. Com. s.a. 483; Anon. Vales. 11. 49 (488); John Ant. fr. 214. 8 (488).

[270] So in 478 when campaigning for the emperor against Theoderic Triarius he asked for land where he and his men might stay and corn to feed them up to next harvest. Clearly they had not been assigned any land personally. See Malchus fr. 16 Müller = 18. 3 Blockley. Previous to this campaign he had been stationed on a more permanent basis far from Thrace towards Scythia (in Dacia Ripensis?). But he abandoned this for the campaign. Malchus fr. 20 p. 444 Blockley.

[271] Malchus fr. 20 p. 446 Blockley τὸ ἄμαχον πλῆθος; 448 Theoderic's mother; 448 2000 waggons; fr. 18. 2 p. 430 Blockley = 15 Müller men and women.

[272] Malchus fr. 20, 438 p. 55 Blockley implies that when circumstances allowed they would sow or harvest.

[273] Malchus fr. 20 p. 438, 446 Blockley. At this point no question of returning to Novae.

[274] Marcell. Com. s.a. 483: 'creditam sibi Ripensis Daciae partem Moesiaeque Inferioris cum suis satellitibus pro tempore tenuit.'

[275] They were presumably not numerous enough to defend a territory as well as campaign. If non-combatants had to be separated from warriors, fortified cities would have been safer than the open countryside, as in Malchus fr. 20 p. 446 1. 213 Blockley.

As in the case of Alaric's band the final settlement only took place after many vicissitudes, heavy casualties,[276] and presumably wide fluctuations in the size of the band. Survivors of the Pannonian Goths who had entered the Eastern Empire under Theodemer and Theoderic in 473, and even their children, are likely to have formed a small proportion of the force that invaded Italy.[277] In many ways the Italian Ostrogoths became a people as a result of their shared experiences under Theoderic.[278]

What is astonishing and in need of explanation is the ease with which all these German groups took to a wandering existence making their living according to circumstances as a huge robber band or as a paid mercenary army. This is the more surprising in view of the good evidence that at least many Goths had lived as farmers in villages before they entered the Empire[279] and that they entered the Empire in the hope of being given land to farm.[280]

But perhaps it is a mistake to interpret the evidence to mean that the Goths were peasants in the same sense as modern peasants or the peasants of the Empire—though we do not know that the latter were as rooted as we like to think. In any case the sharp distinction between peasants and nomads is probably mistaken. To quote from a study of modern Cyrenaica: 'There is no absolute separation between the man who herds and the man who farms. With few exceptions all nomads practice agriculture, and all sedentary farmers maintain at least a small herd of livestock'.[281]

The behaviour of the Goths in many ways is similar to that of past and present tribes of nomads or semi-nomads.[282] The unstructured nature of nomad society means that the position of leader is never secure, but has to be perpetually consolidated by success and largess.

[276] Malchus fr. 18. 2 p. 430 Blockley (AD 478), fr. 20 p. 434 (479), p. 448 (479) loss of 5000 men and 2000 carts.

[277] W. Ensslin (1947) 66, but estimates not based on reliable figures.

[278] Of course Theoderic unlike Alaric and Theoderic Strabo started as a hereditary tribal leader.

[279] Priscus fr. 49 Blockley = 39 Müller: Huns lived on produce of Goths' land. See also description of Gothic village in *Passio S. Sabae Gothi* in H. Delehaye (1912), and E. A. Thompson (1966) 25–28, 64–77. For a comparable example of a peasant people becoming mobile see Caesar's description of the migration of the Helvetii: *BGt* 2–5.

[280] *Pan. Lat.* ii (xii) 22. 3: admitted Goths serve in camp and on fields. SHA *Claud.* 9. 4: Gothic prisoners of war work land in Empire in AD 270. Amm. xxxi. 3. 8: Goths attracted to Thrace because of fertile soil. Amm. xxxi. 4.5: Goths offered land to cultivate. Amm. xxxi. 4. 8: leaders offered land to cultivate. Them. *Or.* xvi. 211 b, 212 b, xxxiv. 22: agreement of 382. Claud. *VI Cons. Hon.* 183: Alaric foiled from farming Etruria.

[281] D. L. Johnson, J. Al-Akhdar (1973) 39.

[282] Jordanes' description of the 'Lesser Goths' is suggestive, but stands alone. They inhabit the territory of Nicopolis stretching towards the Balkan mountains. They are numerous, unwarlike, rich only in flocks and pasture land for cattle and forests for wood. They buy their wine from neighbouring countries but mostly drink milk (*Get.* 267).

The absence of hierarchy affects the behaviour of everybody. Status has to be earned and prowess regularly demonstrated. The normal field in which prowess is demonstrated and respect earned is war. If a situation such as this existed among the Goths this would account for the insatiable thirst of Gothic leaders for gold and silver, as they would need this to distribute to their followers. It would also provide an explanation for the seeming inevitability with which Goths sooner rather than later invariably found themselves at war with surrounding provincials. It goes without saying that nomad or semi-nomad traditions would explain the ease with which Goths adapted to a wandering existence: they would be quite accustomed to spending a great part of the year following flocks from pasture to pasture while crops were growing in a base area watched by only a small part of the population, or perhaps by clients.[283] Other features that recall the life-pattern of nomads are the Goths' seeming ability to absorb outsiders into their tribal society,[284] the way their leaders' prestige depended not only on wealth and birth, but also very largely on their power, outside the tribal organization altogether, in the administration of the Empire.[285] We are told that before the Goths entered the Empire the imposition of an embargo on trade across the Danube had a very serious effect on their condition.[286] This might well have been the result of the nomadic or semi-nomadic economy of the Goths not being self-sufficient, but dependent on exchanges with the sedentary economy of the Empire. Such dependence of nomads or semi-nomads on trade with sedentary neighbours is well attested among contemporary nomads.[287] Nomadic and semi-nomadic tribes are in many ways like armies. Apart from this they tend to produce more young men than can be supported by pastoralism. These today,[288] as in the past,[289] provide manpower for armies—comparable to the federates of the Later Empire.

[283] Cf. D. L. Johnson, J. Al-Ahkdar (1973) 50 ff. on the annual cycle of sowing, nomadic pastoralism, harvesting of Cyrenaica. W. W. Swidler (1973), esp. 32 ff.

[284] See above p. 13, 17, 77, cf. D. P. Cole (1973) 116: 'Whole lineages for example, sometimes change tribal affiliation, while other lineages change from subservient status to equal status if they begin to act like free and independent tribesmen.'

[285] G. J. Obermeyer (1973), esp. 163, D. P. Cole (1973) 120.

[286] E. A. Thompson (1966) 19–20 on Amm. xxvii. 5. 7, which he finds difficult to explain in spite of his survey of the evidence for extensive trade between the Goths and the Empire, ibid. 34–43. They had also received subsidies of grain and clothing from the Empire, ibid. 38 n. 2. Grain sent to nomads in SE Europe: Them. *Or.* xxx. 350 a.

[287] A. Mohammed (1973), esp. 98, 108.

[288] D. P. Cole (1973) 123 ff. on national guard of Saudi Arabia.

[289] T. Asad (1973), esp. 66, on armies of great Arab conquests. On Palmyra as a centre of settled and semi-settled nomads and how this favoured both trade and recruiting, see J. Teixidor (1987).

It would not be reasonable to claim that the analogy between the Goths before entering the Empire and any of the nomads or semi-nomads of the Middle East studied by modern anthropologists is a very close one. One important fact about the Goths, for instance, was that they were a ruling people lording it over earlier sedentary populations of the area.[290] We do not of course know anything at all about the formal structure of this relationship, and the links if any between the subject peoples and the tribal structure of the Goths themselves. Basically we know very little about the organization of Gothic society, and any proposed reconstruction will have to make use of models based on analogies with better-known societies. The analogy with contemporary nomads or semi-nomads of the Near East has the advantage that it helps to explain characteristics which are difficult to explain if the Goths were 'peasants' pure and simple. It makes it easier to understand how they were able to transform themselves into mobile bands of warriors after entering the Empire. Goths serving in the Roman army had long been familiar with the Empire's elaborate organization for paying soldiers their *annona* in kind. They realized that by exploiting this facility they would be able to live not only more plentiful but also more glorious lives. The prospect drew groups as well as individuals into the Empire. That the new life might involve mobility did not worry them in view of their own nomad or semi-nomad traditions. In these circumstances it was easy for an Alaric or one of the Theoderics to provide himself with a personal military following which if everything went well might again become a people and eventually establish permanent settlements once more.

[290] Soz. vi. 37; Priscus fr. 11. 2 p. 410 Blockley: 'The Scythians are a mixed people. In addition to their own languages they cultivate Hunnic or Gothic or (in the case of those who have dealings with the Romans) Latin.'

PART II

The Eastern Government and its Army

6

The Murder of Rufinus

PREVIOUS chapters have illustrated the problems caused by the largely barbarian army in the West. Among these not the least was that power passed from emperor and civil administration to a long series of military commanders, Stilicho, Constantius, Bonifatius, Aetius, until in 476 the general Odoacer deposed Romulus the last Western emperor. In the East the outcome was different: civilian control was maintained and the Empire survived.

In the East, the *praefectus praetorio Orientis* was the most powerful official under the emperor,[1] filling a role comparable with that of the *magister utriusque militiae praesentalis* in the West.[2] This was especially true under a weak emperor, or while the emperor was absent on campaign. So when Theodosius I campaigned in Italy against Maximus the East might have been left in charge of his teenage son Arcadius. To prevent this Theodosius appointed Tatian praetorian prefect of the East,[3] and made his position exceptionally strong by giving Tatian's son Proculus[4] the important office of prefect of Constantinople.[5] Tatian and Proculus were both pagans, but at that critical moment it was more important that they were Easterners from Lycia, and could count on support from members of the Eastern governing class which was growing in confidence, and developing a sense of a Helleno-Roman identity of their own.[6]

Soon after he had returned from Italy victorious, Theodosius replaced Tatian by Rufinus.[7] By now Tatian and Proculus were already so deeply rooted that the change of ministers had features of a palace revolution. Proculus and Tatian were found guilty of treason. Proculus was executed, Tatian banished to Lycia, his property confiscated.[8] All Lycians, Tatian's countrymen, were deprived of office and declared ineligible for official appointments henceforth.[9] It looks as if Tatian had consolidated his position by appointing officials

---

[1] A. H. M. Jones *LRE* 371–2.
[2] Prefect's power in emperor's absence on campaign: John Lydus ii. 11. 3.
[3] *PLRE* i s.v. Tatianus.   [4] *PLRE* i s.v. Proculus.
[5] J. Matthews (1975) 224.
[6] Dagron (1968), cf. also below, p. ooo.
[7] In summer 392 between *CT* xii. 1. 127 and vii. 6. 2.
[8] Condemnation of Tatian and Proculus: Zos. iv. 52, *Chron. Pasch.* s.a. 393; some of Tatian's legislation repealed: *CT* xii. 1. 131, ix. 42. 12–13, ix. 1. 23.
[9] *CT* ix. 38. 9; Claud. *In Ruf.* 1. 237.

from his home province. About the same time Rufinus hurried to Antioch to have the *comes Orientis* Lucianus beaten to death.[10]

Rufinus, the new prefect, whose appointment marked Theodosius' reassertion of his authority in the East, was close to the emperor. Like Theodosius a Westerner, he was born in Elusa in south-western Gaul. He had accompanied Theodosius to Italy holding the position of *magister officiorum*, and rendered his emperor the service of reconciling him to bishop Ambrose of Milan after the massacre of Thessalonica.[11] As a reward, perhaps, he was made consul in 392. The prefecture of Rufinus marks an epoch in the history of the Empire: he was the last Western official to be appointed to govern the East by an emperor of a united Empire.

But Rufinus' policies in many ways foreshadowed the future. He was a dedicated Christian and a patron of ascetics.[12] Naturally he was a strong supporter of Theodosius' policy of alliance with orthodox Christianity. Laws addressed to Rufinus combat paganism no less than heresy,[13] though the new and radical offensive against paganism preceded Rufinus' appointment to the prefecture.[14] Equally important was Rufinus' development of Theodosius' policy with regard to barbarians.

In summer 394 Theodosius marched west against Eugenius, leaving Rufinus in charge of the East. To protect himself in this vital and highly exposed position Rufinus raised a bodyguard of Huns for himself,[15] presumably with Theodosius' permission. He is the first civilian known to have kept such a force. Another exceptional right is implied by the fact that Rufinus issued laws from Constantinople after the emperor, the source of all legislation, had left the city.[16] After Theodosius I had died on 17 January 395[17] Rufinus was left as guardian of the eighteen-year-old Arcadius[18] and *de facto* ruler of the Empire in the East.

While he was striving for the position of principal minister of Theodosius, Rufinus faced the rivalry and competition of the generals Timasius and Promotus who had led Theodosius' armies against Maximus. Rufinus slapped Promotus in the presence of the emperor,

[10] Claud. *In Ruf.* 1. 240, Lib. *Ep.* 1025: as son of Florentius prefect of Constantius Lucianus belonged to the new eastern aristocracy. See *PLRE* i s.v. Lucianus.

[11] J. Matthews (1975) 234–6, *PLRE* i s.v. Rufinus.

[12] e.g. the establishment of a martyr's shrine and monastery at his palace at Chalcedon, see J. Matthews (1975) 134–5, J. Pargoire (1899) 429–77, R. Janin (1964) 161 f., 504 f.

[13] Laws against heretics and pagans: *CT* xvi. 5. 23–26; 10. 12–13.

[14] *CT* xvi. 10. 10 (13. 2. 391); 7. 4–5 (9. 6. 391).

[15] Claud. *In Ruf.* ii. 76, *Chron. Minor* i. 650. 34.

[16] *CT* v. 14. 34 (6. 11. 394), xiii. 8. 1 (9. 1. 395); see also Zos. iv. 57.

[17] Death of Theodosius I: *Cons. Const.* s.a. 395.

[18] Alan Cameron (1970) 38–40, (1968) 247–80.

and when in 392 Promotus was ambushed and killed by barbarians[19] Rufinus was accused of having plotted his death.[20] In 394 Timasius departed to Italy as one of the commanders of the expedition sent against Eugenius. So Rufinus was left without rivals in the East, but also without the support of an adequate field army,[21] and obliged to devise a strategy for keeping barbarians out of the East which did not rely on soldiers. His problems were aggravated by the death of Theodosius. For Stilicho, guardian of Honorius and commander of the combined field armies of East and West, claimed that Theodosius had named him guardian of both sons, and gave every indication that if necessary he would come East to take over the guardianship of Arcadius by force.[22]

Rufinus habitually relied on diplomacy rather than war. We have seen how in 392 he frustrated Stilicho by negotiating a settlement with the 'Goths in the marshes'.[23] At that time he was still acting on behalf of Theodosius. After Theodosius' death, he repeated this performance by reaching an agreement with Alaric before Stilicho had arrived on the scene to force a decisive military solution.[24] He also seems to have made agreements with Huns.[25] Perhaps he hoped if necessary to use Huns against Germans or vice versa. The sources preserve no details of these treaties, but almost all agree in accusing Rufinus of treason. It is claimed that he conspired with Alaric at the expense of the provincials.[26] He was also accused of collusion with the Huns. Soldiers are said to have feared that Rufinus would make them slaves of Huns and Alans.[27] According to the ecclesiastical historians, he invited the Huns into the Empire.[28] That such accusations should be made retrospectively is not surprising: federates were extremely disagreeable and dangerous neighbours at the best of times. In the case of the federate allies of Rufinus, it will have been noted that shortly after the agreements Alaric was plundering Greece, and the Huns raiding deep into the Eastern provinces.[29]

[19] Zos. iv. 51.

[20] Zos. iv. 51; Claud. *In Ruf.* i. 316–17; Alan Cameron (1970) 71–2.

[21] Gildo had close ties with Constantinople since his daughter and her husband lived in the palace there, Jerome *Ep.* 79. 5.

[22] Zos. v. 4; Alan Cameron (1968) 247–80.

[23] See above, p. 54.   [24] See above, p. 58.

[25] Theodosius had settled Huns in Thrace under their own chieftains: Eunapius fr. 60 Blockley = 61 Müller. If Rufinus had actually been responsible, or if he had arranged further settlements, this would explain the accusation that he had invited Huns into the Empire (see nn. 26–27).

[26] Zos. v. 4; Claud. *In Ruf.* i. 308, 319, ii. 9, 501; John Ant. fr. 190; Oros. vii. 37. 1; *Chron. Minor* ii. 64, 395. 4.

[27] Claud. *In Ruf.* ii. 270–1.   [28] Socr. vi. 2, Soz. viii. 1.

[29] Jer. *Ep.* 60. 16 (AD 396); Claud. *In Ruf.* ii. 28–36; Philostorg. xi. 8; Socr. vi. 1. 7; Soz. viii. 1. 2; Josh. Styl. 9.

But these disasters happened too late to account for Rufinus' assassination on 27 November 395.[30] Arcardius had ordered Stilicho to return to the East the eastern units of the field army still under his command. Stilicho had agreed, and the troops under the command of Gainas proceeded to march to Constantinople. When Rufinus accompanied Arcadius to welcome the army at Hebdoman near Constantinople the soldiers turned against the prefect, killing first his personal guard and then himself.[31] At first sight it looks as if the crime had been instigated by Stilicho in an attempt to achieve through murder the guardianship of Arcadius that had eluded him so far. But even if Stilicho had instigated Gainas, he gained no benefit at all from the murder.[32] Rufinus was obviously extremely unpopular in the East. The bitter hostility of all the Greek sources shows this beyond any doubt. In his years of power Rufinus had gained a great deal of wealth, which was resented.[33] He had antagonized the army through his treatment of the generals Promotus and Timasius. Gainas may well have thought of himself as avenger of Promotus. He had waged a cruel vendetta against his predecessor in the prefecture, his family, and his fellow Lycians. He was a Westerner holding a position which the rising aristocracy of Constantinople was beginning to think of as their own.[34] It was feared that he would get Arcadius to marry his daughter[35] and thus to consolidate his position through a link with the imperial family, in the same way as Stilicho's position was established in the West.[36] Opposition to this scheme was organized by Eutropius the eunuch and *praepositus sacri cubiculi* of Arcadius, who managed to arrange a marriage between Arcadius and Eudoxia, daughter of the Frankish general Bauto[37] and possibly sister of Arbogast.[38] She had been brought up in the house of a son of Promotus, and was clearly anything but a friend of Rufinus. It was not Stilicho, but Eutropius in particular and the new aristocracy of Constantinople in general, who benefited from the murder of Rufinus. It is a reflection of the strength of civilian rule in the East that Gainas the Gothic commander of regular troops who had brought about the death of Rufinus did not as a result gain a position in the East comparable to that enjoyed by Stilicho in the West.

[30] Socr. vi. 1. 4.
[31] *Chron. Minor* i. 650. 34; Claud. *In Ruf.* ii. 76.
[32] Alan Cameron (1970) 146–7.
[33] Claud. *In Ruf.* i. 179 ff.; Jer. *Ep.* 60. 16; John Ant. fr. 188; Zos. v. 1.
[34] J. F. Matthews (1975) ch. v, and below, p. 24.
[35] Zos. v. 3.
[36] See above, p. 24.
[37] *PLRE* i s.v. Bauto.
[38] John Ant. fr. 187 = Eunapius fr. 58. 2 Blockley, see above p. 9 n. 24.

7
The Rulers of the East and their Military Policy

AFTER the fall of Rufinus government at Constantinople passed into the hands of Easterners—in which it was to remain. Leading men at Constantinople were determined that they should never again be subject to a Western government. To most observers at the time it appeared that after the fall of Rufinus power in the East had been seized by Eutropius, the *praepositus sacri cubiculi*. Eutropius was a former slave and a eunuch. Although he entered palace service late in life with recommendations from the general Abundantius, he won the confidence of Theodosius, who sent him to Egypt to consult the hermit John as to whether the expedition to suppress Eugenius was likely to be successful.[1] Eutropius was strongly favoured also by the empress Eudoxia.[2] Eutropius' reputation as the most powerful man at the Eastern court led to his becoming the object of vicious attacks by Claudian in the West. For Stilicho, Claudian's patron, assumed that it was mainly the influence of Eutropius which was preventing himself from becoming regent for Arcadius in the East as well as for Honorius in the West.[3] That Eutropius did indeed have great power is shown by the fact that he chose an archbishop of Constantinople,[4] led an army,[5] and was awarded the title of patrician,[6] at that time a very rare distinction, making conspicuous the recipient's exceptional closeness to the emperor.[7] He received statues all over the empire and finally the consulate.[8]

Eutropius' power was made possible by the Eastern system of administration, a centralized civilian bureaucracy controlled by the emperor and his advisers, at Constantinople. The emperor could of course consult anyone he chose. Most often he reached his decision with the help of the *consistorium*, which had taken the place

---

[1] Biography of Eutropius: *PLRE* s. v. Eutropius.

[2] Arrangement of Eudoxia's marriage: Zos. v. 3, Claud. *De Nupt. Hon. et Mar.* 23–7; later she turned strongly against him: Philostorg. xi. 6, a pattern repeated in her relations with Chrysostom, see below, p. 198 ff.

[3] Claud. *In Eutrop.* i and ii, and Alan Cameron (1970) 125 ff., also S. Dopp (1980).

[4] See below, p. 166.   [5] *In Eutrop.* i. 234–86.

[6] Zos. v. 17. 4; Claud. *In Eutrop.* praef. 2.

[7] W. Heil (1966).

[8] *CT* ix. 40. 17; Claud. *In Eutrop.* i. 8 'omnia cesserunt, eunucho consule, monstra'.

of the *consilium* of earlier emperors.[9] It consisted of the principal civilian ministers, the praetorian prefect, the *magister officiorum*, the quaestor, the *comites sacrarum largitionum* and *rei privatae*, and such others as the emperor chose to summon. The commander of the guard, the *comes* or *comites domesticorum* and the two *magistri militum praesentales* were also ex-officio members.[10] The *consistorium* had no defined role apart from that given to its deliberations by the presence of the emperor, and it had no chairman apart from the emperor. A strong emperor dominated it. In the absence of a strong emperor the *consistorium*, and therefore the government of the Empire, was normally swayed by the head of the most powerful department, the praetorian prefect of the East.[11] Under Arcadius there was ruthless and even bloody competition for this position. But sometimes in special circumstances the position of greatest influence could be held by the holder of some other office, the *magister officiorum*,[12] for instance, or, as after the murder of Rufinus, by the *praepositus sacri cubiculi*, the head of the imperial household. But even during the predominance of Eutropius the praetorian prefects Caesarius and Eutychianus[13] were men of stature and influence, or at least so it will be argued.

After the fall of Rufinus the government at Constantinople had at its disposal once more a large regular field army.[14] But while the availability of an army was advantageous, it was also dangerous. The army had eliminated one unpopular minister, and there was an obvious danger that having intervened once it might do so again. Moreover the army's effectiveness when dealing with unruly federates, the most acute problem facing the Empire, had already been shown to be very limited. It was expensive to maintain, and impossible to keep up to strength without resort to the recruiting of unreliable barbarians. Faced with these problems, the government of the Eastern Empire maintained a consistent policy over a considerable period. Their first priority was the preservation of civilian control over the army. This meant above all keeping generals in their place. Secondly they reduced their dependence on the army to a minimum, by solving military problems as far as possible by non-

[9] J. Crook (1955).

[10] A. H. M. Jones *LRE* 333.

[11] *LRE* 333–7; D. A. Graves (1972).

[12] Notably Helio for 13 or 15 years after 414: A. H. M. Jones *LRE* 179, *PLRE* ii s.v. Helio; perhaps Rufinus before his prefecture. Cf. M. Clauss (1980). Claud. *In Eutrop.* ii. 325 ff.: Eutropius' council of war. The emperor is not mentioned. Nevertheless this could be a parody of a meeting of the *consistorium*.

[13] On their respective careers I follow A. H. M. Jones (1964*b*) 80–1 and *PLRE* i. 320, as argued in W. Liebeschuetz (1987) and below, p. 253 ff.

[14] See D. Hoffmann (1969) 30–4, 40–6.

military means. Confident in their ability to do this, they even allowed their newly acquired field army to run down.

The sources are not good enough for the writing of a full history of the Eastern army in these years, but certain features are clear enough. There was suspicion of successful generals. Three–Timasius, Abundantius, and Fravitta[15]–were brought down in treason trials. The promotion of Gainas and Tribigild was obstructed until their personal grievances helped to drive them to rebellion. No attempt was made to built up a fighting force capable of decisive military action. The fighting record of the Eastern army was remarkably unimpressive. Only one invader was decisively defeated by Roman troops, the Huns in 398; and these were raiders rather than potential conquerors, and were defeated only after they had penetrated deep into the Empire. Of two other major enemies of the Empire, Gainas was eventually destroyed by Huns, and Alaric induced to invade the West. Offensive wars were not even attempted. At the same time the government was stingy in its rewards to soldiers, or so at least the troops thought. That was surely an important reason for the breaking loose of the forces of Tribigild and Gainas. The policy had grave drawbacks: Greece and Epirus were devastated by Alaric, Thrace by that part of Gainas' army which was not caught and destroyed in Constantinople. The capital itself saw street fighting. Raids of Huns and Isaurians struck deep. But the important fact remains that the Eastern Empire survived and slowly but steadily grew stronger year by year. That was the justification of a policy which had been more or less forced on Rufinus but which was followed consistently for more than twenty years by the men who ruled the East after his death, starting with Eutropius.

---

[15] Fravitta may have been assassinated. See below, p. 123.

8

The Age of Eutropius

EUTROPIUS owed his pre-eminence to a mutiny, but he and the
leading officials during this period were no more creatures of the
soldiers than Rufinus had been. Quite the reverse. Eutropius almost
immediately demonstrated his independence by successive trials,
disgrace, and exile of two highly distinguished generals, Abundantius
(consul 393)[1] and Timasius (consul 389).[2] As far as we know neither
was replaced. Gainas may well have expected one of the vacant
commands. He did not get it. The affairs are described by Zosimus.[3]
It is significant that neither was of barbarian origin. If Eutropius
rightly or wrongly thought them dangerous, it was because they were
well-known soldiers, not because they were Germans. In charge of
the trial were Saturninus,[4] an even more senior soldier, who favoured
diplomatic means of dealing with the Visigoths,[5] and Procopius, a
relative by marriage of the late emperor Valens.[6] These trials
demonstrated plainly enough that Eutropius and the civilian officials
of the Empire intended to remain masters. More explicitly still,
Eutropius himself was about to try his skill at military leadership.

This was a time of great danger. The East was threatened in
different ways by Alaric and his Goths, by Stilicho and the army of
the West, by Hunnish raids, and even by its own largely barbarian
forces. The danger is reflected in legislation. Cities were ordered to
build walls, and arrangements were made to finance the new
fortifications.[7] Rules were laid down for billeting a field army at
Constantinople.[8] Two laws seek to ensure that the recruit-tax, the
payment which could be demanded as an alternative to the furnishing
of recruits, should be properly collected and that possible collectors
should not enjoy illicitly obtained exemptions from this invidious
duty.[9] Three laws try to bring back soldiers absent from their units
and to punish private individuals who have taken such absentees into

---

[1] Timasius' distinguished career: *PLRE* i. 914; at this time seemingly *magister militum
praesentalis*: Zos. v. 8–9, Eunapius fr. 65. 3–4 Blockley = 70–71 Müller.
[2] Abundantius: *PLRE* i. 4–5, *comes et magister utriusque militiae—praesentalis?* Zos. v. 10,
Eunap. fr. 65. 8 Blockley = 72 Müller.
[3] Zos. v. 9–11.   [4] *PLRE* i. s.v. Saturninus.
[5] See above, p. 28.
[6] Procopius: *PLRE* i. s.v. Procopius 9, Zos. v. 9. 3–5.
[7] *CT* xv. 1. 34; cf. 24. 3 (396).
[8] *CT* vii. 8. 5; cf. 6. 2 (398).   [9] *CT* xi. 23. 3–4.

their employment.[10] Other laws are framed to prevent soldiers from extorting money from the civilians whose duty it was to deliver their payment in kind (*annona*).[11] These laws are in accordance with the policy of keeping the army under control, but they are in an administrative tradition which had already been followed by Rufinus[12] and which went a lot further back[13] since it was directed against abuses inherent in the system of paying government employees their wages in kind.

Measures of this kind, however beneficial to administration and civilians, were not going to overcome a major military crisis such as faced the East in 396. Alaric's Goths broke loose in Greece. Available forces were unable to stop them. The praesental field army does not appear to have been engaged.[14] At the same time the Huns had since 395 been harrying large areas of Asia Minor.[15] What must have seemed as alarming as the barbarian invasions was that Stilicho, the regent of the West, in 397 volunteered to help the Eastern government against Alaric, and took an army to Greece, without having renounced his claim to be rightful regent of the Eastern emperor as well.[16] It is evident from the hostile reaction of the East, that he came not only without asking whether his help was wanted, but directly contrary to the wishes of the Eastern government. The situation was dangerous, but Eutropius managed to master the crisis, and what is more, to do so without a major military effort. He rid himself of Stilicho without fighting, reached an agreement with Alaric diplomatically, and campaigned only against the Huns—but this too in such a way as to give a minimum of glory to the generals.

Stilicho arrived with a large army. He fought Alaric and was fairly successful, if less successful than Claudian was to claim on his behalf. At any rate, Alaric's army, though ejected from the Peloponnese, survived intact. According to Zosimus, Stilicho was prevented from achieving complete success by indiscipline among his troops,[17] possibly encouraged by Gothic bribes.[18] There is no evidence that Stilicho received any military support from the Eastern government. After Stilicho had departed from Greece Eutropius had him declared a public enemy by the senate of Constantinople.[19] What action of Stilicho served as justification? Was it that he had abandoned Greece to Alaric, or perhaps simply that he had taken an army to Greece, a province of the Eastern Empire, without permission of the Eastern

---

[10] *CT* vii. 1. 15, 16. 17.   [11] *CT* vii. 4. 21, 24, 25.   [12] *CT* vii. 4. 18, 20.
[13] *CT* vii. 4. 1 (325).   [14] Zos. v. 5–6.   [15] E. Demougeot (1969) 386–93.
[16] Claud. *de IV cons. Hon.* 459 ff.; *B. Get.* 513–7.   [17] Zos. v. 7.
[18] Claud. *B. Get.* 87–8. On the whole affair: Alan Cameron (1970) 168 ff.
[19] Zos. v. 11; Eunopius fr. 74 (Müller) = 66. 2 (Blockley).

government? Subsequent events make the latter the more likely: they suggest that the East was frightened and hostile, rather than disappointed at being left in the lurch.

In autumn 397 Gildo, the Western military commander in North Africa, transferred his allegiance to the Eastern emperor and his offer was accepted by the East.[20] Since African corn was essential for feeding the population of Rome this was extremely damaging to Stilicho and the West. It is difficult to believe that anticipation of Gildo's rebellion had not contributed to Stilicho's decision to leave Greece with Alaric undefeated,and extremely likely that Eutropius had wooed Gildo precisely in order to force Stilicho to withdraw.[21] Certainly in negotiations that preceded the outbreak of hostilities,[22] that is, the cutting of the Roman corn supply by Gildo late in autumn of 397[23] and the invasion of Africa by a Western army,[24] the Eastern government evidently did not make any concessions. Indeed it is likely that the condemnation of Stilicho was proclaimed as a gesture of support for Gildo.[25] When the Western army invaded North Africa the East did not provide Gildo with military support. But by then the danger that Stilicho might intervene in the East was over.

There remained the problem of Alaric. After Stilicho's withdrawal, Alaric moved his reduced forces into Epirus[26] and proceeded to feed them by plundering the provincials. We have already seen how Eutropius pacified him by characteristically unmilitary means, that is, by giving Alaric the official position of military commander in Illyricum with control not only over his Goths, but over regulars and armament factories, and with some jurisdiction over civilians. At the same time a praetorian prefect headed the civilian administration.[27] For the time being at least order had been restored.

Credit for this policy has always been assigned to Eutropius, but it should be noted that by 4 September 397 Eutychianus was praetorian prefect of the East, after previously in all likelihood holding the prefecture of Illyricum.[28] Eutychianus' subsequent career shows that

[20] Zos. v. 11; *Chron. Gall.* s.a. 397.

[21] That Claudian did not mention Gildo as an excuse for Stilicho's leaving Greece (stressed by Alan Cameron (1970) 173) is not decisive because in *IV Cons. Hon.* 460 ff. Claudian focuses on Stilicho's success and seeks to hide, not to explain, its limits.

[22] *Cons. Stil.* iii. 81–3.   [23] *B. Gild.* 66–7.

[24] Ibid. 415 ff. Gildo defeated and killed 31. 7. 398 (s.a. *Chron. Minor.* i. 298, 528).

[25] *Cons. Stil.* i. 276–8 'hoc coniuratus alebat | insidiis Oriens: illinc edicta meabant | corruptura duces'. Claudian presents the East as using Gildo: *B. Gild.* 276–8; also *Cons. Stil.* i. 7–8 'Lybiae post proelia crimen | concidit Eoum'.

[26] Claud. *In Eutrop.* ii. 215.

[27] See above, p. 59–60.

[28] *CT* vi. 3. 4; cf. 4. 9 (397). See *PLRE* i s.v. Eutychianus 5, and W. Liebeschuetz (1987). He would presumably have been the first prefect appointed after the division of Illyricum (see

he was the outstanding administrator of his generation. It is likely that he played a role in devising the settlement with Alaric, and he may well have been one of the instigators of the very bold policy of supporting Gildo's transfer to the East. Later he was to show himself an extremist in his readiness to cooperate with barbarians.

The outcome of 397 was altogether satisfactory from the point of view of the Eastern government. Without engaging the units recently returned by Stilicho, and indeed without any large scale military operations of any kind, Stilicho had been diverted and Alaric pacified. Of course this was a respite rather than a permanent solution. The important point was that the Eastern Empire was preserved. For the West the consequences were less happy. Not only had the Empire been weakened by a major rebellion in the vital corn-producing provinces of Africa, but in addition a most formidable foe was being preserved and strengthened in the shape of Alaric and his Goths, who in twelve years' time were going to sack Rome itself.

The following year 398 Eutropius was free to concentrate on the Huns and to win another and even more gratifying success. Huns had been penetrating deep into the provinces of Asia Minor since 395.[29] Even Antioch was threatened.[30] It seems to have been a matter of widespread and persistent raiding rather than of an invasion, and the forces of the Empire appear to have been ineffective.[31] In 398 Eutropius was at last in a position to concentrate the military resources of the East[32] on this menace. It can be assumed that he now engaged the field army units returned by the West. But significantly he did not send them out under Gainas, their old commander, who in view of his high command in the Eugenius campaigns and his part in bringing Eutropius to power surely must have felt entitled to supreme command against the Huns. In fact Eutropius did not give the command to any established general but took it himself. What is more, in spite of total lack of military experience he proved equal to the task.[33] The Huns were driven out, and success was won without

above, p. 58). The fact that two laws addressed to Eutychianus (*CT* vi. 4. 30; xvi. 5. 33) concern Constantinople *could* be a result of the version in the Code being derived from the prefect of Illyricum's copy of an original issued on behalf of the prefect of Oriens.

[29] Claud. *In Eutrop.* i. 234–86; Socr. vi. 1; Soz. viii. 1; Philostorg. xi. 8; Josh. Styl. *Chron.* 9 p. 8 ed. Wright; *Chron. Edessenum* ed. I. Guidi in *CSCO* (*Scr. Syr.*) iii. 4, 6. 20–21. Claud. *In Ruf.* ii. 33–5 proves that raids were happening in 395.

[30] Jerome *Ep.* 60. 16, 77. 8; cf. G. Downey, *A History of Antioch in Syria* (Princeton, 1961) 438–9.

[31] F. C. Burkitt, *Euphemia and the Goth, with the Acts of Martyrdom of the Confessors of Edessa* (London, 1913).

[32] Units restored by Stilicho: Claud. *In Eutrop.* ii. 411–16; many Gothic troops: *In Eutrop.* i. 242.

[33] *In Eutrop.* i. 234–86, ii praef. 55–6.

any military man getting glory which might have gone to his head. It was Eutropius who got the deserved rewards for a considerable achievement, outstanding among them the consulate for 399.[34]

The campaign did, however, sow the seeds of future trouble. Trigibild, a Gothic subordinate commander, was left dissatisfied with the recognition and rewards he and his men had received. They mutinied at the moment when Eutropius was enjoying his greatest triumph, and their action set in motion the sequence of events that was to overthrow him. Gainas too was bitterly resentful.[35] It was clearly not easy to repel invaders, and at the same time to keep the army both under restraint and contented.

The mutiny of Tribigild and his Goths promptly demonstrated the risks inherent in solving military problems by non-military means. A mixed body of Ostrogoths and Greuthungi[36] had been settled near Nacoleia in Phrygia in 386.[37] There the men lived with their families and farmed the land.[38] Claudian describes them as a squadron (*ala*), that is, a cavalry unit,[39] although in another passage he refers to these people as a legion.[40] But it is clear that they constituted a potential rather than an actual force. They had taken part in the campaign against the Huns,[41] but were not now in a state of mobilization. They may have been worried that they might lose the status of warriors and end up as nothing more than peasants.[42] But at the time they were still under the command of an officer, the Goth Tribigild,[43] a kinsman of Gainas[44] and therefore not one of their own group. Tribigild had his headquarters at Constantinople[45] and seems to have commanded other federate units besides the Greuthungi at Nacoleia.[46]

Tribigild and his Greuthungi proceeded to rebel. The immediate cause of the rebellion (or mutiny) was a refusal by the government to

[34] *In Eutrop.* i. 284–6.

[35] Eunap. fr. 75 = 66 Blockley; Marcell. Com. s.a. 399; Zos. v. 13. 1 'honours unbecoming a general'; in the circumstances this could only have been the consulate, to which he certainly had a claim on past achievements and which could hardly have been refused if he had led the victorious campaign against the Huns. Instead Eutropius led the campaign and became consul.

[36] Claud. *In Eutrop.* ii. 153–4.   [37] Philostorg. xi. 8.

[38] *Chron. Minor.* i. 244 (381. 1); Claud. *In Eutrop.* ii. 194–206; cf. Zos. iv. 3. 8–9; *In Eutr.* ii. 577–8 'quibus arva domosque praebuimus'.

[39] *In Eutrop.* ii. 176.

[40] Ibid. 576 'legio pridem Romana'. Surely this cannot mean that they were citizens, though perhaps that some of the settlers entered regular units. So G. Albert (1984) 90 n. 19.

[41] At least this is generally assumed; see G. Albert (1984) 89–90. It is difficult to explain their confidence in Tribigild if he had not led them in war.

[42] *In Eutrop.* ii. 195 ff.

[43] *PLRE* ii s.v. Tribigildus. His rank χιλίαρχος = *tribunus* (Socr. vi. 6), with rank of *comes* (Philostorg. xi. 8); perhaps *tribunus gentis Greuthungorum*? Cf. 'tr. gentis Marcomannorum' *ND Oc.* xxxiv. 24.

[44] Soc. vi. 6. 5, Soz. viii. 4. 2.   [45] Zos. v. 13. 2.

[46] Philostorg. xi. 8; Zos. v. 13. 2 ἦρχε . . . Ἰλῶν . . . βαρβάρων ἐπιδρυμένων τῇ Φρυγίᾳ.

provide gifts and treasure.[47] The gifts had been demanded by Tribigild, but it can be assumed that the men expected to get their share, and that their disappointment was a principal motive for the rising.[48] When the mutiny had already broken out Tribigild was offered a higher rank, seemingly that of *magister militum*.[49] As we have seen, high Roman rank was regularly asked by German federate leaders. Now Tribigild refused it. Presumably the Greuthungi and others who had joined him felt that to live by plundering[50] was more profitable and more honourable and manly than any agreement that could be expected from Eutropius at that stage. Claudian suggests that Tribigild and his men were following the example recently set by Alaric[51] and that Eutropius was hoping to achieve a settlement (*foedus*)[52] similar to that accepted by Alaric and other independent federates.[53] At the start the number of mutineers was not very great[54] but, like Alaric's Goths and other war bands both inside and outside the empire, Tribigild's force grew rapidly by absorbing discontented elements among the population,[55] and in all likelihood such reinforcements were not restricted to runaway slaves of Gothic origin.[56] As success produced growth, so defeat resulted in shrinkage. At one stage the band was reduced to three hundred[57] but quickly recovered to become formidable once more to the point of destroying an army of regulars.[58]

The rising of Tribigild was a terrible calamity for the areas of Phrygia and Lydia affected by it.[59] Eutropius was forced to take military counter-measures on a large scale, involving two armies and two commanders, Gainas and Leo.[60] One might conclude that these were the two praesental armies of the *Notitia* under the *magistri militum praesentales*.[61] In fact this does not seem to have been the case. Neither commander had the rank of *magister militum*. Gainas only received the title much later,[62] and meanwhile was merely *comes*

---

[47] *In Eutrop.* ii. 178–9, 189–90. On the alleged conspiracy with Gainas, see below, p. 111.
[48] Convincingly argued by G. Albert (1984) 92–5; see also above, p. 42, and Malchus fr. 18. 1 Blockley = 14 Müller.
[49] Claud. *In Eutrop.* ii. 320–1 'prima . . . cingula dignari'.
[50] Ibid. 318 'notae dulcedine praedae'.   [51] Ibid. 198 ff.
[52] Ibid. 324 'nec spes iam foederis exstat'.   [53] Cf. above, p. 59–60.
[54] *In Eutrop.* ii. 221–2.   [55] Zos. v. 13.
[56] Danger of German slaves: Synesius *De Regno* 20.   [57] Zos. v. 16.
[58] Zos. v. 17. If collusion between Gainas and Tribigild (Zosimus'—i.e. Eunapius'—explanation) is rejected, his evidence suggests large-scale desertion of Germans from Gainas to Tribigild.
[59] Eunapius fr. 66. 2 Blockley = 75.1 Müller; Claud. *In Eutrop.* ii. 275 ff.
[60] Zos. v. 13, both started from Constantinople.   [61] *ND Or.* v, vi.
[62] Soz. viii. 4. 5, Theodoret v. 32. 1: command of both Roman and Gothic units after agreement with emperor. Only Socr. vi. 6. 1 implies that he was *magister militum* from the beginning of the episode. He is probably careless and wrong.

militaris.[63] Leo was Gainas' subordinate,[64] so he cannot have held a superior rank. He was a man of humble origin. At least according to Claudian he had been a weaver.[65] He was a member of the *consistorium* under Eutropius,[66] but no military achievements of his are recorded.[67] His problem illustrates Eutropius' reluctance to give established officers a chance to win glory and power. Of the armies, Leo's was evidently composed of regular units, including regiments that had been returned to the East by Stilicho and that had fought against the Huns. But Gainas' army was composed of federates. Zosimus makes the distinction quite clear,[68] and indeed the original strategy was based on it. Leo's regulars were to confront the mutinous federates in Asia, while Gainas' federates took up position on the European side of the Hellespont in case Tribigild should try to cross.[69] The fact that in the end Leo's army was defeated and destroyed[70] suggests that Eutropius had not built up a powerful regular army around the returned units. He chose instead to keep in being a considerable force of federates. This is a safe deduction from the position of Gainas.

When Gainas was given the mission of guarding Thrace in case Tribigild should cross the Hellespont, he was already holder of an important command. According to Socrates and Sozomen he exploited this to build up an army with personal loyalty to himself, recruiting fellow Goths from his homeland and giving commissions to friends and relatives.[71] It is implied in Sozomen's account that Tribigild's was one such appointment.[72] If this is right Gainas' position was that of head of all federates, corresponding to that of the later *comes foederatorum*.[73] If this was so it is important. Tribigild was not the tribal leader of a group of Greuthungi but a Roman officer of Gothic descent given the command of Greuthungian forces and probably other barbarian units. There is good reason to suppose that he might have become the leader of a tribe if he had been successful and if he had not been overshadowed by Gainas. In any case the fact that Tribigild had been appointed by Gainas would make it easy to

---

[63] Marcell. Com. s.a. 395; also s.a. 399; Jordanes *Rom.* 320, *Get.* 176.

[64] *PLRE* ii s.v. Leo 2; Zos. v. 16. 5.

[65] *In Eutrop.* ii. 381–2.   [66] Ibid. 376 ff.   [67] Zos. v. 14. 2.

[68] v. 17. Leo's forces consistently 'Romans' or 'soldiers' against the 'barbarians' of Gainas here and elsewhere. Units restored by Stilicho: Claud. *In Eutrop.* ii. 409–16. They had been stationed at Constantinople and had taken part in the triumph over the Huns at Ancyra. Gainas only received Roman command of Roman units as *magister militum*: Soc. viii. 4. 5.

[69] Zos. v. 14.   [70] Zos. v. 17; Claud. *In Eutrop.* ii. 432 ff.

[71] Socr. vi. 6. 1; Soz. viii. 4. 1; cf. G. Albert (1984) 110–13. Against Albert I would insist that a Roman officer like Gainas—or Stilicho or Bonifatius—did not need to have a following (*Gefolgschaft*) in order to reach high rank in the army. It was the high rank which enabled them to acquire a following. It was different with men who could offer their service to the Empire because they were leaders of barbarian bands already, like Alaric after 395.

[72] Soz. viii. 4. 1.   [73] See above, p. 31 n. 45.

understand that his rebellion was thought to have been instigated by Gainas.[74] Gainas was a Goth born outside the Empire,[75] but he had served for many years in the Roman army, rising from the ranks.[76] He was a Roman citizen.[77] He owned considerable property at Constantinople so that a district of the city was later called after him.[78] He corresponded on questions of theology with Nilus the hermit.[79] He was an Arian, but otherwise well-established in the society of the capital. He had performed great services for Theodosius and more recently had cleared the route to power for Eutropius. He had good justification to feel entitled to a praesental command and the honour of the consulate.[80] That these were withheld would provide sufficient motive to account for his hostility to Eutropius and his subsequent actions, with the result that a Roman career officer ended as a failed Alaric.

The military operations against Tribigild were remarkably unsuccessful. Leo could not—or dared not—defend Lydia. Rumour magnified the threat represented by Tribigild. Luckily for the Lydians and the inhabitants of the numerous and rich Ionian cities Tribigild led his men into Pamphylia. Here the population was less demilitarized than in other inland areas of the Empire. Frequent attacks by Isaurians had conditioned the peasants of the hill area and also the inhabitants of cities to self-defence.[81] The rebel force was caught in a pass near Selge by a local militia of slaves and peasants organized by a certain Valentinian and suffered heavy losses. It is said that it was reduced to 300 men and that these were blockaded between the rivers Melas and Eurymedon, between Side and Aspendus. Both Roman armies moved into Pamphylia to end the rebellion.[82] But astonishingly enough Tribigild recovered. The next thing we hear is that he destroyed the army of Leo. According to Claudian Leo was attacked when he and his men were totally unprepared.[83] To many contemporaries the only possible explanation was treachery: Gainas had sent Leo German reinforcements and these had turned on their new comrades.[84] But this view does not appear to have been taken by the authorities at Constantinople. They did not treat Gainas as a traitor who had caused the death of a large number of Roman troops: they promoted him.

---

[74] Zosimus-Eunapius and the ecclesiastical historians agree on this. Claudian and Synesius have different explanations. The authorities at Constantinople at the time do not appear to have believed that Gainas had intrigued with Tribigild. See below, p. 111–2.

[75] Zos. v. 21. 9.   [76] Soz. viii. 4. 1.   [77] Socr. vi. 6. 1.

[78] Th. Preger (1901–7) iii. 257.   [79] Nilus *Ep.* i. 70, 79, 114–16, 205–6, 286.

[80] Zos. v. 13, 17.

[81] Brigandage in Asia Minor: E. Patlagean (Paris, 1977) 297–301.

[82] Zos. v. 15–16.   [83] *In Eutrop.* ii. 432 ff.   [84] Zos. v. 17.

9

The Fall of Eutropius and the Prefecture of Aurelian

THE defeat of Leo was the immediate cause of the fall of Eutropius and of his praetorian prefect Eutychianus. According to Zosimus, Gainas sent an ultimatum to the emperor Arcadius to the effect that he would not be able to put an end to Tribigild's mutiny unless Eutropius was surrendered to him. His motive is said to have been jealousy: Eutropius had achieved rank and recognition which had been withheld from Gainas.[1] As we have seen, Gainas had good reason to feel that his services merited the reward of high rank.[2] One might add that Gainas might quite reasonably have feared that he too would eventually share the fate of Timasius and Abundantius. But Gainas had not only his own units, but the army as a whole, behind him. For while Gainas and his troops were in Phrygia,[3] it is clear that there was a violent military demonstration in the capital itself.[4] One suspects that anger at the condemnation of Timasius and Abundantius, resentment at denied promotion, and economies at the expense of the army, especially of the regular units, had united the army against Eutropius, so that Gainas was avenging not only his own grievances but those of the entire army, federates and regulars alike.

In addition, many civilians were thoroughly discontented with Eutropius. The law (addressed to Aurelian), which annulled Eutropius' acts, states as one of its objectives 'that neither these men who by their courage and their wounds extend the Roman boundaries, nor those who guard these territories by preserving the equity of the law, may lament the fact that this vile monster defiled the divine gift of the consulship by his contagion'.[5] Clearly Stilicho and Claudian were not

---

[1] Zos. v. 17. 5. [2] See above, p. 99.

[3] Zos. v. 17; cf. Synesius De Prov. 1220 C-D.

[4] John Chrys. In Eutropium (PG lii. 395); De capto Eutropio, ibid. 397. Alan Cameron (1989) points out discrepancies between accounts of military riot in the two Eutropius sermons, arguing that the second refers to the asylum and arrest not of Eutropius but of Joannes. But Gainas and his men pressing for the surrender of Aurelian, Saturninus, and John were at Chalcedon, not at Constantinople (Zos. v. 18. 7–9). So the traditional title of the second sermon is probably correct. Alternatively perhaps not only Gainas' men but also the troops inside Constantinople (the scholae?) were demanding the surrender of the three civilian politicians.

[5] CT ix. 40. 17, of 17. 8. 399 according to Seeck (MSS 17. 1. 399, which is impossible).

the only ones to be shocked at the consulate being held by an ex-slave and eunuch. It is obvious too that so respectable and senatorial a figure as the former prefect of Constantinople, Aurelian, thoroughly approved of the deposition of the man over whose trial and condemnation he was to preside.[6] John Chrysostom the archbishop too, angry at Eutropius' support of public spectacles,[7] and even more at the laws limiting the Church's right of asylum,[8] obviously acquiesced in the deposition of Eutropius, even if he tried to avert his execution.[9]

Reasons for dissatisfaction with Eutropius can be suggested. After all the policy of relying on Germans and neglecting the regular forces had led to unprecedented devastation in the heartlands of the Empire and growing danger to Constantinople itself. Furthermore a Persian war was threatening.[10] Claudian was probably not exaggerating when he wrote that many Easterners were praying that Stilicho would come to their aid.[11] At any rate they will have felt that the crisis could not be overcome while the Eastern Empire was close to war with the West. If this was not enough, Eutropius had quarrelled with the empress Eudoxia.[12] The Empress' role in politics at Constantinople has regularly been exaggerated but in any discussion of the future of Eutropius, whose official position was after all head of the imperial household, her views are likely to have carried weight. She was a dangerous adversary.

The fall of Eutropius brought Aurelian to power as prefect of the East. This shows how much the senate had been involved, for Aurelian as prefect of the city had conferred benefits on the senate, and he was clearly the senate's man.[13] Many years later the senate was to honour him with a gilded statue in commemoration of the three prefectures, his close relations with successive emperors, and finally the fact that he had put an end to certain 'griefs' of the senate. This could be a reference to his part in the fall of Eutropius.[14]

The appointment of Aurelian has been seen as a victory of an anti-barbarian nationalist party.[15] This is a mistake, a consequence of ignoring the strongly tendentious character of Synesius' *De Regno* and *De Providentia*,[16] and of taking their evidence at its face value. It would be extremely surprising if a coup largely made possible by the armed support of a barbarian general should have given power to a

---

[6] Philostorg. xi. 6.   [7] *In Eutropium* 1 (392).   [8] Ibid. 2 (394).

[9] See below, p. 190.   [10] Threat of Persian war: E. Demougeot (1951) 225–6.

[11] Claud. *In Eutrop.* ii. 506.   [12] Philostorg. xi. 6.

[13] *PLRE* s.v. Aurelianus 3: references to legislation as prefect of Constantinople.

[14] *Anth. Gr.* xvi. 73; alternatively the laws of the urban prefecture or restoration of burnt-down senate house could be meant.

[15] So by O. Seeck (1910–20) v. 315 ff.

[16] *PG* lxv. 1053–1108, 1209–82; Lacombrade (1951).

fanatical opponent of the Germans in the army. In fact Aurelian's position seems to have been extremely ambiguous, not to say devious.

The principal evidence for Aurelian's public attitude is Synesius' *De Regno*. The speech has the form of an oration spoken by an ambassador delivering gold crowns to celebrate an anniversary of the accession of the emperor. But it quite evidently is not that. It is far too undiplomatic.[17] If it was spoken by Synesius while on his delicate mission to Constantinople this could only have been to a small carefully selected gathering composed of men who shared its sentiments and could be relied upon not to wish to make the ambassador's inevitably difficult task of obtaining tax reliefs even more difficult. Obviously the audience was interested in government, and able to understand Synesius' allusive references to individuals. They must also have been men of high position if they were confident that they could afford to listen to a controversial speech of that kind. We know that not long afterwards Synesius considered Aurelian a friend.[18] He is surely the most likely focus of the group that heard—or perhaps only read—the oration. Now the controversial parts of the speech are concerned with two themes: the excessive influence of the officials of the imperial household (the references are extremely allusive), and the need for the Romans to cease to rely on German mercenaries. They should return to the condition of their warlike past, and defend the empire themselves. Both themes are likely to have met the approval of Aurelian at some point in time.[19] The question is when? *De Regno* cannot be dated precisely so that we cannot state with certainty when this audience with its animus against courtiers (presumably freedmen-eunuchs) and German mercenaries came together. In fact the speech could have been held at any time after Synesius' arrival at Constantinople, probably in autumn 397.[20] If it was held soon after that it represented the programme, or perhaps the shared prejudice, of the group which were hoping to bring Aurelian to power. In fact the speech contains hints suggesting that it was composed well before the overthrow of Eutropius (high summer 399). Synesius warns that 'skirmishes' of the kind to be expected to result from reliance on

[17] Alan Cameron, J. Long, L. Sherry (1990) ch. IV, argue conclusively that *De Regno* was spoken to an invited audience, like the political orations of Libanius. It does not claim to be the actual embassy speech. That too was outspoken (*De Insomniis* 14), but later (*De Regno* 1108 c).

[18] Synesius *Ep.* 61; *De Prov.*, *passim*. That this was a real friendship and not simply the 'friendship' of patron and client is argued below, p. 137–8.

[19] Even if he later denied it. After all Gainas did come to think of him as an enemy. Synesius would have been extremely foolish to speak only for himself, and we can link him with no other politician of note.

[20] Alan Cameron, J. Long, L. Sherry (1990) ch. IV. 2; T. Barnes (1986*a*). The interpretation

German soldiers have just begun.[21] This could be an allusion to an early stage in the rising of Tribigild. For the defeat of Leo was surely more than a skirmish. This would suggest a date in early spring 399 or even winter 398/9.[22] It has been argued by P. Heather that the allusions to a German general fit Alaric better than Gainas.[23] If that is right the 'skirmishes' could be some otherwise unknown incident involving Alaric in Illyricum, and the date of the speech could be a year or more earlier. The fact that what seems to be criticism of the influence of Eutropius is so indirect also points to an early date, a time when Eutropius was at the height of his power and dangerous.[24] The anonymity of the criticism would certainly have been quite pointless after Eutropius' fall.[25]

Whenever the speech was delivered[26] it could not have been in July 399 at the time of the coup.[27] At that point Aurelian must have been all things to all men, and Gainas must have received a firm assurance that he and his Germans would be well looked after. If the *De Regno* had already been spoken or published Aurelian must have dissociated himself from the speech completely, and made it abundantly clear that it in no way represented his policy. Presumably he insisted that Synesius had spoken only for himself. In *De Providentia* Synesius treats the suggestion that Aurelian intended to carry out the policy advocated in *De Regno* as a slander, part of an intrigue designed to get Gainas to move against Aurelian.[28]

Whatever assurance Gainas received was insufficient to produce trust. Gainas arrived at Constantinople and insisted that it was not enough to depose and exile Eutropius; he must be brought back and executed. Arcadius and Aurelian yielded once more. They recalled Eutropius and, to keep a promise that they would not kill him while in Constantinople, had him tried and executed at Chalcedon, on the

of P. Heather (1988) would really only fit a date soon after autumn 397, before Gainas or Tribigild had become problematical — or alternatively a rewriting *after* the fall of Gainas to support the ending of subsidies to Alaric.

[21] *De Regno* 1091 D–1092 A.

[22] Leaving enough time for Tribigild's operations in Phrygia and Pamphylia (Zos. v. 15–17).

[23] P. Heather (1988). The argument is plausible, but there is almost (but see below, p. 108 n. 38) no evidence that Alaric played any part in the politics at Constantinople. Gainas is likely to have been in command of federates before the outbreak of the Tribigild revolt (see above, p. 101–2).

[24] Late in 398 Eutropius had won his military victory over the Huns. Was that the appropriate time for advising that the emperor should spend his time with military men rather than courtiers, 'men with small heads and petty minds'? (*De Regno* 1077).

[25] With Alan Cameron, J. Long, L. Sherry (1990) ch. V. 5, and against G. Albert (1984) 43 ff., I can see no evidence for followers of Eutropius remaining in power whom Synesius might have had to placate.

[26] Of course the actual speech may have been edited considerably for publication. *De Prov.* surely was. See below, p. 269.

[27] *CT* ix. 40. 17 of 17. 8. 399 (O. Seeck); on 25. 8. 399 Eutychianus was still in office (*CT* ix. 40. 18).   [28] *De Prov.* i. 15.

other side of the straits.[29] Aurelian presided.[30] Eutropius' execution is
likely to have taken place not many months after his deposition. For
Gainas had come to Constantinople not only to destroy Eutropius,
but also to negotiate an agreement on Tribigild's behalf which would
put an end to Tribigild's rebellion,[31] and it is likely that not only the
killing but also the earlier deposition of Eutropius were successive
concessions in negotiations intended to lead to this treaty. The
interval between them is not likely to have been long. I have argued
elsewhere that the execution happened around 1 October 399.[32]

After this Aurelian and Gainas cooperated,[33] but Gainas' behaviour
suggests that he never trusted Aurelian. Aurelian was nominated to
be the Eastern consul in 400.[34] He did not, however, remain in office
long enough to be inaugurated on 1 January 400.[35] As early as
11 December 399 a law was addressed to his successor in the
prefecture of the East, Eutychianus.[36] What had happened was that,
immediately after achieving a sworn agreement with the emperor,
Gainas left Constantinople for Phrygia, where he got Tribigild to
accept the terms and to obey his orders. They combined forces and
marched or rode via Thyatira towards the Hellespont and Bithynia.
Their armies are said to have plundered the countryside like
enemies.[37] Since Zosimus follows Eunapius, who was a Lydian, the
looting is presumably a fact. But it need not have been worse than the
normal behaviour of a Roman army living on the country. Coastal
Asia Minor was not used to the movement of armies. There was no
question even now of Gainas being treated like an enemy, but there
was great fear at Constantinople. Gainas could insist that the emperor
met him near Chalcedon. Arcadius came and accepted Gainas' demands.
Gainas compelled the emperor not only to depose Aurelian, but to
surrender him, together with the veteran general Saturninus and
John, a young courtier friend of the empress Eudoxia, to be tried in a
court under the presidency of Gainas himself. The court met and
sentenced them to death. The sentence was later commuted to exile[38]—
under guard.[39]

Gainas' reported motive for proceeding against Aurelian is fear
that he himself might be tried for treason—as Timasius and
Abundantius had been. Gainas had come to believe that Aurelian was
strengthening the regular units of the army in order to expel and even

[29] Zos. v. 17–18.   [30] Philostorg. xi. 6.
[31] Zos. v. 18–19.   [32] See below, p. 265.   [33] Zos. v. 19.
[34] Zos. v. 18; Socr. vi. 6 (667 A); Soz. viii. 4 (1521 C), Synesius *De Prov.* (1172 B).
[35] See below, p. 260.   [36] *CT* xii. 1. 163.   [37] Zos. v. 18.
[38] Zos. v. 18, perhaps in territory controlled by Alaric: at any rate they gained their freedom
after *disembarking* in Epirus, Zos. v. 23. 1.
[39] Zos. v. 23.

to destroy the Germans.[40] In other words, Aurelian was accused of putting into practice the policy which he had allowed his friend Synesius to expound some months earlier. Whether Aurelian was really planning anything of the kind, we cannot tell. As the events have been reported by our sources the demand for the surrender of the civilians was Gainas' alone, but it is possible that the call for their punishment came from the army as a whole, including the units stationed inside Constantinople.[41] If that was so, the charge against Aurelian was not that he was opposed to barbarians in the army, but that he was suspicious of the army altogether, and was showing signs of continuing with the policies of Eutropius. Saturninus had certainly offended the army, for he had been responsible for the condemnation and disgrace of the general Timasius.[42] Aurelian was walking a political tightrope. He may well have intended to double-cross Gainas, and perhaps 'the generals' as a group. As it turned out Gainas double-crossed him: he first made use of Aurelian to overthrow Eutropius, and then rapidly got rid of him.

It may seem surprising that Gainas allowed Aurelian to be replaced by Eutychianus, who had been the leading minister of Eutropius, but an explanation can be suggested. Eutropius had offended Gainas and Tribigild personally. He had done worse to other generals and had shown himself stingy to the army as a whole. He had not, however discriminated against federates as compared with regulars. Quite the reverse. He had given an extremely favourable treaty to Alaric. So Gainas may well have decided that, while Eutropius personally was impossible, his principal ministers and his policy were acceptable. There is a suggestion in *De Providentia* that Typhos-Eutychianus had on earlier occasions enjoyed the support of Gainas' Goths.[43] Once in office it seems as if Eutychianus did try to coexist with Gainas, turning a blind eye to undisciplined behaviour of his troops, in much the same way as the Eastern government had learned to coexist with Alaric, and Stilicho was to do not long after.[44]

At this time considerable influence was enjoyed by John Chrysostom. The ecclesiastical historians made much of the bishop's successful— or at least temporarily successful[45]—opposition to Gainas' request for a church in which he and his Arian troops could hold Arian services.[46] From this one might deduce that Chrysostom was in

---

[40] Synesius *De Prov.* 1245 D–1247 A.

[41] See note 4 above on implications of Alan Cameron (1989).

[42] Zos. v. 9. 3–5.   [43] 1248 B.   [44] See below, p. 116 ff.

[45] See below, p. 190–1, on 'church of the Goths'.

[46] Soz. viii. 4, not Socrates, Theodoret *HE* v. 32. Theodoret also praised Chrysostom's resistance in a lost panegyric, Photius *Bibl.* 273, suggesting that he was well informed about Chrysostom.

opposition. This is probably the impression which the historians were trying to create, but there are indications that they have not told the whole story. In itself the fact that Chrysostom was able to prevail over the Gothic general who had recently compelled the emperor to exile his principal ministers shows that the bishop had achieved a remarkable ascendancy. Another indication pointing in the same direction is the account of a council of state held in the bishop's palace ('home of the high priest') after the destruction of the Goths in Constantinople. When the question of the recall of the exiles, that is of Aurelian, John, and Saturninus, was raised, the 'priest', i.e. surely Chrysostom, promised that this would be done.[47] There is good evidence that Chrysostom proceeded to go himself as ambassador to the Goths in Thrace.[48] One of his objectives was to negotiate the return of the exiles,[49] another almost certainly to reach a new agreement between Gainas and the government at Constantinople.[50] Clearly he was trusted by both parties. It is relevant that Eutychianus had been praetorian prefect when Chrysostom was consecrated archbishop of Constantinople, and that Chrysostom had taken a great interest in the spiritual welfare of Goths—even if his concern was that they should be orthodox.[51] On the other hand, it is clear that there was considerable criticism of Chrysostom's role in preventing a church from being put at the disposal of Arian Gothic soldiers.[52] Evidently some thought that his intransigence played no small part in causing the state of war between Gainas' Goths and the Empire. Intervention by a bishop of the capital in the secular affairs of the Roman Empire was of course something new. It was bound to be extremely controversial, and it remained exceptional. It would be a mistake to see Chrysostom's influence at this time as that of an ecclesiastical magnate who was was extending his power into the secular sphere. It was rather the case that his pastoral concern for all, including Goths and even to some extent Arian Goths, allowed him to bridge the divisions which had arisen between Goths and Greeks during the Gothic occupation of Constantinople.

[47] Synesius *de Prov.* 1267 B.   [48] Theodoret *HE* v. 33.

[49] *Hom. cum Saturninus et Aurelianus acti essent in exsilium* (*PG* lii. 413–20) refers to this mission. G. Albert (1984) 153–6 is mistaken to date Chrysostom's intercession to the time of Gaina's coup. Intervention at nearby Chalcedon would not have required Chrysostom to interrupt preaching at Constantinople long enough to need the apology: πολὺ ἐσίγησα χρόνον, καὶ διὰ μακροῦ πάλιν πρὸς τὴν ὑμετέραν ἐπανῆλθον ἀγάπην (opening words). *De Prov.* 1268 B ὁ δὲ ἱερεὺς ἀυτόν τε ὑπέσχετο seems to refer to Chrysostom's announcement that he would go to intercede for Aurelian.

[50] Theodoret *HE* v. 33. 1, and G. Albert (1984) 158–61.   [51] See below, p. 169–70.

[52] F. van Ommeslaeghe (1979) 152. Synesius *De Prov.* 1268 c . . . ὡς ἐλπίσαι θωπείᾳ καὶ χρήμασι τὸν ἱερέα περιελεύσεσθαι suggests that Eutychianus made efforts to secure Chrysostom's support.

10

The Fall of Gainas

AFTER the exiling of Aurelian, Saturninus, and John, Gainas was at the height of his power. He had been appointed commander of the infantry and cavalry by the emperor and commanded not only his own federates but all imperial forces within striking range of Constantinople. A federate leader could hardly achieve more. A large part of Gainas' army was billeted in Constantinople itself. He held at the heart of the Eastern Empire a position very like that which Alaric was holding in Illyricum, and Stilicho in Italy. That Gainas could not maintain this position was a fact of enormous significance for the future of the Eastern Empire.

In spite of his importance Gainas remains a very obscure figure. The reason is that while we have at least four versions of the Gainas affair none is a straightforward report by an impartial and well informed observer.[1] The fullest account, that of Zosimus, is generally agreed to be a summary of the narrative of Eunapius, who was a contemporary and lived at Sardes, close to the events described.[2] This closeness might have enabled him to produce first-rate history, but in fact it had the opposite effect. Sardes had been in great danger from the mutineers,[3] and to an observer from Sardes the appearance of devastating armies in the rich and peaceful countryside of Lydia could only be explained by conspiracy, conspiracy between the mutineers and Gainas, the commander-in-chief of the armies that should have suppressed the mutiny.

According to Zosimus, Gainas was discontented. He demanded and was refused 'honours unbecoming a general'.[4] So he conspired with Tribigild and encouraged him to rebel. Clearly Gainas' complicity remained completely secret because Eutropius gave him one of the two military commands created to suppress Tribigild. Tribigild proceeded to get into trouble, not through imperial troops, but as a result of resistance organized locally.[5] At this point Gainas saved Tribigild by sabotaging Leo's army. He reinforced Leo with

---

[1] Four versions: Zosimus-Eunapius, the ecclesiastical historians, Synesius, and Arcadius' column. On that see below, p. ooo.

[2] On Zosimus: F. Paschoud (1975). On Eunapius: R. Blockley (1981) 1–26, also bibliography, and (1980), R. Goulet (1980), W. Chalmers (1953), I. Opelt (1965), R. T. Ridley (1969–70).

[3] Zos. v. 18.   [4] v. 13.   [5] See above, p. 103.

German federate units with the result—so it is suggested—that Leo's army broke up. The barbarians began to devastate the countryside and to attack the Roman regulars until Leo's force and their commander had been completely destroyed. In Zosmus' Eunapius-based story Leo's disaster was caused entirely by the treacherous reinforcements sent by Gainas. Tribigild's Greuthungi are given no active part at all.[6] The story is extremely unlikely to be true. Treachery on so monumental a scale could not have remained secret. Yet the authorities continued to employ Gainas in a way which would have been unthinkable if they knew that he had recently brought about the destruction of a Roman army.

It might be possible to save the credibility of Zosimus' story by making the assumption that while knowing about Gainas' treachery the emperor, deprived of one of his armies, was completely at the mercy of the other, and complied with Gainas' demands merely from lack of an alternative. However, Zosimus' account continues equally implausibly. Gainas, we are told, used his rank as commander-in-chief of all units to move regular units including palace guards out of Constantinople:[7] he was preparing to take over full control of the city. He was going to attack as soon as all the regulars had left. Barbarians outside the city were to coordinate their assault with those stationed inside it. Unfortunately for him—so Zosimus reports—Gainas let the barbarians outside the city attack the walls before those inside were ready. This gave the Roman soldiers[8] and the population warning to close the gate and hold the walls while they destroyed the Goths within.[9] Thus Gainas' attempt to take control of Constantinople ended in disaster. The story is extremely unlikely. Why should Gainas have planned to attack the walls from the outside when he already had a force of 7000 men inside the city?[10] In fact the other two versions have quite different accounts of the circumstances of the destruction of the Goths inside Constantinople.

The second version is found in the ecclesiastical historians, Sozomen and Socrates.[11] Both almost certainly used Eunapius. That is why their accounts of the earlier stages of the rising of Tribigild are close to that of Zosimus, if much condensed. On the subject of the

---

[6] Zos. v. 17. In Claudian's *In Eutrop.* ii. 432 ff. Leo's army was routed by Tribigild's force through an unexpected attack on the Roman camp.

[7] v. 18. 10; but some palace guards were left in the city, 19. 2. On the palace guards see R. I. Frank (1969).

[8] φύλακες (Zos. v. 19. 3).   [9] v. 19. 3–5.

[10] v. 19. 4; according to Synesius *De Prov.* ii. 2 (1264) a fifth of his whole force. G. Albert (1984) 131 n. 184 suggests that this is too high and wonders whether families (*De Prov.* ii. 1 1260); Soz. viii. 4. 15) are included.

[11] Sources of Socrates: F. Geppert (1898); Sozomen: G. Schoo (1911), see also L. Jeep (1885).

Germans in Constantinople, however, their story is quite different. They certainly had additional sources of information, including an epic poem by an eye-witness, one Eusebius, writing to celebrate the defeat of Gainas soon after the event, and probably also a poem by Ammonius first performed in 438.[12]

In this version religious factors are prominent. This is not only because the authors are historians of the church, but also because divine help was emphasized in official accounts of the defeat of Gainas. Under the Theodosian dynasty Christianity was not only the religion of the emperor, but state religion in the full sense of the word. Its symbols and concepts began to figure prominently in imperial ideology and ceremony.[13]

In Sozomen, but not Socrates,[14] the account of the fall of Gainas begins with a description of how Gainas' plea to be allowed a church for Arian services was successfully resisted by John Chrysostom. In Sozomen's narrative—as in that of Synesius—Gainas' sacrilege, his attempt at religious innovation, like 'hybris' in Greek tragedy, was punished by divinely sent madness driving the sinner to self-destructive acts. In both Sozomen and Socrates the fall of Gainas is preceded by acts of reckless banditry. Gainas is said to have ordered his troops to seize the wealth of the Constantinopolitan silversmiths, and when this failed to set fire to the imperial palace. This attempt too was a failure, since the palace appeared to be defended by mysterious guards of huge stature. This was repeated on three successive nights. Gainas took the supernatural defenders to be real soldiers and decided to leave the city on a pretext. He was accompanied by some of his men who masked the evacuation by hiding their weapons in carts carrying their families. The guard at a city gate discovered[15] the weapons and tried to stop the Goths. This led to fighting which soon spread into the city. At that point the emperor declared Gainas an enemy, and ordered the Goths remaining in the city to be slain. Soldiers[16] attacked the Goths. When they took refuge in a church the Romans threw firebrands down from the roof and burned them.[17] In

[12] Socr. vi. 6, cf. *PLRE* ii s.v. Eusebius 8. But what did they take from the *Gainia*? Hardly any political or military information. Perhaps only the alleged attacks on the silver of the silversmiths and on the palace, the latter defeated by a supernatural intervention.

[13] Eunap. fr. 68 Blockley = 78 Müller mocks the 'hand of God driving off the barbarians' image. See also the conspicuously Christian character of Arcadius' column, on which: E. H. Freshfield (1921–2), J. Kollwitz (1941) 16–62; A. Grabar (1936) 75; S. G. MacCormack (1981) 57–61, G. Becatti (1960) 151–264, and below, p. 277.

[14] Soz. viii. 4 (1524 B); Socr. vi. 5 (637 B) alludes to the episode in a different context.

[15] οἱ φρουροὶ τῶν πυλῶν: Socr. vi. 6 (680B). φύλακες: Soz. viii. 4 (1525 A).

[16] οἱ παρόντες στρατιῶται: Socr. vi. 6 (680 C), Soz. viii. 4 (1025 B).

[17] Socr. vi. 6, Zos. viii. 4; Philostorg. xi. 8 has an independent version of Gainas' escape from Constantinople.

this version the fantastic and miraculously repelled attack on the palace replaces the absurd plan for a concerted operation against the city by Germans inside and outside it. As the story was told by Zosimus, Gainas actually began to carry out his plan for seizing the city. According to Socrates and Sozomen, fighting between barbarians and 'Roman' soldiers and civilians broke out by accident, when the Germans were already demoralized as a result of a mysterious and clearly supernatural intervention. The object of this version was evidently to stress the fundamental contribution of divine help, that God had defended the pious and orthodox emperor and his capital.

The third version is that of Synesius in *De Providentia*. The point of view is different because Synesius' narrative is focused not on Gainas but on the Roman politicians hidden under the names of Osiris and Typhos, i.e. Aurelian, and Eutychianus. The pamphlet is in effect a rewriting of the Egyptian myth of Isis and Osiris as it had been told by Plutarch.[18] In Synesius' version Osiris is made to stand for Aurelian, and Typhos, his villainous adversary, for Aurelian's rival whom A. H. M. Jones identified as Eutychianus.[19] As told by Synesius the myth has acquired features of panegyric in praise of Aurelian and invective against Eutychianus. But it is neither standard panegyric nor invective. The genre is mixed and complex.[20]

Gainas figures in Synesius' myth as a barbarian general who is used by the villain to overthrow the hero. The portrait is much more favourable than one might expect in view of the opinions about barbarian mercenaries Synesius had expressed in *De Regno*.[21] This is not necessarily because he had changed his mind, or even because Gainas was powerful at the time that Synesius wrote the first part of *De Providentia*. It is a common trick of oratory to praise someone the speaker disapproves of in order to accentuate by contrast the even deeper villainy of the immediate target of the speech.[22] The early events of the Gainas crisis are not included in Synesius' fable. Tribigild is alluded to only briefly as a leader of a local uprising. For Synesius the conspiracy began when Gainas was sent to deal with the uprising, but it was not between Gainas and the leader of the revolt, but between Gainas and Typhos the wicked brother of Osiris,[23] that is, the praetorian prefect Eutychianus. The object of their conspiracy was to win for the wicked brother the kingship of Egypt, i.e. the

---

[18] J. G. Griffiths (1970).

[19] A. H. M. Jones (1964*b*), esp. 80–1. Against Alan Cameron, J. Long, L. Sherry (1990) ch. V. 5 and T. Barnes (1986*a*) I have argued that Jones is right. See Appendix I.

[20] As is suggested in the Preface, *PG* xvi. 1212; cf. W. Liebeschuetz (1983) 44–6 and below, p. 138–9.   [21] *De Regno* 21–4.

[22] Cf. praise of Caesar to blacken Antony in Cic. *Phil.* ii. 45. 6.

[23] *De Prov.* 1249 B.

praetorian prefecture of the East, and for the Germans safety from the alleged schemes of Osiris—Aurelian.[24] Typhos-Eutychianus is said to have offered Constantinople to the Germans for plundering.[25] The conspiracy succeeded. Osiris-Aurelian was deposed and exiled, Typhos-Eutychianus took his place, and the Germans entered the city.[26] Synesius briefly alludes to an attempt at religious innovation.[27] As in Sozomen this is rapidly followed by the downfall of Gainas and his Germans.

In Synesius' account the barbarians in Constantinople fell into a kind of unaccountable panic, with the result that they decided to leave the city, taking their wives and children with them. It is likely that when Synesius describes the Germans' unpredictable behaviour in the city, sometimes drawing their swords as if to launch an attack and sometimes fleeing as if pursued by an armed enemy,[28] he is thinking of the events that were to give rise to the story of the supernaturally foiled attack on the palace, or perhaps even of that story itself. As in the ecclesiastical historians, the withdrawal turned into a battle at the end of which the Germans left in Constantinople had been destroyed. As in the ecclesiastical historians, the outbreak was the result of an accident; Synesius' version of the accident is, however, different. While the ecclesiastical historians start the outbreak with Roman soldiers at the gate stopping the Germans from taking weapons out of the city, according to Synesius fighting developed from a brawl provoked by an outspoken beggar woman.[29] Synesius is closer to the ecclesiastical historians than to Zosimus, but his account is clearly independent of theirs. Synesius was an eye-witness, and includes much detail which is best explained on the assumption that Synesius simply related what he knew had happened. On the other hand, Synesius was writing both panegyric and invective, both inevitably sources of distortion. What are we to make of it all?

The most untenable feature is the role of Typhos-Eutychianus. According to Synesius' story Eutychianus' treason was eventually established. This is incredible in view of the fact that Eutychianus was to hold the highest office once more within four years of the expulsion of Gainas, while the 'good' Aurelian had to wait no less than fourteen.[30] Clearly Eutychianus was not discredited by the Gainas affair. The picture of Typhos the traitor is rhetorical distortion. The

---

[24] 1245 D–1248 B.

[25] 1249 B.   [26] 1252.   [27] 1257.

[28] 1260; G. Albert (1984) 130 ff. convincingly suggests a breakdown of discipline among Germans.

[29] 1261 B.

[30] The view of A. H. M. Jones (*PLRE* ii. 1250), see W. Liebeschuetz (1987) and Appendix I.

elder brother has been blackened to serve as a foil to the younger brother whom the writer is magnifying. One might compare the way the portraits of Rufinus and Eutropius were distorted by Claudian in order to glorify Stilicho. There was of course a difference of objective between the rhetorical publicity as practised by Claudian and by Synesius. Claudian's poetry was written in support of Stilicho's policy at the time of writing. The Egyptian Tale does not serve any particular policy. Certainly a version of history which transfers the principal guilt for the outbreak from the Germans to the Roman praetorian prefect was not written to support an anti-German policy.

A second example of distortion is the miraculous character of Synesius' account of the liberation of Constantinople: the expulsion of Gainas is presented as a divine mercy. This, as we have seen, was the official version commemorated in the carvings of the column commemorating the victory,[31] which has also left traces in the ecclesiastical historians. Synesius has accentuated the miraculous nature of the deliverance by insisting that it was brought about by civilians alone. The other accounts mention soldiers.[32] Indeed, no matter how many regular units Gainas had transferred out of the city, the palace guards must have remained.[33] Surely Zosimus and the ecclesiastical historians correctly describe what happened when they give to soldiers an important role both in the annihilation of the Goths in the city, and among the defenders of the gates against the Goths who were trying to break in to the city from outside.

It is worthwhile trying to reconstruct Eutychianus' policy. Clearly it involved cooperation with the Germans. When Leo's army had been wiped out by the mutineers the Roman authorities were in a difficult position: to deal with the rebellious Germans, they only had two armies at hand, both largely composed of Germans. Gainas was certainly less formidable than Alaric. So the first decision was to give the task to Gainas. Gainas made his agreement conditional to the removal of Eutropius. The Roman government accepted the condition, and Aurelian the new praetorian prefect carried it out. The punishment of ex-ministers was a regrettable feature of the ruthless competition for power of this period. The execution of Eutropius was part of a series which began with the exiling of Tatian (and the execution of his son Proculus), continued with the murder of Rufinus, and ended with the exile of Aurelian himself. Gainas proceeded to end the mutiny of Tribigild by diplomatic rather than military means. He then marched north into Bithynia and was able to face the emperor and his ministers from a position of very great strength. On the one

---

[31] See above, p. 113 n. 13.
[32] See above, p. 113 and n. 16.　　　　　[33] Zos. v. 19. 2.

hand he was at the head of the only field army in the neighbourhood of the capital, on the other he had just rendered the state the great service of ending the mutiny. As a result he was in a position to force a bargain. He agreed to move his troops out of Asia into Thrace. In return he demanded and received the surrender of the prominent men whom he considered his enemies (Aurelian, Saturninus, and John) and he was given the title of *Magister militum* of both armies. Eutychianus was the new praetorian prefect who presided over the carrying out of the new agreement, as Aurelian had presided over the carrying out of the old. No doubt he hoped that Gainas would now defend Thrace and Constantinople against external attack—not the least danger being that Alaric might break loose in the Balkans and turn East. The policy might be summed up as balancing one German commander against another. In the absence of a national regular army the only alternative would have been the much more risky one of using one German army to destroy another.

A consequence of this policy was that part of Gainas' force was billeted in Constantinople. It was quite usual for units of the praesental field army to be temporarily lodged in the capital.[34] I do not think that the admission of German troops into the capital was seen as the reception of a garrison of occupation, or that the Germans insisted on it in order to be able to put pressure on the government. Analogy with Germans elsewhere suggests that what the Germans were concerned for was money and food. Eutychianus will have promised them both. The evidence—such as it is—suggests that the Germans were uncomfortable in the big city and, far from doing anything to take control of it, were just moving out their equipment, prior to leaving themselves, when fighting broke out.[35] The camp was some distance away from the city so as to be secure from sudden attacks from inside the walls, with the result that the main body could not come to support their comrades in the city before the gates were closed. Eutychianus' policy collapsed on 12 July 400.[36] Out of some obscure incident, fighting broke out between Germans and Constantinopolitans ending with the destruction of about 7,000 Germans in the city.[37] The

---

[34] Gainas had originally started from Constantinople: Zos. v. 14. Troops at Constantinople in transit: CT vii. 8. 13 (422), 14 (427) refer to billeting of troops at Constantinople.

[35] Permanent stationing of troops in a city had always been thought to endanger discipline: Zos. ii. 34, Amm. xxii. 4. 6–8, other refs. in R. MacMullen (1963a) 84–5. As G. Albert (1984) 130 ff. points out, federates who were not well disciplined to start with were bound to get out of control altogether. This was possibly the reason why Gainas decided to leave. Alan Cameron, J. Long, L. Sherry (1990) ch. VI. 1 suggests that they feared for the safety of their families, and that the barbarians massacred were mainly dependants. According to Synesius (*De Prov.* 1260 ff.) they simply felt insecure. This would not be surprising: they were countrymen and not trained for street fighting.

[36] *Chron. Minor.* ii. 66.   [37] See p. 112 n. 10 above.

killing was not indiscriminate. The victims were all followers of
Gainas, soldiers and civilians left in the city. Other Goths were left
alone. Constantinople continued to house an Arian Gothic community—even one divided by a schism of its own.[38] What happened
on 12 July 400 was not a blind and frenzied attack on everybody
German. What made possible the discrimination was that Gainas'
men, caught in their houses in the centre of the city, realized that the
riot was directed against themselves and decided that in these conditions resistance was useless. They threw away their weapons and
sought asylum. Some were killed singly or in groups in the streets, the
largest number in the church of the Goths.[39] The other Goths at
Constantinople were probably in the main either civilian slaves or
freedmen, or soldiers in regular units. Presumably the civilians stayed
quietly at home, while the soldiers may well have fought against their
fellow Goths. After all, Fravitta, the general chosen to lead the
Roman forces in the now almost inevitable war against Gainas, was
himself a Goth.

For Eutychianus the massacre of Gainas' Goths was of course a
disaster, but it seems from Synesius' Tale that even at this point the
praetorian prefect did not abandon his policy. As well as equipping
the state for war by raising heavy taxes, Eutychianus seems to have
tried to undo the effects of the disastrous misunderstanding at
Constantinople, and to restore the status quo, by negotiations and
diplomacy.[40] Evidently this was in vain and some time later (before
8 December 400) Eutychianus was replaced by Caesarius.[41]

There was now, at last, and probably for the first time, open war
between the East Roman government and its German field army.[42]
The *magister militum* of the East, Fravitta, was by a joint decree of
emperor and senate put in charge of all available military and naval
forces. These were evidently neither large nor well disciplined.[43] The
strategy he adopted was significantly one which avoided pitched
battle.[44] The decisive fact was that Gainas could not feed his army in
Thrace.[45] The crops had been harvested and removed behind the
shelter of city walls. The walls were guarded by the citizens under

---

[38] Socr. v. 23; Soz. vii. 17. It is significant that a Goth, Fravitta, was appointed to resist
Gainas.

[39] *De Prov.* 1264 D, 1268 A.

[40] *De Prov.* 1268 C.   [41] *CT* i. 34. 1.

[42] *De Prov.* 1268 D–1269A; Zos. v. 19. 6.

[43] Fravitta evidently did not bring the Eastern field army. Presumably he took over mainly
the troops that were defending Constantinople. There were no others in the region: Socr. vi. 6
(680 A). Some regular Roman troops were even then with Gainas—who had them killed:
Zos. v. 22. 9).

[44] Zos. v. 20–1.

[45] Zos. v. 19. 7, the usual weakness of wandering barbarian bands. See above, p. 73.

their magistrates.[46] Lack of supplies compelled Gainas to try to cross back into Asia. He forced his way through the long walls into the Chersonese and built rafts to take his troops across to Lampsacus. When the attempt was made, Fravitta rammed the clumsy rafts with boats assembled in anticipation and destroyed them.[47] Gainas gave up the attempt to cross into Asia and retreated first towards, and then across, the Danube, hoping to lead his men back to their home country. Fravitta did not pursue him. After they had crossed the Danube Gainas and his force were destroyed by Uldin, a Hunnish king and sometime ally of the Empire, who controlled territory north of the Danube.[48] Gainas' head was displayed at Constantinople perhaps on 3 January, or more likely February, 401.[49]

The Gainas affair evidently caused much fear, anger, and division among the population of Constantinople. We have just enough evidence to make it likely that one of the most controversial events during the rising was the destruction of the Goths together with the church in which they had taken refuge and the priests that were ministering to them. The destruction marked the culmination of a victory, but it was also an atrocity, and within a very short time came to be seen as such.

Of our two earliest sources Zosimus-Eunapius[50] and Palladius' Dialogue concerning the Life of John Chrysostom[51] only Zosimus-Eunapius mentions it, adding that those 'excessively Christian' thought it a great sacrilege.[52] Palladius not only ignores the destruction of the Goths and their church but also has no more than one indirect allusion to the whole Gainas episode.[53] He does not even mention Chrysostom's stand against the granting of a church for Arian services. This is significant. Eunapius was an outsider, writing from the point of view not of Constantinople but of provincial Sardes, and in addition writing pro-pagan polemic. He was an opposition writer as far as that was possible at the time. Palladius, on the other hand, was writing an apology for Chrysostom to be read by

[46] Zos. v. 19. 6. Cf. resistance by civilians: in Pamphylia, above, p. 103; at Adrianople, Amm. xxxi. 6. 2, cf. Them. *Or.* xiv. 181 b; to Alaric in Greece, L. Robert *Hellenica* iv, 61 nn. 2–3, *IG* v. 2. 153, iii. 636, vii. 93; at Semos, Theophyl. Simoc. vii. 3 ed. de Boor pp. 249–51, Prisc. fr. 9. 3, G. Dagron (1974) 356 n. 1.

[47] Zos. v. 21.

[48] Zos. v. 22.

[49] So O. Seeck (1919) 303, citing *Chron. Minor.* ii. 66. s.a. 401, but Alan Cameron (1989) points out that the Latin version s.a. 400 dates death of Gainas to February.

[50] Eunapius was published after Pulcheria became Augusta in 414 (fr. 72. 1 Blockley = 87 Müller: ἐπὶ Πουλχερίας). F. Paschoud (1975) 173–5 argues for after 423. R. Blockley (1981) and (1980) would emend Pulcheria to Eudoxia, making possible publication soon after 404, but against this Paschoud (1985a).

[51] Published not long after 407.

[52] Zos. v. 19. 5.   [53] See below, p. 259.

the people of Constantinople who had deposed and exiled him. Contentious issues, such as the involvement of the empress in the campaign against him, had to be minimized or ignored. It looks as if Gainas, the Goths, and particularly the destruction of the Goths in Constantinople, were similarly topics too controversial to be mentioned.

Confirmation of this is provided by the historical reliefs on Arcadius' column. The column has been destroyed, and the sculptures are only known from drawings of varying accuracy, by different artists. One set of drawings representing a continuous band of events evidently copies the carvings on the lower half of the column, and the beginning of the narrative sequence. The artist either did not see the carvings very well, or—more likely—merely used them as starting point for variations of his own. At any rate he transformed what was evidently a sculptured narrative of the story of Gainas' Goths from their departure from Constantinople to their final destruction into a triumphal procession of the imperial army, complete with barbarian prisoners.[54] But whatever freedom the artist allowed himself, he could hardly have ignored the depiction of a battle fought in the streets of the city if such a battle had been represented on the column. The fact that his drawings show no street-fighting suggests that no street-fighting was shown on the column. That this was so is confirmed by three so-called Freshfield drawings, dating from 1572–8, which give detailed, and it seems generally reliable, views of the carvings as seen respectively from east, south, and west. Here too there is not the slightest hint of fighting inside Constantinople. The artist shows Goths filing past monumental buildings of the capital, and leaving the city in a peaceful procession through what may be the Golden Gate.[55] The conclusion is unavoidable that the column did not show the rising of the people of Constantinople against the Goths which came to be regarded as the decisive victory achieved miraculously with divine aid. Instead the monument appears to have given space to subsequent events passed over briefly by our written sources. The Goths are shown marching through Thrace. There is a remarkable sequence of rustic scenes depicting the army moving through forest

[54] Printed version in P. L-F. Menestrier (1711), also in A. Banduri (1729), G. Becatti (1960) pl. 78–80 reproduces the drawing in the Louvre. Becatti argues (pp. 111–50) that these drawings represent the column of Theodosius. I am convinced by J. Kollwitz (1941) 21–2 that they are based on Arcadius' column. See also below, pp. 273–4.

[55] J. Kollwitz (1941) 28 and Beilage 4; E. H. Freshfield (1921–2) pl. 16. Basic reliability of the Freshfield drawings is suggested by comparison with the drawing of the column in the Bibliothèque Nationale (G. Becatti (1960) pl. 72–3, J. Kollwitz (1941) pl. 34) and with Lorich's drawing (G. Becatti pl. 63d, J. Kollwitz Beilage 8. 1). For representation of the departure of the Goths see below, pl. 4. 1–3, 5. 1.

and open plain, past herds and herdsmen, through mountainous country and finally past an extraordinary group of tent-like huts occupied by near-naked groups around what might be a low circular table. It is tempting to recognize the dwellings of country folk. But comparison with a miniature in the *Ilias Ambrosiana* suggests that they are military tents, and their occupants Goths relaxing over a meal around a large circular plate. Fravitta's victory over the Goths trying to cross the Hellespont into Asia was represented.[56] The climax of the campaigns as shown on the column was the defeat of the Goths in three great battles involving cavalry on both sides. The victors represented on the column are not identifiable as Huns, but might be taken for the emperor's army. The building of the column and presumably the ordering of its carving may have started as early as 401/2.[57] If so, the column would seem to commemorate an official version earlier than that of our other sources, a version according to which Gainas was destroyed in the way in which it was traditionally fitting for a barbarian to be destroyed, by the leadership of the emperor and the valour of his soldiers. What is not traditional is that carving on the base of the column prominently proclaims that victory had been won in the sign of the Cross.

Contradicted as it is by two contemporary sources of very different tendency, Zosimus–Eunapius and Synesius, the version of the Gainas war shown on Arcadius' column cannot be true. It was inevitable that it should soon be superseded by others which gave an important place to the fighting in Constantinople. A trace of the column story survives in Sozomen's report that Gainas met final defeat and death at the hands of a Roman army.[58]

For the historian the importance of the carvings on the column lies in their implications. It would appear that the battle of Constantinople, glorious as it was from many points of view, was also so controversial that the authorities decided that it should be buried in silence. Who were the men responsible for the 'cover-up'? We do not know, but publicized leadership at that time came from the emperor Arcadius. It was he who proclaimed Gainas a public enemy and ordered the Goths left in the city to be killed.[59] Later he and the senate appointed

---

[56] J. Kollwitz (1941) pl. 3–4. *Ilias Ambrosiana* miniature XXVII is illustrated in G. Becatti (1960) pl. 67.

[57] Theophanes a.m. 5895 (De Boor 77. 24): 402/3 but Theophanes dates Gainas' revolt one year too late. The east side of base shows two Augusti as consuls. This would fit 402. It was dedicated in 421: Marcell Comes s. a. 421, *Chron. Pasch. PG* 796–7.

[58] Soz. viii. 4 (1528 A).

[59] Eunapius-Zosimus v. 19 stresses that the emperor personally ordered the killing in the church; according to Soz. viii. 4 he merely ordered the killing of all Goths in the city. So also Socr. vi. 6.

Fravitta to command the imperial forces at Constantinople. Eutychianus' prestige must have been shaken, but he remained in office.
We cannot tell how far it was still his advice on which the emperor
acted. We are, however, told that Eutychianus criticized the burning
of the Gothic church,[60] an act which many must soon have regretted.

As bishop, Chrysostom must have taken an active part in any
controversy over the burning, whether he led the attack on those
responsible for the outrage, or whether he employed his eloquence to
justify them. Of course we have no explicit evidence for the attitude
actually taken by Chrysostom. We can, however, be sure that,
whatever it was, it won him both friends and enemies and that the
enmities incurred in the controversy over the burnt church played a
significant part two years later, in the conflict which led to his
deposition.

Of course the burning of the church was only one of a number of
causes of recrimination. The whole policy that had brought the Goths
into Constantinople was under attack. Scapegoats were sought and
conspirators suspected. The detail is lacking, but the existence of a
witch-hunt situation is clear. All the sources on the Gainas affair,
even though they differ in important details, agree that there had been
some kind of conspiracy to take over Constantinople in the interest
of some party. There evidently was a great deal of talk of conspiracy
and treachery at Constantinople in the autumn of 400. Synesius gives
a brief and obscure account of events there after the destruction of the
Goths on 12 July, while surviving Goths were still in control of
Thrace: the city was under siege; there was widespread fear of
treason. An investigation was being undertaken in the senate, and
witnesses were questioned, both Greek and barbarian. Many of
the persons interrogated were women. This suggests that the
investigators were concerned to get evidence from the servants of
suspected persons. The inquiry seems to have been held at the same
time as Gainas was unsuccessfully trying to cross into Asia. (Evidence
is said to have been produced that Eutychianus had wished the Goths
to succeed in crossing.) According to Synesius the investigation was
directed specifically against Eutychianus. Presumably it was then that
the accusation that Eutychianus had conspired with Gainas was first
made. The commissioners are said to have called for his arrest and
trial; but the emperor insisted that his punishment should be left to
Hades.[61] Presumably it was on account of this investigation that
Eutychianus lost the praetorian prefecture to Caesarius.[62] It is,

[60] *De Prov.* 1268 A.
[61] *De Prov.* 1269 A-C.
[62] The phrase of the oracle, ἐκποδὼν γενομένου τοῦ Τυφῶνος (*De Prov.* 1256 D)—surely *ex*

however, clear that, whatever evidence was produced by the investigators late in 400, it did not prove conspiracy on the part of Eutychianus, or prevent him from being reappointed to the prefecture a few years later. It looks as if other men were investigated, and fared worse. Two parts of a law issued on 19 January 401 suggest that trials resulting in the confiscation of property had recently taken place.[63] The laws also show that the government at least was viewing the situation calmly, for one of the objects of the legislator was to make possible an act of mercy which would restore the property to its former owners within a period of two years. One might deduce that the authorities had yielded to the demands of a public hysteria which they did not share, and whose consequences they were hoping to mitigate.

Paradoxically Fravitta, the man who had presided over operations which had brought about the destruction of Gainas, fared worse. He was at first criticized for not actively following up his victory on the Hellespont, but the ultimate success of the campaign silenced this criticism.[64] He was rewarded with the consulate, and we hear that he led another campaign in Thrace.[65] But some time before 404 he was killed, probably murdered.[66] Information about the circumstances comes from disconnected fragments of Eunapius.[67] The death of Fravitta occurred as a result of a difference with John, a favourite of the empress Eudoxia and recently a colleague in exile of Aurelian and Saturninus.[68] Fravitta accused John of destroying the unity of the emperors and undermining the whole Empire. John was powerful and influential, and a group of courtiers fearing John and hoping to gain by his favour came together to get rid of Fravitta.[69] The most active part seems to have been played by a man whom Eunapius calls Hierax, i.e. Hawk, on account of his rapacity.[70] Eunapius' account of the carrying out of the plot has been lost. The use of the word φόνος suggests that it culminated in assassination,[71] but it is just possible that Fravitta was accused of treason and executed.[72] A revival of the charge that he had deliberately spared Gainas when it was in his

eventu—together with the account of the trial (1270), must mean that Typho-Eutychianus was deposed shortly before the return of the exiles. See below, p. 263.

[63] *CT* ix. 42. 17, x. 10. 23.
[64] Eunapius fr. 69. 4 Blockley = 82 Müller.
[65] Zos. v. 22. 3; Eunapius fr. 69. 4 Blockley.   [66] Eunapius fr. 71. 4 = 86 Müller.
[67] Fr. 71. 2–4 Blockley = 83–6 Müller, 72. 1–4 Blockley = 87–8 Müller; Zos. v. 25. It looks as if Eunapius treated the killing of Fravitta and related episodes as a scandal of major importance. On this Alan Cameron, J. Long, L. Sherry (1990) ch. VI. 4.
[68] *PLRE* ii s.v. Ioannes 1.   [69] Eunapius fr. 71. 3 Blockley = 85 Müller.
[70] Fr. 71. 2 Blockley = 83 Müller, 71. 3 Blockley = 85 Müller, 71. 4 Blockley = 86 Müller, 72. 1. 45 = 87 Müller; cf. *PLRE* ii s.v. Hierax.
[71] Fr. 72. 1. 47 = 87 Müller.   [72] Fr. 71. 4. See n. 78 below.

power to destroy him[73] would have provided a convenient basis for a prosecution or an excuse for an assassination.

At least two alternative contexts could be constructed. The conflict between John and Fravitta could be linked with Alaric's invasion of Italy in late 401[74] and public debate about the policy that the Eastern governments ought to follow in these circumstances. Should the West be assisted or not? So a date for the killing of Fravitta towards the end of 401 would be attractive.[75] But there is a strong though circumstantial argument against it in the evidence of Eunapius-Zosimus.

Eunapius evidently made a great deal of the death of the heroic and outspokenly pagan[76] Fravitta.[77] Unfortunately none of the fragments of his lost narrative is precisely dateable. But there is enough circumstantial evidence to make possible conjectures. First Hierax, the man responsible for the death of Fravitta searched and plundered Pamphylia after the killing of Fravitta.[78] This was during a period of invasion by Isaurians which was ended by the general Arbacius.[79] Now Arbacius himself escaped treason charges by bribing the empress Eudoxia.[80] So the whole series of events must have happened before Eudoxia's death on 6 October 404. The other hint is provided by the information that Fravitta had openly opposed the *comes* John over a policy which he asserted would destroy the concord and unity of the two emperors with disastrous results.[81] We are not told what the policy was, but we do know that a period of collaboration between East and West ended in the course of 403, with the result that Stilicho refused to recognize the Eastern consul of 404.[82] We have seen earlier that it was at this time that Alaric and his Goths turned up in Eastern Illyricum.[83] It was also towards the end of 403 that a silver statue of the empress Eudoxia was set up close to St Sophia at Constantinople[84] and that official images of the empress were sent out

---

[73] Fr. 69. 4 Blockley = 82 Müller; Stilicho's claim: Claudian *Cons. Stil.* ii. 71–81, and on it Alan Cameron (1970) 152.   [74] On this see above, p. 60 ff.

[75] This is supported by Eunapius fr. 72. 4 Blockley = 88 Müller, referring to killing of 'the consul himself'. Only two men who reached the consulate were killed around this time: Stilicho in 408 (when he was 'former consul') and Fravitta possibly in 401, the year of his consulate. But the fact that Fravitta's consulate was not annulled makes it unlikely that he was condemned for treason in his year as consul. It remains possible that he was murdered.

[76] Fr. 69. 4 Blockley = 82 Müller.

[77] Fr. 71. 1 Blockley = 84 Müller, 71. 2 Blockley = 83 Müller, 71. 3 Blockley = 85 Müller, 72. 1 Blockley = 87 Müller, 72. 4 Blockley = 88 Müller.

[78] Eunapius fr. 71. 4 ἐπὶ τῷ Φραβίθου φόνῳ, 'after' or 'in connection with', or 'with a view to', but in any case *close in time* to 'the killing'.

[79] Zos. v. 25.   [80] Zos. v. 25. 4.   [81] Eunapius fr. 71. 3 Blockley.

[82] See Alan Cameron, R. S. Bagnall, K. A. Worp (1987); O. Seeck (1919) 306.

[83] See above, p. 64.

[84] *CIL* iii. 736; Socr. vi. 18.

to the provinces, including those in the West. Honorius wrote a letter of protest to his brother.[85] It is not clear why precisely Honorius objected to this innovation, but the incident certainly suggests a deterioration of relations between East and West of which Alaric was the ultimate cause. So it is easily conceivable that the conflict between Fravitta and John was over the policy to be followed with regard to Alaric. What the conflicting proposals were we can only conjecture. The eventual outcome was that Alaric and Stilicho made an alliance to attack the East.

Looking back at the Gainas affair it is clear that there existed at Constantinople, as there did in Italy, fear of the German mercenaries, and suspicion of men who cooperated with them. But the significant fact is that this powerful tide of feeling did not result in radical reversals of government policy. The contrast with the West could not be greater. There a consistent policy, not unlike that of the East, was maintained by Stilicho. But in 408 opponents of that policy over-threw Stilicho, and there followed a period marked by repeated changes in personality and reversals of policy in the course of which Rome was sacked, Alaric's Goths consolidated into a nation, and the Empire suffered damage which was never to be made good.[86]

[85] *Coll. Avell.* 38. 1 (*CSEL* xxxv. 1. 85), cf. K. G. Holum (1982a) 66.
[86] J. Matthews (1975) 300–2.

II

After Gainas

THE Gainas episode clearly demonstrated the danger presented by
federates, but it did not prove that the Eastern Empire needed a
powerful regular army. After all, it had rid itself of Gainas without
winning a major land battle. Gainas had been forced out of imperial
territory by starvation and the decisive military victory had been
won—not easily and in several battles[1]—by Uldin, an allied king
beyond the Danube frontier.

The lesson that the Eastern government seems to have learnt was
that it must try to manage as much as possible without Germans,[2]
even though that meant a much weaker army. Fravitta, the Gothic
general, had commanded the Roman forces against Gainas, and in a
subsequent operation against certain runaway slaves and deserters
who said that they were Huns, and who were plundering Thrace,[3] but
he was killed soon after. About the same time Alaric left the territory
of the Eastern Empire to invade Italy. We have seen that he had not
actually been encouraged to do this by the Eastern government. It is
unlikely, however, that he had been given any incentive to stay in its
service.[4] There seems to have been a deliberate effort to keep
Germans out of the commanding position in the army. Most of the
known Eastern generals in the decade following the destruction of
Gainas have Greek or Latin names.[5] Of the generals with barbarian
names Arbazacius was an Isaurian born in Armenia,[6] and Arsacius
and Varanes I[7] were Persians. For the time being the government at
Constantinople was looking to the East for foreign mercenaries.
The use of federates was not totally abandoned: a small force of
Huns met with very great success in Libya.[8] Varanes as *magister
militum praesentalis* in 409 calmed a mob during a bread riot at
Constantinople. He had come from the West where he had actually
for a time been the successor of the murdered Stilicho.[9] His transfer
to the East was perhaps an indication of better relations between the

---

[1] Zos. v. 22.

[2] They were not of course totally dispensable. Fravitta apart, Plintas (consul 419) and
Ardaburius 3 (consul 427) must have begun their military careers in the first decade of the
century.

[3] Zos. v. 22. 4–6.   [4] See above, p. 230.   [5] *PLRE* ii. 1290–3.

[6] Ibid. 127 s.v. Arbazacius 1.

[7] Ibid. 152 s.v. Arsacius 3; 149 s.v. Varanes 1.

[8] See below, p. 230.   [9] Zos. v. 36. 3.

two governments now that the East no longer felt threatened. On 10 December 408 the Western government lifted the embargo on Eastern trade that had been imposed by Stilicho.[10] In 410 six regiments were sent by the Eastern government to assist Honorius in Italy when he was on the point of giving up the struggle against Alaric and his puppet emperor Attalus. This was a small army by the standards of an earlier Rome, but it was large enough to enable Honorius to man the defences of Ravenna and to continue the struggle against Alaric.[11]

The East could spare 4000 men because it had no significant military commitments at the time, and because Anthemius and his advisers were determined not to be forced into any major campaign if they could help it. Like Eutropius, they were ready to risk military weakness if in this way they could avoid the danger to internal stability of a large army and successful generals. Without the federates of either Alaric or Gainas the East was of course even weaker militarily than it had been under Eutropius. Luckily the threat represented by Stilicho had gone, but the Empire had considerable difficulty even in coping with mere bandits. Isaurian raids were resumed in 403–4 and although Arbazacius managed to drive the raiders back into their mountains and to recapture a lot of their plunder, the attacks were resumed soon after and continued to plague neighbouring provinces for many years.[12] In 405 the Ausurians, a nomad tribe, began to raid the Libyan province of Pentapolis, and it was only in autumn of 412 that they were defeated and Libyans enabled to go about their lives without fear. Even so, the frontier security of earlier times does not appear to have been restored.[13]

On 1 May 408 the emperor Arcadius died. Immediately the king of Persia appears to have threatened war if anyone should prevent the succession of Arcadius' son the infant Theodosius. This may have been a demonstration of monarchical solidarity, but it was also a threat of military intervention by Persia in the internal affairs of the Empire.[14] It is surely not a coincidence that the same year brought a dangerous invasion of Thrace by joint armies of Huns and Skiri led by Uldin, king of one group of Huns and destroyer of Gainas. The Empire survived, partly through promises and bribes. The Roman general was able to break up the invading force by inducing some of

---

[10] *CT* vii. 16. 1.

[11] Zos. vi. 8. 2; Socr. viii. 10; Soz. ix. 9; Procop. *B. Vand.* i. 2. 32–36; D. Hoffmann (1969) 46–98 on identity of units.

[12] Isaurian raids: Zos. v. 25.

[13] See below, p. 229.

[14] Procop. *B. Pers.* i. 2. 1–10; Theophanes a.m. 5900. See K. Holum (1982a) 83.

Uldin's officers to desert to the Romans, taking their men with them. The remainder were then routed.[15] The many prisoners taken were not enrolled in the army, nor settled together as potential soldiers, but distributed individually among landowners in Asia Minor for no other employment than that of farmworkers to increase agricultural production in a time of food shortage.[16] Clearly Anthemius wanted to make sure that these barbarians were not able to come together once more as a warrior band like the Greuthungi of Tribigild. In 408 the Empire peacefully came to an agreement with the Persians which, among other terms, set out trading places on each side of the frontier where merchants from the two empires could meet and transact their business.[17] Like Rufinus and Eutropius, Anthemius preferred to keep out invaders by diplomacy and spending money rather than war.

A policy of this kind could not have been followed by the Western government: its frontiers were too long and too exposed to attack. The Eastern Empire had only two vulnerable frontiers, in Mesopotamia and along the Danube. The former was safeguarded for the time being at least by a treaty with the Persians, the latter remained vulnerable,[18] and with it Constantinople. The Eastern government implemented a programme of fortification. City walls were constructed in the Balkan provinces and no one was exempted from the compulsory service needed for the building. From the highest to the lowest all were to contribute in proportion to their property.[19] Constantinople itself received a powerful new wall eleven metres high, with ninety-five towers at intervals of fifty-five metres.[20] These defences, which were strengthened by an outer wall later in the reign of Theodosius II, and by a wall along the sea front later still[21] made Constantinople all but impregnable. Henceforth it presented an insuperable bulwark in the way of invaders across the Danube, which kept people and resources of the rich provinces of Asia Minor safe from war and destruction.

The age of Anthemius was a time of recovery and growing prosperity for the East, to the point that men began to wonder whether the Empire could not afford a more ambitious, and traditionally Roman, military policy. It has been shown by Holum that the end of Anthemius' prefecture was followed by a noticeable change in various

---

[15] Soz. ix. 5. 1–5.

[16] *CT* v. 6. 3 (409); for Anthemius' caution cf. also *CT* v. 6. 2. Food crisis at Constantinople: *Chron. Pasch.* s.a. 412—but in urban prefecture of Monaxius.

[17] *CJ* iv. 63. 4.　　　　　　　[18] *CT* vii. 17. 1 (412): expansion of Danube fleet.

[19] *CT* xi. 17. 4, xv. 1. 49; *CJ* x. 49. 1.

[20] Socr. vii. 1. 3; *CIL* iii. 7484; *CT* xv. 1. 51 (413), vii. 8. 13; R. Janin (1964) 265–83.

[21] R. Janin (1964) 287–300. That the long walls from sea to sea to the west of Constantinople were built shortly after the settlement with the Huns in 447 is argued by M. C. Whitby (1985).

aspects of policy.[22] The group of public men who had guided the East for around twenty years now gave place to others. Even if one does not accept Holum's argument that the change of course was from the start directed by the child emperor's fifteen-year-old sister Pulcheria,[23] it is clear that she eventually emerged as a powerful influence on government. One feature of the new course was a further increase in pressure on pagans, Jews, and heretics in favour of religious uniformity on a basis of orthodoxy.[24] Another departure was a war waged offensively with Persia. The immediate cause, as might have been expected, was religious. In 419 or 420 a bishop in Persian Khuzestan had destroyed a fire altar of the Zoroastrian state religion and the king of Persia had retaliated by executing the bishop and some of his followers. Shortly afterwards refugees appeared at Constantinople asking for support from the Empire. When the Persian government demanded return of the refugees the Roman authorities, eager to assist fellow Christians, rejected the demand.[25] A less pious consideration may have been that a dynasty as unmilitary as the first and second generation of descendants of Theodosius had to demonstrate that the Empire could nevertheless win victories under its rule. In 421 one Roman army supported rebels in Persian Armenia, another invaded Persian Mesopotamia. The operations achieved little, not only because it was always very difficult for Roman forces to achieve a decisive victory against the Persians, but also because Roman military strength was not what it once had been. Many of the troops used in the Persian campaigns had been transferred from Europe,[26] exposing the European provinces to attack, and offering the Huns an opportunity to launch a devastating invasion of Thrace which culminated in a siege of Constantinople itself.[27] The eastern campaign had to be broken off and peace made with Persia. The Empire was no longer capable of carrying on two major wars at the same time.

The empire nevertheless did not give up its more active foreign policy. When Honorius, the Western emperor, died[28] the East took an active interest in the succession. For a short time Theodosius II claimed to be the ruler of both halves of the Empire.[29] Eventually in 425 an Eastern army intervened in the West to depose the usurper

---

[22] K. Holum (1982a) 94 ff., also (1977).

[23] Born 19. 1. 399 (*Chron. Pasch.* s.a. 399).   [24] See below, p. 146 ff.

[25] On the Persian war: Socr. vii. 18–20; Theodoret *HE* v. 39; Theophanes a.m. 5918; K. Holum (1977).

[26] Theophanes a.m. 5943 ed. de Boor, p. 104: troops moved from Europe and the vicinity of Constantinople. *CJ* viii. 10. 10 (420–2): landowners on the eastern frontier permitted to build fortifications, an admission that the army could no longer guarantee their safety.

[27] B. Croke (1977); *Chron. Minor.* ii. 75 s.a. 422.   [28] 15. 8. 423 (Soc. vii. 22).

[29] Socr. vii. 23; Theophanes a.m. 5915; Hydatius: 82 = *Chron. Minor* ii. 20; Prosper Tiro 1283 = *Chron. Minor.* i. 470; Cassiod. *Chron.* 1283 = *Chron. Minor.* ii. 155.

John and put young Valentinian II, son of Galla Placidia and grandson of Theodosius I, on the Western throne.[30] In 431 another large expedition went to the assistance of the West. This time the purpose was to prevent the Vandals from occupying what is now Tunisia and was then proconsular Africa and Numidia.[31] The Eastern army suffered several defeats and could not prevent Vandals occupying almost the whole of the provinces except for the fortified cities of Cirta and Carthage. Eventually the army was withdrawn because once again the Huns, now led by Rua, had exploited the absence of the Eastern striking force to put the Empire under pressure: Rua demanded the Romans' return of peoples who had sought refuge within the Empire; otherwise he would make war. The Empire decided on negotiations but before an agreement could be reached Rua died.[32] This brought little relief to the Romans, since Rua's achievement of building up a great federation of Hunnish tribes was continued and developed with dramatic success by his nephew and successor Attila.[33]

The limited remilitarization of the Eastern Empire after the prefecture of Anthemius involved the reappearance of barbarian generals. In 418 a rebellion in Palestine was suppressed by Plinta, an Arian Goth, who was consul in 419 and *magister militum praesentalis*, perhaps continuously from this year to 438.[34] One of the armies in the Persian war was commanded by Ardaburius, an Alan.[35] Ardaburius together with his son Aspar defeated the usurper John.[36] That these men were qualified to be appointed to high commands suggests that they had considerable service in the Roman army behind them. This in turn shows that even during the period of debarbarization the Eastern Army included soldiers of Gothic or Alan origin. It is a reasonable inference from the fact that a Goth and an Alan were appointed to the highest commands that the enlarging of the army for offensive operations, and later to face the Huns of Attila, involved the recruiting of significant numbers of Alans, Goths, and other non-Romans. It is not a coincidence that Aspar for a considerable time achieved a position at Constantinople comparable with that which Stilicho had once held at Rome, and Gainas briefly in

[30] Olympiod. fr. 46 = 43 Blockley; Socr. vii. 23; Philostorg. xii. 13; John Ant. fr. 195.

[31] Procop. *B. Vand.* i. 3. 35–6; Evagr. *HE* ii. 1; Theophanes a.m. 5931.

[32] Priscus fr. 1.

[33] E. A. Thompson (1948) 70–5.

[34] Marcell. Com. s.a. 418; cf. *PLRE* ii s.v. Fl. Plinta.

[35] *PLRE* ii s.v. Fl. Ardabur 3, Socr. vii. 18, 20, 23: under him served as *comes foederatorum* (Malalas 364) a Goth, Fl. Ariobindus, *PLRE* ii s.v. Fl. Areobindus 2. Two Roman generals, Vitianus and Procopius, are also mentioned.

[36] Olympiod. fr. 43 Blockley = 45–6 Müller. *PLRE* ii s.v. Fl. Ardabur Aspar—also a Roman general, Candidianus.

the Eastern capital.[37] The problem of integrating large bodies of semi-independent federates into a peaceful society also returned to the East.[38]

Though the Eastern Empire did not maintain the degree of de-militarization which it had achieved after the Gainas episode, it never returned to the huge defence forces of the Diocletianic Empire and the *Notitia*. Even when the Eastern Empire was following offensive military policies its field armies were not strong enough to fight successfully on more than one front at a time. The fifth century also saw a running down of the screen of *limitanei* that had been stationed in a continuous chain of forts along the eastern frontier. Archaeological evidence is beginning to suggest,[39] and Procopius' history of the Persian wars confirms,[40] that many of the forts were evacuated in the course of the fifth century and that by the time of Justinian almost all had been abandoned. There was a comparable reduction of the number of units in the Thebaid.[41]

[37] Aspar, Plintas, and Ariobindus formed a close family group, linked to the imperial family, assimilated to Roman ways but kept apart by their Arian religion. See A. H. M. Jones *LRE* 181–2, *PLRE* ii stemma 39.

[38] *PLRE* ii s.v. Triarius, Theoderic Strabo 5, Fl. Theodoricus 7.

[39] S. T. Parker (1980), esp. 873–4, (1986).

[40] W. Liebeschuetz (1977).

[41] R. Rémondon (1961) 80–2.

12

The Arcadian Establishment
AD 392–412

WHEN we look at the military and foreign policy of the Eastern Empire from the prefecture of Rufinus (392–5), or even earlier, to the end of that of Anthemius (405–414), or a little longer, a striking feature is its consistency and continuity. These in turn can be seen to be linked to the fundamental stability of what might be called the 'Arcadian Establishment'. Of course first impressions suggest otherwise: this was a period of violent political conflict. Rufinus was lynched by the army, Eutropius executed, Aurelian exiled, Eutychianus charged with treason and acquitted, or eventually exculpated and reinstated, John Chrysostom the archbishop exiled, recalled, and exiled again amidst riots. But these violent events must be seen in perspective. Radical changes of personnel in leading positions were offset by a homogeneity of attitude and outlook. The men who held the most important offices under Arcadius were remarkably similar in social background. Their rivalry, though intense, seems to have been for power and control of patronage, and does not seem to have involved significant differences over policy or ideology.[1] Moreover the period was characterized not only by the overthrow of ministers but also by continuity of careers.

Continuity of career and homogeneity of background are most evident among the praetorian prefects, the holders of the office which, under weak emperors at any rate, most resembled that of the prime minister of a modern state. When Rufinus was murdered, he was succeeded by Caesarius, who was praetorian prefect of the East under Eutropius in 395–7, consul in 397, and prefect once more after the expulsion of Gainas in 400. He had been *magister officiorum*, the second civil office in importance, as long ago as 386–7.[2] He may well have been a man who had risen through public service and been favoured by Eutropius for that reason,[3] for when Libanius delivered a speech in his praise he claimed to have 'known' him,[4] but said nothing

---

[1] I agree with Alan Cameron (1981) against K. Holum (1982a) 86 n. 1.

[2] *PLRE* i s.v. Caesarius 6; see Appendix I, p. 262, below defending A. H. M. Jones's reconstruction of the career.   [3] Like Hosius, the *magister officiorum* (*PLRE* i. 445).

[4] *Or.* xxi. 6, admittedly a *praeteritio*, i.e. Libanius lists topics which he is not going to take up. That the speech is not formally a panegyric weakens the argument from silence.

about his early life and family. This makes it likely that he had lived in the East for some time, but also that his father and ancestors had not been men of distinction. Caesarius' successor Eutychianus was *comes sacrarum largitionum* in 388, praetorian prefect (in A. H. M. Jones's view) of Illyricum in 396–7, praetorian prefect of the East in 399–9, 399–400, 404–5, and consul in 398.[5] His career in the highest offices spans the whole period of crisis. He probably was the son of Taurus, a self-made man who had been praetorian prefect of Italy and Africa under Constantius and condemned to exile by a military tribunal under Julian. Eventually he settled at Constantinople and founded a great family there. If, as is quite likely, he paid, or his sons paid, for the construction of the forum Tauri at Constantinople, they were very rich indeed.[6] It would also show that the family spent a great deal of money in order to win the favour of Theodosius, for it was in that forum that Theodosius set up a column bearing an equestrian statue of himself. Eutychianus' prefecture of the East was briefly interrupted in 399 by the first praetorian prefecture of his brother Aurelian, another man whose career in highest office spans the whole period. After a succession of obscurely described earlier posts, he was prefect of Constantinople in 393–4, praetorian prefect of the East from August to December 399, consul in 400, and praetorian prefect of the East for a second time in 414–16.[7] The long interval between the prefectures suggests that he was somewhat discredited by his part in the destruction of Eutropius and the rise of Gainas. Another reason why Aurelian had to wait for such a long time for his second prefecture was that from 405 to 414 that office was held by the obviously extremely able Anthemius. Anthemius' career began in 388 when together with Aurelian he carried out a diplomatic mission to Persia. He was *comes sacrarum largitionum* in 400 and *magister officiorum* in 404.[8] His family background was very similar to that of Aurelian and Eutychianus. He was a grandson of Flavius Philippus, like Taurus a self-made man, who had reached the praetorian prefecture and consulate under Constantius and had founded a great family at Constantinople.[9]

[5] See *PLRE* i s.v. Eutychianus 5.

[6] *PLRE* i s.v. Taurus 3. Later members of the dynasty: *PLRE* ii s.v. Fl. Taurus 4 (cos. 428) and Fl. Taurus Clementinus Ammonius Clementinus (cos. 513). Stemma: *PLRE* i. 1146. Forum Tauri: R. Janin (1964) 64–5. Taurus 3 and his sons between them held six praetorian prefectures, providing enormous scope for enrichment. Chrysostom's sermon *Cum Saturninus et Aurelianus acti essent in exsilium* (*PL* lii. 413 ff.), and (if Alan Cameron (1989) is right) *De capto Eutropio et de divitiarum vanitate* (ibid. 395 ff.) can be understood to imply that Aurelian and his colleagues had been notorious for the pursuit of wealth.

[7] *PLRE* i s.v. Aurelianus 3.   [8] *PLRE* ii s.v. Anthemius 1.

[9] *PLRE* i s.v. Philippus 7, ancestor of emperor Anthemius; *PLRE* ii s.v. Anthemius 1; for other descendants see *PLRE* ii. 1311 stemma 5.

Men of similar background held appointments at a slightly lower level. Optatus I, nephew of a consul in 334, was prefect of Egypt under Theodosius I (in 384), an influential member of the senate of Constantinople around 390, and in 404 as prefect of Constantinople persecuted the followers of John Chrysostom.[10] In that year one of the consuls was Aristaenetus II, both of whose grandfathers had been praetorian prefect under Constantius. Aristaenetus himself had been prefect of the city in 392.[11] Another long career was that of Clearchus II who held high office in the East in 386 and was prefect of the city from at least May 400 to March 402, so that his period of office bridged the expulsion of Gainas' German mercenaries and the return of the men exiled by them. It may be that he was already in office in May 399. In that case he had still been appointed by Eutropius. His career culminated in the prefecture of Illyricum some time before 407.[12] His name suggests (though there is no other evidence) that he was the son of Clearchus, consul of 384.[13]

Anthemius was succeeded in 414 by Monaxius, and a new generation took over the prefecture of the East, with only the interruption of the second prefecture of Aurelian. Monaxius resumed office and held it to 420.[14] He was the last prefect for a long time to hold the prefecture for so many years; two or three years became the rule. The prefects of the East ceased to be *de facto* heads of the government. Immediately this role may well have been taken over by Helion, *magister officiorum* 414–27.[15] At the same time Pulcheria, the sister of the young emperor Theodosius II, was steadily gaining influence and power, even if it is difficult to believe that she in any real sense took over the government in 414 at the age of 15.[16] Monaxius and his immediate successors did not belong to the families of the 'Arcadian Establishment'. The next generation of the dynasties of Taurus and of Philippus—and of Tatian, the victim of Rufinus—duly appear in the *fasti* of the praetorian prefecture.[17] But henceforth the establishment of dynasties of that kind was rare. The great majority of prefects of the fifth and sixth century, especially officials of outstanding achievement, were new men, not members of office-holding families.[18]

[10] *PLRE* i s.v. Optatus 1.   [11] *PLRE* i s.v. Aristaenetus 2.

[12] *PLRE* i s.v. Clearchus 2.

[13] *PLRE* i s.v. Clearchus 1.

[14] *PLRE* ii s.v. Fl. Monaxius.

[15] Helion, *PLRE* ii s.v. Helion 1. Another powerful figure was the eunuch Antiochus (*PLRE* ii s.v. Antiochus 5), K. Holum (1982*a*) 80–3. Very influential about 404 (Synesius *Ep.* 110), he was dismissed from post of *praepositus sacri cubiculi* in 421.

[16] Soz. ix. 1 (1593 B) taken literally by A. H. M. Jones *LRE* 179 and Holum (1982*a*) 90 ff.

[17] *PLRE* ii s.v. Fl. Taurus 4, Fl. Taurus Clementinus; see also ibid. stemma 5 (descendants of Anthemius), ibid. s.v. Tatianus 1.

[18] A. H. M. Jones *LRE* 207, 235, 275, 295.

The 'Arcadian Establishment' was made up of the most distinguished individuals of the new East Roman aristocracy which had been consolidating ever since Constantine had set up his capital at Constantinople.[19] It consisted of two layers. First of all there was the senate of Constantinople, which had been consciously built up on the model of the Roman senate by Constantius in cooperation with Themistius the philosopher. Then there was the much more numerous senatorial order, which comprised all men of senatorial rank, whether they had achieved this by virtue of the office they were holding, or as a reward for having held a particular office, or purely honorifically without having held any office at all. The senatorial order was a device for using the traditional prestige of a Roman senator to smooth the working of the Late Roman bureaucracy, senatorial rank being used either to give prestige to imperial officials or to reward them for past services. The number of positions conferring senatorial rank increased steadily, and membership of the order grew accordingly.[20]

Membership of the senatorial order was hereditary. It involved the burden of a special senatorial tax, but also the highly desirable privilege of immunity from service in city councils.[21] The fact that there had come into existence in the East a senate and a senatorial order meant that there was in the East an influential group of men convinced that they had the same duty and right to occupy leading positions in the Empire as the senators of Rome, and eager to ensure the *de facto* independence of their half of an empire which, in theory and law, remained united.

The new senate and senatorial order were drawn in part from the wealthiest citizens of the largest Greek cities of the East. In that sense it represented progress towards Greek self-government. It also involved a drain of men and resources from the provincial cities to Constantinople which was noticed and resented. At city level politics and service in the city council became devalued. The councils lost members and influence. In the cities themselves power came to rest not with councillors but with men of real or honorary rank in the imperial aristocracy,[22] and men discontented with some aspects of their city looked for support to the provincial governor, the emperor's representative, or to the influence of great men at Constantinople. All these effects can be observed in the cities of Cyrenaica as described by Synesius.[23]

[19] See G. Dagron (1974) 147–90.
[20] A. H. M. Jones *LRE* 526–42.
[21] For references to legislation to prevent city councillors escaping into the senate or government service see *LRE* 740–5.
[22] W. Liebeschuetz (1972) 174–92, P. Brown (1978) 48–53.
[23] See below, p. 234.

Though the new senate and senatorial order upheld the emancipation of the Greek East, a significant proportion of their members were of Latin origin. After all, the Empire remained the Roman empire: senate and senatorial orders were Roman concepts. Latin was and remained for a long time the language of command in the Roman army, and a high proportion of the officers, barbarian and Roman, will have been Latin- rather than Greek-speaking.[24] Latin continued to be the official language of administration and law in the East,[25] though in practice most business must have been carried on in Greek.[26] For most of the fourth century men from Latin-speaking provinces continued to be appointed to high positions in the East.[27] All emperors of the fourth century up to and including Theodosius I, with the possible exception of Julian, had been brought up in Latin. Constantinople itself was a bilingual city.[28]

Theodosius I actually strengthened the position of Latin at court by bringing a number of relatives from Spain and the Western provinces into the government of the East.[29] Of these the most outstanding were the praetorian prefects Cynegius[30] and Rufinus.[31] That Theodosius was aware of the gap between leading families of Constantinople and the newcomers, he showed by determined efforts to marry Olympias, a great lady of Constantinople, granddaughter and heiress of Constantine's praetorian prefect Ablabius, first to Nebridius, a Western follower and relative of his own, and after Nebridius' death to Helpidius, another relative.[32]

There seems to have been a real campaign to strengthen Latin in government by appointing candidates who had a training in that language. The sophist Libanius at Antioch feared for the employability of his students, and for the future of Greek rhetoric and of the whole civilization that centred on it.[33] He need not have worried. Among civilians the prestige of Greek culture was overwhelming. The descendants of Theodosius' Western officials cannot be traced, but it can be assumed that they were thoroughly

---

[24] See names in *fasti* of *PLRE* ii. 1290 ff.

[25] Cyrus, *PPO Or.* 439–41, was first to issue edicts of prefecture in Greek: John Lydus *De Mag.* ii. 12. 2. Justinian's *Novels* were the first imperial laws to be issued in Greek: T. Honoré (1978) 125.

[26] W. Liebeschuetz (1972) 247–8.

[27] See *fasti* of prefectures and other high offices in *PLRE* i.

[28] G. Dagron (1969); B. Hemmerdinger (1966); cf. T. F. Carney (1971) ii. 48, 59 on Latin culture of John Lydus.

[29] J. Matthews (1975) 109–14.

[30] *PLRE* i s.v. Maternus Cynegius; also J. Matthews (1967).

[31] *PLRE* i s.v. Fl. Rufinus 18; also above, p. 89.

[32] *PLRE* i s.v. Olympius 2, Nebridius 2, Fl. Ablabius 4.

[33] W. Liebeschuetz (1972) 244–6.

Hellenized, just like the descendants of the Latin-speaking magnates of the courts of Constantine and Constantius. The fathers or grandfathers of leading senators of the 390s were made the objects of abuse by Libanius because they had been men of humble origins—an attendant at public baths,[34] for instance, and a sausage maker,[35] and because they owed their advancement to a knowledge of shorthand rather than of Greek rhetoric.[36] Their sons and grandsons were not only well educated in Greek literature[37] but also extremely snobbish. Libanius' invective was aroused by their refusal to allow into the senate a friend and assistant of his on the grounds that ownership of an arms factory made him unworthy.[38] In the 390s at Constantinople snobbery and rhetorical education were perfectly compatible. Mastery of Greek rhetoric had come to hold high prestige in the capital. His anger and complaints notwithstanding, it was only now that Libanius fulfilled the ambition of getting pupils into the prestigious office of prefect of the city, Aristaenetus in 392,[39] and Severinus in 398–9.[40]

We learn something about the literary culture, the recitations, the friendships based on common interest in Greek literature and philosophy, and the exchange of new writings from the letters of Synesius. Synesius was an aristocrat and landed magnate of Cyrene deeply interested in literature and philosophy. He was sent to Constantinople as ambassador by his province. While in the capital city he recited poems in the Doric dialect to select audiences, some in praise of Aurelian the praetorian prefect, his personal benefactor and benefactor of his province. He assures us that he refrained from putting his praise of Aurelian into writing as long as Aurelian was in power. Only after the prefect had lost office did Synesius take it upon himself to publish his praise and to publicize him, risky as that had now become.[41]

The three letters addressed to Aurelian are extravagantly complimentary.[42] Aurelian is addressed as a near divine being sent down by god or providence to set right the world.[43] This is not the kind of language that one would expect Synesius to have used to an equal.[44] Yet Synesius, writing not very long after his embassy, referred to

---

[34] *Or.* xlii. 24–5 (Datianus).
[36] W. Liebeschuetz (1972) 242 ff.
[37] See below, p. 139.
[39] *PLRE* i s.v. Aristaenetus 2.
[41] *De Prov.* 1253 D.
[42] *Ep.* 31, 34, 38 (Migne) = 31, 47, 35 (Garzya).
[43] *Ep.* 34 οὗ τῇ προνοίᾳ μέλει Ῥωμαίων, ἀλλὰ μέλησει ποτέ. *Ep.* 38 ἐπ' αὐτὸ τοῦτο καταπεμφθεῖσαν. Both letters were written when Aurelian was not in high office but looking forward to it. *Ep.* 31 looks back to a prefecture in which Aurelian benefited all men.
[44] The language is unique among the letters, but then Synesius did not write to anyone else of such rank.

[35] *Or.* xlii. 24–5 (Philippus).
[38] *Or.* xlii. 21.
[40] Ibid. s.v. Severinus 3.

Aurelian as a 'dear friend'.[45] So personal relations did exist between them. This can also be inferred from the general tone of *De Providentia*. Synesius practically tells us that the second part of *De Providentia* was written at the request of Aurelian.[46] It is of course enormously laudatory. It is not, however, a political pamphlet. For the point is made with some emphasis that Osiris-Aurelian could have anticipated and prevented the whole Typhos affair.[47] In fact Osiris-Aurelian is shown to have been better at beating off the attacks of daemons on his soul than at defending his worldly power, even though it affected the lives of so many others.[48] In other words the allegory represents Aurelian as too good a man, perhaps one might even say, as too good a Christian,[49] to be an effective ruler of the Empire. The portrait would hardly help to win Aurelian political supporters,[50] but it might have pleased him personally. In other words the *De Providentia* as we have it is not a panegyric, as I have once mistakenly described it,[51] but a very personal compliment. This interpretation of *De Providentia* would help to explain—and excuse—the language of the letters. Synesius is not simply flattering the great man by describing him as a saviour figure, but he is alluding to Aurelian's role as Osiris in the allegory, a much more subtle and dignified way of paying a compliment.[52]

If this interpretation of *De Providentia* is right Aurelian saw in Synesius more than a man capable of writing highly cultured panegyrical pieces, of the kind that Claudian wrote for Stilicho.[53] The two men were united by genuine literary friendship. Certainly, if Synesius wrote the essay for Aurelian to read, he must have thought of him as a man of high literary education, capable of spotting and

---

[45] *Ep.* 61, and on it T. Barnes (1986*b*).

[46] *De Prov.* praef. 1212. On *De Providentia* see French translation, introduction, and commentary: Ch. Lacombrade, (1951*a*), also Appendix I below.

[47] *De Prov.* 4 (1220): all intelligent men knew Typhos' failings. 8 (1224–5): priests warn Osiris of Typhos 11 (1236): Taurus warns Osiris—previously he has provided a philosophical and 'demonological' explanation of the Typhos phenomenon. 12 (1237): Osiris does not exile Typhos but tries to overcome malice by kindness—in vain. 1236 B: Osiris renounces force.

[48] *De Prov.* 10 (1232): Taurus warns Osiris that he would have to defend against demons not only his soul but his worldly position as well.

[49] On Aurelian's Christianity see below, p. 141.

[50] *De Prov.* 12 (1236 B) χρῆμα ἥκιστα τῆς γῆς ἄξιον.

[51] W. Liebeschuetz (1987).

[52] I suggest that all three letters allude to *De Prov.*, *Ep.* 34 almost explicitly, *Ep.* 38 referring to Aurelian's divine soul having been 'sent down' to do good to all men; cf. *De Prov.* 10 (1229 A) ψυχὰς συγγενεῖς δεῦρο κατακομίσαντες. *Ep.* 31 does not refer to Aurelian's providential mission, but its reference to the prefecture in the past dates it to the same period as Part 2 of *De Prov.* with which (and with *Ep.* 34) it shares the hope of great office in future. The ψυχαὶ τῶν πόλεων are surely saints corresponding to the sacred race of heroes of *De Prov.* 12 (1229 B). The date of *De Prov.* is discussed below, p. 272.

[53] Cf. Alan Cameron (1970) 42 ff.

enjoying allusions to classical literature[54] and philosophy.[55] Above all Synesius must have been quite sure that Aurelian would not misunderstand a message even though it was expressed obliquely through allegory. It would not at all have done if Aurelian had taken *De Providentia* as a pamphlet advocating paganism[56] or, even worse, pointing out that he was himself to blame for his political failure. Besides shared cultural interests Synesius and Aurelian did of course have perfectly practical reasons for cultivating each other's friendship. Aurelian could do with a propagandist. Synesius needed influential supporters at court.

This double aspect is characteristic of the relationships preserved in letter collections of Late Antiquity. Most of the letters of Synesius,[57] like those of Libanius, for instance, were written with the practical objectives of obtaining help of some kind from a man of sufficient power and influence to be able to give favours, or alternatively simply to keep alive a relationship which might one day be useful.[58] At the same time the writing and the appreciation of literary letters was a cultural activity. The letters are filled with quotations and literary allusions which the correspondents are expected to appreciate. The recipient of a letter can be expected to read it out to assembled friends and to subject it to literary criticism.

Characteristically most of the correspondents lived at Constantinople. Synesius had met some of them when they were students at Alexandria, more during the embassy. Most of them were of course men of influence, though Synesius was too much of a provincial to be on close terms with many holders of the highest offices; the principal exception was Aurelian. The *comes* John, Aurelian's colleague in exile, was also a correspondent.[59] The great prefect Anthemius did not receive letters from Synesius. But three men close to Anthemius did. These are Troilus,[60] Theotimus,[61] and Nicander.[62] All were literary men. Troilus was a sophist and poet who reputedly had very great influence with the praetorian prefect.[63] Theotimus was a poet too. Synesius professes respect for Nicander as a critic. A pupil of

---

[54] e.g. to appreciate *De Providentia* fully the reader ought to recognise that the myth is a variation on that in Plutarch's *De Iside et Osiride*, on which J. G. Griffiths (1970). See also Jacqueline Long (1987) and Alan Cameron, J. Long, L. Sherry (1990) Ch. VII. 5.

[55] Above all c. 19 in Taurus's speech.

[56] That Christianity underlies the retelling of the old myth is clearest in 1257 where the defeat of Typhos and his allies is shown to be a consequence of the introduction of Arian worship into Constantinople. On the Egyptian Tale as a 'typology' see below, p. 271.

[57] Now to be read in A. Garzya, *Synesii Cyrenensis Epistolae* (Rome, 1979).

[58] W. Liebeschuetz (1972) 17–23; J. Matthews (1974).

[59] *PLRE* ii s.v. Joannes 1; A. Garzya (1979) 196.

[60] Synesius *Ep.* 26, 73, 91, 112, 118.   [61] *Ep.* 47 (49 G), 49 (51 G).

[62] *Ep.* 1, 75.   [63] Socr. vii. 1; cf. *PLRE* ii s.v. Troilus.

Troilus, called Eusebius, wrote an epic poem about the defeat of
Gainas, in a sense a parallel to Synesius *De Providentia*.[64] Anthemius
was evidently the centre of a literary circle. At Constantinople
literary friends used to meet at the house of Marcian, a former
governor of Pamphylia and a philosopher. Synesius calls it the
Panhellenion[65] and professes to be afraid of the criticism which a
letter of his might receive in that gathering.[66]

It is a reasonable hypothesis that the attitudes found in the circle of
Synesius represent the predominant influence in senatorial circles at
Constantinople for something like twenty years after the murder of
Rufinus.[67] Even after that the high prestige of Greek letters did not
disappear. Theodosius II married a wife remarkable not only for
beauty but also for education[68] and it was subsequently, in 425, that
the 'University' of Constantinople was founded.[69] Nevertheless there
was a change of atmosphere which can be attributed to a further
infusion of Christianity, inspired by the flourishing monastic movement of Constantinople,[70] and also to the ascetic ideals of the emperor's
sister Pulcheria, whose dedication to a life of virginity was an act of
renunciation but also a source of power.[71]

It makes a great difference whether one views the élite of Constantinople through the letters of Synesius or the invectives of Claudian.
In the interest of detraction Claudian has made the most of the
humble birth of two of Eutropius' trusted advisers, Hosius, the
magister officorum, who is said to have started as a slave and cook,[72]
and Leo, the amateur general supposedly once a carder of wool.[73]
Towering above them is of course the caricature of Eutropius himself,
the ex-slave consul. It is likely enough that Eutropius helped some
former colleagues in the domestic service of the emperor to positions
high in the public administration. But most of the commanding
heights of government were held not by such men, but by members
of the group described earlier, many of whom had held office before
the rise of Eutropius and were to continue to do so after his fall. Of

[64] Socr. vi. 6. 36.
[65] See the learned, ingenious, and plausible explanation of this title in Alan Cameron, J. Long,
L. Sherry (1990) Ch. III. 1, n. 108; cf. A. J. Spawforth, S. Walker, 'The world of the
Panhellenion in Athens and Eleusis', *JRS* lxxv (1985) 78–104.
[66] *Ep.* 101 (p. 172 1. 15 ff. Garzya), 119.
[67] Until 'the age of Pulcheria' and her new ministers from around 415. See Holum (1982a)
97 ff.
[68] See *PLRE* ii s.v. Aelia Eudocia (Athenais) 2, and K. Holum (1982a) 112 ff.
[69] *CT* xiv. 9. 3, xv. 1. 53.
[70] G. Dagron (1970).
[71] Soz. ix. 1–3 and K. Holum (1982a) 93 ff., 137 ff.
[72] Claud. *In Eutrop.* ii. 346 ff.; *PLRE* i. 445.
[73] His piety: Synesius *De Prov.* i. 18; the chapel of St. Stephen: *V. Isaacii* iv. 18; cf. K. Holum
(1982a) 86 n. 30.

course even the longest established families at Constantinople were 'new' by the standards of Rome. But that was not why Claudian included them in his biting parody.[74] He did that because they supported Eutropius in his policy of resisting the claims of Stilicho.

The letters of Synesius, so informative in other respects, give little or no explicit indication of the secular correspondents' religion. Yet Synesius was, in this writer's view, born a Christian, and certainly ended his life as a bishop, a persecutor of heretics, and founder of a monastery.[75] The Christianity of Aurelian was similar. He had long supported Isaak, the pioneer of monasticism at Constantinople. Late in life Aurelian built a *martyrium* where he intended to enshrine the recently discovered relics of St Stephen.[76] When he failed to obtain the body of St Stephen he had Isaak buried in the *martyrium* instead.[77] Aurelian's second praetorian prefecture was marked by a spate of legislation against heretics, pagans, and Jews.[78] Reading *De Providentia* and Synesius' letter to Aurelian superficially we would not guess that Aurelian was strongly Christian. The fact is that it was literary convention, not paganism, that kept explicit references to Christianity, as well as Christian technical terms, out of secular correspondence and secular writings of high literary pretension. So evidence for Christianity in the literary classes is inconspicuous. But there is enough to show that Christianity had become the religion of the Eastern ruling élite. Caesarius, twice praetorian prefect, built a church dedicated to St Thrysus,[79] while his wife Eusebia was a patron of a group of Macedonian monks.[80] Eusebia exemplifies a type of Christian piety common among senatorial ladies at Constantinople. Literary circles were on the whole—with some notable exceptions among Neoplatonic philosophers[81]—made up of men. Christianity, however, gave women plenty of opportunities to display piety and employ wealth. Many wives and daughters of the aristocracy in the East and West were ready to devote time and property to the service of the church.[82]

---

[74] Claud. *In Eutrop.* ii. 326 ff.

[75] See W. Liebeschuetz (1985*b*) 159, and Alan Cameron, J. Long, L. Sherry (1990) ch. III. 1; cf. below, p. 233.

[76] *V. Isaacii* iv. 18.

[77] Alan Cameron (1989) quotes an extract from an upublished version of the Life of Isaac from F. Nau, *Rev. de l'orient chrétien* 11 (1906) 199 ff. On the discovery of the body of St Stephen and its use in ecclesiastical politics by John of Jerusalem see E. D. Hunt (1982*a*) 203 ff.

[78] See below, p. 150.

[79] Soz. ix. 2.

[80] Soz. ix. 2.

[81] On Hypatia: J. M. Rist (1965). Women among the select circle of Neoplatonic philosophy: Eunapius *Lives of Philosophers*, Alan Cameron, J. Long, L. Sherry (1990) ch. II. 5.

[82] R. Albrecht (1986); E. Clark (1979), (1983).

What made their prominence possible was a conjunction of the now ancient rights of Roman women and new scope given to their exercise by Christianity. Traditional was the right to own and inherit property, as well as to have a relatively unrestricted social life.[83] Christianity offered an opportunity of using property and the freedom to support the poor and sick, the clergy and bishops. Another use might be to endow monasteries or nunneries.[84] The opportunities were widely taken up. We are especially well informed about senatorial women at Rome,[85] of whom the best known are the two Melanias. The biography of the Younger Melania still allows us to sense her motives, including a deep revulsion from her role as a passive instrument of family continuity through arranged marriage and childbearing, and a positive dislike not only of sex but also of cleanliness, in short a need to defy the older generation. The reader feels Melania's passionate desire to dedicate herself to God, to fulfil the commandment to sell all property to give to the poor, together with her proud awareness that she is performing a vital role as supporter of the Church and maintainer of holy men.[86] The Church, as represented by clergy and bishops, was glad to let women play the new role.[87] These dedicated and unmarried or widowed women exemplified the high valuation the church placed on the control of animal passions by reason and self-discipline, the predominance of man's better nature. They also provided economic resources for charitable work and for the maintenance of the clergy.[88]

The role of these women was not restricted to charity and munificence. They came to play an extremely important part in ecclesiastical diplomacy. Hospitality and wealth which the great ladies of the capital cities could place at the disposal of their preferred ecclesiastics enabled the latter to travel to the capital, to stay there for as long as they thought necessary, and to have the means with which to publicize their views and to influence people.[89] Furthermore the ladies had social connections which the ecclesiastics lacked. In this period bishops

[83] On social life: S. B. Pomeroy, *Goddesses, Whores, Wives and Slaves* (London, 1975) 176–89. On control of property: J. A. Crook, *Law and Life at Rome* (London, 1967) 113–15; B. Rawson (1986) 93–120 by S. Dixon; J. F. Gardner (London, 1986) esp. 71–7.

[84] R. Albrecht (1986). The position of the foundress based on family, wealth, and social status resembled that of a great lady ruling her household: E. Clark (1985).

[85] Thanks to correspondence to St Jerome. See J. N. D. Kelley, *Jerome* (London, 1975), *passim*. E. Clark (1979).

[86] D. Gorce (ed.) *Vie de sainte Mélanie*, Sources Chrétiennes 90 (Paris, 1962).

[87] e.g. *Jean Chrysostom: La virginité*, ed. J. H. Musurillo and B. Grillet, Sources Chrétiennes 125 (Paris, 1966). Id. *À une jeune veuve. Sur le mariage unique*, ed. B. Grillet and G. H. Ettlinger, Sources Chrétiennes 138 (Paris, 1968).

[88] E. D. Hunt (1982a), chs. 7–9.

[89] Olympias financed not only John Chrysostom but also for a time at least his opponents Theophilus of Alexandria and the three Syrian bishops. See *V. Olymp.* 14; Pall. *Dial.* 58. See also P. Brown (1970).

were probably most often sons of curial families, and rarely belonged to the senatorial aristocracy. If they were going to attain their ends, whatever these might be, in the capital, they needed contacts, and for ecclesiastics contact was easier to make with the pious womenfolk of the aristocracy than with the more indifferent (perhaps even only recently converted) men.[90] Thus the ladies were in a position to mediate between the ecclesiastical and secular hierarchies.

The history of Chrysostom introduces us to a number of ladies in this role. Outstandingly the most important was of course the empress Eudoxia.[91] Some ladies of the court used their resources and influence on behalf of Chrysostom's opponents.[92] Other ladies favoured Chrysostom, and of these Olympias was the closest to him. She was the granddaughter of Ablabius, for eight years praetorian prefect of Constantine. In other words she belonged to the new 'establishment' of Constantinople, like Aurelian and Eutychianus and Anthemius. She was also the heiress to very great wealth, with estates in Thrace, Galatia, Cappadocia, and Bithynia, and several mansions in Constantinople and its suburbs.[93] Married when still young, she had soon been widowed, and it was said that she had never ceased to be a virgin. The emperor Theodosius wished to marry her to his kinsman Helpidius, hoping in this way to give Helpidius entrée into the aristocracy of Constantinople, as well as control of her vast wealth. Olympias refused to be used in this way, and turned down the match. Evidently she justified her stand with the precept, preached in so many sermons at the time, that it was better for a Christian widow not to remarry. Theodosius was so angry that he not only put Olympias' property under guardianship, but also forbade her to so much as meet any bishops. After the victory over Maximus, Theodosius relented and gave back to Olympias disposition over her property.[94] Not much later, and in defiance of the law which forbade the consecration of widows less than sixty years old,[95] Nectarius

---

[90] P. Brown (1961*b*).

[91] Eudoxia evidently acted as patron of Chrysostom's enemies, the visiting Syrian bishops Severianus of Gabala and Antiochus of Ptolemais (Soz. viii. 10). But she had also given crucial support to the Tall Brothers (Pall. *Dial*. 26, cf.Soz. viii. 13, 15). The fact that Eudoxia received and offered support to ecclesiastics does not mean that she was equally involved and equally powerful in secular matters.

[92] Marsa (*PRLE* ii. 728), widow of general Promotus (*PLRE* i. 750). The empress Eudoxia had been brought up in the house of one of Promotus' sons. Castricia (*PRLE* ii. 271), widow of the general Saturninus 10 (*PLRE* i. 807), Eugraphia (*PLRE* ii. 417) was the most fanatical opponent (Pall. *Dial*. 17) and offered her house as a meeting place to Chrysostom's enemies (*Dial*. 27).

[93] *Jean Chrysostom: Lettres à Olympias* ed. A. -M. Malingrey, avec le texte grec et la *Vie anonyme d'Olympias*, Sources Chrétiennes 13 bis (Paris, 1968); on it G. Dagron (1974) 503–6.

[94] Pall. *Dial*. 61; *V. Olymp*. 5–6, and comments of G. Dagron (1974) 503–6.

[95] *CT* xvi. 1. 27.

bishop of Constantinople ordained her as a deaconess. Olympias proceeded to reduce her property charitably. She gave money to the
poor, and kept open house for travelling bishops and clergy. Among
those who benefited from her hospitality were the bishops Antiochus,
Accacius, and Severianus, who were to become the core of opposition
to Chrysostom. She rarely visited the baths, and then only for her
health. She did not take off her chemise even in the water.[96] When
Chrysostom became bishop in 398 he immediately attended to the
morals of the 'order' of widows. To those who were not living
chastely he counselled a course of asceticism, consisting of fasting and
abstinence from baths and attractive clothes. If they were not up to
this they were to hasten into a second marriage.[97] Olympias was
advised to use her property more discriminately.[98] She obeyed and
became a close friend. She looked after him and paid most of his
living expenses, so that he cost the Church nothing.[99] In addition she
gave vast donations to the Church of Constantinople.[100]

Christianity was capable of bringing together in a common cause a
much wider spectrum of society than literary education. As we have
seen, soldiers did not usually come from the most highly urbanized
areas of the Empire—if they came from within the Empire at all—
and officers were not as a rule men of high education.[101] Generals
received literary letters from Libanius in which he praised them for
having written at all, not for the literary style of their letters.[102]
Synesius wrote to two generals interested in literature and philosophy,
but he comments on their intellectual interests as unusual.[103] But
inability to write according to the rules of rhetoric did not disqualify
a military man from showing himself a pious Christian. The distinguished generals Victor[104] and Saturninus[105] competed to offer land on
which the monk Isaak could set up his cell and establish a monastery.
The estate of the general Promotus came to be occupied by a monastery of Gothic monks who unlike the great majority of their fellow
tribesmen were orthodox.[106] Gainas corresponded with the hermit
Nilus on questions of theology.[107] Marsa the widow of Promotus was

---

[96] Pall. *Dial.* 61.
[97] Pall. *Dial.* 20.
[98] Soz. viii. 9.
[99] Pall. *Dial.* 61.
[100] *V. Olymp.* 5–6.
[101] See above, p. 23.
[102] W. Liebeschuetz (1972) 114 n. 2.
[103] Simplicius: Synesius *Ep.* 24, 28, 129 (Migne) = 24, 28, 130 (Garzya). Cf. *PLRE* ii s.v.
Simplicius 2. Paeonius: *Ep. ad Paeonium* (1580 b), cf. *Ep.* 142, see *PLRE* ii s.v. Paeonius 1, also
T. D. Barnes (1986a) 109–10.
[104] *V. Isaaci* iii. 10, iv. 15; Theodoret *HE* iv. 33. 3; see *PLRE* i. 959.
[105] *V. Isaaci* iv. 14; see also *PLRE* i. 807.
[106] John Chrys. *Ep.* 207.
[107] Nilus *Ep.* 1. 70, 79, 114–16, 205–6, 286.

an opponent of John Chrysostom,[108] as was the widow of Saturninus.[109] Saturninus and Victor survived from the court of Valens, which had after all already been attended by many sincere Christians.[110] But Theodosius and his Western followers imported a greater degree of aggressiveness, and, as we have seen, his prefects Cynegius[111] and Rufinus[112] took a lead in the suppression of paganism, encouraging the destruction of temples by bishops and monks.

The arrival of Theodosius brought with it not only a more aggressive Christianity but also the dangers of deep divisions between the Christians at court, since Theodosius began his reign by affirming his support of 'orthodoxy' in an area that had for nearly half a century been ruled by emperors with Arian sympathies and from a capital where Arians were certainly in a considerable majority.[113] Men like Saturninus and Victor who had served Arian emperors for most of their lives will have been faced with a dilemma. In these circumstances the reception of relics, the building of churches to house them, and the promotion of monasticism[114] allowed men to demonstrate their religion in a way that was dogmatically neutral, or at least not tainted by past controversy and taking of sides.[115] Support of the monastic movement went back to the time of Valens, and monasticism at Constantinople, characterized by freedom from rules and a strong sense of duty towards the poor, had Arian or more precisely Macedonian roots.[116]

Christianity had the potential to be a great social unifier.[117] The comparatively humble social level of Christian origins and its regular services and sermons, together with its charitable institutions enabled it to reach and influence social levels below the reach of any traditional civic institution.[118] Christianity was a community builder, and in the course of centuries it became the cement of East Roman society.[119] But before that it had also brought deep division.

[108] Pall. *Dial.* 25.
[109] Ibid., loc. cit.
[110] J. Matthews (1975) 128–30.
[111] J. Matthews (1967); *CT* xvi. 5. 13–14, 16; Lib. *Or.* xxx.
[112] On his legislation see below, p. 146.
[113] See below, p. 158.
[114] Patronage of monasticism at court of Theodosius: J. Matthews (1975) 130–9.
[115] Cf. P. Brown (1981) 93 ff. on cult of relics as expression of concord.
[116] John Matthews (1975) 129–31; G. Dagron (1970) 244–53.
[117] S. Mews (1982) esp. 1–20 (S. P. Brock).
[118] See below, p. 251.
[119] N. H. Baynes (1955a) 24–46, Averil Cameron (1979). It also helped to unify Goths and Vandals and to bring into being numerous sectarian communities.

13
Legislation against Heretics, Pagans and Jews

PERHAPS the most conspicuous evidence of the Christian beliefs of members of the 'Arcadian Establishment' is the fact that it maintained and extended legislation penalizing religious dissent, pagan, Jewish, and above all sectarian Christian. A tidal wave of such legislation was let loose by Theodosius I at the very start of his reign, when he proclaimed his support of what became catholic orthodoxy.[1] Theodosius was evidently motivated by sincere belief and a sense of religious responsibility.[2] At any rate, he proclaimed his policy of support for Nicaean orthodoxy at the very beginning of his reign, and proceeded to implement it by means of a mass of legislation as soon as he had entered Constantinople.[3]

After Theodosius' death religious legislation continued to be abundant under the influence of Rufinus. The legislative tide receded somewhat during the later 390s:[4] the Theodosian Code preserves no Eastern laws against heretics issued between 402 and 410.[5] It must, however, be remembered that many fewer Eastern laws of any kind have come down to us from the first decade of the fifth century than from preceding decades.[6] But if fewer laws were issued, existing laws were not repealed. The 'Arcadian Establishment' believed in using the law in favour of religious uniformity on the basis of catholic orthodoxy.

Loyal belief was not punished, nor was mere membership of a heretical group sufficient to incur a penalty—as a rule.[7] What the laws proscribed were specific 'external' acts. Groups declared heretical were deprived of their churches.[8] They might not be allowed to hold meetings,[9] or they were forbidden to consecrate bishops or ordain clergy.[10] It was declared an offence to allow a meeting of a heretical sect to be held on private property.[11] In the case of pagans, the laws were

---

[1] CT xvi. 5. 5 (379), cancelling a recent rescript of toleration of Gratian, cf. Soz. vii. 1.
[2] See below, p. 157.   [3] CT xvi. 5. 6–16, 17–24.
[4] 6 laws in 395, 4 in 396, 1 in 397, 1 in 398, 1 in 399. Survey of whole legislation in P. P. Joannou (1972).
[5] Between CT xvi. 5. 30 (402?) and 48 (21. 2. 410), 49 (1. 3. 410).
[6] See O. Seeck (1919) 297–319.
[7] The Manichaeans were the principal exception, see below, p. 147 n. 24–6.
[8] CT. xvi. 5. 8 (381), 30 (402).   [9] Ibid. 12 (383), 20 (391), 24 (394), 26 (395).
[10] Ibid. 5. 13 (384), 21 (392), 22 (394), 24 (394).   [11] Ibid. 21 (392).

focused on the prohibition of sacrifice.[12] There was no compulsory conversion of individuals. As a rule ordinary members of a proscribed group did not suffer legal disabilities simply because they belonged. Such disabilities normally affected only persons of the highest social class. So various laws excluded pagans,[13] heretics,[14] and Jews[15] from posts in the imperial service.

A tendency to reduce further the civic rights of religious dissenters went against the tradition of Roman administration, and made only slow progress. For instance, Rufinus forbade Eunomians to receive or leave anything by will,[16] but his law was repealed by Caesarius in 395[17] and by Eutychianus in 399.[18] Eventually, however, the Eunomians were disqualified in both respects.[19]

Among Christian sects Novatians generally received the most favourable treatment.[20] They were as a rule allowed to keep their churches,[21] and their bishops at Constantinople were highly respected.[22] This was because the dissent of Novatians was a consequence of moral rigorism,[23] not of distinctive belief: above all they agreed that the Persons of the Trinity were of the same substance.

The worst treated group were the Manichaeans. Not only were they deprived of the right to make wills or to benefit from them, but this penalty was imposed retroactively.[24] Moreover, Manichaeans might be sought out by informers, brought to court and punished, and in the case of sub-groups even executed simply for membership of the group.[25] They were treated as apostates rather than dissenters and altogether appear to have inspired quite extraordinary fear and indignation in the legislators, or rather in the bishops, on whom persecution of Manichaeans depended in practice and who presumably instigated the laws.[26]

Numerically the strongest sect in the East were certainly the Arians, themselves divided into a number of sects who differed among themselves about the relationship of God the Father to Jesus the Son.[27] The central group which had been recognized as orthodox by the emperor

---

[12] *CT* xvi. 10. 11 (391), 12 (392), 13 (395).
[13] *CT* xvi. 10. 21 (Aurelian *PPO Or.* 415).   [14] *CT* xvi. 5. 29 (395), 48 (410).
[15] *CT* xvi. 8. 24 (Palladius *PPO It.* 418).   [16] *CT* xvi. 5. 23.   [17] Ibid. 27.
[18] Ibid. 36.   [19] Ibid. 49 (Anthemius *PPO Or.* 410), 57 (Aurelian *PPO Or.* 415).
[20] Socr. v. 10, 14, 20.
[21] But Leontius of Ancyra deprived Novatians of churches; Soz. viii. 1.
[22] Socr. vi. 22, 25, vii. 39; Soz. viii. 1.   [23] Socr. v. 19, 22.
[24] *CT* xvi. 5. 7. 1 (Eutropius *PPO Or.* 381).
[25] *CT* xvi. 5. 9. 1 (Florus *PPO Or.* 382).
[26] S. N. C. Lieu (1984) 111 ff., 154 ff.; also P. Brown (1969).
[27] On Arians see below, p. 148.

Valens insisted on the 'likeness' of Father and Son. The most moderate Arians, the Macedonians,[28] were close to the Nicaeans in their beliefs about the relationship of Father and Son, but emphasized the subordination of the Holy Ghost. The extreme Arians, sometimes referred to as Neo-Arians, were led by Eunomius. They stressed the unlikeness of Father and Son. The Eunomians were evidently numerous at Constantinople.[29] Gregory of Nazianzus delivered his Theological Orations against them.[30] Eunomius was an impressive speaker and a man of great charisma whose arguments aroused the interest of the emperor Theodosius himself.[31] He evidently represented a considerable threat to orthodoxy. Perhaps the most objectionable feature of the Eunomians from the point of view of the orthodox was that they emphasized their distinctiveness by adopting a specific baptismal rite involving single—instead of threefold—immersion.[32] It is a feature of the anti-Arian legislation that for a great part of our period it was directed explicitly not against Arians as such but against Eunomians. Up to 387 laws were indeed directed against Arians, or Arians and Eunomians.[33] In 423 Arians reappeared.[34] But in the intervening years only Eunomians are mentioned in new legislation.[35] The old anti-Arian laws were of course not repealed, but it looks as if the government was trying to isolate the extreme Arians. Full-blooded persecution of Arians of every kind must have been hampered by the fact that the fathers of the leading public figures at Constantinople had surely at least professed support for Arian doctrines as long as Constantine and Valens were emperors. There was presumably the further consideration that when dealing with Arians the government faced the dilemma that Arian Goths formed a considerable part of the army. The fact that they were not allowed to have a church for Arian services in Constantinople must have caused quite enough discontent. The government could not afford legislation which would compel it to alienate its own soldiers further.[36]

Eunomians, however, were harried unmercifully. Heretics in general could not have churches, and might not hold meetings in

[28] On Macedonius and Macedonians, see below, p. 164, also p. 212.

[29] T. A. Kopecek (1979).

[30] Greg. Naz. *Or.* xxviii–xxxi (Discours Théologiques), Intr., text, transl., notes by P. Gallay, Sources Chrétiennes 250 (Paris, 1978).

[31] Socr. iv. 7, v. 20, 34; Soz. vi. 26, vii. 6, 17. Extant works edited by R. P. Vaggione (1987).

[32] Soz. vi. 26.

[33] *CT* xvi. 5, 6, 8, 11–13, 16. On Eunomius: Socr. iv. 7, v. 20, 34, Soz. vi. 26, vii. 6 (his charisma), vii. 17 (banished by Theodosius).

[34] *CT* xvi. 59, 60, 64.

[35] *CT* xvi. 5, 17, 23, 25, 27, 31–2, 34, 36, 49, 58. In addition there are laws against heretics in general, and against a variety of named heresies, most frequently Manichaeans.

[36] As explained *CJ* I. 5. 12. 17.

Constantinople.[37] But authors, teachers, and clergy of the Eunomian sect are to be tracked down and expelled from all cities of the Empire.[38] Teachers of the Apollinarians must leave Constantinople. Houses where such men have been hidden are to be confiscated.[39] But the unfortunate Eunomians and the Montanists are prohibited from meeting in the country too. If they contravene the law, guilty clergy will be deported for life, and the administrator of the property where the meeting has been held becomes liable to the death penalty. The estate itself is to be confiscated.[40] This was a savage law which was actually superseded by a more moderate, if still severe, enactment a year later.[41] Eunomians,[42] like heretics in general, were excluded from the imperial service, but they were penalized more severely than the others in that they were eventually disqualified from bequeathing or receiving property through wills.[44]

It has been noted that in the first decade of the fifth century there was an interval without legislation against heretics. It may be that first the Gainas crisis[45] and then the controversy over John Chrysostom[46] distracted the government's attention. There was a resumption of legislation against heretics,[47] as against Jews[48] and pagans,[49] in the last years of the prefecture of Anthemius.

The motive at this stage probably was pressure from 'grass roots', that is, a demand for legal support from monks and bishops in the provinces.[50] It is certainly not a coincidence that in 415 Jews were expelled from Alexandria,[51] that in March 415 Hypatia was lynched in the same city,[52] and that in 417 or 418 Severus bishop of Minorca forcefully converted the Jews of Minorca with the help of relics of St Stephen.[53] The monastic movement was making Christianity more aggressive.[54] Meanwhile at court the emperor's sister Pulcheria was steadily increasing her influence on government.

---

[37] *CT* xvi. 5. 30 (Clearchus *Praef. Urb.*, on date see below, p. 255 n. 13).

[38] Ibid. 31 (Caesarius *PPO Or.* 396), 32 (Caesarius *PPO Or.* 396), 34 (Eutychianus *PPO Or.* 398).

[39] Ibid. 33 (Eutychianus 397).   [40] Ibid. 34 (Eutychianus 398).

[41] Ibid. 36 (Eutychianus 399).   [42] Ibid. 25 (Rufinus *PPO Or.* 395).

[43] Ibid. 29 (Marcellus *Mag. Offic.* 395), 48 (Anthemius *PPO Or.* 410).

[44] See above, p. 147, nn. 16–19.   [45] See above, p. 111.

[46] See below, p. 195 ff.

[47] *CT* xvi. 5. 48–50 (410), 6. 6–7 (413), 7. 6 (413), 7 (413).

[48] *CT* xvi. 8. 22 (415), 25. 2 (423), 27 (423), 29 (429), 9. 4 (417), 5 (423).

[49] *CT* xvi. 10. 21 (415), 22 (423), 25 (435), and the law against pagans, Jews, and heretics with abuse and justification of their persecution: *Nov. Theod.* 3 (438).

[50] Bishops' essential role in suppression of Manichaeism: S. N. C. Lieu (1985) 160 ff.; in suppression of Donatists: P. Brown (1972) 321 ff. Bishop uses charge of heresy to defeat rival: ibid. 313 on Socr. vii. 3.

[51] Socr. vii. 13.   [52] Socr. vii. 15; John of Nikiu 84. 88–100.

[53] E. D. Hunt (1982*b*).   [54] Socr. vii. 14, cf. Lib. *Or.*, xxx. 8–12.

She was deeply moved by the ascetic ideals and she exploited her own position and strong personality and the pliable and indecisive character of her brother, the emperor Theodosius, to further her religious ideals and the cause of orthodoxy.[55]

The pattern of anti-pagan legislation was similar to that of legislation against heretics. The heart of it was the prohibition of sacrifice. Since sacrifice was the essential ritual of paganism this amounted to an attempt to suppress paganism altogether. In addition pagans were excluded from the imperial service. There was an abundance of laws under Theodosius,[56] and further laws after Theodosius' death addressed to Rufinus,[57] Caesarius,[58] and Eutychianus.[59] Then came a pause. Legislation was resumed in 416,[60] with further laws in 423[61] and 435.[62] At the same time cultural paganism enjoyed almost complete toleration. The writings of Synesius like those of Claudian are full of allusion to gods, goddesses, and pagan mythology. Yet Synesius almost certainly, and just possibly Claudian too, were Christian when they wrote.[63] But whether they were Christian or pagan, their literary paganism was evidently perfectly acceptable at the Eastern and the Western court. It is also significant that Socrates and Sozomen, the ecclesiastical historians, got much of their secular history from Eunapius, an outspokenly pagan and anti-Christian writer.[64]

In view of the intolerant character of the legislation against heretics and pagans, the tone of legislation about Jews may surprise.[65] A succession of laws is concerned to ensure that the Jews should in fact enjoy the rights which were theirs by law. So we read: 'No person outside the religion of the Jews shall establish prices for the Jews';[66] and 'If any person should dare in public to make an insulting mention of the illustrious patriarchs [of the Jews] he shall be subjected to a sentence of punishment';[67] or again 'Those privileges which are conferred upon the first clerics of the venerable Christian religion shall continue by the consent of Our Imperial Divinity for

---

[55] Soz. ix. 1: Pulcheria's vow of virginity; ix. 4: her way of life; K. Holum (1982*a*) 98–100: influence of Pulcheria.

[56] *CT* xvi. 10. 7 (381)–12 (392).   [57] *CT* xvi. 10. 13.   [58] Ibid. 14.

[59] Ibid. 16.

[60] Ibid. 21, dated 26. 8. 416 but addressed to Aurelian. O. Seeck (1919) 88 redated it 415.

[61] Ibid. 22–23.   [62] Ibid. 24.

[63] On the religion of Synesius see above, p. 141, and now Alan Cameron, J. Long, L. Sherry (1990) ch. II. 2–4. Alan Cameron (1970) 189–227 argued that Claudian was a Christian. This has been opposed by J. Vanderspoel (1986), on the basis of poem 25 'In Iacobum magistrum equitum'. That poem treats intercession by saints humorously, which would be at least unusual for a Christian writer, even if one does not accept the identification of the 'moriens conviva' of line 11 as Christ. August. *CD* v. 26 describes Claudian as pagan. Augustine was in a position to know.

[64] On Eunapius see above, p. ooo.   [65] K. D. Reichardt (1978).

[66] *CT* xvi. 8. 10 (the Jews 396).   [67] Ibid. 11 (*Comes Or.* 396).

those persons who are subject to the power of the Illustrious Patriarchs, for the rulers of the synagogues, the patriarchs and the priests, and for all the rest who are occupied in the ceremonial of that religion'.[68] Compared with the laws against pagans and heretics these laws are remarkable for their tolerance. It may or may not be significant that all of them were issued before John Chrysostom became archbishop of Constantinople.[69] Laws protecting the rights of Jews are not an innovation of the period of Eutropius. They continue a tradition established by Constantine,[70] and recently revived by Theodosius at a time when he happened not to be under the influence of Ambrose.[71] After the fall of Eutropius the policy was maintained by Eutychianus,[72] by Philippus, praetorian prefect of Illyricum in 420,[73] and by Asclepiodotus in 423.[74] By then the legal position of the Jews had deteriorated. Aurelian in 415 had deprived the Jewish patriarch of his honorary praetorian prefecture and ordered him to demolish synagogues that could be destroyed without causing a riot.[75] Later the patriarchate itself was abolished and Jews were forbidden to build new synagogues.[76] Jews were also excluded from the imperial service.[77] Pressure on Jews by their neighbours led by monks or bishops was now increasing. We hear of synagogues being confiscated or destroyed,[78] even though the law continued to protect them and the remaining civic rights of the Jews.

Emperors and officials were eager to give the objective of religious unity very high priority, even though the antagonism aroused by the laws they issued to bring that about would make government quite unnecessarily difficult. Nevertheless the officials of Theodosius and his successors were not prepared to sacrifice to religion all the traditional objectives of Roman administration. For instance, the era of Eutropius produced legislation to limit the use of ecclesiastical asylum,[79] to prevent men using consecration to the priesthood for tax avoidance,[80] and to make sure that monks and clergy who had committed crimes should not escape punishment.[81] These laws

---

[68] Ibid. 13 (Caesarius *PPO Or.* 397).
[69] Socr. vi. 2. 11.   [70] *CT* xvi. 8. 2 (330).
[71] Ibid. 8. 8 (392).   [72] Ibid. 15 (404).   [73] Ibid. 21.
[74] Ibid. 25.   [75] Ibid. 22 (415).   [76] Ibid. 25, 27 (423).
[77] Ibid. 16 (404), 28 (418).
[78] J. Juster (1914) i. 461–9, ii. 200–1; L. C. Ruggini (1959) 192–207, E. D. Hunt (1982*a*), these last two relating to the West.
[79] *CT* ix. 45. 2 (*Praef. Egypt.* 397), 3 (Eutychianus *PPO Or.* 398) = *CJ* i. 3. 12.
[80] *CT* xvi. 2. 32 (Caesarius *PPO Or.* 398), 33 (Eutychianus *PPO Or.* 398).
[81] *CT* ix. 40. 16 (Eutychianus 398). Cf. also laws to prevent ordination being abused to avoid curial duties: *CT* xii. 1. 163 (Eutychianus 399), 172 (Herculius *PPO Ill.* 410), and to ensure that debts to councils or empire should have prior claims on estates left to clerics or monks: *CT* v. 3.1. (Taurus *PPO Or. 434*).

offended Chrysostom, who considered them an attack on the Church.[82] They are likely to have been resented widely among monks and clerics and pious laymen, and may well have contributed to Eutropius' fall from power. They did not, however, discredit the official directly responsible, the prefect Eutychianus. As we have noted, his career continued with only a brief interruption. This is not surprising, for the laws which offended Chrysostom were in the tradition of the Eastern administration. Already in 392 a law had ordered that debtors of the state should be made to pay even if they had to be dragged out of asylum in a church.[83] It is significant that the laws issued by Eutychianus under the influence of Eutropius were not repealed, but were taken into the Code of Justinian, having become part of the permanent law of the Empire. We noted repeated attempts to ensure that Jews should be able to exercise their long-established legal rights. As late as 423 the prefect Asclepiodotus legislated against Christians 'who abuse the authority of religion and dare to lay violent hands on Jews and pagans who are living quietly and attempting nothing disorderly or contrary to law'.[84] The men who governed the East were extremely conscious of the need to maintain the rights of the state against private usurpations of every kind. It is debatable how successful they were in this, but there can be no doubt that they tried very much harder, and were much more successful, than the authorities in the West—for instance, only the East legislated against the patronage of villages.[85]

When we examine the practical consequences of so much religious legislation, it becomes clear that much of it was not enforced: activities contrary to published laws were not systematically sought out and suppressed.[86] For instance, contrary to what a reader of the Theodosian Code might expect, Arians continued to live and worship, even at Constantinople, in considerable numbers. If they had been deprived of recognized churches they nevertheless continued to meet outside the city[87] at regular meeting houses, led by their own clergy and even bishops.[88] In fact they had two sets of houses of prayer[89] and clergy, because they were divided on the question whether it was right to describe God as 'the Father' before Christ the Son had come into

---

[82] See below, p. 189.

[83] *CT* ix. 45. 1 (Romulus *Com. Sac. Larg.*) = *CJ* i. 25. 1.

[84] *CT* xvi. 10. 24 (Asclepiodotus *PPO Or.*) = *CJ* i. 11. 6; cf. xvi. 5. 26 = *CJ* i. 9. 16: protection of synagogues.

[85] *CT* xi. 24. 3 (395)–6 (415).   [86] As noted by Soz. vii. 12.

[87] Socr. vi. 20; Soz. viii. 8.   [88] Socr. vii. 6, 30.

[89] Soz. vii. 17. In 399 at Constantinople the buildings were outside the city. Otherwise the refusal of a church to Gainas (see above, p. 113) would not make sense. But a decade later Nestorius destroyed an Arian church in Constantinople: Socr. vii. 29.

existence. Among the Arians Gothic soldiers were prominent, and the division was eventually ended by the Gothic general Plinta, who in spite of his Arian faith enjoyed great power and influence and achieved the highest distinction with the consulate.[90] If Arian and other dissenting groups survived at Constantinople itself there can be no doubt that they did so too elsewhere, depending on the attitude of the local bishop.[91] In fact one might generalize that these laws represented a demonstration of religious commitment, and of readiness to support bishops or officials who wanted to take action against non-Catholic religion, much more than a set of rules which the government was bound to implement throughout the Empire.[92]

The long-term consequences of the imperial government's commitment to religious unity are too big a subject to discuss here. For the present study it is important that this policy made it easier for Arian Goths and other barbarians to avoid assimilation into the population of the Empire. Arianism became part of their ethnic identity. Conversion to Arianism may even have provided a rite of passage which helped the Arian tribes to absorb Romans into their fellowship. The consequences were far-reaching and disruptive, as we have seen—but also gradual and long term. A much more immediate result of Theodosius' decision to employ the coercive power of the state to favour religious unity on the basis of Nicaean orthodoxy was that he would have to face the religious opposition of the majority of the inhabitants of his capital city.

---

[90] Soz. vii. 17; *PLRE* ii s.v. Fl. Plinta.

[91] Chrysostom deprives Novatians of churches: Socr. vi. 11. Nestorius penalizes Macedonians (Socr. vii. 31), previously tolerated (*CT* xvi. 5. 59–60, 65).

[92] The most striking example of failure to implement religious legislation is Justinian's conniving at Theodora's protection of numerous Monophysites in the Hormisdas palace at Constantinople, who ordained James Baradai, who in turn went out to found Monophysite churches all over the East: Averil Cameron (1985) 78–80 and W. H. C. Frend (1972) 288. On the complex motivation of emperors responsible for religious legislation see P. Brown (1972) 316–20.

PART III

Chrysostom and the Politicians

14

Orthodoxy Imposed at Constantinople

THEODOSIUS I became emperor on 19 January 379 at the height of the Gothic crisis after the disaster of Adrianople.[1] It would be reasonable to assume that Gratian chose him in the first place because of his qualities as a soldier and politician, as the man most likely to lead the Eastern Empire out of its dangerous situation. But it is clear that from the beginning Theodosius considered that his task had an essential component: the restoration of unity in the Church. For already in August 379 an edict was issued jointly by Gratian and Theodosius forbidding all heresies 'by divine and imperial law', and annulling an edict of tolerance which Gratian had issued at Sirmium not long before.[2] It is reasonable to suppose that this dramatic reversal of policy was made under the influence not only of Ambrose, the strong minded bishop of Milan,[3] but also of Gratian's new colleague. In spite of the obvious advantage of facing the crisis in unity based on tolerance, Gratian and Theodosius decided, as Constantine had decided before them, that their responsibility to God for the unity of the Church must have priority.

To take sides in religious controversies was bound to arouse antagonism. This did not matter very much in the West because Nicean orthodoxy had always been dominant there and had recently grown even stronger.[4] But in the East, where Arianism had been very strong for a long time, Theodosius risked serious difficulties by siding with orthodoxy. Above all, Arianism had a powerful following at Constantinople. It might be uncomfortable for Theodosius to live among a people who differed from him in religion. Roman emperors in the past had taken great care to be on good terms with the population of their capital.[5]

As a Westerner, and by family background, Theodosius' allegiance was to Nicaean orthodoxy,[6] and he was evidently willing to face

[1] Accession of Theodosius I: Socr. v. 2, A. Ehrhardt (1964).
[2] *CT* xvi. 5. 5 (issued at Milan 3. 8. 379 to Hesperius *PPO It.*) refers to revoked edict of tolerance; also Socr. v. 2, Soz. vii. 1. On the background of Gratian's edict of tolerance see R. Snee (1985) esp. 410–13.
[3] J.-R. Palanque (1933) 64–7, 71; (1931).
[4] J.-R. Palanque, G. Bardy, P. de Labriolle (1936) 278–81.
[5] Alan Cameron (1976).   [6] Soz. vii. 4.

considerable risks on its behalf. Nevertheless he proceeded with some care. He made inquiries about the religious situation in the East before taking unambiguous action.[7] His information will have confirmed him in the course he favoured in any case. For he learnt that the Arians in the East were divided, and presumably also that the orthodox were organized in two blocks. On the one hand the orthodox bishops of Egypt were led by the aged Peter of Alexandria; on the other those of Syria and Asia Minor, inspired until his death by Basil of Caesarea,[8] were now led by Meletius who had assembled a synod of no fewer than 150 bishops at his see of Antioch in 379.[9] The two groups were on far from good terms. But it would seem that, whether as friends or opponents, the orthodox would be more formidable than the Arians. If his conscience forced him to choose one faction rather than the other, Theodosius had respectable political as well as religious reasons for opting for orthodoxy. So on 27 February 380 he issued an edict addressed to the people of Constantinople ordering them to follow the faith of Peter as now followed by Damasus of Rome and Peter of Alexandria.[10]

This edict was not welcomed by the Constantinopolitans. Constantinople was a Christian city, where all classes are said to have been passionately devoted to theological discussion.[11] The predominant brand of Christianity was Arian,[12] and the lively state of theology had even produced sub-divisions among Arians.[13] Other sects included Apollonarians[14] and Novatians.[15] How hard it was for the orthodox to survive in this environment was shown by the experiences of Gregory of Nazianzus when a group of orthodox clergy and laymen were encouraged by the news of Theodosius' accession to invite him to become their leader.[16] The small community had no church. Gregory was installed in a private house where he held services in a chapel dedicated to St Anastasia,[17] the name of the

---

[7] Soz vii. 4; cf. Basil *Ep.* 91 (372) and 204 (375) with the same information that there was no Arianism in Illyricum.

[8] On the two orthodox factions and their differences in belief, and on the see of Antioch, see A. M. Ritter (1965) 32.

[9] A. M. Ritter (1965), C. H. Turner (1899 ff.) i. 625 ff., G. Bardy (1979).

[10] *CT* xvi. 1. 2.

[11] Greg. Naz. *Or.* xxviii. 1–2 (*PG* xxxvi. 12): popular discord incited by Eunomians everywhere, cf. *De Vita Sua* 1210 ff., ed. C. C. Jungck (1974) 112. Greg. Nyss. *PG* xlvi. 557.

[12] Greg. Naz. *Or.* xlii. 4 ff. on weakness of orthodox; also *Or.* xxxiv. 6, and *Carmen de Vita Sua* 573 ff.

[13] Divisions among Arians: Socr. v. 20, 23–4; Soz. vii. 17, cf. above, p. 000.

[14] Apollinarians: Socr. ii. 46, iii. 16; Soz. vi. 25.

[15] Novatians: Socr. iv. 28, v. 10, 21, 22; Soz. vi. 24, viii. 12, 14, 18, viii. 1.

[16] Summoned by clergy and laymen: *De Vita Sua* 595–7, Jungck 82. He came unwillingly and deceived by misleading arguments: *De Vita Sua* 607–8, Jungck 82.

[17] Socr. iv. 1; Greg. Naz. *Or.* xlii. 26.

patron saint, 'Resurrection', representing a programme: the revival of orthodoxy. The community was so small that the arrival of the corn-fleet from Egypt with its orthodox sailors produced a significant addition to the congregation.[18]

So when Theodosius ordered them to follow the faith now followed by Pope Damasus at Rome and bishop Peter at Alexandria,[19] the Constantinopolitans were not impressed. At Easter they threw stones at Gregory as a pagan.[20] As Theodosius was busy campaigning, Gregory had to cope as well as he could. He had befriended a Christian Cynic from Alexandria called Maximus and even delivered an oration in his praise.[21] Then in July 380 one night, while Gregory was unwell, some Egyptian clerics took over the chapel of St Anastasia, and consecrated Maximus bishop of Constantinople.[22] Maximus could not maintain himself at Constantinople, and Theodosius refused to support him when he appealed to the emperor at Thessalonica.[23] The consecration of Maximus was finally rejected only by the synod of Constantinople in spring 381.[24]

On 24 November 380 Theodosius entered Constantinople,[25] and when Demophilus the Arian bishop refused to sign a declaration of orthodox faith the emperor had him and other Arian priests expelled from all churches in the city.[26] The population was hostile. Soldiers were needed. Constantinople looked like a captured city.[27] Gregory of Nazianzus, the champion of orthodoxy, was conducted to the cathedral by the emperor himself. It had been a bleak day. As they took their places in the choir the sun broke through the clouds. Tactfully Gregory did not occupy the bishop's throne.[28] His formal election to the see had to wait for the decision of the synod in May 381.[29] Subsequently the expulsion of Arians from their churches was enforced all over the East. It is an indication of Theodosius' caution that it was only now, a year after he had ordered the Constantino-politans to follow orthodox belief, that he risked a definition of what orthodox belief was. No longer content to endorse the faith of

[18] *Or.* xxxiv (*PG* xxxvi 241–56).

[19] *CT* xvi. 1. 2 ('ad populum urbis Constantinopolitanae', 27. 2. 380).

[20] *De Vita Sua* 654–78, 1658–9, Jungck 86, 134; *Ep.* 77: monks and the poor involved. Also on hostility: *Or.* xxxiii. 5 (*PG* xxxvi. 220 C–221 B), *Or.* xxiii. 5 (*PG* xxxv. 1156 B–1157 A).

[21] *Or.* xxv–xxvi, J. Mossay, *Grégoire de Nazianze, Discours 24–6*, Sources Chrétiennes 284 (Paris, 1981).

[22] *De Vita Sua* 750 3ff., Jungck 90.   [23] Ibid. 1001 ff., Jungck 102.

[24] A. M. Ritter (1965) 48–53, 4th Canon of the Council of Constantinople, Mansi iii. 56.

[25] Socr. v. 5. 6.

[26] Soz. vii.   5–7; Socr. v. 6–7; Philostorg. ix. 19; Theodoret *HE* v. 8; Marcell. Com. *Chron.* s.a. 380.

[27] *De Vita Sua* 1325–45, Jungck 118.

[28] Ibid. 1353–94—though he did somewhat later: *Or.* xxxvi. 2–3.

[29] See n. 24, and *De Vita Sua* 1525–7, Jungck 128.

Damasus of Rome and Peter of Alexandria he now explicitly referred to the Nicaean creed and paraphrased its most controversial sentences.[30]

Meanwhile the congregations of Gregory at Constantinople had grown considerably, but he was still not popular. While open demonstrations ceased, Gregory was aware of discontent which he compared to the groaning of the giant Typhoeus buried under Mount Aetna.[31]

Soon afterwards Gregory had occasion to pardon a man who confessed to having conspired to assassinate him.[32] The Arians were far from broken. In 388 a rumour that Theodosius had been defeated by the usurper Maximus[33] provoked a series of riots in which the palace of the bishop was burnt. This was Nectarius, Gregory having resigned long ago, in 381.

The resignation of Gregory of Nazianzus was not directly due to the Arians, although their strength must have contributed to the unease which Gregory did not cease to feel as long as he was bishop.[34] He resigned because his election was being attacked at the synod on formal grounds. Basil had years before consecrated him bishop of Sasima in Cappadocia.[35] His opponents now insisted that his election to the see of Constantinople was illegal, since the Fifteenth Canon of Nicaea forbade the translation of a bishop from one see to another. Gregory might well have maintained his position if he had fought for it. He gave up partly for the sake of unity, partly because his role at the centre of ecclesiastical power politics was extremely uncongenial, and partly no doubt because, though obliged to preside over the synod of bishops, he had lost control of it.[36]

He fell victim to an alliance of Damasus, the pope of Rome, and the bishop of Alexandria. The reasons for the hostility of these bishops are interesting because they reflect tensions in the structure of the Empire produced by the growing emancipation of the East and the rise of Constantinople. The pope and the bishops of the West, together with the bishop of Alexandria, had for some time been in conflict with the Eastern orthodox group led by Basil and Meletius, both over dogma and over the filling of the see of Antioch.[37] The

---

[30] *CT* xvi. 5. 6 (10. 1. 381), xvi. 1. 3 (1. 7. 381).
[31] *De Vita Sua* 1404–5, Jungck 122.   [32] Ibid. 1442–74, Jungck 124.
[33] Socr. v. 13.   [34] P. Gallay (1943).
[35] *Carmen de vita sua* 386–525, Jungck 72 ff., notes p. 169 ff.
[36] A. M. Ritter (1965) 97–111.
[37] The difference arose when Athanasius of Alexandria refused to recognize Meletius as bishop of Antioch because he had been ordained by Arian bishops and was suspected of Arian views: Soz. iv. 28, Socr. ii. 44. Basil had tried hard to end the division but was rebuffed. J.-R. Palanque, G. Bardy, P. de Labriolle (1936) 269–74. H. Lietzmann, *Die Zeit der Kirchenväter* (Berlin, 1944) = *Geschichte der alten Kirche*, vol. 4, 13–20, E. Schwartz (1935), esp. 44 ff.

pope recognized Paulinus and refused to acknowledge Meletius. At Antioch and in the East generally support for Meletius was overwhelming. After Basil's death Meletius was the leader of the orthodox group. As such he presided over the synod of Constantinople until he died. But the pope continued to recognize Paulinus and he induced Ascholius of Thessalonica to attack the election of Gregory[38] precisely because Gregory belonged to the Meletian group. The part that had been played by the pope in Eastern affairs over the last decade was bitterly resented, with the result that the synod was seen to be clearly divided between East and West.[39] It was unlucky for Gregory that when he was attacked by the allies of the pope, he was not supported by his own natural Eastern allies. This was because he had spoken in favour of Paulinus, the claimant to the see of Antioch recognised by the West.[40] It is not unreasonable to see a parallel between these conflicts and the reaction against Western influence in the secular affairs of the East after the murder of Rufinus.

The role of Alexandria is even more significant. Gregory had previously suffered from the hostility of Alexandria. The consecration of Maximus represented an attempt by the bishop of Alexandria to place a nominee of his own on the episcopal throne at Constantinople. It was not the last. At the Council of Constantinople it was Timothy, successor of Peter as bishop of Alexandria, who led the attack on Gregory which ended in his resignation. Intervention by Alexandria in the affairs of the see of Constantinople continued. Three more bishops of Constantinople were to be deposed, principally at the instigation of a bishop of Alexandria: John Chrysostom, Nestorius, and Flavian.[41]

The bishop of Constantinople did not enjoy any position of privilege among the bishops of the East before Constantine transformed Byzantium into Constantinople and made it his capital. It was not he, but the bishop of Heraclea, who was the metropolitan of Thrace. But the fact that the bishop of Constantinople was the bishop of the imperial residence made his position unique. So he became the natural judge of appeal for bishops involved in disputes in the provinces of Asia Minor.[42] Unless it could somehow be prevented,

---

[38] Damasus *Ep.* v. 6 (*PL* xiii 368 A–369 A, 370 A).

[39] When Gregory took the Western view and supported the recognition of Paulinus, the young bishops of the East 'croaked like crows and were eager to sting him in the face like angry wasps': *De Vita Sua* 1680–87. When Timothy of Alexandria and his allies arrived they 'blew a sharp westerly wind in the face of the assembly', and they were immediately opposed by the bishops of the East, so that a conflict as between wild boars resulted (ibid. 1802–7). East v. West rhetoric: ibid. 1690 ff).

[40] See A. M. Ritter (1965) 105.   [41] N. H. Baynes (1955b).

[42] Cf. G. Dargon (1974) 461–3 on episodes in AD 383–94.

the bishop of Constantinople was certain to become the leading bishop in the East, threatening the independence of sees not only in the neighbourhood of the capital but all over the eastern provinces.

The bishop of Alexandria had long occupied a special position. He was the unquestioned head of the church in Egypt. He was patron of the Egyptian monks. His see was a long way from the imperial capital. There was a tradition of cooperation between Alexandria and Rome, with the popes treating the bishops of Alexandria almost as their representatives in the East. The personality of Athanasius and his struggles with successive emperors for what he considered, and what eventually became, orthodoxy, had greatly increased the prestige of his see. All this was threatened by the rise of Constantinople.[43] Consequently bishops of Alexandria took great interest in appointments to the see of Constantinople. If a nominee of the bishop of Alexandria was appointed, this would enable Alexandria to benefit from the special position of Constantinople. If a bishop of Alexandria failed to achieve the appointment of a nominee of his own he would be tempted to frustrate, and if possible overthrow, the new bishop of Constantinople, especially if he looked like building up the power of the see.

The intrigues of bishops of Alexandria were assisted by the constitutional position of the Church, which remained an independent institution, separate from the state apparatus. Bishops, elsewhere than at Constantinople, were elected by the people and clergy of their city, and bishops deliberating collectively in a synod were guided, in theory at any rate, by the Holy Spirit, so that it was not proper for an outsider to dictate their decisions.[44] In private the emperor had great influence. He usually appointed the bishop of the capital, and he also had considerable influence over Empire-wide synods. This was not only because of his physical power and patronage, but also because gatherings of bishops, reaching their decisions by consensus under the influence of the Holy Spirit, had no procedure for dealing with disagreements. They did not, for instance, employ majority voting, so that it was left to the emperor, through his representative, to make sure that there was a decision. Besides, invitations to general synods were sent out by the emperor, and it was he who decided who was summoned and who was not.[45] So in a general way synods reached

---

[43] G. Dagron (1974) 101–3.

[44] Divine guidance of Councils was repeatedly asserted (without being dogmatically defined or necessarily recognized in practice), e.g. by Constantine after Nicaea in Theodoret HE i. 9, Socr. i. 9, cf. A. v. Harnack, *Lehrbuch der Dogmengeschichte* (Freiburg, 1987) ii. 91–5. F. Dvornik (1934), E. Schwartz (1921).

[45] The emperor issued invitations to Council of Constantinople: Mansi iii. 557; bishops from

decisions in accordance with imperial policy. Nevertheless emperors were ready to leave assembled bishops some freedom.

It followed that Councils could to some extent be manipulated, or even terrorized, by interested parties other than the emperor[46] particularly when the Empire had a weak ruler, as under the successors of Theodosius I. This situation gave the bishops of Alexandria their chance to intervene at Constantinople. In the case of the synod of 381 and the controversy around Gregory of Nazianzus one factor which helped the Alexandrian intrigue to succeed was a feeling shared by Theodosius and council that Rome and Alexandria should receive some consolation for the Second and Third Canons, which had limited to Egypt the right of the bishop of Alexandria to intervene in the affairs of other sees, and had given to the bishop of Constantinople a 'primacy of honour' second only to that of Rome. Another factor was the reluctance of Gregory to fight for his position.

The competition between the Churches of Constantinople and Alexandria was paralleled by secular tensions. As we have seen the establishment of an imperial capital at Constantinople caused resentment in the leading cities of the East whose resources, human, economic, and cultural were drained to the city on the Bosphorus. The cities could not resist, but the churches, or at least the biggest and most remote of the churches, could—in their way.

The resignation of Gregory of Nazianzus did not of course alter the ecclesiastical situation of Constantinople, an Arian city whose churches were controlled by orthodox clergy. In handling this problem Theodosius showed himself much more sensitive than the tone of his laws would suggest.[47] From a list of possible successors to Gregory submitted by the synod, Theodosius chose Nectarius, a candidate whom no one had expected to succeed.[48] Nectarius was a layman, a senator, and he had not yet been baptized. But he was a good choice, being a diplomat rather than a churchman and, unlike Gregory, neither an orator nor a theologian. He actually got a Novatian bishop to produce a statement of orthodox belief in preparation for a meeting with Arians and others to discuss union. He kept a low profile, and gave the citizens of Constantinople a

the Western half of empire and from areas of Asia Minor where Arians predominated were not invited. Lists in L. H. Turner (1899) ii. 3 (1939) 433–63. Mansi iii. 567–72. Finally the canons were submitted to emperor for confirmation, Mansi iii. 577.

[46] See esp. T. Gregory (1979) 102 and K. G. Holum (1982a) 162 ff. on Council of Ephesus.

[47] See also the attempt to achieve unity without discussing dogma on the basis of acceptance of ancient writings: Soz. vii. 12, Socr. v. 10.

[48] Socr. v. 8, Soz. vii. 8; he was a friend of Diodorus of Tarsus and belonged to the circle of Basil and Meletius.

chance to get used to the new situation. Ritual and familiarity would succeed where compulsion and argument would probably have failed.

A symbolic ceremony celebrated the victory of orthodoxy. Theodosius had the bones of Paulus, orthodox bishop of Constantinople after 337, who had died, possibly by violence, in exile in Armenia, brought back to Constantinople, and had them buried with great ceremony in what had been the principal church of the Macedonians.[49] The building had been put up by Macedonius, the Arian rival of Paul, before his consecration as bishop. When Macedonius became bishop he was consecrated in the church, which continued to be used by his followers until they were deprived of it by the edict of Theodosius. Now Theodosius turned it into a monument and *martyrium* for Macedonius' orthodox rival and victim.[50]

The circumstances of Paulus' death, as indeed of his life, were little known. It was possible for a hagiographer to compose his biography on the pattern of the career of Athanasius of Alexandria, and to end it with the sensational allegation that Paulus was strangled by the Arians.[51] So the bones that Theodosius brought back in triumph were the relics of a martyr of orthodoxy. The new cult seems not to have caught on, however. In Sozomen's time most people believed that the bones were those of Paul the Apostle. A more effective demonstration of divine support for orthodoxy was provided by the tombs of Martyrius and Marcian, two clerics of Paulus, executed for their part in a riot occasioned by Paulus' deposition which had resulted in the death of the general Hermogenes. The two men were buried in the place of execution. In time the belief spread that the relics of the two clerics had driven off the lingering ghosts haunting the place and thus proved themselves the bones of holy martyrs. John Chrysostom began the building of a church on the spot. Miracles were duly reported.[52]

In 391 Theodosius transferred the head of John the Baptist to Constantinople. According to the story as it was later told. Mardonius, the *primicerius sacri cubiculi*, had urged Valens to have the head taken to Constantinople. When the transport had reached the neighbourhood of Chalcedon the mules absolutely refused to go on. This was taken to be a sign from God, and the relics were left where they had stopped in a village belonging to Mardonius watched

[49] Soz. vii. 10.
[50] Socr. v. 9, Soz. vii. 10; was this the church used for services for Orthodox Goths (Theodoret *HE* v. 30, John Chrys. *Hom.* 8 (*PG* lxiii. 499–510))?
[51] G. Dagron (1974) 422 ff. On the church: R. Janin (1969) 394.
[52] Soz. iv. 1; G. Dagron (1974); R. Janin (:1969) 377–8.

over by Macedonian clergy. Theodosius approached the custodians in person for permission to transfer the relics. He failed to persuade a woman in charge of the relics but succeeded with a priest, arguing that if what he intended was against the will of God it would not be possible to move the relic. Then he took off his purple cloak and wrapped the box containing the head in it. So he moved the relic to Hebdomon outside Constantinople and built a great church to house it. The translation went without a hitch. By humbling himself before the relic Theodosius had been able to prove his closeness to God, for he had been allowed to do what had been refused to the Arian Valens and his Macedonian monks.[53] Not long afterwards Theodosius prayed in the new church before setting out against Eugenius, and in due course a miracle confirmed that St John had taken notice of his piety.[54]

[53] Socr. vii. 21. On the church's later part in coronation ritual: R. Janin (1969) 413–15.
[54] Socr. vii. 24, cf. N. H. Baynes (1955a) 233–60, on supernatural defenders of Constantinople.

15

The Election and Preaching of John Chrysostom

WHEN Nectarius died in 397 there were many candidates eager to succeed him. The decisive voice at Constantinople was of course the emperor's. At this time, however, the emperor was the ineffective Arcadius, and the real ruler was Eutropius, then at the height of his influence. It was he who seems to have decided that the time had come for orthodoxy in the capital to be given a more conspicuous head, and who chose John Chrysostom as the most suitable man. Chrysostom had made a reputation as an exceedingly popular preacher at Antioch.[1] Like Gregory of Nazianzus he was a master of rhetoric, whose sermons could be enjoyed by the most fastidious admirer of classical language.[2] Compared with Gregory he was much less of a poet and theologian, and more of a teacher, in fact a born teacher. He was a publicist, but also a man of action, if perhaps in an unworldly way. Eutropius seems to have first persuaded the clergy and people of Constantinople to elect John. Next he had the election confirmed by the emperor. Only then did he bring John to Constantinople. Since it was feared that Chrysostom's departure from Antioch might provoke a riot, the commanding general brought him out of the city in secret. At Constantinople Chrysostom was consecrated by a synod of bishops summoned from a wide area, as if he was to be proclaimed bishop not only of Constantinople but of the East. Not surprisingly this aroused opposition. Theophilus, the bishop of Alexandria, opposed the ordination of Chrysostom, and proposed that one of his own clergy, a priest called Isidore, should be elected. Eutropius then informed Theophilus that his many enemies would be allowed to prosecute him unless he yielded. So Theophilus gave way, but did not forget.[3]

Once installed at Constantinople Chrysostom showed himself an extremely active bishop. His next urgent task was of course to win the population for the orthodox religion of the emperor and Empire, and this he proceeded to do—but not by attacking Arian beliefs head-on. At Antioch he had held a series of sermons against 'those

---

[1] Still P. C. Baur (1929–3). R. L. Wilken (1983).
[2] On the language of Chrysostom see below, p. 184, nn. 150–1.
[3] Socr. vi. 2; Soz. viii. 2; Pall. *Dial.* 19.

who believe that the Son is dissimilar from the Father', the so-called Anomoeans, extreme Arians who included the followers of Eunomius.[4] At Constantinople one of his first sermons was directed against the Anomoeans,[5] but he held no other such series. There are not a few dogmatic passages, including some polemic against Arian doctrines, scattered through Chrysostom's Constantinopolitan sermons.[6] But overall, dogma occupies a small place in his huge output of pulpit oratory;[7] his immediate aim was to propagate Christian morality, and to persuade his hearers to let Christianity play a larger part in their lives and thoughts. Presumably he assumed that if this objective was achieved allegiance to state orthodox religion would follow automatically.

In winning converts from Arianism Chrysostom seems to have been more concerned to occupy people with orthodox activities than to persuade them of the truth of particular doctrines. So he encouraged the cult of the 'Holy Notaries', a pair of orthodox martyrs.[8] He also organized nocturnal processions to counter processions of the Arians. In all his efforts Chrysostom had the enthusiastic support of the empress Eudoxia. We have a sermon which Chrysostom gave on the morning after a procession in which Eudoxia had been a conspicuous participant. Her financial contributions were equally useful. Chrysostom could afford to outdo the Arians in pomp and circumstance, with silver crosses and an abundance of torches. Not surprisingly fighting broke out between rival processions. A eunuch of the empress was wounded. Thereupon the emperor prohibited all Arian processions,[9] and for the time being at least all Eunomian meetings, even outside the city.[10] Chrysostom could scarcely have hoped for more. Of course this was not the end of the Arians. Arian beliefs continued to have a significant number of adherents at Constantinople. But as Arianism lost followers among the citizens of Constantinople it became increasingly the religion of Gothic inhabitants. Besides, the community was weakened by internal divisions. So before long Arianism ceased to represent a challenge to orthodoxy. The orthodox kept the ritual innovations

[4] *Hom. I–X Contra Anomaeos* (*PG* xlviii. 701–96) = A.-M. Malingrey, R. Flacelière, *Jean Chrysostome, sur l'incomprehensibilité de dieu*, vol. 1, Sources Chrétiennes 282. There are numerous polemics against the Manichaeans in the homilies on Matthew and against Arians in the homilies on John, both series delivered at Antioch.

[5] *Hom. XI–XII contra Anomaeos* (*PG* xlviii. 796–812).

[6] See *PG* lxiv. 165–6 (index s.v. Arius, Arii, etc.); *Hom.* vi (*PG* lxiii. 491 ff.) against Novatians.

[7] Low priority for teaching of dogma: *Hom. IV. 2 in Joann.* (*PG* lix. 48).

[8] See above, p. 164. Chrysostom introduced vigils: Pall. *Dial.* 31–2.

[9] Socr. vi. 8; Soz. viii. 8.

[10] *CT* xvi. 5. 34 (398).

introduced in rivalry with Arianism, above all processions and hymn singing.[11]

We have seen that on one occasion at least the empress herself took part in a procession. This was a great torchlight procession accompanying certain relics from the Cathedral to the Church of St Thomas.[12] Although this occasion was presumably part of the campaign against the Arians, Chrysostom's sermon shows that he was concerned to make it above all a demonstration of social solidarity. He points out that the relics were followed by persons of all ranks, officials, priests, monks, virgins, rich, poor, Greeks, Syrians, and barbarians, all processing and singing psalms together. In the midsts of them all Eudoxia demonstrated her piety and her closeness to the people. She served the relics like a handmaid—at least so Chrysostom tells us—carried the shrine herself, and touched the relics again and again to receive their blessings for herself.[13] As they marched beside the sea for nine miles the light of torches was reflected in the water like a river of fire.[14] They arrived at sunrise. Then Chrysostom delivered a sermon full of rejoicing and praise of the congregation, and above all of the empress. Later there was another service which the emperor Arcadius himself attended. Chrysostom points out that the emperor had come into church without his crown, and the imperial guard without their weapons. They have entered humbly as they would heaven, where pomp and display are rejected and only goodness of life counts.[15]

In the sermon Chrystotom rhapsodized over the piety of the empress, contrasting her, whose virtues were known all over the world, with a courtesan notorious over as wide an area. It is not perhaps surprising that the close alliance between empress and archbishop soon turned to hostility.[16]

There is little in Chrysostom's sermons to suggest that he was worried about paganism at Constantinople. He found objects for his missionary zeal elsewhere. In 398 he is reported to have supported Marc the Deacon, who had been sent by his bishop to win the emperor's support for the closure of the temples at Gaza in Palestine. Marc took a letter from the bishop to Chrysostom, who passed the letter to Eutropius, who in turn worked on the emperor. The result was that Marc got an edict closing the temples, and the dispatch of an

---

[11] Socr. vi. 8; Soz. viii. 8; cf. Soz. iv. 29 (hymn singing at Antioch). Arius had won converts through songs: Philostorg. ii. 2, Socr. i. 9.

[12] Were they relics of St Phocas of Pontus (*PG* l. 699–706) or, as argued by J. Vanderspoel (1986) 247–8, of the martyrs of Anaunia (*PL* xiii. 552)?

[13] *PG* lxiii. 468–72, 699–706.

[14] Ibid. 470.

[15] Ibid. 743. The emperor left before the sermon.   [16] Ibid.

official to enforce the edict.[17] There is considerable doubt about the historicity of the activities of Porphyry of Gaza as reported by Marc the Deacon.[18] But there is no reason to disbelieve Chrysostom's letters which show him organizing missionary work among the pagans of Lebanon from exile.[19]

Chrysostom refused to allow a church to be used by Goths for Arian services.[20] But he did feel responsible for the souls of the Goths in Constantinople, and he did assign one church—perhaps the church dedicated to the orthodox bishop Paul[21]—to the Goths for orthodox services. He appointed Gothic-speaking priests, deacons, and readers to preach to them.[22] We have a sermon which Chrysostom himself preached at that church, after there had been readings and a sermon in Gothic by a Gothic priest. It has been suggested that the sermon was held at Easter 399,[23] but there is no datable detail. We cannot even be certain that the congregation consisted mainly of soldiers. Chrysostom's sermon touches on a number of topics. He improvised, and one topic led to another. But the principal theme is that for the Church there is no difference between Greek and barbarian.[24] Chrysostom emphasises that Christianity is practised among many barbarian peoples and that its teachings have been translated into their languages—an allusion to the Gothic bible. Christianity depends on the power of its doctrines, and on their realization in deeds, not on the artistic use of language. When Isaiah prophesied that the wolf would feed with the lamb,[25] he meant that the fiercest of men would become so gentle that they could be herded with the mildest. The congregation could observe this happening on that very day since the most barbarian of barbarians (i.e. the Goths, hardly a tactful way of describing the bulk of the congregation) 'were standing together with the sheep of the Church, with a common pasture and one fold, and the same table set before all alike'. The word was preached to all alike. Abraham, patriarch of both Church and synagogue, had been a barbarian who received the call in what was now Persia. Moses had grown up and been educated in a barbarian home. The first men called to proclaim the new-born Jesus were the Magi from barbarian Persia. Nobody should therefore think it disgraceful for a barbarian to get up to speak in church.[26] Chrysostom's sermon is by no means without that sense

---

[17] Marc. D. *V Porphyr.* 26.

[18] See H. Grégoire, M. A. Kugener (1930), xxxiii–xxxvii, and below, p. 199, P. Peeters (1940–7).

[19] I. Auf der Mauer (1959). Theodoret *HE* v. 29.

[20] See below, p. 190.

[21] So B. Battifol (1899); E. A. Thompson (1966) 131 n. 1: a church next to the church of St Paul.

[22] Theodoret *HE* v. 30.   [23] P. C. Baur (1929–30) ii. 77.

[24] *PG* lxiii. 499 ff.   [25] Ibid. 502.   [26] Ibid. 501.

of superiority over barbarians which he was trying to combat. Its tone is paternalistic and patronizing, recalling the liberalism of the early rather than the late twentieth century. But in the atmosphere of Constantinople in 399 it would suggest to Goths that Chrysostom was their friend and a prominent public figure whom they could trust.

Chrysostom organized missionary work among the nomadic Goths along the Danube.[27] He consecrated a Goth named Unila to be bishop of the Goths in the Crimea,[28] and when Unila died Chrysostom, though in exile, was concerned that he should receive a worthy successor.[29] He kept in touch with the Crimean Goths through certain Gothic monks whose monastery was situated on an estate near Constantinople that had belonged to the general Promotus. These monks evidently had a say in the appointment of the Crimean bishop. Indeed it is likely that he was chosen from among them. Chrysostom was worried that his ecclesiastical opponents, now in control of the Church of Constantinople, would choose somebody unsuitable who would only cause trouble when he took up his duties in the Crimea. He hoped that the monks could prevent this by delaying the selection of the new bishop.[30] Chrysostom's interest in missionary work among barbarians was unusual. Clergy, whether Greek- or Latin-speaking, were not normally ready to become missionaries.[31] Chrysostom's zeal was the expression of a personality exceptionally determined not to be swayed by the cultural (not racial) prejudice which induced the educated inhabitants of the Empire to despise mere barbarians.

Perhaps surprisingly Chrysostom, who was so enthusiastic a teacher and missionary, was also interested in administration. He examined the accounts of the *economicus* of his church and stopped certain grants.[32] He reduced expenditure on the bishop's palace and transferred it to a hospital.[33] He founded new hospitals, including one for lepers.[34] He encouraged a more ascetic morality. He tried to persuade the clergy not to live under the same roof with their housekeepers,[35] and he urged the widows enrolled on the Church's register to fast regularly and to abstain from bathing and dressing attractively or, failing this, to remarry as soon as possible.[36] He also

---

[27] Theodoret *HE* v. 31.   [28] E. A. Thompson (1966) 114.

[29] *Lettres à Olympias* (A.-M. Malingrey, *ep.* 9. 5 = *PG* lii. 618, *ep.* 14. 5).

[30] *PG* lii. 726–7, *ep.* 217.   [31] E. A. Thompson (1963a).

[32] Pall. *Dial.* 5 (p. 20).   [33] *Dial.* loc. cit.

[34] F. van Ommeslaeghe (1977) 396 on 'Martyrius' 491 b–495 b, 499 a–b.

[35] Pall. *Dial.* loc. cit. The sermons *Adversus Syneisactes* (*PG* xlvii. 495–532) were written at Antioch.

[36] See above, p. 144.

advised them how to use their very considerable fortunes in the service of the Church.[37]

Chrysostom strove to realize the primacy of Constantinople over Churches in other provinces which had been proclaimed—in a purely honorary sense—at the Council of Constaninople in 381. As bishop of Constantinople he may have obtained an imperial edict for the suppression of paganism at Gaza. He was certainly confident of being able to get one against Marcionism for a bishop of Cyrrhus in Syria.[38] His active interest thus extended far beyond the boundaries of his see. Chrysostom's most sensational initiative was taken in 402.[39] Invited to consecrate a new bishop of Ephesus, Chrysostom travelled to Ephesus, convoked a council of 70 bishops of the diocese of Asia, and faced with two rival candidates, appointed a third, his own deacon Heraclides. He then proceeded, with the collaboration of the synod, to replace at least six, perhaps as many as sixteen bishops.[40] He also expelled Novatian and Quartodeciman sectarians from a number of their churches.[41] Finally on his way home he replaced the bishop of Nicomedia in the diocese of Pontus.[42] Chrysostom was establishing disciplinary supervision over the bishops of neighbouring dioceses.[43] He did this with the full backing of the emperor, since he was able to offer deposed bishops the consolation of immunity from curial service.[44] Moreover only the emperor could have provided the armed force needed to enforce the decisions of Chrysostom's synod.

No matter how active Chrysostom was in other fields, his central interest and the source of his fame was preaching. We know a great deal about this. Chrysostom's sermons were taken down by shorthand writers.[45] Moreover the long series of sermons providing a continuous commentary on books of the Bible, or Epistles of St Paul look as if they have been designed also to be read as a comprehensive interpretation of these texts.[46] Chrysostom had already produced treatises for reading, as well as a large number of sermons at Antioch. He continued to be extremely productive at Constantinople.

---

[37] Soz. viii. 9.

[38] Theodoret *HE* v. 31; V. Grumel (1958) 18.

[39] Alan Cameron (1987) proves conclusively against P. C. Baur, *St. John Chrysostom* ii (1959) 145, 155, n. 13, and myself, (1985) 5, that this was in 402, not 401.

[40] Pall. *Dial.* 47 (p. 82).

[41] Socr. vi. 2, cf. *PG* lxiii. 491 ff., against the Novatians.

[42] Appointing Pansophius tutor of Eudoxia: Soz. viii. 6.

[43] Pall. *Dial.* 47 (p. 83. 6): six bishops deposed, all in Asia. He has ignored Gerontius of Nicomedia in Pontus. Soz. viii. 6: 13 bishops deposed in Lycia, Phrygia, and Asia, as well as Gerontius of Nicomedia. Theophil alleged deposition of 16 (Pall. *Dial.* 47 (p. 82. 24)).

[44] Pall. *Dial.* (p. 51. 16).   [45] B. Goodall (1979) 62–78.

[46] P. C. Baur (1929–30) 234 ff. = i. 222 ff. in tr. by M. Gonzaga, corrected by B. Goodall (1979).

Throughout his episcopate he appears to have been busy on one or the other of his commentaries. We have a series of fifteen sermons on the Epistle of Paul to the Philippians (spring-early summer 399), twelve sermons on the Epistle to Colossians (autumn 399), fifty-five sermons on the Acts of the Apostles (second half of 400 to spring 401),[47] eleven sermons on 1 Thessalonians, five on 2 Thessalonians, (402) thirty-four sermons on Hebrews (winter 402–3). They are thoughtful, eloquent, and in many ways of timeless relevance. They provided a remarkable record of the way the people of Constantinople were educated by means of Christian sermons, often twice a week, week after week, month after month, year after year.[48]

Sermons have been so familiar for so long that it requires an effort to realize that this form of education was a Christian innovation. No doubt there had been predecessors of a kind: moral lectures in the lecture theatres of philosophers, more informal discourses in streets and public places by more popular preachers,[49] the implicit moralizing of set speeches of rhetoricians. But these could not compare in social range of audience, or in regularity with the Christian sermon.[50] Naturally the question arises what precisely was achieved by this unprecedentedly intensive educational effort. We shall return to this latter.

Although he would have been reluctant to admit it, there is no doubt that John Chrysostom was a great entertainer. As a preacher he followed in the tradition of the great rhetors of the past. Like them he entertained an audience and aroused its enthusiasm by sheer eloquence. Like any successful rhetor Chrysostom was extremely sensitive to the feelings of his hearers and able to build up close rapport between them and himself. Like Libanius and other sophists he enjoyed the applause he was so skilful at eliciting.[51] The declamation of secular rhetors included a considerable element of moralizing. Libanius, and no doubt many another sophist, insisted that rhetorical education had a moral objective.[52] The Graeco-Roman world had long been familiar with philosophers who had lectured on moral topics. What was new was the regularity of the Christian sermon, the passion with which moral commands were expounded as divine commandments, and the claim to universal attendance. Another innovation was the fact that the Christian preacher did not base his teaching on Greek or Latin classics, but on a book whose

[47] Alan Cameron (1987) 344–51. *Hom.* 41 was later than 26. 1. 401.
[48] M. von Bonsdorf (1922).
[49] Jewish sermons: F. Siegert (1980), the Jewish homiletic tradition: C. Raphael (1968), 53–83.
[50] Preaching part of Christian meetings from the beginning: see W. A. Meeks (1983) 146–7.
[51] Applause: *Hom. xxx. 4 in Act. Apost.* (*PG* lx. 226–28); cf. P. C. Baur (1929–30) 188–90.
[52] Moralizing in declamations of Libanius: B. Schouler (1984) 942–1000.

authors were Jews rather than Greeks, and whose language was popular rather than literary.

Congregations were socially mixed. The poor were certainly there, and might even have spent the night sheltering in the church.[53] But one gets the impression that the rich were very strongly represented. A great deal of what Chrysostom said was addressed to members of the servant-and-property-owning class. As typical areas of occupation for men he names law-courts, council chambers, the market place, and war—the traditional scenes of upper-class public service.[54] He calls on absentee landowners to build churches in their villages, drawing attention to both the secular and the spiritual benefits that they would derived from this expenditure.[55] He frequently warns his audience against wearing rich garments, pearls, or jewels.[56] He dissuades men over-eager to become bishops by explaining the heavy burdens and responsibilities of the office.[57] Presumably these words were addressed to well-to-do and educated members of his congregation. Chrysostom calls on his hearers to offer hospitality.[58] He assumed that they normally conversed about money. 'We have no mind for such themes' (i.e. national defence, which is left to the emperor and his advisers). 'But how we may buy land or slaves or make our property greater, these are subjects we can talk about every day and never be tired of them'.[59] Chrysostom attacks social pride and snobbery. He emphasizes that Paul stayed at the house of a woman who was a seller of purple and a foreigner, Peter at the house of a tanner: obviously many of his congregation looked down on shopkeepers and craftsmen.[60] Palladius, John's biographer, could refer with contempt to the opinions of a certain tanner 'who takes the stench of his workshop home to live with him'.[61]

But Chrysostom was emphatically not an élitist. The contrast with Synesius,[62] or the pagan philosophers commemorated in Eunapius' *Lives of the Philosophers*, could not be greater. Again and again he stresses that Christianity is available to all and that within the Church all social distinctions disappear. Christianity had not been taught by the wealthy and educated. The triumph of Christianity means that fishermen have triumphed over philosophers. Plato is silent, while

[53] J. Dumortier (1972) on *Hom. in Hoseam* (*PG* lvi. 120) spoken at Antioch.
[54] e.g. *Hom. de studio praesentium* 3 (*PG* lxiii. 488).
[55] *Hom. XVIII. 4–5 in Act. Apost.* (*PG* lx. 147–8).
[56] *Hom. VIII. 2–3 in I Tim.* (*PG* lxii. 541–2).
[57] *Hom. I. 3–4 in Titum* (*PG* lxii. 668–70).
[58] *Hom. XLV. 4 in Act. Apost.* (*PG* lx. 319–20).
[59] *Hom. XXXII. 2 in Act. Apost.* (*PG* lx. 237).
[60] *Hom. XXXV. 1 in Act. Apost.* (*PG* lx. 254).
[61] Pall. *Dial.* 67.
[62] See below, p. 228 ff.

Peter is heard even among distant Parthians, Medes, and Indians. Where now is Greece? Where Athens?[63] He dwells on the poverty of Jesus' disciples: eleven men without rank, illiterate, poor, unknown, 'naked', owning no more than one tunic, one belt, not a stick, not a penny. These are the men chosen by Jesus to carry his message.[64] Paul, a tentmaker, prevailed over a proconsul and a magician. Christianity does not need beauty of language. Its truth is enough. Only ugly women need make up, in order to draw attention away from their unattractive bodies. The word is preached to all. Abraham had received it in Persia, Moses in Egypt. Goths, Thracians, Sarmatians, Moors, and Indians were now receiving it.[65] When the congregation assembles in church all distinction disappears, young, old, rich and poor, free and slaves, officials and humble citizens, are all made equal when they join in singing psalms. Men and women have different spheres in life, respectively inside and outside the home, but as far as virtue and piety are concerned there is no distinction between them.[66] The Christian religion even bridges the widest distinction in the world, that between emperor and subject. The empress mingles with her people high and low in a nocturnal procession to escort relics from the cathedral to the church of St Thomas.[67] No doubt pomp and circumstance surrounded emperor and empress in church as elsewhere, but when facing God, or even the martyrs, the emperor is as much a suppliant as any of his subjects. He comes to receive favours, not to give them. He comes humbly, as he will one day when hoping to enter heaven.[68]

References to the emperor or empress are very general and correct. Chrysostom was careful to avoid any comment that might be taken to be political. In a sermon on the anniversary of the death of Theodosius I he recalls how the usurper Eugenius was defeated by the prayers of Theodosius.[69] This is the new Christian view of the role of the emperor, who is victorious not because of his generalship but through his Christian piety.[70] From time to time Chrysostom seems to have felt the need to show that not even the palace was beyond the range of episcopal admonition. So he alludes to violent events that have happened in the palace since the time of Constantine[71] and in

[63] *Hom. IV. 3 in Act. Apost.* (*PG* lx. 47).
[64] *Hom. X. 3 in illud messis quidem multa* (*PG* lxiii. 520).
[65] *Hom. VIII. 2 habita postquam presbyter Gothus* (*PG* lxiii. 501).
[66] *Hom. de studio praesentium* (*PG* lxiii. 488).
[67] *Hom. II postquam reliquiae martyrum* (*PG* lxiii. 469); cf. above, p. 000.
[68] *Hom. III dicta praesente imperatore* (*PG* lxiii. 673).
[69] *Hom. VI habita in ecclesia apostolorum* (*PG* lxiii. 491).
[70] K. Holum. (1982a) 50–51.
[71] *Hom. XV in Ep. ad Philip.* (*PG* lxii. 295–6).

another sermon points out that the empress decked in gold as she is would not have impressed spectators as much as Paul the Apostle. Indeed if Paul in chains and the empress had entered the church at the same time all eyes would have turned from her to him.[72] Nevertheless he did not explicitly refer to, never mind criticize, any specific act of the reigning emperor or empress before his condemnation at the Synod of the Oak.[73]

A striking feature of the sermons of Chrysostom is his constant repetition that the essential Christian virtue is care for the needy. Again and again he takes up the theme of Matthew 25: 31–46, insisting that Jesus is alive in strangers, in the naked, the poor, the sick and so on, and that whatever has been done for those in need has been done to Jesus.[74]

In sermon after sermon those with wealth are called upon to use it for the benefit of those without. Chrysostom employed all his rhetorical skills to make the rich feel guilty. At times his sermons achieve an astonishing virulence. The ravening thirst for money is a disease.[75] All wealth has been evilly acquired. If you have inherited wealth this only means that you have not yourself sinned to acquire it. You are benefiting from the thefts of others.[76] Riches are acquired by petty deceits,[77] or by hoarding of corn in times of famine,[78] or by usury.[79] The rich are worse than wild beasts, ready to plunder widows and orphans, pitiless towards the weak and the poor.[80] All human evils can be derived from those old words 'yours' and 'mine'.[81] One does not quarrel about what belongs to all: sun, water, air.

This is not to be taken in a political sense. Chrysostom does not recommend collective action, whether by the government or by the people, to dispossess the rich and to share out their wealth. He seeks to evoke feelings of guilt which are to lead to voluntary action. The rich are to abandon conspicuous consumption, give up splendid clothes and household furnishings. Women are to stop wearing gold:[82] 'Have you come to pray to God with broidered hair and ornaments of gold? Do you think you are going to a dance? Don't imitate the courtesans who wear dresses of this kind to allure lovers. . . . And if Paul asks us to get rid of objects which are merely an

---

[72] *Hom. X in Ep. ad Coloss.* (PG lxii. 371), cf. *Hom. III. 2 ad pop. Ant.*, (PG xlix. 50).
[73] See below, p. 177 and 201.   [74] R. Brändle (1979).
[75] eg *Hom. LXIII in Matt. 3–4* (PG lvii. 606–10).
[76] *Hom. XII. 3–4 in I Ep. ad Tim.* (PG lxii. 562–3).
[77] *Hom. X. 4 in I Ep. ad Thess.* (PG lxii. 460).
[78] *Hom. XXXIX. 7 in I Ep. ad Cor.* (PG lxi. 343) from Antioch.
[79] *Hom. LVI. 5 in Matt.* (PG lxi. 555–8).
[80] *Hom. II. 5 ad Hebr.* (PG lxiii. 26).
[81] *Hom. XII. 4 in I Ep. ad Tim* (PG lxii. 543–4).
[82] *Hom. VIII in I Ep. ad Tim.* (PG lxii. 541–4).

indication of wealth such as gold, pearls, and expensive garments how much more urgent it is to abandon things which imply deliberate beautification such as make up, eye shadow, an elegant belt or close-fitting shoes.'[83] He calls on masters to have their numerous superfluous slaves taught a trade and then to set them free.[84]

Instead of wasting it in display the rich are to give their wealth in charity to the poor. 'Do you pay such honour to your excrements as to receive them in a silver chamber-pot when another man made in the image of God is perishing of cold?'[85] They are not to withhold alms because they might be assisting a wilfully idle layabout. God offers sun and moon, earth and water to workers and non-workers alike.[86] It is Christ who is clothed and fed in the person of the poor man.[87] What does charity require? Gifts to beggars in the street, sharing out of left-overs after a meal, giving away of old clothing, saving for future acts of giving, to help debtors in difficulties with creditors.[88] A doctor ought to give his professional services free.[89] Anyone might leave legacies to the Church.[90] His hearers are to set aside a guest room with a bed, table, and candlestick so as always to be in a position to offer hospitality to a stranger. 'Receive him in the upper part of the house. If not that, in the lower where the mules are kept. . . . Provide lodgings for a poor man or woman. You have a room for a chariot, room for a litter but not one for Christ'.[91]

Chrysostom was obviously a fearless fighter, not afraid of stirring up controversy or of arousing dangerous hostility. He achieved both. Some of the rich resented his attacks on their means of gaining wealth.[92] The clergy were angered by his criticism of the practice of clergy living under the same roof with their housekeepers.[93] Occasionally he risked language which might—and in the end did—give offence at court. But it would be a mistake to conclude that he chose his words without at all considering the hostility that they might arouse. His freedom of speech (παρρησία) was restrained in two very important respects. In the first place admonitions were always framed in terms of great generality, rarely making reference to individuals. This seems to be a rigidly adhered rule of his preaching.[94]

---

[83] *Hom. VIII in I Ep. ad Tim.* 541.
[84] *Hom. XL. 5 in I Ep. ad Cor.* (PG lxi. 553–4) from Antioch.
[85] *Hom. VII. 5 in Ep. ad Coloss.* (PG lxii. 350).
[86] *Hom. XXXV. 3 in Matt.* (PG lvii. 409).
[87] *Hom. XV. 6 in Ep. ad Rom.* (PG lx. 547–8), ibid. *Hom.* xviii. 7 (PG lx. 582–3).
[88] Pall. *Dial.* 21.   [89] *Hom. XXV. 4 in Act. Apost.* (PG lx. 196).
[90] *Hom. XVIII. 6–7 in Ep. ad Rom.* (PG lx. 581–2).
[91] *Hom. XLV. 4 in Act. Apost.* (PG lx. 319–20).
[92] 'Martyrius' p. 480 a; cf. F. van Ommeslaeghe (1981) 347.
[93] Palladius' defence (*Dial.* 65–6) proves that sermons were resented.
[94] Confirmed by Pall. *Dial.* 66.

But his hearers could sometimes spot the individual who had provoked the critical generalizations. So people thought that a sermon full of criticism of the behaviour of women generally reflected the preacher's annoyance with the Empress Eudoxia.[95] Again, we are told that certain individuals dared not come to church after he had drawn attention to them in sermons against avarice.[96]

In the second place he refrained from taking sides in political controversies, or even mentioning them. The problem of German mercenaries clearly aroused powerful emotions at Constantinople in 399–400. Chrysostom himself was deeply involved in the politics of this time. Nevertheless the sermons of the period are practically without allusion to political anxieties. In the sermons military or political crises are not caused by bad policies, but by sin which has drawn upon itself inevitable divine punishment. When in 395 the Huns were threatening Antioch, and even in church people were talking about the dangers and the failures of the government, John refused to be diverted to a political theme, insisting that the dangers were caused not by failures of the authorities but 'by our sins'—and he continued to provide his regular Sunday mixture of biblical exegesis and moral exhortation.[97] He did not consider it his duty to tell the authorities how to deal with the Huns. The only explanation of the Gainas crisis and the subsequent uneasy situation that Chrysostom allowed himself in sermons is that it was all a consequence of excessive love of money[98]—and that only by implication. Allusions to political issues or events are extraordinarily rare in the sermons, which as a result are impossible to date at all precisely.[99] Eloquent and great-hearted as Chrysostom undoubtedly was, he was anything but a popular agitator.

The absence of political comment, even of allusions to topical events, is characteristic of the Christian sermon generally and not peculiar to Chrysostom. The sermon was an integral part of the Christian service from the beginning. Its function was to proclaim the significance of Jesus, to explain the meaning of the sacred scriptures, to celebrate martyrs, saints, and festivals.[100] From an early period Christian sermons were composed in a heightened language. Inevitably

---

[95] *Socr. vi. 15.*

[96] 'Martyrius' p. 480 a–b; reference in F. van Ommeslaeghe (1979).

[97] *In Hoseam (PG* lvi. 103).

[98] *In Eutropium* 1 (*PG* lii. 392), *De capto Eutropio* 3 (*PG* lii. 398–9).

[99] Allusions to natural events are rare too. There are few passages like *PG* lvi. 263 describing how after three days of rain the population, fearing for the harvest, rushed first to worship in the church of the Holy Apostles and then crossed the Bosporus to celebrate the festival of Peter and Paul. It is quite likely that merely topical allusions have at some stage been edited out.

[100] E. Norden (1898) 529–73, largely stylistic, but takes the history of Greek sermon up to Basil and Chrysostom. The Christian sermon is a neglected topic.

this meant the use of the rhetorical techniques taught in schools and used by secular orators.[101] One effect of this was to bring the tone of the sermon closer to the formality and rhythm of liturgical prayer. Christianity had from the beginning demanded very high moral standards from its followers, and moral teaching was an integral part of Christian worship.[102] It fell to the bishop not only to conduct services but also to enforce the moral discipline in his community.[103] So Christian sermons from the start had much to say about conduct. What concerned a Christian preacher was the standard of behaviour inside the community. How outsiders behaved was not his business. For centuries the outer world could be assumed to be indifferent, if not positively hostile.

Chrysostom's preaching followed conventions which had been established when Christianity was the religion of minority groups, long before it became the religion of emperor and Empire. Most of his sermons start with a long section of biblical exegesis and end with a shorter passage of moral teaching. Both are strictly parts of a service, not of a campaign for improving the world. Chrysostom was a born teacher, with a special enthusiasm for moral education. His sermons are a continuing challenge to moral self-improvement. He taught virtues like self-restraint, forbearance, justice, and most of all care and consideration for those in need. He called for never-ending effort to overcome sin. He preached the unimportance of widely sought-after ends such as wealth, fame, and success. To summarize one passage out of innumerable others of the same kind: the worshipper leaving church should take with him a cure for his passions, or at least an eager determination to overcome them. Above all, he should strive to vanquish anger. He should fight to overcome love of money and pride. He should practise justice and temperance and be ready to undertake repentance through confessions and almsgiving. At each stage of life he should do his utmost to overcome the vices which that age was most prone to. His aims should be nothing less than perfection. 'In what way are you better off if though you be no fornicator yet you are covetous? It matters not to a sparrow caught in a snare if he is not tied in every part but only by the foot'.[104]

Chrysostom's moral principles were in many ways not very different from those propounded by secular philosophers, especially

---

[101] S. G. Hall (1979).
[102] R. Lane Fox (1986) ch. 10, esp. 501 ff.
[103] P. Brown (1987), 259 ff.
[104] *Hom. XXIX. 4 in Act. Apost.* (PG lx. 219).

of the Stoic school. But the total effect was quite different. The reiterated insistence on the importance of humility, the call to repentance, the offering of hope of eternal life, and the warning of hell,[105] not to mention the constant underpinning with quotations from the scriptures produces an effect which is Christian and new.

If the message of Chrysostom's preaching developed over the years, the story of his intellectual and spiritual development has not yet been written. But on some issues his views have been shown to have evolved, the role of women, for instance.[106] There are plenty of passages in sermons of Chrysostom which express an extremely restrictive attitude to women. Their place is in the home, their task the education of their children.[107] Women should remain silent in church. They have no public teaching role.[108] Just as man was created for God, so woman was made for man.[109] The highest praise for a woman is to have become like a man.[110] It is probably not a coincidence that Chrysostom shows no sign at all of veneration for the Virgin Mary. Rather the reverse. He stresses her humanity and human weaknesses, such as vanity.[111]

Now Chrysostom may well have held these theoretical attitudes all his life. The fact remains that the writings in which he expresses them most sharply all date from his Antiochene period,[112] that is, they express the views of an inexperienced idealist recently converted to the values of the ascetic movement. In due course, life taught him to modify his attitudes in practice, even if he did not abandon his principles. It was not only that the empress was his ally during the first years of his episcopate, but that quite a number of women played an important role on the interface between church and state. There was the additional circumstance that he developed a close Platonic relationship with Olympia,[113] a relationship in which enjoyment of

---

[105] Heaven: *Hom. XXVIII. 5 in Ep. ad Hebr.* (*PG* lxiii. 199); *Hom. VI. 4 in I Ep. ad Thessal.* (*PG* lxii. 434); *Hom. X. 3 in I Ep. ad Tim.* (*PG* lxii. 553–4). Hell: *Hom. X. 3 in I Ep. ad Tim.* (*PG* lxii. 552); *Hom. V. 4 in Act. Apost.* (*PG* lx. 65–6); *Hom. V in Ep. ad Rom.* (*PG* lx. 432); ibid. *Hom. XXV. 6* (*PG* lx. 635. 6).

[106] E. Clark (1979).

[107] Mother and education of children: *Hom. in illud: vidua eligatur* (*PG* li. 321–38); *De Anna* (*PG* liv. 631–76).

[108] *Hom. XXVII in I Ep. ad Ocr.* (*PG* lxi. 315–16); *Hom. IX in I Ep. ad Tim.* (*PG* lxii. 543–48); *De Sacerdotio* iii. 9. (*PG* lxviii. 646).

[109] *Hom. XXVI. 2 ff. in I Ep. ad Cor.* (*PG* lxi. 214 ff.).

[110] e.g. *Hom. V. 3 De studio praesentium* (*PG* lxiii. 487).

[111] *Hom. XLIV. 1 in Matth.* (*PG* lviii. 464–5); ibid. *Hom. IV. 5* (*PG* lvii. 45); *Hom. XXI. 2 in Ioann.* (*PG* lix. 13); ibid. lxxx. 2 (*PG* lix. 467).

[112] *Hom. viii. 4 in Genes.* (*PG* liii. 73); ibid. xv. 3 (*PG* liii. 121–2); ibid. xviii. 8 (*PG* liii. 144–5).

[113] A.-M. Malingrey (1968).

the power to manipulate one of the great ladies of the city seems to have played a much smaller part than in comparable friendships of Jerome. Through experience Chrysostom came to see that some of his favourite quotations from Paul, 'the head of the woman is man',[114] or 'neither was man created for the woman but woman for the man',[115] or 'but I suffer not the woman to teach nor to have authority over man'[116] gave an incomplete account of the respective roles of the sexes, even in the work of the Church. Through experience Chrysostom began to appreciate the importance of women as partners of the apostles, more specifically of Priscilla and Phoebe, the female helpers of Paul, and also of the mother of the Maccabees.[117] He came to agree that the 'full panoply of Christ' fits women as well as men.[118]

Chrysostom's attitudes can be shown to have evolved in other areas. As a young man he had spent six years living as an anchorite in the desert.[119] At this time he felt that a Christian could only be saved if he lived as a monk.[120] Later he came to see that the essential duty for a Christian was care for his fellow men. He could state that the life of a priest or missionary was better than that of a solitary ascetic.[121] Fasting and celibacy, an austere way of life, are forms of discipline of benefit to the person who practises them but to nobody else. Aiding the poor is worth much more. Pity and mercy cause sins to be forgiven and make man godlike.[122] Every situation affords opportunity to help those in need.[123]

One activity which he learnt to value later in life was financial administration. As a preacher at Antioch he complained that bishop and clergy had to spend far too much time managing the property and collecting the revenues of the church. They spend their days like tax collectors or customs officials; they negotiate with innkeepers and corn merchants. They have to be present at the harvest and at the selling of crops.[124] Chrysostom wished the clergy to be liberated from the care for property and to be free to look after people, the poor, the oppressed, the sick, widows, and orphans. It is the laity's task to provide the clergy with a steady income which will enable them to

---

[114] *1 Cor.* 11: 3.   [115] *1 Cor.* 11: 9.   [116] *1 Tim.* 2: 12.

[117] *Hom. V. 3 de studio praesentium* (*PG* lxiii. 488–9).

[118] Ibid., 488, quoting *Eph.* 6: 13; cf. also ibid. 487: men and women equal in worship.

[119] Pall. *Dial.* 19.

[120] *Advers. oppugn. vit. monast.* iii 15 (*PG* xlvii. 376).

[121] *De Sacerdotio* vi. 7 (*PG* xlviii. 683).

[122] *Hom. VI. 2 in Ep. ad Tit.* (*PG* lxii. 698); *Hom. XXV. 3 in 1 Ep. ad Cor.* (*PG* lxi. 208).

[123] *Hom. XIV. 6 in 1 Ep. ad Tim.* (*PG* lxii. 578); *Hom. XII in Ep. ad Coloss.* (*PG* lxii. 387): marriage a figure of the Church of Christ. See R. Brändle (1979) 159–72.

[124] *De Sacerdotio* iii. 16 (*PG* xlviii. 656); *Hom. LXXXV–LXXXVI in Matth.* (*PG* lviii. 761–4); R. Brändle (1979) 108–11.

perform these charitable duties.[125] A few years later, at Constantinople, when Chrysostom had become bishop, and was himself deeply involved in the checking of accounts,[126] a task which Gregory of Nazianzus, for instance, had neglected,[127] he ceased to complain about such chores. Presumably he realized that the Church could not do its work without property, and that, this being so, it was right that clergy should give time to its administration.[128]

Chrysostom was very conscious that it was not enough for him to make general and abstract demands. If the sermon is not to be wasted it must be followed by action—if only the passing on of what the preacher has said in church to those who had been unable to be there. What was most frequently and earnestly demanded was almsgiving. Another demand made with a frequency that surprises the modern reader is that members of his congregation must not in any circumstances swear.[129] John was of course only repeating the biblical commandment not to take the Lord's name in vain, but at the same time refusal to take an oath was something simple and concrete that a man could do to start himself on the journey of moral improvement.

Another way in which the preaching could lead to straightforward and conspicuous action was through the shunning of public entertainments. Chrysostom produced some of his most eloquent prose for attacks on the evils of the theatre and the chariot races, the two entertainments which brought passion and excitement into the lives of the masses in cities like Antioch and Constantinople. Following a long tradition of Christian preachers[130] he regarded these shows as unmitigated evils. The races were bad, the theatres worse. Members of his congregation are urged to stay away from them.

Chrysostom's hostility to the shows was motivated by the anxiety of a moral teacher. Like many generations of moralists before him. Chrysostom saw it to be the principal object of moral education to establish control of human passions. The public spectacles had precisely the opposite effect; they provided occasion to indulge passion. The chariot races—like football matches today—aroused huge crowds of spectators to intense experiences of joy, anxiety, or grief according to whether their favourite was winning, struggling, or losing. The passionate partisanship of the spectators often culminated in furious brawls.[131] In the preacher's view the experience of watching would exercise and strengthen irrational and dangerous emotions

---

[125] *Hom. LXXXVI. 4 in Matth.* (PG lviii. 762).   [126] Pall. *Dial.* 20.
[127] *Carmen de vita sua* 1475 ff.   [128] R. Brändle (1979) 107–14.
[129] e.g. *Hom. VIII–XI in Act. Apost.* (PG lx. 69–100).
[130] See e.g. C. J. Cadoux (1925) 440–2; O. Pasquato (1976).
[131] *Hom. X. 2 in illud, messis quidem multa* (PG lxiii. 518).

until they became dominant and uncontrollable. And the effect of the theatre was even more dangerous than that of the hippodrome. Erotic scenes, attractive dances, suggestive attitudes, immoral songs arouse adulterous passions which remain after the show has ended, and by comparison make the love of wife and family appear humdrum and unattractive.[132] Needless to say the theatre produces resistance to church attendance. A man whose lusts have been aroused in the theatre does not want to listen to sermons advocating self-restraint and chastity.[133]

In the sermons of Chrysostom and others the opposition of Church and spectacles was extreme. But if one looks at both in a social context the gap between them can be seen to be less than it seemed from the preacher's point of view. Mass entertainments—if in some respects demoralizing—in others express real human values and contribute to the cohesion of society. The fact of the survival of the shows in the face of attack by generations of preachers and moral philosophers shows that the ancients realized this too. But for the preachers the spectacles were rivals. Naturally, since people chose to go to them instead of going to church, or alternatively, after hearing a sermon advocating discipline and self-restraint, turned to enjoy an emotional orgy, watching the chariot races or the dancers.

Church and the public shows had more in common than a preacher could be expected to agree. A sermon of Chrysostom's was a performance. Rhetoric had long been at the centre of Graeco-Roman culture. Chrysostom was a master of every rhetorical technique. His sermons offer lively comparisons, vivid descriptions, the whole range of figures of speech, passionate denunciations, enthusiastic praise, and every trick that will move an audience to enjoyable emotion. His style could be appreciated by the educated for its pure classicism, but he was also careful to keep his verbal structures simple, so that they would have a very wide appeal. Besides he always had something to say. So it is not surprising that people came to hear him for enjoyment, that he was in fact something like a superstar whose transfer from Antioch to Constantinople had to be kept secret in case news of it started a riot.[134] Apart from the sermon, a service could be a highly emotional experience, taking the worshipper through a wide range of emotions from fear and self-abasement to the joy of assured

[132] *Contra ludos et theatra PG* lvi. 266–7 held on 3 July 399 according to J. Pargoire (1899–1900) 151 ff. *CT* ii. 8. 23 of 27. 8. 399 forbidding plays and horse races on Sundays may be a response to Chrysostom's protest.

[133] *De Davide et Saule Hom. III. 2* (*PG* liv. 696–7).

[134] *De Sacerdotio* v. 1 (*PG* xlviii. 673); Pall. *Dial.* 19: riots feared when Chrysostom moved from Antioch to Constantinople. On rhetorical technique of Chrysostom see R. L. Wilken (1983) 95–127.

salvation. Some members of the congregation accompanied their chanting by contortions of the body and twisting of their raised arms. Chrysostom discouraged such behaviour, but the significant fact is that he did have occasion to reprimand it.[135] We have seen that he organized nocturnal processions with hymn singing to combat similar activities of the Arians. These too were highly emotional mass demonstrations, and as likely to escalate into riot as any theatre audience.[136]

Chrysostom was a popular educator in the full sense. Week after week he systematically explained books of the Old and New Testaments.[137] Of course the sermons are more than literary exegesis. Almost all of them end with a moral discourse only loosely connected with the text explained earlier. Nevertheless the bulk of the sermon is simply an explanation of the biblical story and words. A whole series of sermons amounts to a lecture course on some part of biblical literature. Chrysostom wanted his congregation to become thoroughly familiar with the sacred writing and for the sake of his objective employed timeless educational tricks of the trade. He deliberately withheld information so that his hearers should look it up for themselves. Who, for instance, was the king of Babylon alluded to by Isaiah 14: 12?[138] He explains his method: 'Birds do not put food into the mouths of their young as they grow older, but let it drop so that the young birds learn to pick it up.' This is how he taught the bible.[139] He wants his hearers to think about what he has said when they have left the church. Not only are they to think about what he has said, and to talk about it to people who have not attended the service; they must also read the bible—in spite of a widespread belief that bible reading was only required of monks.[140] He will accept the excuse that they do not own a copy only from the poorest.[141] The bible is the working tool of the Christian, for whom the ownership of a bible is more essential than it is for copper- and silver-smiths to own the tools of their trade, and yet the craftsmen consider tools are so vital that they refrain from selling them even in famine.[142] It was not necessary to buy the whole bible at once as its books were available separately.[143] John Chrysostom recommends the time after meals as

135 *In illud vidi dominum Hom. I* (*PG* lvi. 99).   136 See above, p. 167.
137 Suggesting that a lesson from the bible was a regular part of the service, cf. F. van der Paverd (1970) 115, R. Zerfass (1963), and (1968).
138 *VIII Hom. habita postquam presbyter Gothus . . .* (*PG* lxiii. 506).
139 *Hom. I. 4 de mutat. nom.* (*PG* li. 119).
140 *Hom. II. 6 in Matth.* (*PG* lvii. 30–2).
141 *Hom. XXI. 1 in Ep. ad Ephes.* (*PG* lxii. 150); *Hom. VII. 4. in Ep. ad Hebr.* (*PG* lxiii. 67); *Hom. XXI. 6 in Genes.* (*PG* liii. 183).
142 *Hom. XI. 1 in Ioann.* (*PG* lix. 78); *De Laz. III. 2* (*PG* xlviii. 993).
143 *Hom. IX. 1 in Ep. ad Coloss.* (*PG* lxii. 361).

particularly suitable for bible reading. This could be followed by discussion of the passages read, which would be an improvement on the endless gossip about actors, dancers, and charioteers that usually occupied people after their meal about this time.[144] Reading and discussion he recommended above all for women, for whom the home would become a kind of spiritual school.[145]

The fruit of reading and discussions would be the accumulation of a stock of general knowledge of biblical topics. A Christian ought to know the number of letters written by Paul,[146] the number and names of prophets and apostles.[147] Once Chrysostom set a kind of general knowledge test. What is a narrative? What is a prophecy? What is a parable? What is a type? What is an allegory? What is a symbol? What are Gospels? Why are they called Gospels, even though they contain much that is sad?[148] He complains that too many of his congregation have their heads full of the names of actors, horses, and charioteers and may not be aware even of the existence of the Acts of the Apostles.[149]

The aim of all this is no doubt to get the laity thoroughly acquainted with the doctrines and moral teachings of Christianity, but an incidental effect is to inculcate deep knowledge of a large body of literature. Making allowances for the pastoral bias of the author, Chrysostom's commentaries on various books of scripture are not at all unlike modern editions of literary texts annotated for use in schools. They stimulate questions why Paul, or other scriptural authors, wrote precisely what they did, in the way they did, and lay the foundation of an interest that could last a lifetime. Preaching like that of John Chrysostom would encourage the spread of literacy among a wider segment of the population, and among women. It also offered to all Christians who made the effort possession of a literature to provide a common frame of reference such as classical Greek literature was providing for the literary élite.

If sermons offered a literary education, it was a restricted one. Even though we know, and would in any case be able to deduce from the quality of his Greek,[150] that John Chrysostom himself had been steeped in the traditional rhetorical education, secular classics did not figure in his sermons, except now and again as the butt of derogatory

[144] *Hom. X. 8 in Genes* (PG liii. 90); *Hom. XVIII. 3–4 in Ioann.* (PG lix. 118); *Hom. VI. 6 in Genes* (PG liii. 61).

[145] *Hom. LXI. 3 in Ioann.* (PG lix. 340); *Hom. XXXV. 2 in Genes.* (PG liii. 323).

[146] *In illud salutate Priscillam et Aquilam 1* (PG li. 187 ff.); *Hom. I. 1 in Ep. ad Roman.* (PG lx. 391).

[147] *Hom. LVIII. 4 in Ioann.* (PG lix. 320).

[148] *Hom. XIX in Act. Apost.* (PG lx. 156).

[149] *Hom. in inscriptionem altaris 3* (PG li. 71).   [150] M. Soffrey (1939), (1947–8).

comments.[151] Nevertheless there were as yet no Christian schools.[152] Literacy still had to be acquired at secular schools and through reading of secular authors. But for the good life or salvation they were dispensable. The bible provided all that was needed.[153]

Chrysostom can have been in no doubt that his preaching was a conspicuous success as entertainment. Sermons, like public shows, aroused emotions intensified by the large number of people sharing them.[154] Chrysostom disliked the expression of emotions during the service. Yet there can be no doubt that his sermons did more than anything else to rouse the congregation.[155] Rhetoric was one of the oldest forms of public entertainment in the Graeco-Roman world, and Chrysostom was an acknowledged past-master of rhetoric. He was appreciated. He frequently asked the congregation not to interrupt him with applause.[156] 'When as I speak I hear myself applauded, at the moment indeed I feel it as a man: for why should I not own the truth? I am delighted . . . but when I go home and think to myself that those who applauded received no benefit from my discourse, but that whatever benefits they ought to have got they lost while applauding and praising, I am in pain and groan and weep, and feel as if I had spoken in vain'. So he proposes the rule: no applause except at the end of a sermon.[157]

Certainly he did not always preach to a full house. Congregations were adversely affected by bad weather and the rival attractions of the theatre and chariot races. Attendances were largest at Easter. Chrysostom fears that at this and some other festivals church attendance has become an empty social form.[158] Needless to say, he fought to maintain his audience. He attacks the moral dangers of attending the chariot races or the theatre. He threatens to ex-communicate men who miss the service in order to enjoy themselves at the public entertainment.[159] He takes particular care over a sermon given to a small audience so that those who have not come shall think that they have missed something. The fact that a law issued in August

---

[151] C. Fabricius (1962); J. Dumortier (1953).

[152] H.-I. Marrou, *A History of Education in Antiquity* (London, 1958).

[153] Apart from the bible Chrysostom recommends only Athanasius' *Life of Antony: Hom. VIII. 5 in Matt.* (*PG* lviii. 88).

[154] Cf. C. L. Critcher (1971); P. Veyne (1976).

[155] *De Sacerdotio* v. 2 (*PG* xlviii. 673); *Ad pop. Ant.* ii. 10. 4 (*PG* xlix. 38); *Hom. XVII. 7 in Matt.* (*PG* lvii. 264).

[156] *Hom. XXX. 4 in Act. Apost.* (*PG* lx. 226–28).

[157] Ibid. (*PG* lx. 228).

[158] *Hom. XXIX. 3 in Act. Apost.* (*PG* lx. 218); *Hom. in illud si esurierit inimicus 3* (*PG* lii. 177); *Hom. VIII in Genes. 1* (*PG* liv. 67); *Hom. XI. 1 in Joann.* (*PG* lix. 78). Christians compared unfavourably with Jews: *Hom. in inscriptionem altaris* (*PG* li. 70).

[159] *Hom. contra ludos et theatra 1* (*PG* lvi. 263 ff.); on date see n. 132 above; *Hom. IX. 1 in Ioann. 5.17* (*PG* lxiii. 512).

399 prohibited the holding of shows on Sunday suggests that he used his influence at court to combat the rival attractions.[160]

Accounts of the careers of famous preachers inevitably raise the question whether so much preaching made any difference to the behaviour of the people subjected to it. Chrysostom formulated the question with characteristic honesty: who has become a better man by attending service for a whole month? If you were getting any profit by sermons and services you ought to have been long leading the life of true wisdom, with so many prophets twice in every week discoursing to you. Soldiers, wrestlers, doctors became more proficient through training. What about church attenders? Our forefathers did not build churches merely to bring us together from our private houses and show us to one another, since this could have been done also in the market place and in baths and in public processions, but to bring together learner and teacher and to make the one better by the other. With us it has all become mere customary routine, formal discharge of duty, a thing we are used to. Easter occasions a great assembly, tumult, and bad behaviour, but no good is left behind. As for vigils and hymn singing many do it merely out of vanity. 'Think how sick at heart it must make me to see it all like so much water poured into a cask with holes in it. The Church is a dyer's vat: if time after time perpetually ye go hence without receiving dye what is the use of coming here continuously.'[161]

If it is impossible to assess to what extent the sermons of Chrysostom and others changed the behaviour of their hearers, we can observe unambiguous symptoms of the deepening Christianization of the population of the Empire, and it is reasonable to assume that regular sermons were an important factor in bringing this about. By the end of the fourth century the Empire had acquired a consciously Christian ruling class with consequences in legislation which have been examined.[162] There was a strong commitment to ascetic ideals and Christian charity among upper class women.[163] These years saw the foundation of charitable institutions at Constantinople and elsewhere. One might talk of the beginnings of a stream which was to grow into a flood from the mid fifth century.[164]

City life had always required rich and poor to coexist in a confined space and therefore inevitably involved the risk of disastrous conflicts.[165] Thus there had always been pressure on the rich not to

---

[160] *CT* ii. 8. 23 (27. 8. 399).

[161] *Hom. XXXIX. 3 in Act. Apost. (PG* lx. 218).

[162] See above, p. 141.   [163] See above, p. 142–3.

[164] Soz. iv. 20. 2, v. 19. 2–3; Theodoret *HE* v. 19. 2–3; Greg. Naz..*De Vita Sua* 1500–1502. Chrysostom's foundation: Pall. *Dial.* 5. Many monasteries: Callinicus *V. Hypat.* 11. 1.

[165] A. H. M. Jones (1940) 250.

flaunt their wealth, and to share its benefit through semi-compulsory expenditure on behalf of the community. At Athens this had produced a significant levelling of property.[166] This was long ago. Roman rule had everywhere eroded democratic institutions and relaxed the popular pressure on the rich. In the changed circumstance of the fourth and fifth centuries AD the Christian preacher—together with the hippodrome and the odd riot—assumed the role of the popular assembly, and made it easier for classes to live together. It is not a coincidence that precisely in sermons held in the crisis of 399–400 John Chrysostom persistently dwelt on the evils of love of money, and on the proper use of it.[167] The German threat called for social coherence. As Palladius, Chrysostom's apologetic biographer, put it: 'He put his hand to the sword of correction of the rich, lancing the abscesses of their souls, and teaching them humility and courtesy towards others.'[168]

But Christian giving was different from the traditional munificence expected from the wealthy inhabitants of cities.[169] Christian charity was not directed towards fellow citizens or political supporters but towards the poor, whoever they might be. It was given to them precisely because they were poor or sick, and because God wants Christians to look after those in need. In fact this was one way in which men might atone for the sins with which they were inevitably contaminated.[170] The idea that the poor and the sick and the old ought to be helped because they were there, and were God's creatures, is not classical. Moreover Christian charity did not provide the same range of services as had been—and to some extent were still— provided by *curiales* for their fellow citizens. Christian charity did not provide amenities like shows and baths and colonnades which were of benefit to rich and poor alike. It was focused on basic needs of food and shelter. Christian giving was quite independent of the secular institutions of the city. If charity was not given to the beneficiary directly, it was channelled through the Church or through a religious institution like a hospital or a monastery. The scale of Christian charity cannot be quantified, but the rapid growth in the number of monasteries and other charitable institutions at Constantinople[171] suggests that it was cumulatively very considerable. It was of course not restricted to Constantinople, nor even, like curial

---

[166] M. I. Finley (1983) 34–70.

[167] *In Eutropium (PG lii. 391–6); De Capto Eutropio* (ibid. 396–413); *Cum Saturninus et Aurelianus . . .* (ibid. 413–20).

[168] Pall. *Dial.* 21. [169] P. Veyne (1976) 44–67.

[170] E. Patlagean (1977*b*) 181–96; P. Brown (1987) 276–82.

[171] See above p. 144–5, and G. Dagron (1974) 510–13, D. J. Constantelos (1968), R. Janin (1964) 564–82, (1969) 550–69.

munificence, to cities. Remains of monasteries in areas where the thinness of later occupation has preserved much late Roman building show that they were extremely numerous everywhere, and particularly in the countryside.[172] The foundation of monasteries involved another development of very great and lasting significance, the widespread acceptance of the superior holiness of the unmarried life. This pervaded all classes, with the result that very large numbers of men and women chose to live celibate lives whether singly as hermits, or communally within the monasteries founded by the wealthiest among them. The ascetic life was dedicated to the service of God, but the ascetes still had to have at least a minimum of the necessities of life. So the realization of the ascetic ideal required the devising of new structures and organizations which would provide food and shelter at the same time as isolation from the disturbing world. Different forms of monasticism did in fact represent a new way of life which enabled men and women to pray, but also to live and work, outside the traditional framework of home and family.[173] Together Christian charity and Christian asceticism affected many aspects of social and even economic life.[174] They were essential constituents of the society that was coming into existence among the remains of Graeco-Roman civilization.

The causal connection between these wider developments and the preaching of precisely John Chrysostom is of course very slight. But the fact that such profound changes of attitude did take place suggests that regular and sustained preaching did not go without effect. More immediately and conspicuously Chrysostom's preaching won him a personal following. This was clearly shown during the events leading to his deposition and exile. Chrysostom's support at Constantinople was not strong enough to keep him in office once the emperor had decided that he would have to go. But there was rioting and civil disobedience to imperial commands. Arcadius was evidently reluctant to force a confrontation, for he hesitated six months before he compelled Chrysostom to leave Constantinople for his second and permanent exile. Under the emperors of the principate no individual was ever in a position to establish a comparable power base in the capital.

---

[172] G. Tchalenko (1953) i. 145–54.
[173] E. Patlagean (1977*b*) 315–24, 338–40.
[174] See E. Patlagean (1977*b*) ch. 5. 3, 'Le don stimulant de la production'.

16

Chrysostom in the Gainas Crisis

CHRYSOSTOM was a non-political bishop, who was careful to keep completely clear of involvement in secular political controversy. Nevertheless it was inevitable that his influence with important individuals, his popularity with many inhabitants of the capital, and his connections in the provinces, not least with the Goths, should make him a man of power. This appeared very clearly at the time of the fall of Eutropius, and throughout the ensuing Gainas crisis. When Eutropius had lost the favour of emperor and empress he sought asylum in church, and Chrysostom for a time protected him from the soldiers demanding his execution. The fallen favourite cowered under the altar while Chrysostom preached a sermon on moral lessons to be derived from his fall.[1] Considering that Eutropius had made Chrysostom bishop of Constantinople, the sermon shows remarkably little sympathy with the eunuch's fate. One must assume that he had felt recent disagreement between himself and Eutropius deeply. Chrysostom states that 'this persistent enemy of the Church is receiving the punishment which he deserves'. He describes him as accursed, greedy and rapacious,[2] making him the target of a volley of rhetorical invective, but with the political circumstances which have brought about the fall of the eunuch he does not concern himself at all. Instead he preached on the text 'Oh vanity of vanities, all is vanity'. He makes the fallen minister an example of the truth of his favourite theme. Men must not make wealth and power the principal objects of their lives. Both are 'vanity', transitory and, as shown by the fate of Eutropius, potentially deadly.[3] This is a point he has made in innumerable sermons at Constantinople, and earlier at Antioch, with the motive of getting the rich to part with their wealth, in order to alleviate the sufferings of the poor. Now the catastrophe suffered by Eutropius, and his cowering presence at the altar, is made into a confirmation of the teaching, a warning to the rich and a consolation to the poor.[4] Chrysostom refers to his earlier relations with Eutropius. The remarks are of the 'Why didn't you listen to my advice?' kind, and from them we can derive some hints as to the advice the bishop had given to his powerful parishioner. We gather

[1] *In Eutropium* 4 (PG lii. 391–6).   [2] *In Eutropium* 3 (PG lii. 394).
[3] *De capto Eutropio et divitiarum vanitate* 3 (PG lii. 398).
[4] *In Eutropium* 4 (PG lii. 395).

that he warned him of the dangers of wealth, and that he had opposed him in the interest of the Church.[5] This is obviously a reference to Chrysostom's opposition to Eutropius' law limiting asylum. He does not admit to political counsel in a wider sense.

Eventually Eutropius left asylum, perhaps on receiving the promise that he would not be executed—a promise which was not in the end kept. In a second sermon Chrysostom defended himself against the charge of having surrendered Eutropius.[6] Later he was attacked for the sermons. He was criticized—reasonably enough—for lack of charity in that he had abused a man in the depth of misfortune.[7]

In the following year while Gainas and his army were quartered in Constantinople Chrysostom was conspicuously influential. This was probably in part a result of links between bishop and Goths created by Chrysostom's interest in missionary work among the Goths living along the Danube.[8] That he had put a church in the capital at their disposal—even if only for orthodox services—and had preached there himself[9] must also have made for good relations between him and the Gothic soldiers. This must be borne in mind if one tries to evaluate the dramatic incident in which Chrysostom played an Ambrose-like role opposing the might of the state,[10] when emperor and praetorian prefect[11] were ready to allow the Goths to use a church for Arian services. Chrysostom assembled all the bishops who happened to be at Constantinople and confronted Gainas in the presence of the emperor with a formal speech of protest. He won his point without having to stage a 'sit in' in the church, as Ambrose had done at Milan. Theodoret and Sozomen have made much of this triumph.[12] Socrates, whose attitude to Chrysostom was ambivalent, made much less of it.[13] Palladius, the contemporary source, does not mention it at all. It may be that the incident came to be amplified by writers favourable to Chrysostom to counter the charge that he had been excessively pro-Gothic, and more specifically that he had allowed the Goths to hold Arian services in the church which he had given them ostensibly for orthodox worship.

It certainly looks as if the 'Gothic church' was eventually used for Arian services, so that Chrysostom's victory appears to have been temporary only. According to Synesius' account permission to hold Arian services in the city marked the beginning of the end of Gothic occupation. Subsequently Synesius was able to treat the church,

---

[5] Ibid. 1 (*PG* lii. 391).   [6] *De capto Eutropio* 1 (*PG* lii. 397).
[7] Socr. viii. 5.   [8] See above, p. 000.
[9] *Hom. VIII, Postquam presbyter Gothus . . .* (*PG* lxiii. 499–510).
[10] Ambrose *Ep.* 20.   [11] Synesius *De Prov.* 1257.
[12] Soz. viii. 4; Theodoret *HE* v. 32, and in a lost work mentioned Photius *Bibl.* 273.
[13] Socr. vi. 4.

which was destroyed together with seven thousand Goths who had taken refuge in it, as an Arian church.[14] We have seen that this act became so controversial that the immediate official reaction was to bury it in silence. As a result we do not know how the leading men at Constantinople divided in the ensuing controversy. Chrystostom must have been deeply involved. He had broken with Eutropius over the Church's right of asylum. He was responsible for the Goths having been given a church. Quite apart from his personal involvement, the burning of a church together with its priests and a large number of those who had sought asylum there was a dreadful act of sacrilege which a bishop could hardly pass over in silence.[15] It is difficult to believe that he kept silent. If he spoke out at that very tense time he must have made enemies. The official 'news blackout' has kept from us all detail of charges and countercharges. But it may be that Chrysostom's stand against giving a church to the Arians was exaggerated to defend the bishop against accusations made in the course of the controversy over the burning of the Gothic church.

The destruction of the church did not end Chrysostom's influence in secular affairs. After the destruction of the Goths a council of state was held in the bishop's palace, and when certain men demanded that Aurelian and the other exiles should now be recalled, it was the bishop who promised that this would be done. Evidently he was still the man in the best position to negotiate with Gainas. We are also told that even after the battle and massacre in Constantinople Typhos, that is, the praetorian prefect Eutychianus, still hoped to come to an agreement with Gainas. He is said to have tried—and failed—to bribe Chrysostom to support this policy.[16]

In fact Chrysostom cannot have been opposed to what Eutychianus was trying to achieve, for when envoys were sent to Gainas Chrysostom was among them.[17] He was away for a considerable time. When he returned he held the sermon *Cum Saturninus et Aurelianus acti essent in exsilium*.[18] His explanation of his long

[14] Socr. vi. 6, Soz. viii. 4, Synesius *De Prov.* 1268, Zos. v. 19. 3–4: 'The Christian church near the palace'. Marcell. Com. s.a. 400: 'the church of the Goths'. The implication of Synesius is that the church was Arian, which would suggest that in spite of his public protest Chrysostom was ready to overlook the fact that Arians might use the church which he had put at the disposal of Goths.

[15] Clergy killed: Synesius *De Prov.* 1268. Sacrilege: Zos. v. 19. 5.

[16] Synesius *De Prov.* 1268 (assuming that the 'high-priest' is the bishop).

[17] Theodoret *HE* v. 33 and a lost work mentioned by Photius *Bibl.* 273.

[18] *PG* lii. 413–20. G. Albert (1984) and others have dated this sermon to the time of Gainas' 'coup'. Crysostom, it is argued, persuaded Gainas to spare the lives of Aurelian, Saturninus, and John, and to be content with exiling them. But Theodoret *HE* v. 33 makes it quite clear that Chrysostom's embassy to Gainas happened later than his protest over the Arian church, at a time when Gainas was openly an enemy in Thrace. This must have been after 12 July 400. In any case negotiations at the time of the 'coup' could not have kept John from preaching at

absence is shrouded in metaphor. 'He has been away calming a storm, drawing those being shipwrecked out of the water . . . leading those who were sinking to a harbour and calm water.' More concretely he related that he had left the city and gone from one place to another exhorting, requesting, begging that 'the calamity should be removed from our masters', and 'now that the gloomy circumstances have ended' he has returned to the people of Constantinople.[19] The disaster from which 'our masters' were to be freed has always been understood to mean the life in exile under military guard of Aurelian, Saturninus, and John. If that is right, and it is difficult to see what else could be meant, Chrysostom claims that he has been on a mission into territory controlled by the Gothic army in order to negotiate the return of the exiles. In this he succeeded. The exiles came back, sometime in autumn 400.[20] But they were not grateful. Quite the reverse. They appear to have blamed Chrysostom for the fact that they had been sent into exile at all. When his enemies eventually succeeded in bringing him before a court the accusation of having betrayed John to the Germans figured among the charges.[21] Chrysostom says nothing about any wider diplomatic aims of his mission. If he had hoped to negotiate another agreement between the government and the federates the hope came to nothing. War continued, and the federates were eventually destroyed.

Chrysostom was far from discredited. The 37th homily on the Acts of the Apostles, which was probably held early in 401 soon after the final destruction of Gainas, suggests that Chrysostom now publicly approved of the expulsion of the Goths.[22] Synesius' account of the burning of the church shows that at the time of writing it was the prefect Eutychianus who was blamed for the Goths having a church at all.[23] He had of course been deprived of office.[24] Less than a year later, in autumn of 401, around November, Chrysostom left for Ephesus to replace its bishop, and generally to set to rights the churches of Asia.[25] As we have seen, this involved a considerable

Constantinople for any length of time, since they took place at Chalcedon, just across the straits. Theodoret *HE* v. 33 suggests that John's mission ὑπὲρ τῶν κοινῶν τῆς πολιτείας . . . πραγμάτων was not restricted to the release of the exiles.

[19] Ibid. 414–15. The city was divided by suspicion. So also Synesius *De Prov.* 1269, cf. above, p. 122.

[20] Zos. v. 23. A hiatus leaves the circumstances of the return obscure. They returned by boat as far as Epirus. Where had they been? The were back at Constantinople not too late for the year to be named after Aurelian as consul, i.e. in 400, and before the end of the sailing season (Synesius *Ep.* 61 and Alan Cameron (1987), i.e. perhaps October or early November.

[21] Photius *Bibl.* 273.

[22] *PG* lx. 267, and on it Alan Cameron (1987) 347–8.

[23] Synesius *De Prov.* 1268.

[24] See above, p. 122.   [25] See Alan Cameron (1987).

extension of the prerogatives of the bishop of Constantinople. We have also seen that he acted with the full support of the emperor. He was still at the height of his power. At the same time there can be no doubt that Chrysostom's prominence during a period of such bitter controversy had made him many enemies.

Apart from the ill-feeling produced by the special circumstances of the Gainas crisis, the experience of watching an able and popular bishop of Constantinople realizing the potential powers of his office must have alarmed many. It was impossible to tell where this might lead. The nearest recent parallel was the position Ambrose had built up at Milan. At Constantinople the only previous bishop who had attempted to become a power in the city and neighbouring provinces was the Arian, or semi-Arian, Macedonius.[26] It was not a reassuring precedent. Macedonius' position in the city was based on his patronage of a particular branch of the monastic movement which carried on a great deal of charitable activities.[27] He was capable of instigating large-scale riots.[28] Outside Constantinople he deposed and appointed bishops and clergy with the support of imperial edicts. The immediate objective was religious unity on the basis of a particular formula of belief.[29] An inevitable effect was to give the bishop of Constantinople supervision over bishops of a wide area. Finally, Macedonius on his own initiative moved the body of the emperor Constantine from the church of the Holy Apostles to that of St Acacius. This was probably intended as a temporary measure during building works in the former church. But Macedonius had not consulted the emperor Constantius, and for Constantius this was the last straw.[30] Macedonius was deposed together with a number of his followers among the bishops of neighbouring churches.[31] A bishop of the sort Macedonius had been, and as Chrysostom—even allowing for the fact that he was a very different kind of man—might become, or might encourage successors to become, must have been an extremely worrying prospect, not only for fellow bishops but even for the emperor and his ministers. We have seen that in our period Arcadius tended to be a figurehead, while men of the secular establishment ran the Empire.

Chrysostom's centralizing activities at Constantinople threatened in the first place the monasteries which had developed in the Macedonian tradition beyond the control of the bishop. Outside

[26] G. Dagron (1974) 436–42.
[27] Soz. iv. 2. 3, 20. 2, 27; Socr. ii. 38.   [28] Socr. ii. 16; Soz. iii. 7, 9.
[29] Socr. ii. 27, 38. Like Chrysostom, Macedonius persecuted Novatians: ibid. 38.
[30] Socr. ii. 38; Soz. iv. 21. Relics of SS. Andrew and Timothy had been transferred there recently: Jerome *Chron.* s.a. 356 and 357, Philostorg. ii. 2.
[31] Socr. ii. 42; Soz. iv. 21.

Constantinople churches of neighbouring provinces and even dioceses had reason to fear that they might be subordinated to Constantinople. It is not surprising that a lot of people began to look for means of resisting. Of course the man best placed to lead resistance was Theophilus, bishop of Alexandria.

17

Enemies and Friends of John Chrysostom: The Problem

EARLIER chapters have shown that Chrysostom was a formidable bishop of Constantinople. He had a mass following in the city. He was extending the authority of the bishop of Constantinople over bishops of the cities of neighbouring dioceses. In a dangerous crisis he had shown himself to be a serious factor in secular affairs as well. This was something new. The East was not used to having a bishop of Constantinople who could be an independent power in its politics. There was no room for such a figure. He was bound to incur the hostility of all existing established powers, first of all his fellow bishops, but also the secular authorities. This, it will be argued, was the basic cause of the deposition of John Chrysostom.

We have seen that in spring 402 the position of Chrysostom was stronger than ever. He seemed set for a long and successful episcopacy. Yet a little more than a year later, in his sixth year as bishop, he was summoned to appear before the so-called Synod of the Oak in order to answer a long list of charges. He refused to appear and was formally deposed. This was in autumn 403. The first exile was brief. He was recalled after only one day. He did not enter the city and resume his duties as bishop immediately, but after a not very long interval he did both. His opponents, however, remained as determined as ever, and soon resumed their attacks. By Christmas 403 the emperor again refused to take communion with him. Just before Easter 404 Chrysostom was forbidden to officiate at services, and on 20 June 404 he was escorted into exile. This time there was no recall. He died on 14 September 407, while he was being moved to an even more remote place of exile at Pityus on the Black Sea.[1] How can this disastrous conclusion after so promising a beginning be explained?

According to the generally accepted view, a view which goes back to contemporary sources, the cause of the deposition was basically trivial: the empress Eudoxia was offended by one of John's sermons. So she combined with some others who had grievances against Chrysostom, and together they persuaded the emperor to ensure his

[1] W. Liebeschuetz (1985).

dismissal. The view is not satisfactory. Eudoxia no doubt was passionate and easily offended. But she had also been a great admirer of Chrysostom, and after his final exile her hostility ceased very rapidly.[2] One would not have expected her to show the steady and relentless hostility which ensured the second and final exiling. There is also the fact that persecution of John and his followers continued long after her death in October 404. Again, two of the bishops who figure in the sources as the local leaders of the plot, Severianus of Gabala and Antiochus of Ptolemais, were skilled preachers but otherwise second-rate figures.[3] Acacius of Beroea was a man of high standing in Syria and the ascetic movement,[4] but he, like the others, was absent from his see and episcopal duties and vulnerable for that reason. Theophilus of Alexandria on the other hand was formidable. But while he was a determined and persistent enemy of Chrysostom he returned to Alexandria soon after John's return from his first exile,[5] and was never again in Constantinople where the crucial decisions were taken. Clearly Chrysostom had other powerful opponents. Nevertheless the fact that bishops of Alexandria helped to pull down no fewer than four bishops of Constantinople in less than seventy years shows that the intervention of Theophilus represents the working of deep-seated and persistent factors: the threat posed to the traditional position of the bishop of Alexandria by the rise of Constantinople, and the vulnerability of the bishop of Constantinople to the kind of attack a bishop of Alexandria might launch against him.

The sources for the deposition of Chrysostom are good, but have very definite limitations. The principal texts are more or less hagiographical, and tend to personalize the narrative. Chrysostom's opponents are represented as villains. Their motivation is seen in terms of human resentment and jealousies. The ecclesiastical historians, Socrates and Sozomen, in accordance with the rules of their genre, say very little about secular politics—even where secular considerations are likely to have influenced ecclesiastical affairs. While both Socrates and Sozomen sympathize with Chrysostom, Socrates is the more detached, and has included material derived from the propaganda of Chrysostom's enemies. Sozomen wrote a little later than Socrates. His account is fuller, and frequently he seems to have tried to

---

[2] Soz. viii. 18.

[3] On Severianus see *RE* ii A (1930) s.v. Severianus 17; on Antiochus see *Dictionnaire d'histoire et de géographie ecclésiastique* iii. 707 s.v. Antiochus 6.

[4] Theodoret admired him: *HE* v. 27; source for *Historia Religiosa* 1313 C, 1324 B, 1344 D. In 398 Acacius went on an embassy to Rome to report the consecration of Chrysostom and to ask the pope to recognize Flavian as bishop of Antioch. At that time he must have favoured Chrysostom. See Ch. Piétri (1976) 1287.

[5] Soz. viii. 19.

supplement or correct his predecessor.[6] Palladius wrote his *Dialogue on the Life of John Chrysostom* not long after the events, of some of which he had been an eye witness. He probably wrote in exile at Syene in Egypt.[7] Theophilus is the villain of his history. Like the ecclesiastical historians he has little about secular politics. In fact he has gone further, and tried as far as possible to keep the empress out of the story (although he was aware of her role).[8] It must also be borne in mind that Palladius had few dates and does not always indicate the passage of time.[9] It is also important to remember that the *Dialogue* is not a narrative in chronological order, but is composed of thematic as well as chronological sections. The reader who wants to reconstruct how things really happened must constantly turn back or forward from one section to another. Palladius' narrative is selective. Fact and events have been omitted from both apologetic and literary motives. An argument from Palladius' silence is often a weak one. F. van Ommeslaeghe has recently drawn attention to the value of a hitherto neglected source, the biography of John Chrysostom by his contemporary 'Martyrius'. The reassessment of Socrates, Sozomen, and most of all Palladius which he has set in motion will only be completed when historians have studied and absorbed the new edition of 'Martyrius'.[10]

---

[6] Cf. F. van Ommeslaeghe (1979) and (1981), esp. 332.

[7] Palladius, *Dialogus de vita S. Joanni Chrysostomi* ed. P. R. Coleman-Norton (Cambridge, 1928); cf. E. D. Hunt (1973).

[8] *Dial.* 30 (p. 51): Chrysostom said to have called Eudoxia 'Jezebel'. But Palladius blames ladies of court rather than Eudoxia: ibid. 16 (p. 25), 27 (p. 45).

[9] Even Chrysostom's death is not dated.

[10] F. van Ommeslaeghe (1975), (1977) and the edition itself (1989).

18

The Three Bishops and Eudoxia

ANY analysis of the forces that brought down John Chrysostom must start with the group whom all sources show to have been the active organizers at Constantinople of the machinations to bring him down, the three bishops, Severianus, Antiochus, and Acacius, and the empress Eudoxia. The role of the bishops was that of a group of lobbyists determined, partly no doubt from personal motives, to keep the grievance of a much wider range of ecclesiastics before the eyes of the emperor and his ministers. Eudoxia performed the vital role of a link between the dissatisfied clerics and the palace.

Eudoxia's role was essential but its nature must be correctly understood. Eudoxia was a romantic figure, and this has led historians, both ancient and modern, to magnify her part in the politics of her time. The process was begun by the ecclesiastical historians describing the fall of Eutropius. According to Socrates, Sozomen, and most vividly Philostorgius, Eutropius fell because he had offended Eudoxia.[1] We have seen that opposition to Eutropius was vastly more widespread, and above all that Gainas and the army as a whole demanded his deposition and punishment.[2] The incident is a warning to historians to make allowance for the simplification and personalization that events tended to undergo when they were related by ecclesiastical historians.

It has often been stated that Eudoxia was a determined opponent of Gainas and a leader of an anti-barbarian party at Constantinople.[3] In fact there is not a word of explicit evidence for Eudoxia's attitude to this crisis. There is only evidence that she was on good terms with the men whom Gainas sent into exile in spring 400. She was said to have been on terms of extreme intimacy with the *comes* John, to the point that it was rumoured—certainly falsely—that he had fathered her son, who was to reign as Theodosius II.[4] Furthermore we hear that on returning from exile John and Aurelian influenced Eudoxia against Chrysostom and helped to bring about his downfall.[5] So the link was real enough, but it is pure conjecture to suppose that the link was

[1] e.g. K. Holum (1982a), Philostorg. xi. 6.
[2] See above, p. 104.
[3] E. Demougeot (1951) 221 ff.; but K. Holum (1982a) 68 ff. argues that for Eudoxia the issue was 'dynastic security and independence'.
[4] Zos. v. 18. Cf. ch. 21 n. 8.   [5] Zos. v. 23.

based on shared opposition to Germans. After all Eudoxia was of German parentage herself. The fact that she received the title Augusta on 9 January 400[6] at a time when Gainas and his army were inside Constantinople suggests that they had hopes of winning her support. But even if we assume the unproved proposition that Eudoxia was 'anti-German' it does not follow that she intervened actively in the military policy of the Empire. It is much more likely that this was firmly in the hands of the secular officials and their peers whom I have called the 'Arcadian establishment'. At the most she could have served as an intermediary between ministers and emperor.

As we have seen, the Christianization of the Roman aristocracy in the East and West offered new scope to aristocratic women who could employ their wealth, influence, and personal qualities in the service of the Church and of charitable work.[7] Eudoxia was a woman who made full use of these new opportunities. When Chrysostom became bishop she was one of a number of society ladies who helped his work. We have seen how empress and archbishop cooperated in the organization of nocturnal processions to counter demonstrations by the Arians.[8]

The development of the relationship of Eudoxia and Chrysostom cannot be reconstructed from the writings of Chrysostom or from the ecclesiastical historians alone. It requires the use of more questionable sources. Of these seemingly the most authentic is Mark the Deacon's *Life of Porphyry*, bishop of Gaza.[9] According to this *Life* Chrysostom had lost the favour of the empress in autumn 400 because he had criticized her because she had (like Jezebel) coveted and seized someone's private property.[10] In consequence Chrysostom was not in a position to help bishop Porphyry to obtain an imperial edict authorizing him to destroy pagan temples in his diocese. Even if this is true, the first loss of favour was not of long duration, for only a year later in winter and spring 402 Chrysostom had the full backing of the court for his drastic intervention in the affairs of the Churches of Asia.[11] But in any case it is difficult to reconcile Mark the Deacon's evidence that John had lost favour with the role he is known to have played in public affairs precisely at this time in autumn 400, after the destruction of the Goths in Constantinople.[12]

In fact, appearance notwithstanding, Mark the Deacon's *Life of Porphyry* seems to be a highly unreliable source. It purports to be the report of an eye witness and participant in the events described.

---

[6] *Chron. Pasch.* s.a. 400.   [7] See above, p. 141 ff.   [8] See above, p. 167.
[9] Edition, French translation, and commentary in H. Grégoire, H. Kugener (1930).
[10] *v. Porph.* 37. 15, with editor's note.
[11] See above, p. 171.   [12] See above, p. 191.

Unfortunately there is decisive evidence that it cannot be, most strikingly because it includes unacknowledged quotations from Theodoret's *Religious History* written about fifty years after the events described. In addition it contains errors of fact which it would be difficult for a Palestinian priest writing about his own time to commit.[13] It seems that we have to do with an example of a genre of late Roman writing, of which there are not a few examples, but which has not been studied systematically, the fictional biography of a saint, set in a more or less authentic historical context.[14] It may well be that the compiler of the *Life of Porphyry* did incorporate authentic contemporary material, but we cannot be sure that he did, or which parts of the *Life* are based on it. So the value of the *Life* lies in the vivid description of background detail that would have been as true at the time of the compiler as at that of John Chrysostom. Above all it is unique as an account of the kind of intrigue that must have been employed by many to get a reluctant emperor to issue an edict in their favour.[15] But we certainly cannot rely on it as an account of the origins of the break between Chrysostom and Eudoxia.

The same is true to an even greater extent of the *Lives of Chrysostom* written by Theodore of Trimithus about AD 680 and George of Alexandria about 700, who have elaborated the Jezebel allusion in Mark the Deacon into a full anecdote, which is only one of several illustrating Chrysostom's courageous efforts to restrain the rapacity of the empress.[16] G. Dagron has accepted the fundamental reality of this conflict, transferred it from the area of personality to that of politics, and used these passages as a foundation of his explanation of the conflict between Eudoxia and Chrysostom. In his view the real issue between them was the growth of Church property through donations by pious ladies which Chrysostom encouraged assiduously. According to Dagron Eudoxia maintained the rights of the state, whose resources were threatened by the growing economic power of the Church.[17] This will not do. Apart from the low value as evidence of the passages used to support it, the theory is anachronistic in that the growth of the wealth of the Church relative to that of the state was not seen as a problem early in fifth century.[18]

---

[13] See H. Grégoire, H. Kugener (1930) xxxiii–xliv.

[14] For an example of this see C. Mango (1984), cf. also likely *spuria* among sermons of Chrysostom sufficiently in character for their authorship to be in doubt.

[15] A. H. M. Jones *LRE* 344–6 makes the episode the centrepiece of his discussion of court intrigue. *Vita Melaniae* 11–13 has a closely comparable situation.

[16] F. Halkin (1977).

[17] G. Dagron (1974) 498–505.

[18] In the *Life of Porphyry* (for what it is worth) Eudoxia is totally indifferent to financial interests of state; see ch. 41.

Another political cause of the estrangement of the empress from the bishop has been put forward. K. Holum has argued that Chrysostom challenged Eudoxia's *basileia*, a new and more active political role for the empress which was being developed by and for the Augustae of the Theodosian dynasty and which Eudoxia is said to have exploited to enable her to take an open and active part in the government of the Empire.[19] Now there is practically no evidence that Eudoxia ever performed any of the public acts of government of a reigning emperor. The new role of the empress seems to have been a matter of ceremonial; as far as the exercise of power is concerned her role continued to be restricted to influence behind the scenes, the traditional sphere of women in Roman senatorial society. Moreover it cannot be shown that Chrysostom attacked the political role of the empress in any of the very numerous surviving sermons.[20]

Holum has cited 'You who are in the flesh make war against the incorporeal one, you who enjoy balls and perfumes, and sex with a male, do battle with the pure and untouched church.' Later in the same sermon Chrysostom likens himself to John the Baptist and Elias, and Eudoxia to Herodias and Jezebel. Holum is probably right to think that the sermon is genuine, but he has not given enough weight to the circumstance that it was spoken after John had been condemned at the Synod of the Oak, and was anticipating exile or worse. The sermon has all the defiance of a martyr's reply to the judge who has condemned him. It is extraordinarily militant and suggests that Chrysostom for a day or so contemplated the possibility of defying his condemnation, and refusing to go into exile. The references to Herodias and Jezebel imply that Chrysostom thought that his position was similar to that of Ambrose of Milan when he defended his church from being handed over to Arians on the order of the empress Justina.[21] The sermon should not be cited as evidence for a campaign against the political role of the empress before Chrysostom's condemnation.

Palladius, Socrates, and Sozomen agree that the incident which caused the decisive and finally irreparable break between Chrysostom and Eudoxia was a particular sermon against vices of women generally, in which the empress was not named, but which was reported to her as if she had been.[22] This misrepresentation was not totally unjust. Chrysostom was already engaged in conflict with

[19] K. Holum (1982a) 70–8.
[20] The recorded attacks on the empress, whether the veiled attack of Socr. vi. 15—was this when he mentioned Jezebel, Pall. *Dial.* 8 (p. 50–51)?—or the open ones of Socr. vi. 18, have nothing to do with her political role. Chrysostom was angry at slights to himself.
[21] Ambrose *Ep.* 20. Rioting delays exile by three days: Soz. viii. 18; Socr. vi. 15.
[22] Socr. vi. 15; Soz. viii. 16.

Theophilus of Alexandria, and was angry that Eudoxia had, as he believed, encouraged Theophilus' ally Epiphanius in an intrigue to have Chrysostom declared a heretic.[23] But what had annoyed Chrysostom was not the political role of the empress, but behaviour which in other circumstances he might have praised extravagantly, namely her hospitality towards a visiting ecclesiastic. Eudoxia playing her approved role of patroness of churchmen had given the benefit of her protection to an enemy of Chrysostom.

The full story of the estrangement between Eudoxia and Chrysostom cannot be written. Conjectures are possible. A relationship between two extremely strong-willed and at the same time hypersensitive personalities was bound to be difficult. Besides, there was an element of ambiguity in the empress's position when seen through the eyes of an ascetic. Eudoxia was a committed Christian and her role religious, pious, and charitable. But the symbolic expression of her role was through elaborate dress, jewels, and court ceremony, including a retinue of gorgeously dressed women. In other words the ceremonial magnification of the empress could be said to emphasize and develop that worldly and frivolous aspect of female nature that Chrysostom had berated in so many sermons.[24]

[23] Soz. viii. 14–15.
[24] e.g. *Hom. VIII ad Tim. 1.* (PG lxii. 539–44).

19
Theophilus

THE factor which made Chrysostom's quarrel with Eudoxia so dangerous for himself was that he was already involved in a dispute with the powerful Theophilus, bishop of Alexandria. We have seen that bishops of Alexandria were chronically worried by the widening influence of the see of Constantinople. Theophilus had tried to prevent the election of Chrysostom and to bring about the election of Isidore, one of his own clergy, instead. He seems to have become reconciled to Chrysostom's election, for the two bishops combined to send Isidore on a diplomatic mission to Rome to get the pope to recognize Flavian as bishop of Antioch.[1] The initiative succeeded. Theophilus was an exceedingly violent prelate, but in the conflict with Chrysostom he does not seem to have taken the initiative.

The conflict started as an internal matter of the Egyptian church. In a dispute between the majority of the monks of Egypt who insisted that God had human form, and a minority of intellectuals who held that God must be incorporeal as had been argued by Origen, Theophilus thought it politic to take the side of the majority. With the support of an episcopal synod meeting at Alexandria, he condemned the Tall Brothers as followers of Origen. He then proceeded to organize an attack on their monasteries and to drive them out. The fugitives first tried to settle in Palestine, but Theophilus had them expelled from there also. In the end the refugees, by now reduced to fifty, sailed to Constantinople, hoping that the emperor would arrange for their case to be tried. At Constantinople everybody knew that to support the monks meant a conflict with the bishop of Alexandria, something not to be undertaken lightly. So Chrysostom allowed them to pray in churches of Constantinople but did not admit them to communion.[2] They managed to meet the empress while she was out driving in her carriage, and Eudoxia promised that she would cause a council to be convened before which Theophilus would be summoned.[3] But no immediate action followed. The monks came to Constantinople in autumn 400.[4] The summons to Theophilus seems to have been issued in summer 402, nearly two years later.[5]

---

[1] Pall. *Dial.* 22–4; Socr. vi. 7, 13; Soz. viii. 11–12; J. N. D. Kelly (1975) 243–5, 259–61.
[2] *Dial.* 24–5; Socr. vi. 9; Soz. viii. 13.   [3] *Dial.* 26.   [4] K. Holl (1928) 327.
[5] Jerome *Ep.* 98, translating Theophilus' Easter letter of 402, has no reference to the summons.

In autumn 400–401, of course, emperor and bishop had more urgent preoccupations. This was when Gainas was operating in Thrace,[6] and a year later Chrysostom was deeply involved in the ecclesiastical affairs of the diocese of Asia.[7] It was only after Chrysostom's return from Asia in spring 402 that Theophilus was summoned.

Meanwhile there was diplomatic activity. The Tall Brothers continued to press their grievances—not with immediate success. The pastoral circular sent out by Theophilus at Easter 402[8] mentions that the Tall Brothers are canvassing the powerful at Contantinople. Theophilus himself was sufficiently worried to offer to forgive the monks.[9] There is no hint that the monks' efforts had met with any success so far.

Not very long after, the Tall Brothers petitioned the empress while the imperial couple were attending a service in the church of St John the Baptist.[10] If this was on the festival of the patron saint it was on 24 June. [11] The imperial reply was that Theophilus would be summoned to Constantinople to be tried by Chrysostom, while the accusers from Egypt would be required to substantiate their charges against the Tall Brothers before a secular court.[12] The accusers sent by Theophilus were put in court to prove their charges or to face punishment for false accusation.[13] They were eventually condemned.[14] An official was sent to fetch Theophilus to Constantinople.[15] Theophilus was in no hurry; in fact he did not appear at Constantinople for another year.

But he did not waste the time. He was in a very serious situation, and fought ruthlessly and skilfully to get out of it. Theophilus could not attack the emperor who had ordered him to stand trial, but he could discredit the proposed judge, Chrysostom. So he proceeded to smear Chrysostom with the charge which he had brought against the monks whom Chrysostom seemed to be supporting, the charge of holding the heretical views of Origen. Chrysostom's links with so many former associates of the Tall Brothers made the charge more plausible. Theophilus had an ally in the very old and widely revered Epiphanius, bishop of Salamis in Cyprus, an enthusiastic pursuer of

[6] See above, p. 118.

[7] Alan Cameron (1987) 349–50 with ref. to *PG* lii. 421 (Latin) and A. Wenger, 'L'homélie de saint Jean Chrysostome à son retour d'Asie', *REB* xix (1961) 110–23 (Greek text).

[8] Jerome *Ep.* 98.   [9] Ibid. 98. 23.

[10] *Dial.* 26 (p. 43. 10).   [11] P. C. Baur (1929–30) ii. 184.

[12] *Dial.* 26 (p. 43. 14).   [13] Ibid. (p. 43. 15).

[14] Ibid. pp. 43. 21 ff. Photius *Bibl.* 59. 18 a, 18 b, 19 a: Chrysostom charged with having caused imprisonment of the accusers of the Tall Brothers.

[15] *Dial.* p. 43. 19.

heresy who was motivated by obsessive hostility to the teachings of Origen. Theophilus had induced him to hold a synod in Cyprus to condemn Origenism, and to publicize its decrees on the mainland of Asia Minor.[16] Then he urged Epiphanius to travel to Constantinople, to proclaim the condemnation of Origen before an assembly of bishops and clergy, and to involve Chrysostom in the charges against the Tall Brothers whom he was said to be protecting. Epiphanius travelled to Constantinople, and once there proceeded to boycott Chrysostom as if he was tainted with heresy. But he won over neither the empress[17] nor the emperor. Eventually he abandoned his scheme. He died on the way back to Cyprus on 12 May 403.[18] It is evident that at this point the authorities were still backing Chrysostom.

But this was about to change. As we have seen, Socrates and Sozomen link Chrysostom's loss of favour with a sermon he preached against the vices of women, shortly after the departure of Epiphanius.[19] This was widely understood as a veiled attack on the empress and was brought to her notice by enemies of the bishop.[20] That audiences were in the habit of reading between the lines of sermons, we know from the fact that some of Chrysostom's very generalized criticisms of the rich was understood as criticism of the behaviour of particular individuals, who recognized themselves in the bishop's description, and stayed away from church. Since the text of the sermon has been lost we cannot now judge how provocative it was. But whatever the character of the sermon, Socrates and Sozomen are agreed on its consequences. Eudoxia complained to the emperor that Chrysostom had deliberately attacked her, and requested that Theophilus should be summoned to hold a council to try John. According to Socrates, and less explicitly Sozomen[21] the emperor agreed to his wife's request. If they are right, it was at this point, i.e. soon after the departure of Epiphanius in May 403, that Chrysostom's fate was decided, and the sermon was the principal cause why the emperor made up his mind to back not John, but his enemies.

But Palladius' very much fuller and more circumstantial version suggests that the ecclesiastical historians have simplified the story. He confirms that the sermon was strongly resented. In fact it came to form the basis of a charge of treason.[22] But according to Palladius the emperor convoked a council because at this point he still intended Theophilus to be tried, and not because he had decided on a trial of Chrysostom. It was only after Theophilus had arrived at

[16] Jerome *Ep.* 90.
[17] Soz. viii. 15.
[18] *RE* vi. 193 s.v. Epiphanius 3.
[19] Socr. vi. 15; Soz. viii. 16.
[20] 'Martyrius' 480 a–b, cited by F. van Ommeslaeghe (1979) 150.
[21] Socr. vi. 15; Soz. viii. 16.
[22] *Dial.* 30 (p. 50. 25).

Constantinople and rallied Chrysostom's many enemies in autumn 403[23] that Arcadius turned against Chrysostom. Palladius' version is supported by a letter of Chrysostom to Pope Innocent I in which he related that on the arrival of Theophilus at Constantinople, Arcadius had asked him to investigate the charges against the bishop of Alexandria. This Chrysostom had refused to do, since it was not proper for a bishop to be tried outside his province.[24] It was only after that, that Theophilus won over the clergy of Constantinople, and began to draw up charges against Chrysostom.[25]

The narrative of the letter is elaborated in Palladius' main narrative. First Theophilus and his supporters gained widespread support. Then they drew up a list of charges. Finally they petitioned the emperor to order Chrysostom to appear before Theophilus' synod.[26] Their petition was granted, for when Theophilus' synod of bishops met[27] and summoned Chrysostom, the summons was brought by an imperial notary,[28] and its judgement was enforced by an *agens in rebus*.[29] Chrysostom had the support of forty bishops,[30] but since the emperor supported the other side this was no use to him at all.

There are very strong reasons for preferring Palladius' version to that of Socrates and Sozomen. But if we reject the version of Socrates and Sozomen, it becomes necessary to suggest an alternative motive for the change of imperial policy. I would suggest that the motive was provided by the widespread and powerful hostility to Chrysostom both at Constantinople and in the provinces of Asia.[31] Theophilus was extremely skilful at fanning and exploiting this latent hostility. He arranged to arrive at Constantinople in autumn 403 some time after the grain fleet from Alexandria[32] so that he would find a crowd of Egyptian supporters in the city. He had travelled at least the last part of the journey from Lycia by land[33] rallying opponents of Chrysostom in Asia. When he reached Chalcedon he was already followed by many bishops.[34] Eventually he was to achieve a following of 36 (or 45) bishops at the Synod of the Oak.[35] At Constantinople he spent the next three weeks canvassing for further support and gathering material which could form the basis for formal accusations

---

[23] Not dated in sources. Autumn 430 according to P. C. Baur (1929–30) ii. 202.

[24] *Dial.* 9 (pp. 9. 16 ff.).   [25] Ibid. pp. 9. 25 ff.

[26] *Dial.* 27 (pp. 44.19–45. 25); also 'Martyrius', quoted by F. van Ommeslaeghe (1979) 150–1.

[27] *Dial.* 29 (p. 48. 18): 36 bishops from Egypt; 12 (pp. 16. 15–17): 29 bishops from Egypt, 7 from elsewhere; Photius *Bibl.* 59. 19 b: 46 bishops.

[28] *Dial.* 29 (p. 49. 28).   [29] *Dial.* 9 (p. 11): the *curiosus* of the city.

[30] *Dial.* 29.   [31] See below, p. 208 ff.   [32] Soz. viii. 16, cf. 14.

[33] Soz. viii. 14; P. C. Baur (1929–30) ii. 198; Pall. *Dial.* 29. 14. According to 'Martyrius', reported by F. van Ommeslaeghe (1977) 402, he travelled by land all the way.

[34] Soz. viii. 14, Socr. vi. 15.

[35] *Dial.* 12, 28: 36 bishops; Photius *Bibl.* 59: 45 bishops.

at the trial of Chrysostom. He joined forces with three provincial bishops, Severianus of Gabala, Antiochus of Ptolemais, and Acacius of Beroea, whom Chrysostom had antagonized and who seem to have resided almost permanently in the capital. Eugraphia, a great lady and friend of Eudoxia, offered her home for meetings of the faction. Two deacons whom Chrysostom had expelled from the church,[36] as well as Isaac, the revered leader of monks at Constantinople, furnished accusations.[37] They won over Chrysostom's archdeacon and through him a great part of the clergy at Constantinople. In his letter to Innocent Chrysostom even used the word 'all'.[38] Among the supporters of Theophilus were the two men who were to succeed John as bishop of Constantinople, Arsacius, brother of John's predecessor, and Atticus, who was to be highly respected as bishop.[39] Support for Chrysostom's enemies was evidently growing like an avalanche. In the circumstances the very considerable support which Chrysostom retained among the episcopate[40] and the general public of Constantinople could easily be overlooked. It might appear that he was doomed. At the same time Theophilus managed to make his peace with the surviving Tall Brothers.[41] After this it would have been extremely difficult to bring charges against Theophilus. In these circumstances I would suggest that his counsellors advised Arcadius to abandon the case against Theophilus and to support proceedings aimed at deposing Chrysostom. His own clergy were against him. He had not shown respect for the imperial dignity. In spite of his holiness and his eloquence it seemed sensible to drop him. So Theophilus was authorized to preside over a trial of Chrysostom and to condemn him. In the event Chrysostom refused to appear before the synod and was condemned in his absence. Theophilus had achieved his objective, the exiling of Chrysostom, in a way in which it could not have been achieved without him. It is, however, significant that Theophilus played no part in the second half of the story of the fall of Chrysostom. Chrysostom was recalled a very short time after he had gone into exile. The recall provoked riots and street fighting. This induced Theophilus to return to Alexandria. While he was to write a violent invective against Chrysostom, he watched from Alexandria the rest of the campaign against him. Chrysostom had enough enemies at Constantinople. Theophilus' presence was no longer needed.[42]

[36] *Dial.* 27, see also 21.

[37] *Dial.* 21 (p. 34. 6); cf. G. Dagron (1970) 229–76, esp. 262 ff.   [38] *Dial.* 9 (p. 9. 27).

[39] Photius *Bibl.* 59. 19 a.   [40] See above, p. 206 n. 30.

[41] Soz. viii. 16: agreement before trial. Socr. vi. 16: Theophilus took communion with the monks immediately after deposition of Chrysostom.

[42] For full account see W. Liebeschuetz (1985*a*).

20

Clerical Opposition in Constantinople and in Neighbouring Provinces

THEOPHILUS would not have succeeded in mobilizing so formidable an attack on Chrysostom if there had not been a great deal of latent hostility. After so many generations have felt sympathy and admiration for the personality of John Chrysostom, it is difficult to believe that he was disliked by many of his contemporaries, and not only the wicked, jealous, or ambitious. But there is plenty of evidence of hostility among the clergy of Constantinople and neighbouring provinces. These were the people whom the four dissident bishops could most easily organize into a pressure group against their bishop. The charges brought against Chrysostom at the Synod of the Oak show that his ecclesiastical administration had been extremely contentious. He had—so it was claimed—unjustly dismissed a deacon for striking a servant.[1] He had been abusive of some of his clergy, describing them as dishonourable, corrupt, capable of anything, and not worth three obols.[2] He had written a slanderous pamphlet bringing his clergy into disrepute.[3] He had allowed clerics to be tried in public courts and to die in prison.[4] A number of charges concern his financial administration.[5] To most of us the charges seem trivial, as they did to contemporaries at Rome.[6] But this does not mean that they seemed trivial to the clergy of Constantinople: in fact one can be sure that Theophilus and the other bishops masterminding the trial would not have accepted (or perhaps helped to compile)[7] this particular charge-sheet, unless they had thought that it would win them support and do damage to Chrysostom. It is clear even from the sympathetic accounts of the ecclesiastical historians and Palladius that Chrysostom's government of the Church of Constantinople left many people discontented. He was a strict disciplinarian. He expelled a considerable number of clerics from the Church. He appointed the

---

[1] Photius *Bibl.* 59. 18 a. 1: charge 1.
[2] Ibid. 18 a. 24: charge 5.　　　　[3] Ibid. 18 a. 13: charge 8.
[4] Ibid. 18 a. 31: charge 10; also 18 a. 2: charge 2; 19 a. 22: Isaac's charge 15.
[5] Ibid: charges 3, 4, 16, 17.　　　　[6] Pall. *Dial.* 12 (pp. 16, 18).
[7] *Dial.* 27 (p. 45): many charges are in area of 'personnel management'.

stern and unpopular deacon Serapion as his second in command.[8] He tried to prevent the clergy from living under the same roof with their housekeepers, usually dedicated virgins of good family.[9] This arrangement was evidently widespread. It seems to have been related to the ideals of Eustathius of Sebaste one of the leaders of the ascetic movement in Asia Minor.[10] In this branch of the monastic movement women sought to overcome the distinctiveness of their sex by themselves becoming as much as possible like sexless men, cutting their hair, wearing masculine clothing, and sometimes living in mixed monasteries of men and women.[11] The chaste cohabitation of male and female couples was another way in which ascetics could achieve a state in which 'there is neither male nor female'.[12] Eustathius of Sebaste was a close ally of Macedonius,[13] Arian bishop of Constantinople, and patron of an Eustathian form of monasticism in the city.[14] The συνείσακτοι, were therefore well established at Constantinople, and Chrysostom's attempt to suppress them caused widespread indignation.[15] So, right at the start of his episcopate, he was involved in a controversy which was related to the much more serious conflict he was to have with the monks of Constantinople.[16]

Chrysostom had overhauled the finances of the Church of Constantinople in a way that was resented. He personally intervened regularly in the way the funds of the Church were spent.[17] He checked the extent to which the clergy kept the offerings of the faithful. There is no evidence to assess how far he was trying to subordinate the minor churches to the Great Church of Constantinople—if such was his aim at all.[18] He certainly cut expenditure in the bishop's household and transferred the money saved to the upkeep of a hospital. Presumably this caused redundancies among the household staff, as the men dismissed from the household were not necessarily the same as the doctors, cooks, and celibate workers whom he appointed to the hospital.[19] He abolished episcopal banquets, which had provided perquisites for the church's stewards

---

[8] Socr. vi. 4.

[9] *Dial.* 20. The two surviving pamphlets on this problem, *PG* xlvii. 496 ff., edition and French translation: J. Dumortier, *Les cohabitations suspectes, comment observer la virginité* (Paris, 1955), seem to have been written at Antioch.

[10] R. Albrecht (1986) 174 ff., E. Patlagean (1976).

[11] J. Anson (1974).   [12] Galatians 4: 28.

[13] Jerome *De viris illustr.* iii. 80: alliance of Basil of Ancyra, Eustathius of Sebaste, and Macedonius.

[14] Soz. iv. 24, cf. 10 (1174 A).

[15] Pall. *Dial.* 19 (p. 31), G. Dagron (1974) 514 n. 2, on Photius *Bibl.* 59. 18 a. 13: charge 8.

[16] See below, p. 210.

[17] Photius *Bibl.* 59. 18 a. 28: charge 17.

[18] G. Dagron (1974) 498.

[19] Pall. *Dial.* 20 (pp. 32. 9 ff.).

(οἰκουροί).[20] Chrysostom gave very high priority to helping the poor. He refused to use marble which his predecessors had bought for the decoration of the Holy Apostles, and sold it.[21] He also sold many valuable items from the treasury of the church.[22] The men who had looked after finance under his predecessor considered this irresponsible and improvident—or worse. At any rate, both items figured among the charges at the Synod of the Oak, and Arsacius, brother of the late bishop Nectarius, gave evidence against John on the charge of selling valuables.[23] Chrysostom was accused of having sold an inheritance left to the Church by a lady called Thecla[24] and also failing to produce accounts for his expenditure of ecclesiastical revenues.[25] It is obvious that there was great dissatisfaction with the financial side of Chrysostom's administration.

Hostility to John Chrysostom was by no means restricted to members of his clergy. There is evidence that the monks of Constantinople were to a large extent against him. We have no satisfactory account of the origin of this antagonism, because the fact of it was as embarrassing to Palladius as an apologist for Chrysostom, as it was to the biographers of the monks Isaac and Hypatius, who wrote after John had been rehabilitated.[26] Nevertheless, there can be no question about the hostile attitude of the Constantinopolitan monks.[27]

Palladius described Isaac as the leader of false monks, who spent all his time abusing bishops, and as one of the principal conspirators against John.[28] In fact Isaac was very unlikely to represent only himself when he took so prominent a part in the attack on Chrysostom.[29] At the trial Isaac produced his own list of seventeen charges,[30] and he was one of the men who brought the final summons for John to appear before the Synod.[31] One of the charges was that

[20] Pall. *Dial.* 40 (p. 70. 5).
[21] Photius *Bibl.* 59. 18. 5: charge 4.
[22] Ibid. 18 a. 4: charge 3. Church treasures checked after John's second exile: *Dial.* 13.
[23] Ibid. 19 a. 34.   [24] Ibid. 18 a. 27: charge 16.
[25] Ibid. 18 a. 20: charge 17.
[26] G. Karo and other pupils of F. Buecheler, eds. *Callinicus, Vita S. Hypatii* (Leipzig, 1895) xiii–xv proved that Isaac the enemy of Chrysostom was identical with the father of monasticism at Constantinople. AD 383, which according to the *Vita Isaacii, AASS* May, vii. 258 d was the year of Isaac's death, was the year when his successor Dalmatius entered the monastery. Isaac almost certainly died after 3. 12. 415, for he was buried in Aurelian's *martyrium* of St Stephen, which could hardly have been built before the body had been found. On this E. D. Hunt (1982a) 211–18 and Alan Cameron and others (1989). But the Novatians had a church of St Stephen in 404 (Soz. viii. 24).
[27] See the important G. Dagron (1970), esp. 263.
[28] *Dial.* 21.
[29] On *Vita Isaacii, AASS* May, vii, see R. Snee (1985).
[30] Photius *Bibl.* 59 (18 b. 33 ff.).   [31] *Dial.* 40.

Chrysostom had caused a lot of unpleasantness to Isaac personally.[32] Sozomen explains the cause of this hostility:

John had several disputes with many of the monks, particularly with Isaac. He highly commended those who remained in quietude in the monasteries and practised philosophy there . . . but the monks who went out of doors and made their appearance in the city he reproached and regarded as insulting philosophy. For these causes he incurred the hatred of the clergy and of many of the monks, who called him a hard, passionate, morose, and arrogant man. They therefore attempted to bring his life into disrepute, by stating confidently that he would 'eat with no-one, and that he refused every invitation to a meal'.[33]

It is significant that while our sources mention Isaac as leader of the false monks they do not mention any corresponding leader of the good monks. The ascetics belonging to John's party, that is, Olympias and her home of dedicated virgins,[34] the Gothic monks living on the property that had belonged to Promotus,[35] and the Tall Brothers and their sympathizers[36] were, none of them, typical Constantinopolitans. There were no mass demonstrations by monks in favour of Chrysostom to compare with the violent rioting of monks to prevent his return from his first exile.[37] It is also significant that one of Chrysostom's principal enemies among the bishops was Acacius of Beroea, a Syrian like Isaac, and an ex-monk highly respected by the monks of his native province. When Chrysostom was on his way into exile, he was actually attacked by monks as he was staying at Caesarea in Cappadocia.[38] There is every reason to believe that 'the monks' were against Chrysostom.

Unfortunately we have no account written from the monks' point of view. Most of the monks were probably illiterate, and if literate, were not concerned with writing. The oldest hagiographic source, Callinicus' *Life of Hypatius*, written about 447–50,[39] i.e. after the rehabilitation of Chrysostom, is carefully neutral between Isaac and Chrysostom. Each is given a paragraph of praise. Not a word is said of the conflict between them, or of any part that Hypatius himself

[32] Photius *Bibl.* 59 (19a. 28).

[33] Soz. viii. 9, translation by C. D. Hartrauft in vol. 2 of the Postnicene Fathers series.

[34] A.-M. Malingrey, ed. *Jean Chrysostome, Lettres à Olympias et la Vie anonyme d'Olympias* (Paris, 1968) 418 ff.

[35] John Chrys. *Ep.* 5, 14, 207.

[36] Soz. viii. 11 ff.; Socr. vi. 7; Pall. *Dial.* 23 ff. Bibliography: G. Dagron (1970) 259 n. 152. Doctrines and intellectual background: A. Guillaumont (1962).

[37] T. E. Gregory (1973) 61–83.

[38] John Chrys. *Ep.* 14. 2.

[39] G. J. M. Bartellink, *Callinicos, Vie d'Hypatios*, Sources Chrétiennes 177 (Paris, 1971) 11–12.

might have played in those troubles.[40] Incidentally the early part of the *Life* amply illustrates the informality of monasticism at Constantinople around 400, and this helps to explain the antagonism between those uncontrolled monks and their administratively active bishop. In his Constantinopolitan writings Chrysostom occasionally mentions monks with approval. But the references are not to urban monks. The monks are described as 'those of the hills',[41] the 'brothers of the hills',[42] 'those who dwell in the mountains',[43] 'those who have embraced life in the desert'.[44] The passages look like nostalgic memories of the hermits of the hills on the desert edge around Antioch.[45] He says nothing either in praise or blame that might be applicable to monks roaming the streets of the capital.

So the history of the conflict between Chrysostom and the monks of Constantinople has to rely heavily on the passages of Sozomen already cited and some inferences based on scraps of very interesting but totally inadequate evidence on the nature of monasticism at Constantinople. Dagron has pointed out that monasticism at Constantinople was started by Eleusius and Marathonius, assistants of the semi-Arian bishop Macedonius, and was strongly influenced by the ideas of Eustathius of Sebaste. It had features which some contemporaries, and certainly the leaders of the more disciplined and controlled monasticism of later years, found discreditable. The theology might be semi-Arian.[46] Some monasteries contained both men and women. There was little discipline. Monks moved in and out of monasteries, changed monasteries, retired from monastic life almost as it pleased themselves, certainly without reference to any ecclesiastical authority. They wandered among the urban population. They had a strong social conscience.[47] While the founders and financial supporters of monasteries belonged to the official class the bulk of the monks were ordinary people, who like much of the population of the city were recent arrivals from the provinces.[48]

One can see that the monks might be considered a threat to public order—indeed they were. They also offered a challenge to any bishop

---

[40] G. J. M. Bartellink, *Callinicos, Vie d'Hypatios*, 11.

[41] *Hom. VII. 4 in Act. Apost.* (PG lx. 68).

[42] *Hom. XIII. 4 in Act. Apost.* (PG lx. 110).   [43] *Hom. X. 4 in Hebr.* (PG lxiii. 87).

[44] *Hom. XXXIV. 3 in Hebr.* (PG lxiii. 236).

[45] But Isaac and the bishops Antiochus, Severianus, and Acacius were all Syrians.

[46] Soz. iv. 27; an example: ibid. ix. 2. The Macedonian origin of Constantinopolitan monasticism is surely the reason why so little was remembered about it. Maybe the real importance of Isaac lay in that he was an Orthodox follower of the Nicaean creed (Soz. vi. 40) and that he persuaded other monks to accept it too. Episcopal discipline was another matter.

[47] On 'Eustathian' monsticism at Constantinople see G. Dagron (1970), J. Gribomont (1957). For a description of monastic life see Callinicus, *Life of Hypatius*, editions cited nn.26 and 39 above.   [48] G. Dagron (1970) 255.

who took a monarchical view of the government of his Church. After all they were largely outside his jurisdiction. Sozomen suggests that this was precisely the point where they clashed with Chrysostom. The behaviour of the monks at Constantinople did not correspond to what Chrysostom thought proper. He tried to confine monks to monasteries and to subject them to the control of their bishop. This provoked resentment. Dagron goes as far as to interpret Chrysostom's charitable foundations as an attempt to transfer welfare work from monks to the episcopal Church.[49] There is no evidence for this motive. That the monks of Constantinople maintained hospitals or other social institutions is an inference from what is known of the monks of Eustathius of Sebaste. But Chrysostom's own passionate interest in helping the poor went back to his Antioch days and was certainly not simply a reaction to the charitable works of the monks of Constantinople.[50]

It is difficult to estimate the importance of Chrysostom's conflict with the monks since we know so little about their numbers and influence. According to Callinicus there existed crowds of monasteries in and around Constantinople, each with around 150 monks, at the turn of the century.[51] If this was so, a conflict between monks and bishops would cause endless disturbances of a kind which would seriously worry the administration. We know that the opposition of the monks of Constantinople was to contribute significantly to the fall of Nestorius thirty years later.[52] We simply lack the evidence to assert that the monks' contribution to the fall of Chrysostom was comparable. But it is likely.

The disaffected monks certainly were natural allies of Theophilus, and therefore made his task of building up opposition to Chrysostom much easier. Just as Chrysostom was the natural protector of the Tall Brothers, the intellectual monks of Egypt, so Theophilus was the natural ally of the ordinary monks of Constantinople. After all, he seems to have quite deliberately chosen to side with the un-sophisticated.[53]

It is certainly not a coincidence that two of the most prominent laymen among the opponents of John Chrysostom, the general Saturninus,[54] and Aurelian,[55] twice praetorian prefect, had close links with the monk Isaac. Saturninus had given him the land for his first cell, and indeed built the cell itself.[56] Aurelian arranged for Isaac to be buried in the *martyrium* of Stephen which he had built.[57] Perhaps the

[49] G. Dagron (1970) 264.
[50] P. C. Baur (1929–30) i. 312–16; R. Brändle (1979).
[51] *V. Hypatii* 11. 1.
[52] T. E. Gregory (1979) 129–43.
[53] Soz. viii. 11.
[54] *PLRE* i s.v. Saturninus 10; his widow continued the enmity.
[55] Ibid. s.v. Aurelianus 3.
[56] *V. Isaacii* 4. 11.
[57] Ibid. 4. 18.

body of Isaac was a substitute for relics of the body of Stephen himself which Aurelian had failed to obtain.[58] The ability of monks to combine with ordinary people to make an extremely powerful pressure group had already been demonstrated in the events leading to the abdication from the see of Constantinople of Gregory of Nazianzus.[59] In antagonizing the monks Chrysostom had made formidable enemies.

Chrysostom's clerical enemies were unfortunately not restricted to Constantinople and its immediate environs. In the first quarter of 402[60] John travelled to Ephesus in answer to an invitation by the local clergy, and proceeded to exercise patriarchal authority in the ecclesiastical province of Asia in a way which was unprecedented, and extremely controversial.[61] Since the Council of Constantinople of 381 the bishop of Constantinople had enjoyed a 'seniority of honour' second only to that of the bishop of Rome,[62] but he had no unambiguously recognized regular jurisdiction even over the bishops of the cities of the diocese in which Constantinople was situated, Thrace,[63] let alone the bishops of the diocese of Asia. The outcome was certainly dramatic. Invited to consecrate a new bishop of Ephesus, Chrysostom travelled to Ephesus and convoked a council of seventy bishops.[64] He also expelled Novatian and Quartodeciman sectarians from a number of churches.[65] Finally, on his way home, he replaced the bishop of Nicomedia in the diocese of Pontus.[66] Chrysostom was asserting the disciplinary authority of the bishop of Constantinople over the bishops of neighbouring dioceses.[67] It is clear that he did this with the full consent and backing of the emperor. For he was able to offer deposed bishops the consolation that they would probably receive immunity from curial service,[68] a privilege which would require the imperial signature. Moreover, only the emperor could provide any armed force needed to enforce the decisions of Chrysostom's synod. The depositions and consecrations

[58] Alan Cameron and others (1989) cite extract from an otherwise unpublished Life of Isaac cited by F. Nau in *Revue de l'orient chrétien* xi (1906) 199 ff.

[59] G. Dagron (1970) 262; Greg. Naz. *Ep.* 77. 1.

[60] For date see Alan Cameron (1987), correcting P. C. Baur (1929–30) ii. 127. Chrysostom was away over 100 days, returning soon after Easter. See *Oratio post reditum* (PG lii. 421).

[61] G. Dagron (1974) 466–9.   [62] Mansi iii. 560.

[63] G. Dagron (1974) 458–9.

[64] Pall. *Dial.* 47 (p. 82): 16 bishops deposed, according to Theophilus; Soz. viii. 6: 13 bishops; *Dial.* 47 (p. 83. 6): 6 bishops.

[65] Socr. viii. 11.

[66] Soz. viii. 6. Pansophius, former tutor of Eudoxia, was appointed.

[67] According to Soz. viii. 6 bishops were deposed in Lycia, Phrygia, and Asia, as well as Nicomedia in Pontus.

[68] Pall. *Dial.* 51 (p. 51. 16).

decided at Ephesus angered and worried very many people. Citizens naturally resented the imposition of a bishop. The Nicomedians wanted Gerontius back,[69] and there were riots against Heraclides, the newly appointed bishop of Ephesus.[70] Bishops must have been deeply worried by such empire-building on the part of the bishop of Constantinople. Where would it end? Events showed that many bishops did become hostile to Chrysostom. For the time being the emperor was with Chrysostom, but perhaps not wholeheartedly: after all, a year earlier he had prevented Chrysostom from going to Ephesus to depose its bishop.[71] But if Chrysostom were ever to lose imperial support his unpopularity with many bishops would be extremely serious. After all, the future of an accused bishop would be decided by his fellow bishops sitting in synod.[72]

Chrysostom's way of life did not help to reconcile those he had alienated. He preferred solitude to sociability. He evidently made a habit of dining alone.[73] His motives were admirable: to spend the Church's money on any other object than the poor was sacrilege.[74] He was of course very busy. In addition to carrying out his duties as an administrator and preacher with extreme conscientiousness he was also a prolific writer. No doubt he thought he had better uses for his time than communal dining. Furthermore, as a result of prolonged asceticism in his youth he had acquired a weak stomach which could not stand elaborate food. The fact remains that his dining habits made it much more difficult for people, whether clergy or laymen, to meet him. This was bound to cause resentment. People expected to be able to meet their bishop in order to call on his assistance and patronage.[75] Patronage was required of a bishop. Moreover conversation over a meal has always been a good way of discussing contentious situations, and calming passions aroused by them. Chrysostom's zeal produced lots of such situations, but his way of life made it more difficult to discuss them with the people involved. His aversion to sociability was listed among the accusations of the Synod of the Oak, and Palladius felt obliged to include a very long defence of it in his *Dialogue*.[76] The solitary habits of Chrysostom made it easier for the

[69] Soz. viii. 6.
[70] Socr. vi. 11 (alternative version). He was a pupil of Evagrius Ponticus and a former monk of Scetis (Soz. viii. 6), and therefore close to the 'Tall Brothers'.
[71] Pall. *Dial.* 49 (p. 86. 22).
[72] Mansi iii. 560–64; V. Grumel, *Les regestes des actes du patriarchat de Constantinople* (Istanbul 1932–   ) i. 4, no. 5.
[73] Photius *Bibl.* 59 (18 b): charge 25; Pall. *Dial.* 39–45 is a lengthy defence.
[74] *Dial.* 40 (p. 70. 4).
[75] A. H. M. Jones *LRE* 915. On the use and abuse of meals and other forms of social intercourse between governor and governed, see Lib. *Or.* 51 and 52.
[76] See n. 73 above.

visiting bishops and Theophilus to isolate him and to organize a strong pressure group for his deposition, and indeed to turn a large part of the clergy of Constantinople against him.[77]

Now the existence of a large body of ecclesiastical opinion, including a significant number of bishops, was something the imperial government would take into account. In accordance with a tradition going back to Constantine, Christian emperors felt responsibility for the discipline and unity of the Church, but preferred to base their policy on the advice of ecclesiastics, and especially of councils of bishops.[78] If it happened that the Church spoke with two voices, it was left to the emperor to decide which to support and enforce. This was the situation in the case of Chrysostom. The Church was divided. The bishop of Constantinople had fervent supporters as well as determined opponents. The emperor had to make up his mind between them. In a situation like this he would consult with his officials, especially those who would be concerned with enforcement of any decision reached.[79] Unless the emperor was a man of strong personality, holding strong views on the issue concerned, the opinions of the great secular officials were obviously going to be very influential. Arcadius was not a strong emperor, and on the subject of Chrysostom he seems to have been uncertain what course to follow. So the advice of the officials is likely to have been decisive.

[77] *Dial.* 9 (p. 8. 27).
[78] J. Gaudemet (1958) 457–60; see also above, p. 162.
[79] See A. H. M. Jones *LRE* 361.

21

Enemies in the Establishment

ANOTHER consideration makes it almost certain that an important group of officials threw its influence on the side of Chrysostom's opponents. Only so can it be explained that after the bishop's return from his first exile Chrysostom's enemies not only resumed their attack after a very short time, but were strong enough to prevent the case for Chrysostom from receiving any formal hearing at all. In consequence of our principal sources being ecclesiastical we are comparatively badly informed about the attitudes of laymen. There is, however, enough evidence to show that important members of what I have called the 'Arcadian establishment'[1] were hostile.

In the case of Aurelian, the praetorian prefect in autumn 399, we have explicit evidence of positive hostility to John Chrysostom. He, together with the general Saturninus and the *comes* John, had been handed over to Gainas and sent into exile by that German general. According to Zosimus it was after the return of the exiles to Constantinople that Eudoxia's hostility to Chrysostom became manifest.[2]

We do not know what precise role Aurelian played in the controversies over John Chrysostom. As a former prefect of the city and praetorian prefect of the East, he is likely to have held an influential position in the consistory of Arcadius. He did not hold office in these years, and had to wait until 414 for his second praetorian prefecture. But he was rich and highly respected. As praetorian prefect in 414 he decorated the newly rebuilt senate house with busts of Arcadius, Honorius, and Pulcheria. In 415 he added one of Theodosius II. He also received one himself. A district of Constantinople came to be known after him—presumably the district where his mansion had been situated.[3] He is likely to have been a man of influence, and a dangerous enemy even when not in office.[4] Of the other two exiles, Saturninus seems to have died soon after his return from exile, but his widow was a prominent opponent of Chrysostom.[5] We have seen that both Aurelian and Saturninus had links with the monk Isaac.[6]

The *comes* John, the third of the exiles, had a particular grievance against Chrysostom. At the Synod of the Oak Chrysostom was

[1] See above p. 132.   [2] Zos. v. 23.   [3] R. Janin (1964) 155–6.
[4] On Aurelian see also above, p. 133.   [5] Pall. *Dial.* 17.   [6] See above, p. 213.

charged with having informed against him during the 'mutiny of the soldiers'.[7] In all probability the 'mutiny' refers to the occasion when the troops under Gainas demanded the surrender of the later exiles. John was a dangerous enemy since already at the time of his exile, early in 400, he enjoyed the confidence of both emperor and empress, and was even rumoured to have been the father of the little Theodosius II.[8] At the time of the Synod of the Oak he held the title of *comes*, and after the final exile of Chrysostom he was one of a number of magistrates who witnessed the receipt of valuables belonging to the church of Constantinople from the clergy of the exiled archbishop.[9]

One would expect the grievances of the 'exiles' to have been shared by others who had suffered at that time. We have seen that Chrysostom was active and influential in the days when Gainas and his Goths were in occupation of Constantinople.[10] The Gainas episode left behind it much bitterness and resentment. But others who had collaborated with Gainas were forgiven. Eudoxia herself had been proclaimed Augusta during the period of Gainas' greatest influence.[11] There were at least two occasions during the Gainas episode when Chrysostom is likely to have clashed with the authorities. The first was the controversy over the proposal to allow Gainas the use of a church for Arian services. After Chrysostom had blocked this proposal Eutychianus, the praetorian prefect, may well have felt that the bishop had irresponsibly sabotaged his policy of collaboration with the Goths.[12] Subsequently the burning of the church can hardly have failed to produce a crisis in the relations between Chrysostom and the praetornian prefect. Eutychianus, an 'establishment figure' if anyone ever was, was again prefect when Chrysostom was exiled for the second time.[13] Together with the *comes* John and others he signed the receipt of church valuables deposited with magistrates investigating the charges against Chrysostom's financial administration.[14] Eutychianus was the principal adviser of Arcadius, one might almost say his first minister. He must have agreed with the attack on Chrysostom; more than likely he advised it. We know the names of a few others who took part in the suppression of Chrysostom's followers. Of these the most important

---

[7] Photius *bibl.* 59 (17b. 19): charge 11. Against Alan Cameron (1988) I still believe that the homily 'de capto Eutropio' does refer to Eutropius and not to the *comes* John.

[8] Theodosius, born 10 April 401, must have been conceived during John's exile.

[9] *Dial.* 13.   [10] See above, p. 189.

[11] *Chron. Pasch.* s.a. 400: 9 Jan 400.

[12] F. van Ommeslaeghe (1979) 152.

[13] *PLRE* i s.v. Flavius Eutychianus 5. There can be no doubt that he was prefect 404–5.

[14] *Dial.* 13.

was Anthemius.[15] It is practically certain that he was 'the *magister*' (i.e. *magister officiorum*)[16] who gave orders to Lucius, commander of the *schola scutariorum* to break up congregations of Joannites on the night before Easter Sunday 404. Anthemius' record of public service, especially of the nine years during which he practically governed the empire, does not suggest that he was the kind of man to be duped by three fairly obscure bishops. Troops were not normally used against civilians at Constantinople or in other cities of the East,[17] and an able and responsible official is unlikely to have given the order to engage the troops inadvertently. If Anthemius gave the order we can conclude that at this time at least he favoured the suppression of the Joannites. This deduction receives some confirmation from the fact that when Anthemius became praetorian he did not recall the exiled bishop. On the contrary, he made the conditions of exile more severe. Chryosostom was first moved to Arabissus—this was probably on account of Isaurian raids—but he was then moved to Pityus on the edge of the Caucasus, to make it more difficult for followers to visit him.[18] Anthemius made no attempt whatsoever to reconcile Chrysostom and his enemies. It is significant that when Chrysostom was posthumously rehabilitated in 416[19] Anthemius was no longer praetorian prefect.

Soon after Chrysostom had returned from his first exile Simplicius, the urban prefect, put up a silver statue of Eudoxia in the immediate neighbourhood of St Sophia, and provoked Chryosostom into two disastrously tactless sermons.[20] What actually caused the bishop's wrath was a noisy festival that disturbed the service inside the cathedral. One wonders whether the provocation might have been deliberate. Simplicius was a kinsman of Anthemius, probably a brother or a cousin. Perhaps Simplicius had intended that his action should cause discord between Eudoxia and John. In that case he represents yet another member of the new aristocracy of Constantinople who was hostile to the bishop.[21] But the silver statue of Augusta Eudoxia had wider significance since it was part of a

[15] *PLRE* ii x.v. Anthemius 1. John Chrys. *Ep.* 147 (from exile) congratulates him on the prefecture, a diplomatic gesture, not an indication of friendship.

[16] *Dial.* 13. The *magister officiorum* was often described as simply 'the *magister*'. In spring 404 Anthemius held the office. The *scholae* were under the command of the *magister officiorum*. See A. H. M. Jones *LRE* 613. Anthemius will therefore have been one of the 'two or three courtiers' who aided the bishops with military force: *Dial.* 16 (p. 25. 6).

[17] W. Liebeschuetz (1972) 117–18, 125.

[18] *Dial.* 37–8, P. C. Bauer (1929–30) ii. 313 ff., 352 ff.

[19] Socr. vii. 25; Theodoret *HE* v. 34; *Ep. ad Cyril.* 75 (*PG* lxxvi. 348–9). P. C. Bauer (1929–30) ii. 373–77.

[20] *PLRE* ii s.v. Simplicius 4.

[21] Stemma of descendants of Philippus 7: see *PLRE* i. 696–7.

policy involving Empire-wide display of images of Eudoxia. This was in some way felt to be offensive by the Western emperor. For when Arcadius sent out official images of the empress into the provinces Honorius protested.[22]

Among the officials who persecuted the followers of Chrysostom, the urban prefect Optatus earned the most lurid reputation. In fact of the three urban prefects known to have held office during the relevant period he alone seems to have displayed vindictiveness towards the Joannites.

The turnover of officials was high during this troubled period. Paianius was appointed during the first month or so of Chrysostom's exile.[23] Chrysostom clearly considered him a friend.[24] He must have started the investigations into the cause of the fire that destroyed St Sophia and the senate house. Perhaps he did not show sufficient ruthlessness. At any rate he was very quickly replaced by Studius,[25] who received laws on the 29 August and 11 September. He continued the investigation into the fire, and discovered nothing. One of the laws instructs him to release imprisoned clerics, since the sought-for fire-raisers had not been found.[26] The law will have been issued in the usual way at the suggestion of the official to which it is addressed. Studius may have shown too much sympathy for the Joannites.[27] At any rate, by 24 November at the latest he too had lost his office, and was replaced by Optatus who was to hold the office at least until 12 June 405.[28]

While Paianius and Studius seem to have been well disposed towards Chrysostom, Optatus is represented as a persecutor who employed heavy fines and torture to compel dedicated virgins, including Olympias and ladies like her, and also some hermits, to abandon Chrysostom and take communion with his successor.[29] We know nothing of the family backgrounds of Paianius and Studius. This may suggest that their ancestors were not particularly distinguished. But Optatus was a senior senator and nephew of the consul of 334.[30] In other words he had the same kind of background as Eutychianus, Anthemius, Aurelian, and Simplicius. He was a member of the new establishment. Socrates calls him a pagan, but (as Dagron has pointed out) urban prefects were liable to this allegation,

[22] Honorius' letter: *Ep. 38* (*CSEL* xxxv. 85), cf. K. Holum (1982a) 66–7, 127–8.
[23] *PLRE* ii s.v. Paianius. John Chrys. *Ep.* 220 congratulates him on an unnamed appointment in 404. The phrasing would fit the urban prefecture.
[24] John Chrys. *Ep.* 95, 193, 204, 220, 14. 1.
[25] *PLRE* ii s.v. Studius 1.   [26] *CT* xvi. 2. 37.
[27] Note impartiality of *CT* xvi. 2. 37; see also John Chrys. *Ep.* 197.
[28] *PLRE* i s.v. Optatus 1.
[29] *Dial.* 14; Socr. vi. 18; Soz. viii. 23.   [30] *PLRE* i s.v. Optatus 3.

particularly if, like Optatus, they had 'intervened' in an ecclesiastical dispute.[31]

The list of men who for different reasons may be thought to have been opponents of Chrysostom—Aurelian, John, Anthemius, Eutychianus, Simplicius, and Optatus—is an impressive one. They represent the core of the new senatorial aristocracy of Constantinople.

The question next arises why precisely the 'establishment' should have decided that Chrysostom was impossible. We have seen that the Gainas episode aroused the hostility of several important figures, including the highly respected Aurelian. It is also worth noting that even political interventions that were to be praised by our historical sources aroused considerable criticism among some sections of opinion at the time when they happened. Both Chrysostom's behaviour towards the fallen eunuch Eutropius, and his at least temporarily successful resistance to Gainas' demand for a church in which his soldiers could hold Arian services, were to furnish material for hostile propaganda by his enemies.[32]

There was one aspect of Chrysostom's behaviour which directly affected the families who were seeking to build up great senatorial fortunes: his successful efforts to mobilize the property of wealthy women into the service of the Church. Palladius thought it necessary to defend at length John's relationship with Olympias which evidently had aroused a great deal of criticism.[33]

Something has already been said about Olympias, her charitable expenditure and her friendship with Chrysostom.[34] It is clear that their relationship was one of deep personal friendship, without any trace of a physical relationship. Indeed sexual scandal was not even alleged by Chrysostom's opponents. The scandal was not sexual but financial.

One of the reasons why the relationship became controversial, to the extent that Olympias suffered severe persecution after Chrysostom's exile, was the fact that she remained one of his most prominent and dedicated supporters, firmly refusing to take communion with his successor, Arsacius.[35] Another reason has been suggested by Dagron. Outlining the vast resources which under the influence of Chrysostom Olympias put at the disposal of the Church of Constantinople, he argues that the opponents of Chrysostom, notably the empress Eudoxia, were seriously concerned at the rapid growth of the economic resources of the Church when compared

[31] G. Dagron (1974) 291–4.
[32] Socr. VI. 5; Soz. VIII. 4; F. van Ommeslaeghe (1979) 152.
[33] *Dial.* 55 ff., a reply to a specific attack by Theophilus, cf. ibid. 60–61.
[34] See above p. 143.   [35] Soz. viii. 24.

with those of the state.[36] But this is to look at the situation anachronistically. Rapidly as the Church's wealth was growing, it was still very small in comparison with the enormous resources of the Empire, and there is no evidence that its economic power was regarded as a threat to the state.[37] It is true that there was legislation to prevent the wealth of wealthy ladies passing to members of the clergy, either through the ladies' wills or intestacy,[38] but what worried the legislators was the fact that the influence of clerics over pious ladies was depriving heirs of property to which they were entitled, not that the Church was becoming too rich. In other words, the point of view is that of the great families whose social position depended on inherited wealth.[39]

We obtain an idea of how the great families resented the pious donations of some of the womenfolk when we consider the indignation displayed by the senatorial kinsmen of Melania the Younger when she and her husband Pinianus sold their estates and gave the proceeds to the poor or the Church.[40] There is no reason to believe that the senatorial families of Constantinople felt differently about Olympias. Such feelings will have been strongest among families that were seeking to build up an economic and social position to rival that of the great senatorial houses of Rome, in other words among precisely members of the new 'establishment' of Constantinople.

---

[36] G. Dagron (1974) 501 ff.

[37] Wealth of Church of Constantinople: Greg. Naz. *De vita sua* 1475–8. Yet Chrysostom found only *one* hospital, and proceeded to establish others (*Dial.* 20). Whether the Church should own property at all was still controversial. At Constantinople Chrysostom had come to accept that the Church had to administer property. But the development was still in its beginning. R. Brändle (1979) 114–21.

[38] *CT* xvi. 2. 20 (AD 370, West), 27 and 28 (AD 390, East).

[39] Jill Harries (1983), cf. Ausonius *Ep.* 27. 115, mourning the prospect of the dispersal of ancestral senatorial property.

[40] Pall. *Hist. Laus.* 54. 5; *V. Melaniae* 8–14; Ambrose *Ep.* 58.3. See J. Matthews (1975) 152.

22

The Rich, the Poor, and the West

CHRYSOSTOM antagonized some very wealthy and powerful persons, and no doubt others who were simply rich. According to 'Martyrius' at least some of the wealthy claimed that they dared not go to church because when he preached about the misdeeds of the rich all the congregation looked at them. Others complained that by words and deeds Chrysostom was preventing them from making money in their customary way.[1] There is no reason to doubt that his outspoken attempts to awaken the social conscience of the well-to-do caused irritation and annoyance. 'Martyrius' further gives the impression that the poor and the sick were behind Chrysostom. This is likely enough. After all, he had constantly called on those who had money to spare to give it to those in need, and had preached one virtue more frequently than any other, readiness to make sacrifices in order to help the destitute. 'Martyrius' was able to contrast the behaviour of Chrysostom in helping the poor with that of Theophilus who intrigued with the rich.[2] He describes how landowners opposed Chrysostom's efforts to establish a leper hospital in their neighbourhood, and notes that they managed to get the project stopped even before Chrysostom was exiled.[3]

But if Chrysostom aroused the hostility of some of the rich, he was certainly not without wealthy followers. When the Joannite congregations were broken up at Easter 404, some *honestiores*, or even *honorati*, were expelled from the city or imprisoned.[4] Their wives were robbed of jewellery.[5] The crowds that demonstrated on Chrysostom's behalf were not composed of beggars. The law of January 404 forbids staff of the imperial civil service departments from attending tumultuous meetings. They were threatened with dismissal and confiscation of their property if they ignored the prohibition.[6] The law of September 404 threatens masters who let their slaves take part in 'tumultuous conventicles'. The fine is three pounds of gold per slave found taking part in such a meeting. Guilds were held responsible for the behaviour of their members and

[1] F. van Ommeslaeghe (1979) 150, cites p. 480 a–b.
[2] *Id.* (1981) 347.   [3] *Id.* (1979) 151 cites 491 b–495 a.
[4] Pall. *Dial.* 34 οἱ δὲ ἀξιωματικοὶ τοῦ λαοῦ. A later edict was delivered against officials and soldiers as well as ordinary people (*Dial.* 37).
[5] Soz. viii. 28; cf. also the wealthy wife of Eutherius (*Dial.* 34), and Nicarete (Soz. viii. 23).
[6] *CT* xvi. 4. 4.

threatened with a fine of no less that 50 pounds of gold if one of them was to take part in a 'tumultuous conventicle'. One guild is specially named: the money lenders.[7] There is some evidence that demonstrations were organized purposefully. At any rate when the verdict of the Synod of the Oak was announced a crowd gathered and demanded that the case ought to be tried again by a larger synod. This was precisely what John and his followers were demanding and continued to demand to the end.[8]

Chrysostom had wealthy supporters, both at Constantinople and in the provinces. In exile he received offers of help from numerous wealthy people. One Arabius offered the use of a villa at Sebaste in Armenia.[9] Seleucia, wife of Rufinus of Caesarea in Cappadocia, invited Chrysostom to her villa. She also offered him the use of a fortified tower and the protection of her peasants and tenants against the attacks of monks. It was only when threatened by the bishop of Caesarea that she abandoned him.[10] Other persons who showed friendship were Dioscurus, a landowner of Cucusus,[11] Sopater *praeses* of Armenia Secunda,[12] and in the capital itself the *comes* Theophilus and the lady Carteria.[13] These examples show that it is far from true that the 'rich' as such were against Chrysostom. If he was afraid of any one class of people at the time of his exile, it was bishops.[14]

We hear of other sympathizers who were officials or had close links with the official classes. There was Paianius who briefly held the office of prefect of the city immediately after John's exile.[15] Brison, *cubicularius* of Eudoxia, not a senator but no less influential for that, received two friendly letters from the exiled bishop,[16] and one Theodotus, 'ex-consularibus', sent him presents.[17] Anatolius, described as Greek ἐπαρχικός (*praefectianus*), continued to work for the exiled bishop at Constantinople.[18] To this rather ramshackle list of high-ranking sympathizers must be added a number of senatorial wives and widows. Before leaving Constantinople for ever Chrysostom said farewell to four pious and extremely aristocratic ladies: Olympias, Salvina, Pentadia, and Procle.[19] Nothing is known of the background of Procle, but we have information about the others which suggests that all three had connections with the West.

---

[7] *CT* xvi. 4. 5. [9] John Chrys. *Ep.* 121. [8] Socr. vi. 15; Soz. viii. 18.

[10] *Ep.* 14 = 9. 2. 68 ed. A.-M. Malingrey.

[11] *Ep.* 13 = 6. 1. 23 ed. A.-M. Malingrey.

[12] *Ep.* 64, cf. *PLRE* ii s.v. Sopater 1.

[13] *Ep.* 4, cf. *PLRE* ii s.v. Theophilus 2; for Carteria see *Ep.* 232.

[14] *Ep.* 14. 4 = 9. 4. 26 ed. A.-M. Malingrey: even Isaurians are to be feared less.

[15] See above, p. 220. [16] *PLRE* ii s.v. Brison; *Epp.* 190 and 234.

[17] *Epp.* 61 and 141.

[18] *Ep.* 205; *PLRE* ii s.v. Anatolius 5. [19] *Dial.* 35.

Olympias belonged to the new Eastern aristocracy,[20] but she was a widow of Nebridius II,[21] a kinsman of Flacilla, the Spanish wife of Theodosius I. Olympias' charity was inspired by that of the Elder Melania, a great senatorial lady of Rome,[22] whose granddaughter the 'Younger Melania'[23] was to support Palladius and other followers of John Chrysostom when they sought refuge and diplomatic assistance at Rome after the deposition of their bishop.[24] Salvina was a daughter of the North African chieftain and *comes et magister utriusque militiae per Africam*, Gildo. She was the widow of Nebridius III, nephew of the empress Flacilla and perhaps stepson of Olympias.[25] Pentadia was the widow of Timasius, a general of Theodosius I and victim of the eunuch Eutropius.[26] That their son was called Syagrius suggests that the mother came from a great family of Gaul.[27]

It is difficult to estimate the significance of the fact that some of Chrysostom's most important supporters had Western links.[28] They did indeed belong to the group that had governed the united empire for Theodosius I. His leading opponents, on the other hand, belonged to the new ruling class of the Roman Empire of the East. They were conscious of the Greek roots of its civilization and extremely jealous of its political independence. It would be tempting to interpret the deposition of John Chrysostom as one aspect of the emancipation of the Eastern Empire. It might be suggested that the Eastern 'establishment' opposed Chrysostom because he was too Western, and that it was for precisely the same reason that he was to receive wholehearted support from the Pope and Western Emperor. In fact there is little evidence of this. What was more important was that the Joannites had a particular advantage in appealing for sympathy to the West in the fact that the attack on Chrysostom was originally linked with the persecution of the Origenist monks of Egypt and their cosmopolitan imitators. When the Tall Brothers and their admirers, who included Palladius the biographer[29] and John

[20] *PLRE* i s.v. Olympias 1.
[21] *Ibid.* s.v. Nebridius 2.
[22] Pall. *Hist. Laus.* 41. 5; 61. 7. See also E. D. Hunt (1973) 477. *PLRE* i s.v. Melania 1.
[23] *PLRE* i s.v. Melania 2.
[24] Pall. *Hist. Laus.* 41. 5, 61. 7.
[25] *PLRE* i. s.v. Salvina.
[26] Ibid. s.v. Timasius.
[27] Ibid. s.v. Syagrius 1.
[28] Ch. Pietri (1975) 293 ff. One of Chrysostom's first acts as bishop had been to send Acacius of Beroea to Rome to end the Antiochene schism: P. C. Baur (1929–30), ii. 20–23. Chrysostom's friend Evagrius, who according to Socr. vi. 3 ordained him, is unlikely to be identical with Evagrius, the friend of Jerome (*PLRE* i s.v. Evagrius 3) who was influential at the Western court in the 370s. Socrates' account is confused. According to Palladius *Dial.* 19 Chrysostom was ordained by Flavianus. Evagrius was quite a common name.
[29] E. D. Hunt (1973), cf. (1972).

Cassian and Germanus,[30] found patronage and shelter with John Chrysostom at Constantinople, he gained the potential support of the monks' powerful patrons in Italy, notably the ladies and senatorial menfolk of the family of the Elder Melania and of the ecclesiastics associated with them.[31] It was clearly not a coincidence that Palladius, Germanus, and Cassianus came to Rome to report on the persecution of the Joannites,[32] or that John's envoys lodged with Melania the Younger,[33] or that the leader of the unlucky Western embassy to Constantinople was Aemilius bishop of Beneventum, a city of which Publicola, a son of Melania the Elder, was *patronus ex origine.*[34] It is likely that it was through Melania and her friends that Chrysostom gained the support of two ladies of the great Anician family, of Proba widow of Claudius Petronius Probus,[35] four times praetorian prefect, of Iuliana,[36] perhaps her daughter-in-law and wife of the consul of 395, and also of Italica.[37]

Such connections gained for Chrysostom the support of Western bishops, Pope, and Emperor, but this did not help him at all with the authorities of the East. Quite the reverse. The strength of Western support, at a time when Stilicho was threatening the East with war for the sake of the control of Illyricum[38] certainly stiffened the determination of his enemies of Constantinople. It may well account for the harshness of some of the measures taken against the Joannites.

To sum up. John Chrysostom was unpopular with many of his clergy at Constantinople. His interventions in the affairs of neighbouring sees caused anxiety among bishops and resentment among the citizens whose bishops John had deposed. He attempted to discipline the monks living in or near Constantinople and in this way made enemies of a formidable body of men. For the monks were influential with ordinary people as well as with some of the leaders of society. They could riot themselves and could induce the people to riot. In fact they had already once before allied with the bishop of Alexandria to bring down a bishop of Constantinople. At the same time Chrysostom's way of life tended to isolate him. This itself caused resentment. It also helped the intrigues of his opponents. It is clear that these circumstances made him vulnerable when a group of

---

[30] John Cassian ordained by Chrysostom: *De incarnatione Christi 7. 31* (PL l. 269). Germanus: *Dial.* 9, 13, 28; his biography in *DCB* s.v. Germanus 32.

[31] P. Brown (1970), esp. 56–68 = (1972) 210–15.

[32] *Dial.* 13.   [33] Pall. *Hist. Laus.* 61.   [34] *CIL* ix. 1591.

[35] *PLRE* i s.v. Anicia Fultonia Proba; John Chrys. *Ep.* 169.

[36] John Chrys. *Ep.* 169, cf. *PLRE* i s.v. Anicia Juliana 2.

[37] *Ep.* 170, probably *PLRE* ii s.v. Anicia Italica 2, but see P. Brown (1961*b*) 5–6 = (1972) 171.

[38] J. F. Matthews (1975) 274–5, and above, p. 64.

bishops and laymen began to work for his deposition. The clique that worked for his overthrow included two powerful figures, the empress Eudoxia, and Theophilus, the bishop of Alexandria. Eudoxia was volatile and changeable, and she died soon after the second and final exiling of Chrysostom; but Theophilus continued to be associated with the attack, though he did not again leave Egypt. That this group nevertheless succeeded in keeping the imperial government favourable to its objectives for thirteen years was due to the fact that they won the support of the ministers Eutychianus, Aurelianus, and Anthemius who dominated public life between AD 394 and 416. How and why they won it is not altogether clear, but some relevant factors can be identified. Chrysostom had incurred the bitter hostility of the 'exiles' Aurelian, Saturninus, and John during the Gainas affair. Moreover Aurelian and Saturninus were closely associated with Isaac, the leader of the monks whose enmity Chrysostom had aroused. We can conjecture that men like Aurelian and Anthemius, members of recently enriched families that were now dominating the political and social life of Constantinople, resented the activities of a bishop who was successfully urging senatorial women to disperse the property on which the power of senatorial houses depended. Finally, as Western support for Chrysostom developed these men are likely to have seen the conflict with John and his followers as part of their struggle to maintain Eastern independence, and particularly Eastern control of Illyricum, in the face of the pressure of the Western government directed by Stilicho.

23
Bishop and Public Life in the Cyrenaica of Synesius

THIS study has dealt with two aspects of the transformation of society in Late Antiquity: demilitarization and Christianization. The first resulted in the inability or unwillingness of the inhabitants of the Later Empire to rally to the defence of the Empire against foreign invaders. One consequence of the second was the growth of the power of the bishops which introduced new possibilities and new tensions. Of the nature of these possibilities and tensions the career of John Chrysostom provides an unusually well documented illustration. Chrysostom, however, was scarcely typical. As bishop of the capital he occupied a unique position, and in any case he was an exceptional man. We come closer to average experience by looking at the life and career of Synesius—even though Synesius was in many ways an unusual man to become bishop.

Synesius was a citizen of Cyrene. His family was one of the leading families, if not the leading family, in the city, claiming descent from the original Dorian settlers. He and his brother belonged to a group of magnates who under the governor of the province of Pentapolis— and sometimes in opposition to him—ran the affairs of city and province. Cyrene had a city council, and Synesius and his brother were *curiales*.[1] But for Synesius public service and service of his city were not synonymous with service in the council. The council appears as a body obliged to perform burdensome duties for the imperial administration from whose membership Synesius and his brother liked to be exempted.[2] One gets the impression, although there is not enough evidence to be certain, that Synesius dealt with governors directly, not through mediation of the council or as representative of the council. He surely had a residence in the city, but it seems that he and his brother spent a great deal of time on their

[1] On the general background Ch. Lacombrade (1951*b*) is still essential. Fuller documentation of the subject matter of this chapter is found in W. Liebeschuetz (1985*b*), (1986).

[2] Synesius *Ep.* 93, 100. The letters of Synesius are, as generally, cited in the numeration of R. Hercher, *Epistolographi Graeci* (Paris, 1873), 638–739, which has been followed by A. FitzGerald in his translation *The Letters of Synesius of Cyrene* (Oxford, 1926). The numbering of J. P. Migne, *PG* lxvi (Paris, 1864) is given in brackets where it differs from Hercher, as is the numbering of A. Garzya, *Synesii Cyrenensis Epistolae*, (Rome, 1979).

estates. Unlike the 'Hellenes' of the past Synesius did not identify civilization with life in a town.

The picture of the organization of Pentapolis that can be constructed from the surviving letters of Synesius' correspondence is fragmentary and in many details uncertain. But whatever the deficiencies of the evidence, there can be no uncertainty about the prominence in his picture of the two principal topics of this study, defence and the growing power of the bishop.

Cyrenaica, like the provinces troubled by northern barbarians, suffered from the inability of the regular Roman army to prevent the lands inside the frontier from being invaded. The invaders were the Macetae and Ausurians, nomads or semi-nomads[3] whose home territory was in Southern Numidia and Tripolitania.[4] They seem to have moved on horseback, though on one occasion they are said to have brought in 5000 camels to carry off their booty.[5] The fact that they had camels may well be the factor which made the nomads so much more dangerous than they had been in earlier centuries.[6] Ironically the fact that they had taken to the use of camels is likely to have been a consequence of the Roman peace. Provided they were able to use some land on the Cyrenaican plateau, nomads could subsist without camels. It was the pressure of expanding peasant occupation on the plateau which forced the adoption of the camel which could exploit the more marginal pastoral areas outside the range of sheep and goats.[7]

From 404 to 411 the countryside was regularly overrun by these raiders. There was another and even more severe invasion in 412, which culminated in a period of occupation of the countryside by the invader. While on each occasion the raiders were eventually defeated the garrison of the province evidently had great difficulty in coping with them. The instinctive tactics seem to have been to disperse the units of the garrison among cities and other fortified localities of the province, leaving the open countryside at the mercy of the invaders.[8] Synesius blames the bad generalship of individual commanders, but the situation is sufficiently like that in the Balkans and Italy when facing invasion by Alaric to suggest that the failure was not simply that of individuals.

The invaders were not very numerous. The force which was eventually defeated in 411 amounted to something over 1000 men,[9]

---

[3] D. L. Johnson (1969), M. M. Kikha (1968).
[4] D. Roques (1983).   [5] *Catastasis*, *PG* lxvi 1569. A.
[6] O. Brogan (1954), M. W. Mikesell (1955), E. Demougeot (1960).
[7] D. L. Johnson and J. Al-Akhdar (1973), 138–40.
[8] *Ep.* 130, p. 224 (Garzya) = 129 (Migne). *Catastasis*, *PG* lxvi. 1568 A.
[9] *Constitutio*, *PG* lxvi. 1576 B.

and in their defeat a decisive part was played by a unit of the so-called Unnigardae amounting to no more than 40 cavalrymen. If the 40 were reinforced by 200 the commander would be able to take the war into the invaders' home territory.[10] To defeat the great invasion of the following year Synesius thought that four centuries of Unnigardae would be needed.[11] We have seen earlier that the use of small units— not the regiments of 600 or 1000 of the Early Empire—was a characteristic of the Late Roman military organization.[12] So was the difficulty of assembling even these in sufficiently large numbers to enable them to face barbarian invaders.

It is also characteristic that the most effective troops, the Unnigardae, were not part of the regular garrison but an élite unit, recruited from Huns if their name is anything to go by, with special donatives, extra pay, special equipment, and relays of horses. They were a kind of federates, the only unit of this type available in the province and in a different category from all other units.[13] The remaining garrison consisted of two types of units: local troops (ἐπιχώριοι = *limitanei*)[14] and 'strangers' (ξένοι perhaps *comitatenses*).[15] We know of the difference because the two classes of soldiers offered different possibilities of illegal or semi-legal profit to the *dux Libyae*. In the case of the local troops the duke was in a position to retain a share of their pay. In the case of the strangers he could not do this, but he could exploit their mobility by demanding money from the towns where he had temporarily stationed the troops, in return for moving them somewhere else.[16] The 'local' troops had been in the province since time immemorial and they were probably stationed permanently in the same locality, from which they will often have taken their names. So the Balgritae were mounted archers stationed at Balgrae, not far from Synesius' estate.[17] The 'foreign' troops on the other hand had at one time or other been transferred to Cyrene from elsewhere.[18] Regimental names like Marcomanni[19] or Thracians[20] presumably recall the foreign origins even if the units were now being kept up by local recruitment. In Synesius' view the Unnigardae provided the cutting edge of the provincial army.[21] This role might be compared with, for instance,

[10] *Constitutio*, PG lxvi. 1576 c.
[11] Ibid. 1563.   [12] See above, p. 41.   [13] *Ep.* 78.
[14] *Ep.* 78, p. 136. 6, p. 137. 11 (Garzya).
[15] *Ep.* 85, p. 162. 1 (Garzya), cf. *Ep.* 78. p. 136. 7–8.
[16] *Ep.* 130, p. 222. 6–13 (Garzya).   [17] *Ep.* 132, p. 228. 7–11 (Garzya).
[18] *Ep.* 78, p. 136. 7–8 (Garzya); 'they arrive', which I take to mean 'as reinforcements', rather than 'federates'.
[19] *Ep.* 110, p. 195. 12 (Garzya).
[20] Thracians: *Catastasis*, PG lxvi. 1568 b; Dalmatians: *Ep.* 87.
[21] *Catastasis*, PG lxvi. 1568.

that of the Hun and Gothic federates in the army which Stilicho led against Radagaisus.

The inability of the Roman army to protect the countryside led to the widespread fortification of towns, villages, and estates.[22] But the defence of these walls was to a considerable extent in the hands of the civilian population, a leading part being taken by magnates like Synesius himself.

Synesius' estate had a fortified residence which could withstand a siege.[23] His brother seems to have had a fortified villa too. After 404 when the army failed to protect the countryside Synesius assembled a militia from the peasantry, appointed officers and proceeded to patrol the countryside.[24] He had spears and axes made locally.[25] He bought bows, but asks a friend in Syria to send him arrows as the Egyptian kind are unsatisfactory.[26] When his brother reminds Synesius of the imperial law forbidding civilians to carry arms he insists on the justification of self-defence.[27] Synesius tells us that the clergy of the village of Anxomis were organizing the peasantry and leading them against the invaders.[28] There are likely to have been many more local nuclei of resistance. We are reminded of the countryfolk of Phrygia, whose experience in resisting Isaurian raiders enabled them to inflict severe losses on Tribigild, and also of the citizens who manned the walls of their Thracian cities against Gainas.[29] Taking the evidence for the invasion period as a whole there are not many references to locally organized resistance, but this may well be a consequence of the thinness of our evidence. The efforts of a Synesius or his like could not have held up an army or a people on the move. Such little local difficulties as they might cause an invader will have been too insignificant to find their way into such sources as we must rely on. In any case the fact that it was *resistance* that individual magnates of Cyrenaica organized may be less significant than that it was *the magnates*, and neither the cities nor the imperial administration, that did the organizing. We are witnessing a weakening of the administrative structure of the Empire. This remains true even if Synesius' latest piece of information about the nomads is that the Roman army has gained a decisive victory and restored peace to the province.[30] In the long run the old state of security was not restored.

---

[22] R. G. Goodchild (1976), 195–209, G. Barker (1985), 130.

[23] *Ep.* 130, p. 223. 2 (Garzya); cf. R. S. O. Tomlin (1979).   [24] *Ep.* 125.   [25] *Ep.* 108.

[26] *Ep.* 133, p. 231 (Garzya) = 132 *PG* lxvi. 1520 c: Synesius is building catapults and needs arrows.

[27] *Ep.* 107.

[28] *Ep.* 122, numerous nuclei of resistance or refuge: *Ep.* 66, p. 112–13 (Garzya) = 67 *PG* lxvi. 1420 B–C.

[29] See above p. 103 and p. 119.   [30] *Ep.* 62.

Fortification of villages and estate centres continued and cities continued to shrink.[31]

For six or seven years Synesius participated in the defence of his province in the capacity of a man of high social standing and a landowner. Then early in 411 or thereabouts he was elected bishop of Ptolemais and metropolitan of the province of Pentapolis.[32] He became a bishop extremely reluctantly—not because he lacked respect for the office but because he felt insufficiently qualified to perform the role of mediator between his charges and God. Besides, he was aware of the wide range of responsibilities, secular as well as religious, that bore upon a bishop, and was reluctant to take on this full-time occupation for the rest of his life. But once he was bishop, he did his utmost to perform what was expected of him. This included many of the tasks he had performed as a magnate, for instance taking up the cases of *curiales* victimized by the governor.[33] He was one of the speakers who thanked the retiring general Anysius on behalf of the cities of Cyrene and Ptolemais[34] and subsequently sent to Anysius, now at Constantinople, a petition from his former soldiers the Unnigardae who were threatened with a loss of status.[35] When the governor Andronicus became unbearable Synesius led opposition against him.[36] Eventually he excommunicated the official. This act carried with it not only exclusion from church but complete social ostracism. 'I exhort every private individual and official not to be under the same roof as them [Andronicus and his agents], not to be seated at the same table; particularly priests, for these shall neither speak to them while living nor join in their funeral procession when dead.'[37] Andronicus was dismissed from his governorship after perhaps a year in office, and it was only thanks to the physical intervention of Synesius that he avoided prosecution.[38] When, late in summer or autumn 412, the Ausurians resumed their attack on a larger scale than before, Synesius took an active part in the defence of his city, sharing guard duty at night and posting pickets.[39] As bishop he was in effect the representative civic leader of Ptolemais, occupying a position which had once been occupied by civic magistrates.

[31] Urban decline at Cyrene: S. Stucchi (1965), i. 322–4; see also L. Bacchielli (1981), 183 and 190 ff. For history of Cyrene see R. G. Goodchild (1971), on Cyrenaica generally G. Barker, J. Lloyd, J. Reynolds (1985).

[32] W. Liebeschuetz (1986); T. D. Barnes (1986b) argues that Synesius was consecrated in 407. Alan Cameron (1989) makes a very strong case that Synesius was a Christian from birth and baptized after his return from Constantinople.

[33] e.g. *Ep.* 72, 79.

[34] *Constitutio, PG* lxvi. 1573–6.   [35] *Ep.* 78.

[36] *Ep.* 58 = 42 (Garzya), *Ep.* 57 = 41 (Garzya).

[37] *Ep.* 72.   [38] *Ep.* 90 (89).   [39] *Catastasis, PG* lxvi. 1572 C.

It was part of the strength of the bishop's position that he belonged to the larger organization of the Church. As far as the metropolitan of Pentapolis was concerned the Church for practical purposes was the patriarchate of Alexandria under its formidable head Theophilus, the opponent of John Chrysostom. Theophilus had officiated at Synesius' marriage, which was held at Alexandria.[40] Theophilus consecrated Synesius as bishop—in all likelihood he had played a considerable part in persuading Synesius to accept consecration.[41] Theophilus was Synesius' superior as metropolitan of Pentapolis.

The village of Palaebisca in Western Cyrenaica had been part of the diocese of Erythrum, but as the bishop was old and weak and incapable of protecting them the villagers seceded, and managed to get a separate bishop consecrated for their village, choosing Siderius, a retired officer, who had the reputation of being able to injure his enemies and aid his friends. The secession and consecration seems to have been recognized by Theophilus. One can see how the church could have a decisive influence on civil administration by creating or recognizing new sees and thus helping to break up city-territories. When Siderius died Theophilus wished to continue the new arrangement and appointed a successor. Unfortunately the villagers had put themselves back into the diocese of Erythrum since it was now governed by a popular and effective bishop. Theophilus gave Synesius the invidious task of persuading the villagers of Palaebisca to accept Theophilus' nominee. He failed.[42]

Synesius had a rich aristocrat's self-confidence. He made up his own mind, and was not prepared to accept the literal truth of Christian dogmas if they were incompatible with philosophy.[43] But he did accept ecclesiastical discipline. One Alexander had been consecrated bishop of Basilinopolis in Bithynia by John Chrysostom. When Chrysostom was deposed Alexander was driven from his see. Later an amnesty would have allowed Alexander to return to Basilinopolis, but he did not return, preferring to live in his native Cyrenaica. This faced Synesius with a dilemma. Should he treat Alexander as excommunicated and impose ecclesiastical and social ostracism or, at the other extreme, should he behave towards him as to a colleague in office? Synesius was anxious to do whatever was correct. At first he compromised: he excluded Alexander from church and ignored him in public places—but he received him hospitably in his own home. This solution left him uneasy, however: he honoured the memory of Chrysostom and believed in good

---

[40] *Ep.* 105.
[41] *Ep.* 105 is addressed to Synesius' brother, but the arguments are meant for Theophilus.
[42] *Ep.* 67 (*PG* lxvi. 1412 ff.) = 66 p. 105 ff. (Garzya).   [43] *Ep.* 105.

manners. So he asked Theophilus for a ruling. Clearly he was going to do whatever Theophilus would instruct him to do.[44]

Synesius, philosopher that he was, fully joined in the war of words against the 'godless heresy' of Eunomius, whose followers were said to be using influence at court to 'sully' the church. Their 'false teachers' were 'spreading their net' to catch weaker brethren. Their elders were an 'adulterous generation, modern apostles of the devil'. It was well known which estates harboured these 'bandits'. Synesius was in no doubt that Church discipline, what he calls the law of the Church, must be maintained, and that after he had argued his view of the matter, the last and decisive word must be that of Theophilus, his ecclesiastical superior.[45]

The experience of Synesius illustrates how a bishop could step into a position of civic leadership, filling a gap left by the weakening of the city councils. But the fact that a man was bishop was not enough to give him this leadership. A number of factors were involved. Synesius had been a magnate before he was a bishop, and he had occupied a leading position among the frequently quarrelling magnates of the province. He had some influential connections in the capital. He was supported by the powerful patriarch of Alexandria. With all these factors in his favour he was able to bring about the deposition and subsequent prosecution of an imperial governor, and to take the lead in the defence of Ptolemais. But his position was vulnerable. His latest letters written late in 412 or early in 413 express deep depression.[46] Sadness was natural enough in view of the fact that he had lost all three of his sons, and that his occupation as bishop was profoundly uncongenial. But there was a political reason too. Synesius felt abandoned by his friends and deprived of his former influence. What had gone wrong? Perhaps the starting point was that he had overreached himself when he excommunicated the governor Andronicus. At any rate, about this time he lost the friendship of one of his most influential contacts at Constantinople, Anastasius, tutor of the imperial children.[47] That he had lost influence in Pentapolis too is suggested by the fact that his brother Eutropius went into voluntary exile at Alexandria. It seems that he fled to avoid membership of the council. Synesius had interceded for him with the governor Hesychius in vain.[48] In October 412 came the death of Theophilus, bishop of Alexandria.[49] The letters only give isolated

[44] *Ep.* 67, and W. Liebeschuetz (1986), 181–2. Basilinopolis is an emendation of T. D. Barnes (1986*b*).

[45] *Ep.* 5 = 4 (Garzya).

[46] *Epp.* 10, 15, 16, 81 (80).

[47] *Ep.* 56 = 48 (Garzya); cf. *Ep.* 79 (78).

[48] *Ep.* 93 (92); cf. *Ep.* 98.

[49] *Ep.* 12, and W. Liebeschuetz (1986), 180–1; T. D. Barnes (1986*b*) has a different interpretation on the basis that the addressee Cyril is not a bishop but a parish priest.

glimpses of the process by which Synesius became politically isolated. It is clear that his combination of the power of a landed magnate with the prestige of a bishop was not enough to ensure continuance of the influence and power to which he was accustomed. Bishops and notables between them could not provide the continuity of administration of city and territory.

It might be asked whether the evidence of Synesius should be treated as typical. Cyrenaica was not a typical province and Synesius was a very remarkable and unusual man. But there is evidence that the role of Synesius in the secular affairs of Ptolemais and Pentapolis could be paralleled in many cities of the Empire, and that the number of such cities was growing.[50] After all, the bishop was now the only civic dignitary to come near to being an elected leader. He was the only functionary in the city who controlled communal resources independent of the imperial administration.[51] Bishops had long been accustomed to settle disputes between members of their community. The fact that it was up to the bishop to interpret and enforce religious legislation gave him disciplinary power not only over the orthodox, but over heretics, pagans and Jews as well.[52] It is not surprising to find evidence of bishops taking a conspicuous part in famine relief or public building, or efforts to obtain a reduction of imperial taxation. Above all bishops regularly exercised leadership in times of military emergency. Bishops negotiated the surrender of their cities to the Persians, and, as it turned out irreversibly, to the Arab invaders.[53]

In the years after 535 Justinian made a determined attempt to strengthen the system of provincial administration.[54] The detail of the legislation shows that the emperor clearly recognized the secular importance of bishops and attempted to build on it—particularly in the area of jurisdiction.[55] What worried Justinian was not so much the state of city-government, as evidence that the imperial administration was becoming ineffective and failing to sustain the Empire. In fact problems of city and Empire were related. The imperial administration could only provide for the needs of the Empire if it received effective cooperation at city level. Events of subsequent years suggests that Justinian's reforms did not achieve this objective. Bishops and notables could not be an adequate substitute for the political institutions of the city state.

[50] W. Liebeschuetz (1972), 260–3.
[51] J. Gaudemet (1958), 322–68; R. Lizzi (1987).
[52] R. Van Dam (1985), 84–6.
[53] F. Donner (1981).
[54] For a complete survey see A. H. M. Jones, *LRE* 279–83.
[55] H. Jaeger (1960); A. Steinwerter (1956).

Conclusion
The Historians' Post-Mortem

IN his famous *Considérations sur les causes de la grandeur des Romains*, published in 1739, Montesquieu argued that the Romans' reliance on barbarians for the defence of the Empire was the principal cause of its fall. In his view, outstanding military discipline and a highly developed art of war had been the principal reasons for the greatness of Rome. When the Romans began to rely on barbarian recruits they allowed military traditions to decay within the Empire and encouraged the development of the techniques of war among potential enemies across the frontier. Subsequently it proved that traditional discipline and training could not be enforced in the barbarized armies. Roman troops could no longer be relied upon to obey orders, and they no longer displayed the discipline in battle which had given Roman infantry its immense superiority over numerically larger, but much less well disciplined, bands of barbarians. Montesquieu repeats with emphasis the information provided by Vegetius that Roman soldiers were no longer being given the physically strenuous training programme, including long route-marches with full equipment, and that as a result they were no longer fit enough to wear the heavy helmet and armour which had formerly made an intact Roman battle line almost unassailable by unarmoured northern barbarians. Deprived of these advantages Roman armies were no better than their opponents, and the Empire in the West was doomed.[1]

What Montesquieu has to say about the way Christianity influenced the history of the Later Empire is much less significant, both in quantity and acuteness, than his analysis of the role of the army. No doubt he did blame Christianity for a decline in the martial spirit and patriotism of the Romans. He points out, though without elaborating this idea, that the ancestral religion had given a religious dimension to Roman patriotism.[2] But it is possible to gauge his views from a lengthy passage in which worship of images, intervention by priests and, worst of all, monks in secular affairs, and overall feeble

[1] C. L. Montesquieu, *Considérations sur les causes de la grandeur des Romains et de leur décadence*, cited from edition of C. Jullian (Paris, 1900). See ch. 10, 'de la corruption des romains', and ch. 18, 'nouvelles maximes prises par les Romains', esp. 203–4, 206–7; in contrast ch. 2 describes the military traditions that had made Rome great.

[2] Ch. 10, p. 103: 'Il y avait ceci de particulier chez les Romains, qu'ils mêlaient quelque sentiment religieux à l'amour qu'ils avaient pour leur patrie'.

soft-heartedness are held responsible for the failures of the Eastern Empire against the Arabs and later.[3]

Montesquieu's analysis seems to reflect the attitudes of a highly militarized and warlike aristocracy, for whom military qualities of personality and the ability to maintain an efficient capacity for waging war and winning glory seemed to be necessary features of a healthy and self-respecting society. At the same time he believed in a free and just society whose laws were established in accordance with reason, taking into account the special character and spirit of the people whose life they were designed to regulate. He was a predecessor of the philosophers of the French enlightenment,[4] and like them, though in a more moderate way, he advocated a reduction of the influence of the Church in secular affairs.[5] Consequently he had a sharp eye for the harm that the influence of ecclesiastics and monks might have done in the Roman Empire, but was not interested in the way religion, even pagan religion, might have contributed to the political and military strength of Rome in the days of the free republic when she won her empire.

Gibbons's *Decline and Fall*,[6] completed in 1787, is a different kind of book from Montesquieu's *Considérations*.[7] It is on a vastly greater scale, and it is based on much more comprehensive knowledge of the sources. It is narrative history rather than social analysis, but it is interspersed with generalizations based on a very wide range of observations and expressed in memorable phrases.

On the topics of demilitarization and Christianity Gibbon's views seem not to have been very different from those of Montesquieu: he considered both to be primary causes of the decline and fall. But the balance of his interest was very much more civilian. For Gibbon the demilitarization of the Romans was ultimately a consequence of loss of republican freedom:

In proportion as the public freedom was lost in extent of conquest war was gradually improved into an art, and degraded into a trade . . . That public virtue which among the ancients was denominated patriotism is derived from a strong sense of our own interest in the preservation and prosperity of the free government of which we are members.[8]

---

[3] Ch. 22, 'faiblesse de l'empire de l'orient', esp. 250 ff.

[4] D. Mornet, *Les origines intellectuelles de la révolution Française 1715–1787* (Paris, 1933).

[5] T. L. Pangle, *Montesquieu's Philosophy of Liberalism* (Chicago, 1973), esp. 249–59.

[6] E. Gibbon (1787), *The History of the Decline and Fall of the Roman Empire* (London), is cited from the edition of J. B. Bury which first appeared in 1897.

[7] But see Gibbon's *Autobiography*, p. 99: 'My delight was in the frequent perusal of Montesquieu, whose energy of style, and boldness of hypothesis, were powerful to awake and stimulate the genius of the age.' He also 'engaged with Bayle'.

[8] E. Gibbon (1787) i. 1. 9.

It could not therefore survive the death of that freedom. The decline of Roman military art Gibbon ascribed to mistaken policies of Constantine, the separation of frontier guards (*limitanei*) from the field armies, with the latter being given higher pay and status and being quartered in cities with demoralizing effect, and the division of legions into several smaller units. The recruiting of barbarians is seen as a disastrous but inevitable consequence of the unwillingness of the inhabitants of the Empire to serve.[9]

Gibbon gave very much more space to Christianity than to military problems. Indeed it is a special feature of his history which distinguishes it from history as written by his predecessors going back to Late Antiquity[10] that he treats ecclesiastical history together with, and as part of, secular history.[11] But Gibbon's views on the social effect of Christianity were not very different from those of Montesquieu, as can be seen from numerous anticlerical generalizations which are the most frequently cited passages in the History. Montesquieu would surely have approved of a passage like the following: 'The clergy successfully preached the doctrines of patience and pusillanimity; the active virtues of society were discouraged; and the last remains of military spirit were buried in the cloister, a large portion of public and private wealth was consecrated to the specious demands of charity and devotion; and the soldiers' pay was lavished on the useless multitude of both sexes, who could only plead the merits of abstinence and chastity.'[12]

Compared with Montesquieu Gibbon seems to have been less worried by the influence of the Church in secular life; after all, he was writing in Protestant England. But he was just as eager to promote rationalism and above all tolerance.[13] The effect on his *History* is similar. Gibbon is very sharp and eloquent on the subject of Christianity undermining the strength of the Empire. He has very little to say about any positive contribution it might have made to Graeco-Roman society, or its contribution to the survival of the Empire in the East. He, like Montesquieu, was concerned to increase the scope for debate and rational change in public life and to diminish the importance of ritual, ceremony, and symbolism. Consequently he was not very much interested in describing the constructive effects of

[9] E. Gibbon (1787) ii. 17. 176 ff.   [10] Averil Cameron (1985) 36.

[11] See A. Momigliano (1954) = (1966) 40–55.

[12] *Decline and Fall* iv. 38 ('Observations on the fall of the Roman Empire in the West'). 163. See also ch. 31, a most unsympathetic account of monasticism.

[13] Gibbon says relatively little about Roman paganism, but he praises its tolerance: 'the various modes of worship, which prevailed in the Roman world, were all considered by the people as equally true, by the philosopher as equally false and by the magistrate as equally useful' (2. 28).

these irrational and conservative factors. This bias has characterized some of the most important work on Late Antiquity to the present day.

The two hundred years since the completion of Gibbon's *Decline and Fall* has seen an incredible growth of publicly paid scholarship, and in the ocean of books published over these years there has been a whole small literature on Late Antiquity. So the present work represents the inevitably provisional drawing together of threads of an extremely lively, many-voiced, and unfinished discussion. When the author came to define his own position with regard to *grandeur et décadence* he did so principally in relation to the views of two scholars, A. H. M. Jones and G. E. M. de Ste Croix. The reason for this is partly autobiographical. But it also is the case that they are the recent historians who have dealt with themes closest to those treated in this book.

Of all modern works dealing with Gibbon's period it is safe to say that none is more distinguished than A. H. M. Jones's *Later Roman Empire*.[14] If one wants to estimate the success of Jones's book, it is only necessary to compare his book with the principal older studies, the histories of Seeck[15] and Stein.[16] The advance is enormous. The intellectual achievement is the more impressive in that the book has no loose ends. Every fact has a place in the answer to a particular question which the author has set out to answer. Jones did not scatter facts about in order to create an impressionistic picture. There is no attempt to evoke the rich variety of life of the Mediterranean area. There is loss of vividness, but there is the gain that Jones has solved an amazing number of problems. In the sixteen or so years that he worked on the *Later Roman Empire* he completed what would be the life-work of three or four more ordinary scholars. The impact of the *Later Roman Empire* has been vividly expounded by Peter Brown; 'in the present state of Late Roman Studies this book is like the arrival of a steel plant in a region that has of late been given over to light industry'.[17]

The third volume of the *Later Roman Empire* contains references to the sources on which the narrative and descriptive chapters are founded. It contains vast numbers of Greek and Latin texts, scarcely any references to modern literature. This is, in the words of J. Crook, a very scientific history.[18] But if Jones did not engage in much discussion with earlier scholars, and if he did not look at the Roman Empire from any particular philosophical or theoretical point of view, his *Later Roman Empire* does fall into a definite recognizable

[14] A. H. M. Jones (1964).   [15] O. Seeck (1911–20).
[16] E. Stein (1949).   [17] P. Brown (1967).   [18] J. Crook (1971).

tradition of discourse. The conventions are not so much those of any particular school of history as those within which the main central line of political debate has been carried out in Britain at least since Victorian times. The *Later Roman Empire* is extremely undogmatic. Conclusions are based on facts and on commonsense assumptions about unchanging human nature. When constructing his survey of the Roman Empire Jones did not make use of theories whether of psychologists or sociologists or economists. He did not judge Roman institutions by comparison with any ideal of how society should be organized.

Thus the *Later Roman Empire* is extremely unsentimental. Many scholars writing about the Greeks and the Romans seem to have been motivated by admiration of Athenian democracy, for instance, or classical art or literature, or of the Roman Empire or the Augustan peace. Innumerable times the Greeks and Romans have been upheld as models for modern man. Not by A. H. M. Jones. His survey is so critical that one sometimes wonders whether he did not really dislike the Empire and welcome its destruction. I think that one can recognize the unsentimental side of British politics which, for instance, within most of our lifetimes made the jettisoning of the British Empire comparatively painless. It is a tradition which is concerned with justice for individuals, but does not weep for institutions or organizations.

A. Momigliano, who drew attention to this aspect of the *Later Roman Empire*,[19] noted that the work seemed to be written in the tradition of British government White Papers, and more specifically 'in the direct line of the Webbs and Hammonds, indeed of Booth and Beveridge. His work deserves to go down as the Jones Report on the state of the Roman Empire.'

The *Later Roman Empire* is state- and administration-centred. It is assumed that both the achievements and the failings of Roman society were largely due to the quality or defects of its public machinery. Within the public service Jones believed in professionalism. Officials and officers should be appointed for merit rather than on grounds of birth. He is for justice and against corruption.

Jones sympathized with the peasantry and resented the vast and conspicuous consumption of the governing classes, especially of the Western senators. He felt that it must have been enjoyed at the expense of the rest of the population, and especially of the peasants. For the upper classes, he believed in high taxes, honestly collected and responsibly spent. He was indignant at tax evasion. His

[19] A. Momigliano (1965).

sympathies were with productive workers in the towns and on the land, and against recipients of unearned income, whether senators, or decurions, or bishops.

He was particularly hard on decurions. In an earlier work[20] he had himself shown that the downfall of this class of civic notables, which had been mourned by many earlier historians, was self-inflicted, in that wealthy members of the local councils had managed to improve their status by entering the senatorial order or the imperial civil service:

The *curiales* were not, and never had been, creators of wealth. They were rentiers, landlords who were often absentees, and did not on the whole, so far as we know, take any active interest in their estates. They were, many of them, men of culture and education, and in so far as they gave their unpaid services to the government and contributed to its cost, fulfilled a social role: but they did not increase the wealth of the empire.[21]

There is much truth in this. Nevertheless this grudging attitude to the Roman bourgeoisie has prevented Jones from examining the full significance of what happened to the cities in Late Antiquity.

Unlike Gibbon's famous work, the *Later Roman Empire* is not focused on 'decline and fall'. It is concerned with the functioning of the empire as it lived. But the fact is that it did end, and Jones has duly given his views on the reasons why it declined. His basic reason is characteristically simple and commonsensical. He notes that when the Western Empire collapsed in the middle of the fifth century, the Eastern Empire survived. The frontiers of the Eastern Empire were less vulnerable strategically, and down to the end of the fifth century they were also subjected to less pressure than those of the West. This suggests, in Jones's own words, 'that the simple but rather unfashionable view that the barbarian played a considerable part in the decline and fall of the Western Empire may have some truth in it'.[22] In other words, to quote A. Piganiol, 'the Empire did not die of old age, it was assassinated'.[23]

Even though Jones came out with a verdict of murder, rather than death from natural causes, he nevertheless uncovered a lot of failings which a wise and all-powerful emperor would have reformed. The most fundamental is that the superstructure of the Empire was too heavy for its agricultural base. 'The basic economic weakness of the

---

[20] A. H. M. Jones (1940), 192–210.   [21] *LRE* 1053.
[22] *LRE* 1027.   [23] A. Piganiol (1972), last words.

Empire was that too few producers supported too many idle mouths.'[24]. Most conspicuously among these were of course the members of the imperial senate. 'Each senator directly maintained an army of slaves to minister to his wants, and inevitably employed a great number of artists, craftsmen and merchants to supply him with luxury goods.'[25] Also included among the parasites were the local aristocracies, the decurions, who held a monopoly of political power in the hundreds of cities that made up the Empire.

In addition to the senators and decurions, the economically idle mouths were those of civil servants, Christian clergy, and soldiers. When the barbarian pressure necessitated a great increase—possibly a doubling—of the army, the combination of taxes and rents rose to a level which the rural population simply could not support. Peasants could no longer afford to bring up children. The population declined. Land went out of cultivation. This was a vicious circle. As the peasantry declined in numbers the pressure on those remaining grew greater.[26]

This theory seems to fit striking features of the Later Roman Empire. A reduced population would explain the mass of legislation freezing a large part of the inhabitants of the Empire, soldiers, peasants, minor civil servants, armament workers, decurions, into hereditary occupations. It also accounts for the extraordinary degree to which the Later Empire depended for its defence on Germans and other barbarians rather than its own citizens.

As an explanation this theory is also very Jonesian in that it is simple and involves only factors that are sharply defined and whose impact would be direct and in theory at least clearly observable. It does not involve unmeasurable concepts such as mental states and their interrelation with social institutions. Jones did not think it worthwhile to analyse attitudes, say, to military service or to glory, or concepts of citizens' rights and duties, or possible correlation between changes in ideas and changes in social organization, for instance, between the disintegration of the concept of the citizen and the structure of landowning.

More recently the theme of the decline and fall has been taken up by G. E. M. de Ste. Croix, a pupil of Jones, in the last part of the massive *The Class Struggle in the Ancient Greek World*.[27] De Ste. Croix's starting point is A. H. M. Jones's view of the peasantry crushed by a combination of landlords' dues, officials' perquisites, and taxes. But, unlike Jones, he does consider it a part of a historian's task to examine

[24] *LRE* 1045.   [25] *LRE* 1045, more fully 554–7.
[26] *LRE* 1040–45, 1047; some qualification 822–3.
[27] G. E. M. de Ste. Croix (1981), reviewed by R. Browning (1983).

attitudes, and he has set out to trace the invisible, but not therefore insignificant, connections between the failings of the Late Empire and developments in political institutions and economic organization.

De Ste. Croix has strengthened Jones's case for depopulation by assembling a great deal of evidence for the settlement of barbarians within the Empire.[28] This calls for the almost irresistible inference that there was empty land in many places, at least in frontier areas. But de Ste. Croix's explanation of the failure to defend the Empire is basically a mental one: the peasantry, resentful of exploitation, were profoundly indifferent whether their masters were Romans or barbarians. To support this view he has marshalled a great deal of evidence bearing on topics such as deserters from the army, civilians choosing to live under barbarian rule, and Bagaudic peasant risings. He also points out how few are the recorded cases of resistance to barbarian invaders by other than imperial troops.[29] De Ste. Croix's analysis also goes beyond Jones in that he has tried to explain this monumental state of apathy by linking it with social and political developments far back in the history of the Empire. For him the ultimate source of demoralization was the destruction, at the insistence of the Roman conquerors, of democratic constitutions which were widespread in the cities of the Greek world at the time of the conquest. This deprived the mass of the population, that is, of course above all the peasantry, of the institutions which enabled them to defend their rights and status by political means.[30] A parallel trend was the devaluation of the status of the Roman citizen which had once given even a comparatively humble Roman a good chance of avoiding arbitrary punishment or humiliation at the hands of a Roman official. Thus Paul, simply by proclaiming the fact of his Roman citizenship, escaped a summary beating ordered by a Roman officer. Later he appealed to Caesar, with the result that instead of facing trial at Jerusalem where he could not expect a fair hearing he was despatched for trial to Rome itself. In the second century AD the privileging of *honestiores* over *humiliores*, that is, of members of the 'respectable' over the lower classes, came to be more significant than citizenship. So the ordinary Roman citizen lost immunity from examination under torture and the more savage punishments.[31] He became more vulnerable in dealings with officials and social superiors, especially in disputes with a landowner who could influence a judge to put pressure on the peasants. According to de Ste. Croix it was no coincidence that free-born tenants were subsequently tied to their holdings, and that their condition was

[28] Ibid. 509–18.   [29] Ibid. 474–88.
[30] Ibid. 300–26, with impressive documentation 518–37. [31] Ibid. 453–62.

reduced to one of hereditary serfdom.[32] This development, which was paralleled by the loss of independence of many previously independent peasants,[33] was the background and principal cause of the discontent and apathy which obstructed the defence of the Empire.[34]

De Ste. Croix has certainly focused on a development of first-rate importance. It had been a fundamental characteristic of the Graeco-Roman city, of Rome herself no less than of the cities subjected to her, that the peasant enjoyed a definite role in the government of his community, even if the range of his constitutional rights varied from city to city. There can be no question that the peasant lost these rights under the Empire. In fact in important respects, for instance, liability to torture, his condition came to resemble that of a slave. This was a radical change and one which could be expected to have far-reaching consequences.[35]

That the peasantry was edged out of political society, or in other words the peasant's loss of his share in the *respublica*, de Ste. Croix explains in Marxist terms as a consequence of a reduction in the availability and cheapness of slaves. To simplify a little: faced with increased production costs as a result of a decline in the numbers and the higher costs of slaves landowners were anxious to restore their profit margins by pressing higher rents out of free tenants.[36] This would be easier if they were deprived of their political and legal rights. So de Ste. Croix sees the running down of popular participation in government and of the legal privileges of Roman citizenship as 'primarily a development that would facilitate exploitation and as brought about by the propertied classes for precisely that purpose'.[37]

This explanation has the merit of focusing the historian's investigation on agriculture, the basic 'industry' of the ancient world which provided the occupation of the vast majority of the population. In theory at least so profound a change as the decline of slavery and its direct consequence should have left observable traces. In practice it has proved very difficult for historians to make progress in this area. Ancient writers do not show awareness of any decline in slavery, and modern historians have so far been unable to find sufficient evidence to be able to assess the significance of the crisis, if any, in slave holding on the basis of agreed facts. Historians are still far from

[32] G. E. M. de Ste. Croix (1981), reviewed by R. Browning (1983), 249–55. The fullest compact account of the tied colonate is in A. H. M. Jones *LRE* 795–83.
[33] The extent to which free peasants lost their independence in different parts of the Empire is still very obscure, cf. above p. 21.
[34] G. E. M. de Ste. Croix (1981) 475, A. H. M. Jones *LRE* 1058–64.
[35] See remarks of M. I. Finley (1980) 144; R. MacMullen (1986).
[36] G. E. M. de Ste. Croix (1981) 226–62.   [37] Ibid. 463.

having established even in very rough and approximate outline the trends in such key factors as the numbers, prices, or range of deployment of slaves.[38]

The present study, like the later chapters of de Ste. Croix's book, starts from Jones's analysis of the Later Empire. But instead of focusing on the slave system of production, or indeed production at all. I have gone back to Montesquieu and concentrated on the military system. One advantage of this approach is that the sources provide far more evidence about the army than about slavery. At the same time it can be argued that when it comes to explaining the development of the Graeco-Roman city, and territorial states composed of such cities, changes in military organization seem to have had as great or indeed greater influence than changes in production.[39] After all, the city state had started very largely as an organization by the inhabitants of a compact territory for mutual defence. It was the fact that participation by the peasantry was needed for hoplite infantry tactics that gave the Greek and Italian peasants the political leverage necessary to force themselves into the political system, and to get themselves recognized as fellow citizens by the propertied leaders of their society. Indeed it might be argued that it was the requirements of hoplite tactics that produced the concept of citizenship. Under the Early Empire defence ceased to be the duty of all citizens and was entrusted to a professional army. It is no coincidence that the same period also saw the fading out of popular assemblies, jury courts, and indeed the concept of equal rights of citizens as citizens. One result was to make it easier for the propertied to keep control of their city, and no doubt to exploit the peasantry, as de Ste. Croix has argued.

At the same time the imperial administration tightened its supervision of the cities. One can think of a variety of reasons for that. No doubt the local aristocracies needed to be supervised by somebody. From the end of the second century the external pressure on the Empire grew and with it the demands made by the government on the decurions. After the reorganization of Diocletian the demands were enforced by a much tighter system of provincial administration. Concurrently the needs and interests of the imperial administration itself became an independent factor in the evolution of the organization

[38] M. I. Finley (1980) 123–149 on 'the decline of ancient slavery' brings out difficulties in establishing trends in number and cost of slaves; p. 129 refers to I. Biezunska Malowist, *L'esclavage dans l'Égypte gréco-romaine* 2 vols. (Warsaw, 1974–7) ii. 165–7 to show that the cost of slaves did *not* rise in Egypt.

[39] I am thinking of the part played by hoplites in the rise of Greek democracy, of the secession of the plebeians in the Roman 'struggle of the orders', and of the professionalization of the army in the destruction of the Roman Republic.

of the cities. The existence of a centralized administration inevitably resulted in the downgrading of the status, and even the security, of decurions. Equally inevitably such decurions as were able left their city councils for positions of greater honour and security. That this was damaging to the cities was obvious to all. But in the circumstances nothing effective could be done to stop the trend.

Already the distinction between *honestiores* and *humiliores* and the privileging of the former was more directly in the interest of the imperial administration and its members than of simply 'the propertied'. Senators, knights, curiales, soldiers, and veterans, who made up the *honestiores*,[40] had in common that they were all in one way or another concerned with the maintenance of imperial rule. As the imperial administration developed in the course of the fourth century and after, there arose an elaborate hierarchy of ceremonial precedence, status, and privilege. A man's place in this order of rank was determined by his position in the imperial administration or his closeness to the emperor—or to corrupt influence.[41] Most, or all, of these men of rank were property owners. But there would not have been so many of them, and their property would not have been so great, if the Empire had not been obliged to become bureaucratic. Decurions over many generations took advantage of this oppor-tunity.[42] They can hardly be blamed. Their dilemma was a result of the incompatibility of effective local self-government with an active and interventionist central administration.

This development—the rise of the *potentes* and the decline of the *curiales*—illustrates not so much the 'complete control exercised over the whole Graeco-Roman world by the very highest class, of senators and equestrians',[43] as the progressive breaking down of control by city authorities, with the eventual consequence that the the central administration, which had worked through cities, lost control as well.[44] The impression given by the letters of Synesius is that in Cyrenaica the cities came to be dominated by a small number of powerful men who were much less involved in the affairs of their city than decurions had been. In fact they seem to have spent much of their time carrying on feuds among themselves and setting members of the imperial administration against each other.[45] The running down of city self-government certainly affected recruiting and defence.

---

[40] P. Garnsey (1970) 235–59 lists the privileged groups, whose degree of privilege was not identical. *Honestiores* is a blanket term covering all the privileged and distinguishing them from the non-privileged, the *humiliores*.

[41] A. H. M. Jones *LRE* 543–6, 586 (rank); 487–94 (*praescriptio fori*).

[42] *LRE* 740 ff.   [43] G. E. M. de Ste. Croix (1981) 473.

[44] See the acute and stimulating formulations of P. Brown (1978) 27–53.

[45] See J. H. W. G. Liebeschuetz (1985b).

When the regular troops were no longer able to keep invaders out of the provinces it was left to magnates to mobilize the population around their estates. We do not hear of communal action by cities to defend their territories.[46]

The circumstances of the recruiting of foreigners into the Roman army do not suggest that this was caused principally by heavy taxation and consequent depopulation. We do not know at what rate taxes were levied in the fourth century.[47] While there certainly was a reduction in population in some areas, but not everywhere in the West,[48] the fourth century saw the beginning of a long period of population growth in the East—taxation notwithstanding.[49] So clearly other factors played a part too—for instance, the weakening of the political organization of cities. Large estates also are likely to have been an important factor wherever they developed. A great landowner could resist recruiting more effectively than a small peasant. The relative strength of different factors varied in different parts of the empire,[50] but the recruiting difficulty seems to have been almost universal. There certainly was an important element of cultural demilitarization. This was not simply a matter of resentment of exploitation. After all the old officer class, the *curiales* and senators, had become just as demilitarized as the peasants.[51]

Certainly de Ste. Croix is right to focus on the devaluation of the status of the citizen. But the loss of legal protection for the peasants was only one aspect of this. Another was weakening of the pride, solidarity, and sense of superiority of men conscious of their status as Romans. It is only necessary to visit the site of a Roman *colonia*, and to look at monuments with their inscriptions of civil or military careers in the service of the Empire, to realize how important these little Romes must have been as centres of Romanization in distant provinces, and as breeding grounds for future generations of soldiers and officials.[52] In the Late Empire this spirit was dead. Law continued to differentiate between citizens and non-citizens (*peregrini*), but in practice the distinction seems to have made very little difference. The

---

[46] See above, p. 231.

[47] A. H. M. Jones's calculations of very high rates of taxes under Justinian (*LRE* 464) is based on the single P. Cairo 67059 (cf. *JHS*. lxxi (1951) 271–2) from Antaeopolis. Yet R. Rémondon (1965) shows that taxes at Aphrodito continued to rise until the Arab conquest. So there was room for tax rises after Justianian, and the figures from Antaeopolis are either untypical or misleading.

[48] See above, p. 19.   [49] See above, p. 16.

[50] Large estates did not dominate everywhere: see above, p. 000. The tied colonate may not have come to Egypt.

[51] See above, p. 23.

[52] J. C. Mann (1983) 56. The use of Roman honorific nomenclature seem to have survived longest in North Africa.

Theodosian Code has very few laws about relations between Romans and non-Romans, even though the very large number of non-Romans, or at least of men born as non-citizens, in all ranks of the army would surely have produced numerous legal problems if citizenship had retained anything like its former importance. There was a law prohibiting marriage between citizens and *gentiles*. This was evidently valued by both parties, since it was taken over into the law codes of the German successor states. But one suspects that the prohibition mattered because it preserved the distinction between federates and regulars, rather than because it was needed to keep a boundary between citizen and foreigner within the Empire.[53] As Roman citizenship and local citizenship came to matter less other groupings became important. In the senatorial order there arose an important distinction between 'illustrious' senators and senators of lower rank, in the cities between ordinary curiales, principal curiales (*principales*), and men of imperial rank (*honorati*).[54] The departments of the imperial administration developed a cohesion of their own symbolized by the entitlement of officials to face criminal charges, and sometimes even to have civil cases heard, in a court presided over by their head of department.[55] In the countryside there was the consolidation of smaller peasants around the great landowner who gave protection and acquired control as patron, tax collector, and even judge. This development was partly a result of coercion, but partly voluntary.[56] Most far-reaching of all, large bodies of federate mercenaries, instead of being assimilated into the nationhood of the state employing them, developed a new sense of tribal nationhood of their own.[57]

Federates constituted a great danger to imperial government. In the West the commander-in-chief of the army became *de facto* ruler of the Empire. But in the East the end of the fourth century saw the consolidation at Constantinople of a new culturally Greek ruling group, who realized the danger and responded by adopting a policy of solving military problems as far as possible by non-military means. They reduced the size of the army and frustrated the ambition of generals. The Gainas affair was a reaction against this policy. Once the crisis had been passed the civilian policy was resumed. The Eastern government consolidated its control over the army, and the Eastern provinces embarked upon an age of stability and prosperity.

[53] See above, p. 13.
[54] A. H. M. Jones *LRE* 552-4, W. Liebeschuetz (1972).   [55] *LRE* 484-94.
[56] E. Patlagean (1977b) 288-96; I. Hahn, 'Das bäuerliche *patrocinium* in Ost und West', *Klio* 1 (1968) 261-76 = H. Schneider (ed.), *Sozial und Wirtschaftsgeschichte der römischen Kaiserzeit*, Wege der Forschung 552 (Darmstadt, 1981) 234-57.
[57] See above, p. 48-85.

The society of the Eastern Empire became conspicuously Christian. Churches came to dominate cities; the liturgical calendar guided men and women through their lives. It is a fair assumption that Christianity contributed to the functioning of this society. But the nature of its contribution is not easy to assess, because religion achieves its effects not principally as a result of explicit teachings being strictly obeyed, but through the influence of ritual and symbols which work on worshippers by evocation, association, and habit, whose effects are not easily defined. This is one reason why a main tradition of historical research into Late Antiquity has been markedly secular in its approach; another is surely that the tradition is rooted in the French enlightenment.[58]

In a well-known aphorism Gibbon summed up the fall of the Roman Empire as the triumph of barbarism and religion.[59] Jones noted that Christianity, for all its preaching, failed to make men demonstrably better.[60] He points out that it was considerably more expensive than the paganism it replaced, and that this expense was ultimately borne, like all other public expense, by the already overburdened peasantry.[61] Jones regretted the fact that Christianity did not provide a code of conduct for officials. Christian prohibition of killing made life more difficult for judges and soldiers, facing them with moral dilemmas in the course of their regular duties.[62] Jones's negative view of the effect of Christianity on the Empire is moderated only by the fact that he did not consider that any belief or ritual affected human behaviour very greatly. Rejecting the view that Christianity sapped the Empire's morale, Jones commented that 'there is little to show that pagan worship promoted patriotic spirit. . . . For the vast majority of ordinary men Christianity caused no fundamental change in attitude'.[63]

[58] One ought also to mention O. Seeck's *Geschichte des Untergangs der antiken Welt*, which gives a lot of space to religion, but from a crudely evolutionary point of view, and E. Stein's *Histoire du Bas-Empire*, which is almost entirely secular, even though its author was a convert from Judaism to Catholicism. One can draw another line, from Fustel de Coulanges and Durkheim (see A. Momigliano 1970) through N. H. Baynes to Peter Brown, Averil Cameron, and E. Patlagean, of writers who integrate religion into their reconstruction of society and take into account the social effect of ritual and symbolic arts, while not necessarily writing as committed Christians.

[59] *Decline and Fall* vii. 71. 308, but see his note (*Autobiography*, p. 187): 'I have sometimes thought of writing a dialogue of the dead, in which Lucian, Erasmus, and Voltaire should mutually acknowledge the danger of exposing an old superstition to the contempt of the blind and fanatic multitude.'

[60] *LRE* 1063, but he notes the large scale of almsgiving (972) and strict sexual standards (973–4).

[61] *LRE* 1046.   [62] *LRE* 1063–4.

[63] *LRE* 1062–3; cf. *Decline and Fall* iv. 38 ('Observations on the fall of the Roman empire in the West'): 'If superstition had not afforded a decent retreat, the same vices would have tempted the unworthy Romans to desert from baser motives the standard of the republic'.

De Ste. Croix certainly does not underestimate the effects of Christianization, but he sees them as largely negative. Christianity was expensive.[64] It created division between followers of different versions of Christian religion.[65] It encouraged men to deal with poverty through charity, not through a political system that produced communal action to support the weaker members of society.[66] He also notes that Christianity did nothing to end, or even prevent the growth, of great evils such as the use of torture and barbarous punishment, vast extremes of wealth and poverty, and above all, slavery.[67]

There is truth in these observations but they are one-sided. De Ste. Croix is out of sympathy with the Christian-dominated Byzantine society which was coming into being; he believes that the development was regressive and castigates it, as a warning to the present. This has been a time-honoured role for a historian since Antiquity.[68] But it is not the only possible role. The impact of Christianity on Late Roman society is so complex and far-reaching that it calls for comprehensive analysis and mapping. But for this one has to go to historians of another school.[69]

It is seriously to underestimate the significance of the Christian ideal of charity to treat it as nothing more than a doctrine which would salve the conscience of the rich. In the Classical World the idea that man owed a duty to support his fellow men simply because they were fellow creatures of God was something new.[70] The Christian duty of giving was defined quite unclassically as an obligation to help the neighbour in need, with all the poor, the sick, prisoners, widows and orphans, and the aged coming under the definition of neighbours. The politically motivated giving of the city had not been so comprehensively defined. Its recipients were the political citizens as a whole, voters, clients, and other individuals who could be expected to do a favour in return. Slaves or foreigners were not included. The Christian ideal meant progress. In any case the social context of traditional munificence was no longer available. Politically motivated giving had almost ceased. As local politics was fading away, there was no incentive for giving with an expectation of political return. There was need for a new idea of mutual help.

Meanwhile the annual cycle of festivals of the Church was uniting the inhabitants of a city in 'ceremonies of consensus'[71] of a kind

---

[64] (1981) 495–7.   [65] Ibid. 488 ff.

[66] Ibid. 438.

[67] Ibid. 439.   [68] e.g. Livy *Praef.* 10.   [69] See above, n. 58.

[70] A. R. Hands (1968) chs. iii–vi.

[71] D. Cannadine (1982) illustrates that concept with a Victorian example.

which traditional paganism had long provided,[72] but which had declined with other institutions of the self-governing, *curia*-led, city.[73] Sermons calling on the wealthy to give to the poor led only in exceptional cases to a rich individual actually liquidating his wealth,[74] but they did provide continuous moral pressure, which to some extent replaced the political pressure of the many on the few in the political city. The effect cannot be quantified, but it was not insignificant. Solidarity based on the Christian concept of charity surely contributed a great deal to preserving the cohesion of cities, particularly in the East,[75] and thus helped them to survive for about two centuries the decay of their political institutions.

It is easy simply to dismiss Christian asceticism. So Jones saw it as only affecting 'a minority who took the Christian message seriously to heart, and regarding the things of the world as of no account, devoted themselves to achieving eternal life in the world to come'.[76] Earlier, Gibbon had been both impressed and shocked by the scale of the phenomenon; nevertheless when he mocked 'the useless multitude of both sexes who could only plead the merit of abstinence and chastity'[77] he too closed his eyes to the far-reaching effects of the monastic movement. Neither he nor Jones could do full justice to it.

The ascetic ideal inspired new ways of life which, among other things, enabled men or women to make a living as well as meditate and pray unencumbered by family and household. The ascetic life appealed to different individuals for different reasons, but altogether many thousands were attracted.[78] No less important was the fact that self-denial of every kind was thought to confer authority. The idea seems strange in a society where late-Roman values have been turned upside down, so that celibacy is a cause of suspicion, not a recommendation when a man or woman seeks a position of authority. But in Late Antiquity the idea of chastity was a dynamic force. Hermits and monks established a new kind of leadership in the countryside.[79] Pulcheria, sister of Theodosius II, exercised a degree of influence and scarcely concealed power quite unprecedented among

---

[72] R. Lane Fox (1986) 80–82; cf. P. Brown (1978) 35 ff., 'the public worship of traditional gods still activated strong collective images of concord and parity.'

[73] Most strikingly demonstrated by a sudden break in civic inscriptions, religious and secular, around AD 240, described by J. Geffken (tr. Sabine G. MacCormack, 1978) 25; cf. R. Lane Fox (1986) 574 ff.

[74] Not necessarily agreeable to the slaves working the estates about to be given away: *V. Melaniae* 10 ff.

[75] It is likely that the West with shrinking towns and a shrinking population generally did not have the same problem of poverty.

[76] *LRE* 1063.

[77] *Decline and Fall* iv. 38 ('Observations on the fall of the Roman Empire in the West') 163.

[78] A. Grillmeyer, H. Bacht (1951–4) ii. 292–96. [79] P. Brown (1971).

female members of imperial dynasties,[80] and the foundation of Pulcheria's authority was a reputation for holiness derived from the fact that she had formally renounced marriage. Chrysostom spent six years with a hermit on the edge of the Syrian desert. No doubt this experience deeply influenced his personality and thought. It is likely that his independence, abrasiveness, and concern for the poor owed something to the experience of ascetic living. In cities all over the Empire bishops, a male celibate élite,[81] were teaching their congregations week after week, year after year. In the capital, the patriarch, potentially a rival, was normally a valuable ally of the emperor who had appointed him. The traditional limits of a bishop's role and the continuing overwhelming power of a Roman emperor kept the bishop of Constantinople in his place. As Chrysostom experienced, the bishop of the capital could not hold his see against the will of the emperor. But in the provinces, as civic institutions decayed, bishops like Synesius were well on the way to taking control of their cities.[82]

De Ste. Croix's book is 'an attempt to see the Greek world in very close relation with our own, and is inspired by the belief that we can learn much about each by careful study of the other'.[83] If we look at older writing it becomes obvious that great historians of the past, Montesquieu, Gibbon, Fustel de Coulanges, and Jones, have written in the same way, though perhaps they were not all equally conscious that they were doing so.[84] Homer understood the nature of historical research. When Odysseus had lost his way in the present, he consulted the past, that is, the dead seer Teiresias, but the dead prophet could only prophesy after he had drunk the blood of a recently living creature.[85] It is more difficult to recognize the relationship between history and the historian's own world in contemporary writing. But if some of the most interesting work has been about the social implications of holy men, relics, images, and ritual this may be because historians of the present day are aware of disintegration at national, local, and family level,[86] and therefore interested in the devices by which integration and unity were achieved in the past; and especially in the disintegrating world of the Later Empire.[87]

---

[80] Cf. K. Holum (1982*a*), 93. [81] Peter Brown (1987), 269 ff.

[82] See above, p. 232. [83] (1981) xi.

[84] Cf. E. H. Carr (1961) 38: '. . . the historian who is most conscious of his own situation is also more capable of transcending it, and more capable of appreciating the essential nature of the differences between his own society and outlook and those of other periods . . .'

[85] Homer, *Od.* xi. 95 ff.

[86] Cf. A. Momigliano (1977) 372: '. . . by becoming irrelevant to theology, bible criticism risks becoming irrelevant to everything else . . . On a different (perhaps lower) level, the disappearance of national history as a meaningful notion is embarrassing to the historian.'

[87] Perhaps surprisingly there has been little work on the 'demilitarization' of the Romans in spite of the fact that a comparable development has taken place in Western Europe in this century.

Appendix I
The Identity of Typhos in Synesius' *De Providentia*

IT has long been recognized that the Egyptian Tale also known as *De Providentia* of Synesius is an allegory of the events that brought about first the occupation of Constantinople by Gainas the Goth and his largely Gothic mercenaries, and subsequently the destruction of the Goths and their leader. It is agreed that the Osiris of the Tale is to be identified with the praetorian prefect Aurelian. But what historical personage is represented by the villain of the story, Osiris' brother and rival, Typhos, has been much debated. Two men have been principally considered, each sometime praetorian prefect of the East; Caesarius and Eutychianus. O. Seeck identified Typhos with Caesarius;[1] more recently A. H. M. Jones identified him with Eutychianus.[2] More recently still G. Albert,[3] M. Clauss,[4] R. von Haehling, T. D. Barnes, and Alan Cameron[5] have returned with variations to the reconstruction of Seeck. So my continued acceptance of Jones's view requires justification.[6]

Could the prefecture of the East be a collegial office?

The core of Jones's argument is a demonstration that the laws of AD 337–408 can be plausibly assigned to different prefects without any need to assume that any one of the prefectures was ever held collegially by two individuals. Jones concluded that the praetorian prefecture of the period concerned was never a collegial office.[7] If Jones is right, then Typhos must be identified with Eutychianus. For

[1] O. Seeck, 'Studien zu Synesius', *Philologus* lii (1893) 442–83; 'Die Reichspräfektur des vierten Jahrhunderts', *RhM* NF lxix (1914) 1–39; *Die Regesten der Kaiser und Päpste für die Jahre 311–476 n. Chr.* (Stuttgart, 1919), esp. 148, 299–301.

[2] A. H. M. Jones (1964*b*), esp. 80–1. So also in A. H. M. Jones, J. R. Martindale, and J. Morris, *The Prosopography of the Later Roman Empire* i (Cambridge, 1970) and ii (ed. J. R. Martindale, Cambridge, 1980).

[3] G. Albert, 'Zur Chronologie der Empörung des Gainas im Jahre 400 n. Chr', *Historia* xxix (1980) 504–8; (1984) 182–5.

[4] M. Clauss (1980), 133–8.

[5] R. von Haehling, *Die Religionszugehörigkeit der hohen Amtsträger des römischen Reiches seit Constantins I, Alleinherrschaft bis zum Ende der Theodosianischen Dynastie—324 bis 455 n. Chr.*, (Bonn 1978); also T. Barnes (1986*a*), and by far the most thorough of all Alan Cameron, J. Long, L. Sherry (1990).

[6] *De Providentia* cited from J-P Migne, *Patrologia Graeca* lxvi. 1211–82.

[7] 1964*b*.

in autumn of 399 three laws of Aurelian[8] were followed by three laws addressed to Eutychianus.[9] If collegiality is rejected, Eutychianus must have been the successor of Aurelian, as Typhos was of Osiris. The only way to avoid this conclusion would be to re-date the laws of Eutychianus, but since this would mean altering three different, if not widely separated, dates, it would require strong justification.

That the praetorian prefecture of the fourth century was not a collegial office is in itself likely. The administration of a prefecture calls for a single head. None of the other great civilian departments of state was collegially headed. Admittedly we know of one occasion when two individuals held the office of prefect jointly. This was in 378–9, when Ausonius and his son Hesperius were joint prefects of the Gauls and of Italy, Africa, and Illyricum.[10] But this was not a case of a single prefecture being governed collegially by two prefects, but of two prefects having joint administration of two prefectures. It was an exceptional arrangement, by means of which the emperor Gratian conferred a conspicuous honour on his aged tutor. The exception comes near to proving Jones's rule.

But while Jones's rejection of collegial prefectures is plausible on general grounds as well as compatible with a great deal of the evidence, there yet remains doubt, at least as far as the years 396–405 are concerned. The most serious difficulty is presented by *CT* xvi. 2. 32, addressed to the praetorian prefect Caesarius on 26 July 398 when without collegiality there would have been no room for him as prefect, since Anatolius was prefect of Illyricum, and Eutychianus was the second Eastern prefect, i.e. the prefect of Oriens, as is witnessed by numerous laws addressed to him.[11] It is true that many laws in the Theodosian Code have been misdated, but in the case of *CT* xvi. 2. 32 there is no obvious reason why it should have been.[12] So it is just possible that Caesarius was praetorian prefect of the East jointly with Eutychianus. An explanation has been suggested by Albert. The eunuch Eutropius divided the prefecture of the East because he feared the excessive power of the undivided office. One may still wonder why, if the two men held office jointly, between 13. 7. 397 and 25. 7. 399 only one law was addressed to Caesarius, against

---

[8] *CT* ix. 40. 17 (17 Aug.), ii. 8. 23 (27 Aug.), xxv. 6. 2 (2 Oct.).

[9] *CT* xii. 1. 163 (11 Dec.), xii. 1. 164 (28 Dec.), xii. 1. 165 (30 Dec.).

[10] *PLRE* i s.v. Ausonius. Joint-prefect: *Grat. Act.* ii. 11.

[11] Anatolius still prefect of Illyricum in July 398: *CT* vi. 28. 6 of 12. 11. 399. None of the laws addressed to Eutychianus specifies his prefecture—in fact the prefecture of Oriens is rarely specified. Anatolius' prefecture is specified as of Illyricum, and specification continues for later holders of *that* office.

[12] A. H. M. Jones (1964*b*), 81 n. 3: 'This consulship (*Honorio IV et Eutychiano*) seems sound, but must be a mistake.' On likely and unlikely dates in the Theodosian Code see O. Seeck (1919), esp. 18–66.

20 addressed to Eutychianus. The more likely explanation is surely that either the address or the date of *CT* xvi. 2. 32 is mistaken, appearances notwithstanding.[13] Nevertheless the *possibility* of collegial tenure cannot be denied.

Once we allow that collegial prefecture was possible, we are compelled to consider the possibility that this arrangement survived the fall of Eutropius in July 399.[14] If·that was the case, the college must have consisted of Aurelian and Eutychianus, who, as we have seen, between them received six laws in late summer and autumn of 399. If Eutychianus and Aurelian were colleagues, then Typhos cannot be Eutychianus, since in Synesius' Tale Typhos was out of office during Osiris–Aurelian's kingship of Egypt (the prefecture of the East)[15] and only resumed office after Osiris had been overthrown. So if Eutychianus and Aurelian were colleagues Typhos must be identified with Caesarius.[16]

The theory that Eutychianus and Aurelian were colleagues in the prefecture of the East is insecurely founded, but it has consequences which make it attractive. If Aurelian and Eutychianus were colleagues Aurelian's prefecture can be extended beyond the three laws addressed to Eutychianus in December 399. Thus it would become possible for Aurelian to have been in office on 1 January 400, and to have been inaugurated as consul on that date. There are statements in the sources which quite strongly suggest that he did become consul at the beginning of 400.[17] But it remains the case that a collegiality of Typhos–Eutychianus and Osiris–Aurelian would seem a direct contradiction of Synesius' Tale. According to this, the election of Osiris meant the defeat of Typhos,[18] and in a later passage Typhos is said to have resented the fact that he had lost office.[19] Both on general considerations and in view of the relevant evidence it would therefore be preferable to abandon the theory of a collegial prefecture.

---

[13] *CJ* xii. 57. 9, addressed to Clearchus as *PPO Ill.*, and dated by Seeck between February 396 and June 397 (when according to Jones Eutychianus was *PPO Ill.*), is not a serious obstacle to acceptance of Jones's reconstruction. Jones's moving of it into a vacancy 402–7 is perfectly convincing, because during the first years of his nominal reign Theodosius II was frequently omitted from '*Idem AA*' headings of laws, e.g. *CT* xvi. 2. 37, 8. 15–17, 5.37, xv. 1. 42–6, xii, 6. 29–30. See also O. Seeck, (1919) iii.

[14] Perhaps around 25 July when *CT* ix. 14. 3, threatening even the relatives of conspirators against 'illustrious' members of the consistory, was in effect repealed by ix. 40. 18.

[15] *De Prov.* 1241 A: Osiris's election meant τῆς βασιλείας ἐκπεπτωκέναι τὸν ἄνδρα (i.e. Typhos); 1223 B: the election of Osiris was equivalent to the rejection of Typhos.

[16] See n. 3 above for reference to G. Albert's full development of this argument.

[17] Socr. vi. 6; Soz. viii. 45; Zos. v. 17. 8; John Ant., *FHG* iv. 61 *b*; these are discussed below, p. 259.

[18] *De Prov.* 1225.

[19] Ibid. 1241.

The chronology of Gainas' occupation of Constantinople and the date of the deposition of Aurelian

The abandonment of the possibility of a joint prefecture of Aurelian and Eutychianus leaves us with the problem of how Aurelian could have become consul on 1 January 400, even though the dates of three laws in the Code suggest that Eutychianus had succeeded him in the praetorian prefecture of the East by 11. 12. 399.[20] His exile ought to have followed immediately after. It seems certain that if Eutychianus was in office from 11. 12. 399 Aurelian could not have been inaugurated as consul on 1. 1. 400. There seems to be no way out of this dilemma, unless either the dates of the laws of Eutychianus, or that of the consulate of Aurelian are wrong. Later in this appendix I shall argue that it is the statement about the consulate of Aurelian which is mistaken, or rather, imprecise.[21] But it is certainly the case that very many laws in the Theodosian Code have wrong dates. Moreover Alan Cameron has produced a strong case for the proposition that the three laws addressed to Eutychianus in December 399 are really all part of the same law, and that they really belong to autumn 398, when Eutychianus was undeniably praetorian prefect of the East, and legislating on the subject of decurions.[22] Alan Cameron's argument is plausible, though not conclusive. But the transmitted dates of the laws should only be rejected if they are incompatible with an otherwise well-documented chronology of events, that is, if the bulk of the evidence for the events following Aurelian's exile is impossible to reconcile with Eutychianus' accession to the prefecture, Gainas' coup, and Aurelian's exile having taken place in December 399.

Now Gainas' occupation was in any case short, 8 months (11. 12. 399–12. 7. 400) on Jones' chronology,[23] 4 months (March 400–12. 7. 400) on the alternative view.[24] Within the long periods covered by Zosimus and the ecclesiastical historians this is an almost insignificant interval of time, and it is not surprising that their narratives make the Gothic occupation appear a very brief episode, and thus seem to support a very short chronology. But in Synesius' Egyptian Tale the Gothic occupation of Constantinople represents the central episode. It therefore gives a less telescoped account of the events following Gainas' coup than the other sources, which only describe the coup itself and the events leading up to the destruction of the Goths. It is

[20] *CT* xii. 1. 1163 (11 Dec.), 164 (28 Dec.), 165 (30 Dec.).   [21] See below, p. 260.
[22] Alan Cameron, J. Long, L. Sherry (1990), ch. v. 5.
[23] A. H. M. Jones (1964*b*), 81.
[24] e.g. T. D. Barnes (1986) 99, Alan Cameron, J. Long, L. Sherry (1990), ch. V.

from Synesius alone that we can derive any estimate of the length of the occupation.

Synesius' account shows that the reign of Typhos cannot have been very short. He remained in office long enough to increase the tax burden of cities, to call in arrears of taxation, and (as Synesius himself experienced) to cancel exemptions from curial duties.[25] Typhos was in office long enough for his strict financial policy to be credited with results—if only causing widespread distress.[26] Synesius notes that even when the disagreeable consequences of his policy began to be felt Typhos was not deposed immediately—since the gods wished to impress even the dullest wits to appreciate the difference between good and wicked men.[27] This is all very vague, but I would suggest that in view of the slowness of communication in the Roman Empire it would take something like three months at least for a new fiscal policy to be put into effect and to provide a response from the taxpayer. But since, as Synesius insists, the gods made Typhos' victims endure their miseries for some time longer,[28] it looks as if the reign of Typhos lasted significantly longer than three months.

The Egyptian Tale contains a second and less vague survey of events of the reign of Typhos. Synesius relates the experience of a certain stranger, a thinly veiled account of his own experiences at Constantinople under Typhos. When Typhos had seized power Synesius proceeded to make speeches in praise of Osiris, the last in the presence of Typhos himself. Typhos went from bad to worse. The good conditions created by Osiris disappeared. The concessions which Osiris had granted to the cities of Synesius' home province and to Synesius personally were cancelled, and Synesius was in the depths of despondency when a divine oracle promised relief,[29] but not immediate relief, relief 'not in a period of years but of months'.[30] The implication of the narrative is that at the time of the oracle Typhos' tyranny had already lasted some time, and that it would be some further months (surely at least two) before there could be a turning point for the better.

The incident forecast as the turning point, namely, 'when those in power should attempt to introduce innovations in our religious rites',[31] duly came to pass, and the oracle which was surely *ex eventu* was fulfilled. The incident is known also from other sources and, what is more, it can be dated.

---

[25] *De Prov.* 1252 B–53. Synesius' loss of recently gained privileges: 1256 A–B and *PLRE* s.v. Synesius.

[26] 1252 D.   [27] Ibid.   [28] 1252.

[29] 1253 C–1256 B.

[30] 1256 B οὐ γὰρ ἐνιαυτοὺς ἀλλὰ μῆνας.   [31] 1256 C.

According to Synesius Typhos tried to give a temple to the foreigners where rites were to be celebrated which an old law had forbidden to be celebrated in cities.[32] This must be the episode related by Socrates, Sozomen, and Theodoret, when Chrysostom resisted before the emperor a proposal that a church should be given to the Gothic soldiers for Arian services.[33] According to Sozomen and Theoderet Chrysostom's opposition was successful, and according to Sozomen it was precisely at this point that a huge comet was seen in the sky. Now it seems that the sighting of a comet was actually recorded in China from 19 March well into April of AD 400. So this was the time of the year when things began to go wrong for Typhos. It follows that he must have been in power and flourishing for several months before 19 March.[34] In other words a date in December 399 for the coup and the exiling of Aurelian would fit the evidence very well.

The destruction of the Goths did not follow instantly after the controversy over the Arian church; Synesius and the ecclesiastical historians are in agreement on that. According to Synesius what followed immediately was a succession of irrational panics among the foreigners, 'at one moment attempting to draw their swords, and behaving as about to deliver an immediate attack, at another, on the contrary claiming pity and asking to be spared . . . they seemed alternately like pursuers and pursued, as though some hostile force had been secretly conveyed into the town'.[35] Socrates and Sozomen report that the Goths first set out to raid the shops of the silversmiths, and then repeatedly made attacks on the imperial palace, only to be repelled by a vision of supernatural defenders.[36] Synesius and the ecclesiastical historians surely refer to the same events. They are also in agreement that these disturbing experiences induced the Goths to begin to withdraw from Constantinople, and that an incident in the course of this evacuation led to fighting and to the destruction of the Goths still left inside the walls.[37]

I would therefore argue that *De Providentia*, the Egyptian Tale, does provide a definite chronology for the Gothic occupation of Constantinople. Destruction of the Goths: 12 July 400. Demand for an Arian church: about 19 March 400. Beginning of Typhos' reign, that is, Gainas' coup: at least three months earlier. About 11 December 399 would be a perfectly reasonable, and even likely, date for Gainas' coup and Aurelian's exile. There is therefore no reason to emend the dates of the three laws of Eutychianus. It follows that

---

[32] 1256 D.   [33] Socr. vi. 6; Soz. viii. 4; Theodoret *HE* v. 32.
[34] D. J. Schove (1984) 68.   [35] *De Prov.* 1260, tr. FitzGerald.
[36] Socr. iv. 6; Soz. viii. 4; cf. John Ant. fr. 190 (*FHG* iv. 611); Philostorg. xi. 8.
[37] See above, p. 113–14.

Eutychianus was the prefect who succeeded Aurelian, and Typhos of *De Providentia* should be identified with him. There does however remain the difficulty of Aurelian's consulate.

The consulate of Aurelian

All sources agree that Aurelian was driven out of office and into exile by Gainas.[38] We are told by Zosimus that this happened in the year in which he was consul, that is, in 400. Furthermore we learn from Palladius' *Dialogue concerning the Life of John Chrysostom* that at a time which must have been around 1 April 400 Chrysostom was prevented from leaving Constantinople because the bishop and 'guardian of souls' ought not to leave the city during 'the anticipation of so great a tumult'—the 'anticipated tumult' being identified with Gainas, the barbarian.[39] Albert has identified the 'anticipated tumult' with the arrival of Gainas opposite Constantinople and the coup in which Aurelian was overthrown and replaced by Typhos.[40]

At first sight the conclusion that Aurelian was prefect until spring 400 seems unavoidable. On further examination, however, doubts arise. To start with the consulate: in Synesius' *De Providentia* the honour to have the year named after him is listed among the distinctions conferred on Osiris–Aurelian *after* he had returned from exile, that is, as we shall see, probably late in autumn 400.[41] Now this should be taken extremely seriously. Synesius had after all been at Constantinople at the time: he knew what had happened. Why should he have named the 'eponymous year', together with the welcoming crowds, the torch processions, the distribution of gifts (surely marking the inauguration),[42] and the pardoning of his wicked brother, if these events did not all happen at the same time? It must of course have been almost unique for an eponymous consul to be inaugurated close to the end of his year, but in this case the fact of Aurelian's exile would provide an explanation. Consuls were normally designated in September or thereabouts. This gave the consul-designate time to make preparations and to send out invitations to friends for the formal inauguration on 1 January.[43] If Aurelian was inaugurated towards the end of his year, this can only have been because on 1 January he had already been sent into exile.

---

[38] Zos. v. 18 ὁ τὴν ὕπατον ἔχων ἐν ἐκείνῳ τῷ ἔτει τιμῆν; Socr. vi. 6 (677 A); Soz. viii. 4 (1521 C).

[39] Pall. *Dial.* 14 (p. 86. 24–6, 87. 1–3).

[40] G. Albert (1984) 154–6, and *Historia* xxix (1980) 504–8.

[41] 1272 B.

[42] On consular largesse see R. MacMullen, 'The emperor's largesses', *Latomus* xxi (1962) 160 f., Averil Cameron (1976), 197.

[43] e.g. Symmachus *Ep.* i. 101, iii. 21, ix. 113 of autumn 380. Cf. Libanius *Ep.* 1021.

When weighing up the evidence of Synesius on the one hand and of Zosimus and the two ecclesiastical historians on the other, the fact that Synesius was an eye-witness, while the others wrote narratives based on earlier accounts which they very much condensed, must be given due weight. Where their testimony differs, Synesius should be believed. In any case the discrepancy between the two versions is not great. Zosimus does not state that Aurelian was consul at the time when he was exiled, but only that he was eponymous consul of that year—as indeed he did become before the year was out. Zosimus' error is only one of over-simplification. He should have written that at the time of exiling Aurelian was consul-designate. In any case the error is a very small one. Aurelian cannot have missed being exiled while actually consul by more than three weeks. The other sources are demonstrably imprecise. Sozomen describes both men as ex-consuls,[44] Socrates as consulars[45], whilst John of Antioch describes both as consuls.[46] But it does not follow that their source or sources dated the exile firmly into 400, the year of the consulate. After all, the human story in the episode of the exiling of Aurelian is that a man spent in exile much of the year in which he should have held the highest honour in the Roman state. Compared with this pathetic fact the question whether he had actually been inaugurated or not at the moment when he was sent into exile might seem a trivial detail.

The previous paragraph has not of course disproved the strong implication of our sources that Aurelian was exiled after his inauguration during the year of his consulate. The argument is rather that the implication is not so unavoidable as to compel us to disqualify the literal meaning of a statement of Synesius, an eye-witness, the strong chronological indications of Synesius's narrative, and the transmitted dates of one—or even three—laws.

There remains Palladius. According to him Chrysostom was prevented from leaving Constantinople because of an 'anticipated tumult'[47] a tumult which 'was' Gainas.[48] This seems to have been around 1 April 400.[49] Now this *could* mean that the tumult was expected to follow the anticipated arrival of Gainas at Constantinople, but it surely need not do so. The whole stay of the Goths in Constantinople was filled with both rumours and anticipation of tumult. It was feared that the Goths would attack the palace, for

[44] Soz. viii. 4 ὑπατικοὺς ἄνδρας.
[45] Socr. vi. 6 δύω τῶν πρώτων τῆς συγκλήτου ἄνδρας ἀφ' ὑπάτων.
[46] John Ant. fr. 190 λαβεῖν ἀπὸ τῶν ὑπάτων ἀνδρῶν.
[47] *Dial.* loc. cit. (n. 39) ἐν τοσαύτῃ προσδοκίᾳ θορύβου.
[48] ἦν δὲ ὁ Γαινᾶς . . . . ὁ προσδοκώμενος θόρυβος.
[49] Date: G. Albert loc. cit. (n. 3); Alan Cameron, J. Lang, L. Sherry (1990) ch. V. 4.

instance, and that they intended to launch an assault on the city itself. Gainas' request to be allowed to hold Arian services in a church inside Constantinople[50] may well have been anticipated. Certainly, when it came, it was seen as an attempt to cause 'tumult' in the Church.[51] As we have seen, the demand for a church was actually made precisely at this time. Any of these feared operations, above all the last, might have been thought to require the presence of the bishop, the 'guardian of souls', in the midst of his community. We know quite a lot about the personality of John Chrysostom. Was he the kind of man who would wish to leave his congregation when its city might at any day be attacked by seditious barbarian mercenaries? It is much more likely that Chrysostom felt free to leave the city at a time when the crisis had, as it were, stabilized, and the Constantino-politans had got to some extent used to the presence of the unwelcome and unpredictable Gothic soldiers. This would have been the case if the occupation had already lasted some months. In other words Palladius need not, and in my opinion should not, be taken to refer to Gainas' coup. The passage is not relevant to the dating of Aurelian's exile or his inauguration as consul. Aurelian's consulate is not an insuperable obstacle to the identification of Typhos with Eutychianus.

The career and deposition of Typhos

The next step must be to have a closer look at the career of Typhos as described in *De Providentia* with a view to testing whether it really corresponds to what is known about the career of Eutychianus (as A. H. M. Jones thought), or whether it bears a closer resemblance to that of Caesarius, the only other serious candidate.[52] Typhos' earliest office was one of financial administration, perhaps that of *comes sacrarum largitionum*.[53] There is nothing to suggest that he ever held the important office of *magister officiorum*, an office which Caesarius is known to have held.[54] Next Typhos is said to have held successively two administrative posts. The first he held for one year only.[55] The second, which was important enough to involve the assignment of governorships (ἀρχαί), he lost when Osiris–Aurelian was elected to the 'kingship of Egypt', i.e. the prefecture of the East.[56] This sequence of offices would fit the career of Eutychianus as

[50] Soc. vi. 8; Soz. viii. 4; Theodoret *HE* v. 32.
[51] Soz. viii. 4 (1524 A) ἐκκλησίαν θορυβεῖν ἐπεχείρησε.
[52] *PLRE* ii s.v. Caesarius 7, Eutychianus 5.
[53] *De Prov.* 1217 A ταμίας χρημάτων.   [54] *CT* viii. 5. 49.
[55] ἐνιαυτὸν ὅλον ἀποφράδα ἤγαγεν.   [56] *De Prov.* 1241 A, see n. 15 above.

reconstructed by Jones, but not that of Caesarius, who, as far as we know, held only one office, namely the prefecture of the East, between his period as *magister officiorum* and Aurelian's appointment to the prefecture around the beginning of August 399. Caesarius is last mentioned in the prefecture about a year before the appointment of Aurelian,[57] so he cannot be said to have lost it as a result of Aurelian's appointment. During the Osiris–Aurelian 'kingship' Typhos was out of office until with the aid of the barbarian mercenaries he managed to overthrow his rival and replace him.

The greater part of Typhos' period in office, up to the controversy over the Arian church and the beginning of demoralization among the barbarians, has been discussed already. It provides no evidence for the identification of Typhos. The subsequent story provides all but conclusive evidence. The unrest among the barbarians culminated in their actually moving out of the city. Fighting broke out by accident, and ended only when all Goths still left within the walls had been killed. Typhos survived the destruction of his barbarian allies, and even continued in office for some time longer.[58] But not very long afterwards he was subjected to an investigation and placed under arrest. Eventually it was decided not to punish him. Synesius' narrative seems to give a clear description of the circumstances in which the end of Typhos' 'reign' took place. The war between the barbarians outside the city and the 'Egyptians' (i.e. the Empire) was still going on. There was fear that the city might be betrayed from within. On the other hand an attempt by the barbarians to cross 'the river' (i.e. the Hellespont) had been defeated. Osiris–Aurelian returned in time to pardon his brother.[59] All this suggests a date before 3 January 401, when the head of Gainas was brought to Constantinople.[60] If this is right Typhos cannot be identified with Caesarius, because Caesarius was praetorian prefect of the East as late as June 11 403.[61] He must have been the successor of Typhos, not Typhos himself. Alan Cameron has argued that the fantastic detail of the trial of Typhos, for instance, the participation of gods,[62] is intended as a signal that the trial of Typhos is not to be taken seriously, that it is in fact what Synesius and Aurelian hoped would happen, not what did happen. This will not do. The account of the

---

[57] *CT* xvi. 2. 32 of 26. 7. 98. [58] *De Prov.* 1268 B ff.

[59] 1258 D, 1272 B. The defeat of barbarians in the Hellespont (Zos. v. 21) is not mentioned but surely implied.

[60] O. Seeck (1919) 303, citing Marcell. Com. *Chron. Min.* ii. 66 (ed. Th. Mommsen); or, perhaps in February: Marcell. Com. s.a. 400 (Latin version).

[61] *CJ* vii. 41. 2.

[62] Alan Cameron, J. Long, L. Sherry (1990) ch. v. 7. The gods also escort the returning Osiris into Constantinople (1272 B). Surely they stand for the emperor.

trial[63] stands within that part of the Tale which is history dressed up as myth. It is built into the last but one chapter of this section, and it has a definite place in the chronology of the section, that is, after the time when Gainas was trying to cross the Hellespont into Asia[64] and before the return of the exiles, but close enough for Aurelian to be able to ask that his brother should receive a pardon.[65] The trial of Typhos and therefore his deposition are as unambiguously attested in *De Providentia* as any historical event is attested in that ambiguous pamphlet. It will not do to overrule this evidence except in the face of overwhelming contrary evidence.[66]

There is an earlier reference to the fall of Typhos. 'Whenever we shall purify the air encircling the earth by water and fire . . . straightaway expect the better disposition after the removal of Typhos'.[67] This is the second of the three prophecies concluding Part I of *De Providentia*. If we could be sure that it was written *ex eventu*, it would confirm the implication of the trial narrative that Typhos had fallen from power around the time of the return of the exiles. Unfortunately we cannot be sure of this. According to Synesius' preface, Part I of *De Providentia* 'up to the prophecy of the wolf' was written while Typhos was still in power.[68] If this statement is entirely true, the prophecy of the fall of Typhos is mere wishful thinking and does not confirm that Typhos had actually fallen. Alan Cameron has produced quite a strong argument that Synesius did not change the end of Part I when he added Part II. In my view the sentence in the preface should not rule out the possibility that Synesius made some small alterations to Part I—such as, for instance, the inclusion of the second oracle—in order to produce a better fit between the old and the new. In any case, however, the evidence of the trial chapter in Part II is sufficient to make a very strong case in favour of the proposition that Typhos was actually tried, and by implication also deposed from office at the time indicated in the narrative. But if Typhos was deposed and tried towards the end of AD 400, he cannot be identified with Caesarius who was still in office in January 403.[69]

---

[63] 1269 B–C.

[64] Ibid. σπουδή τε πᾶσα ἐφ᾽ ᾧ διαβῆναι τους Σκύθας καὶ τοῦ ῥεύματος ἐπί θάτερα.

[65] 1272 B.

[66] Alan Cameron J. Long, L. Sherry (1990) ch. V. 7 is to my mind methodologically wrong. The fall of Typhos is documented more firmly than the theory about the circumstances of composition. Plausible though the theory is in many respects, it must be rejected precisely because of the account of the trial of Typhos.

[67] 1256 D ἐκποδὼν γενομένου τοῦ Τυφῶνος.

[68] Praef. 1209 A καθ᾽ ὅν μάλιστα καιρὸν ὁ χείρων ἐκράτει. On this see Alan Cameron, J. Long, L. Sherry (1990), ch vii. 6 and below, p. 269.

[69] CJ vii. 41. 2.

Is Jones's reconstruction chronologically possible?

Various kinds of evidence bearing on the identification of Typhos and the date of his coup have been examined, with the outcome that most of them appear to favour Eutychianus and December 399, some very strongly, but perhaps none quite conclusively. The verdict in favour of Eutychianus might therefore still be reversed by some preponderantly powerful argument in favour of Caesarius at the later date. Now it may seem that an extremely powerful objection to the Jonesian view is presented by chronology. Aurelian cannot have become praetorian prefect much before 1 August 399.[70] If he was deposed before 11 December of the same year,[71] as he must have been on Jones's reconstruction, this would leave very little time for the events known to have happened while he was prefect. Within this time Eutropius must have been condemned to disgrace and exile, sent to Cyprus, brought back, condemned to death, and executed.[72] At the time of the execution Gainas was at Constantinople and negotiated a treaty (σπονδάς) between Tribigild and the emperor.[73] After oaths had been exchanged, Gainas returned through Phrygia to Thyatira, presumably via Dorilaeum.[74] Then he returned to Chalcedon through the province of Asia, maintaining his army by plundering. While still on the march, he demanded that the emperor should surrender Aurelian and Saturninus to him.[75] When he arrived at Chalcedon he met the emperor, and the surrender of the men was agreed. At this point Aurelian must have been deposed from the prefecture, and Gainas' army crossed over to Constantinople.

The distances covered successively by Eutropius and Gainas make it inevitable that these events were spread over a considerable time. The distance by sea from Constantinople to Cyprus is around 800 miles. Gainas' route from Constantinople to Thyatira and back must have been around 780 miles.[76] Could these journeys and accompanying negotiations have been completed between, say, 17 August and 11 December 399? When we try to make the calculation there is one important unknown. We do not know anything about the date of the

---

[70] Between *CT* ix. 40. 18 of 25. 7. 400 and ix. 40. 17, probably of 17. 8. 400 (see Seeck (1919) 103).

[71] *CT* xii. 1. 163.

[72] Zos. v. 18; Socr. vii. 21; Soz. viii. 7. 5; Philostorg. xi. 6: Aurelian was one of the judges. Asterius of Amaseia *Hom.* 4. 9, 1 (*PG* xl. 224): execution before 1 January 401. The circumstances of the decision to execute Eutropius are obscure.

[73] Zos. v. 18. 4.

[74] See route map, K. Miller, *Itineraria Romana* (Stuttgart, 1916) 628.

[75] Zos. v. 18; more briefly Soz. viii. 4.

[76] The route is taken from K. Miller, op. cit. 628, fig. 203. The distance is the sum of the component distances according to the itinerary as corrected by Miller.

execution of Eutropius other than that it happened before 1 January 400.[77] Albert argues that it had happened not long before that, and that the second trial could only have happened after a further shift in the political balance at Constantinople had weakened Eutropius' supporters and strengthened his enemies.[78] This is not necessary. The violent language of the edict of 17 August[79] shows that even then there was very strong feeling against Eutropius, not only in the army but among senators as well.[80] It need not have required much further pressure to force a second trial and a death sentence. News of some threatening operation by Tribigild, for instance, might have given Gainas a decisive argument to persuade Arcadius to have the case against Eutropius reopened.[81] The interval need only have been a matter of days. If the decision to recall Eutropius was made on, say, 1 September, we can perhaps place his execution around 1 October.[82] This would leave a little over two months for Gainas' journey of 780 miles, an average of 12 miles a day—if we assume for sake of easy calculation that the arrival was on 4 December. This is feasible, bearing in mind that the Goths were cavalry.[83] It must also be remembered that Gainas will not have travelled all the way in the company of an army.[84] He may well have made most of his

---

[77] Asterius *Hom.* 4 (*PG* xl. 225).   [78] G. Albert (1984) 44–5.

[79] *CT* ix. 40. 17; the month is Seeck's emendation for the impossible MS January.

[80] Ibid. 'qui sua virtute ac vulneribus Romanos propagant' (soldiers), as well as 'qui eosdem servandi iuris aequitate custodiunt' (civilian officials). The soldiers rioted against Eutropius: John Chrys. *In Eutropium* (*PG* lii. 395). *De capto Eutropio* (ibid. 397). The troops were Roman regular units, since Gainas was not yet at Constantinople when Eutropius was deposed (Zos. v. 17. 5), and Synesius explicitly tells us that foreign troops did not witness the election of Osiris–Aurelian (*De Prov.* 1220 C–D). Aurelian, *praefectus urbi* 393–4, represented the senatorial enemies of Eutropius. The empress Eudoxia too was against the eunuch: Philostorg. xi. 6.

[81] Zos. v. 18. 2.

[82] Allowing ten days to Cyprus, twenty days back against the wind; cf. the times of longer journeys in *Marc le Diacre, vie de Poryphyre*, ed. H. Gregoire and M-A. Kugener (Paris, 1930):

   1. Gaza to Constantinople 20 days, return 10 days (ch. 26–27);

   2. Caesarea, Rhodes, Constantinople 20 days (ch. 34 and 37);

   3. Constantinople, Rhodes, Gaza 12 days (ch. 55 and 57).

The speeds agree with those of other ancient voyages. See L. Casson, *Ships and Seamanship in the Ancient World* (Princeton, 1971) 281–96.

[83] It has been calculated that Alexander the Great's army averaged about 13 miles per day, including day-long halts every five or seven days (D. W. Engels, *Alexander the Great and the Logistics of the Macedonian Army* (Berkeley, 1978) 153–6). For short distances cavalry or even lightly armed infantry of his army moved much faster. In 1355 the Black Prince led a raid from Bordeaux to Narbonne and back (900 kms.) in less than two months—an average of 15 kms a day. The return was slowed down by booty, and towns were taken by assault—as they were not by Gainas. See P. Contamine, *War in the Middle Ages*, tr. M. Jones (Oxford, 1984) 225. Data on speed of ancient armies: P. Vigneron (1968) 157–9.

[84] The ruin of Eutropius—unlike the exiling of Aurelian and Saturninus—was achieved by persuasion, not by pressure of Gainas's army (Zos. v. 18). The German federates played no direct part in the earlier change of regime (*De Prov.* 1220 C–D, and n. 60 above). So it is unlikely that he left Constantinople with a huge force of barbarians, as Socrates states (vi. 6. (676 C)). The bulk of his force is likely to have stayed in Phrygia watching Tribigild.

southward journey as an imperial general on horseback or by *cursus publicus*, accompanied only by a mounted escort of followers. In those circumstances he might have travelled very much faster than 12 miles a day. Once he had met his army, which was presumably facing the forces of Tribigild somewhere in Phrygia, he must have slowed down, as the men were fed off the country and the army was slowed down by carts carrying families and plunder. But provided an average of around 12 miles a day was maintained over the whole route, the operation could have been fitted into the available time.[85]

The schedule would nevertheless have been tight and could have been maintained only if Gainas hurried deliberately. There is good reason to suppose that he did so, for at least the first and the last part of his operation. We are expressly told that he left Constantinople immediately after making the agreement on Tribigild's behalf. Gainas is likely to have been in a hurry to get Tribigild's agreement to the treaty which he had just negotiated. Then, after the abortive raid on Sardes and after the forces of Gainas and Tribigild had separated, he seems to have got news suggesting that these authorities at Constantinople were preparing to get rid of him.[86] This must have induced him to accelerate his advance in order to forestall his opponents. After all, the Empire had other armies, the field-army of Fravitta in the East and the federates of Alaric in the West, which might have been moved to protect Constantinople if he wasted time. Of course we do not know when precisely Gainas changed from being an obedient general of the Empire to one who was determined to force a change of ministers. It may be that the projected plundering of Sardes was given up not only because a phenomenal fall of rain made rivers difficult to cross,[87] but also because the need to get to Constantinople quickly made it seem unwise to wait until the flood had subsided. If that was so, most of the 300 or so miles of the return

[85] Say roughly 386 miles from Chalcedon to Philadelphia at twenty miles per day (the *cursus publicus* or a small force of cavalry with spare horses could have done it considerably faster): 19.3 days. Again roughly 386 miles from Philadelphia to Chalcedon at, say, ten miles per day: 38.6 days. Total 58 days. At this rate Gainas, setting out on 1. 10. 399, might have arrived back at Chalcedon on 27. 11. 399, leaving around 13 days for the abortive raid on Sardes (we do not know how far the plundering force got or how large it was), and for negotiations leading to the replacement of Aurelian first witnessed on 11. 12. 399. The negotiations started while Gainas was still on the way (Soc. vi. 6 (676 c)). The distances are in Roman miles which are 142 yards shorter than English ones. In English miles the distance would be around sixty miles less.

[86] Prompt departures: Socr. vi. 6 (676 c). Warnings from wife still at Constantinople: *De Prov.* 1245 D, mentioning separation of the armies also reported by Zos. v. 18. 6. The warning as given in *De Prov.* 1245 D and 1248 A–B recalls Synesius' *De Regno*, whose contents might well have persuaded Gainas that he was in danger.

[87] Zos. v. 18. 5 ὄμβρος ἐξαίσιος The season of maximum rain in the area is from November to February. See W. B. Fisher, *The Middle East* (London, 1963), 311. *B.R. Geographical Handbooks Series: Turkey* (London, 1939–45) i. 414.

from Thyatira will have been made in a hurry. Be that as it may, I hope to have shown that it was quite possible for Gainas to have been back at Chalcedon soon after 1 December 399 and to have forced Arcadius to depose Aurelian and to replace him by Eutychianus before 11 December.

Demonstration of possibility is not proof. In this case, however, since other evidence, above all that of the eye-witness Synesius' *De Providentia*, very strongly supports the hypothesis that Aurelian was overthrown well before March/April 400, and that he was not succeeded by Caesarius but by Eutychianus, a demonstration that this would have been chronologically possible makes it extremely likely, or rather almost certain, that the hypothesis is correct.[88].

The Tradition about Gainas

By the standards of ancient history the events at Constantinople in 399–400 are well documented. So it is in a way surprising that the identity of one of the principal characters should be so obscure. The reason may be that, while the destruction of Gainas was an extremely important event, worthy to be commemorated by a column[89] and at least two epic poems,[90] few of the principal characters could look back on their behaviour with unmixed feelings. Eutychianus was certainly not the villain drawn by Synesius; the fact that he returned to the praetorian prefecture in 404–5 is proof of that. Nevertheless his policy towards Gainas had been a complete failure. Disaster had only been averted by street fighting in Constantinople, followed by full-scale war. This had certainly not been intended. Aurelian too had cooperated with Gainas. In fact he had combined with him against Eutropius in precisely the way Synesius accuses Typhos–Eutychianus of having conspired against Osiris–Aurelian. Since the victims of Typhos survived while Eutropius was executed, Aurelian's behaviour had been the more discreditable. No wonder Synesius obscured the manoeuvres through which Aurelian became prefect with the description of a fantastic procedure of election—which he agrees was not used in this case—and a lengthy speech of Osiris' father.[91] It is not surprising that Aurelian had to wait until 414 before returning to

[88] Circumstantial evidence argued in favour of Caesarius must be interpreted in some other way, e.g. the fact that Asterius of Amaseia in a sermon of 6. 1. 400 did not list Aurelian with other consuls who had come to grief (*PG* xl. 223–5; C. Datema, Asterius of Amaseia: *Homilies* i–xiv (Leiden, 1970) 39–43 and notes), or that Caesarius' wife had Arian sympathies (Soz. ix. 2. 4), or that Eudoxia, the friend of John, one of the exiles, was proclaimed Augusta on 9. 1. 400 (*Chron. Pasch* s.a. 400).

[89] J. Kollwitz (1941) 17–62.   [90] Socr. vi. 6 (681 A).

[91] The procedure: *De Prov.* 6 (1221); that it was not used: 1221 D.

office. John Chrysostom's behaviour too was controversial. He owed his election to the see of Constantinople to Eutropius, and his part in the fall of Eutropius was criticized. True, he offered him sanctuary, but while Eutropius was still in the church Chrysostom made his fall the starting point of a sermon, and when eventually Eutropius left the church only to be arrested Chrysostom was evidently thought to have let him down.[92] Later he seems to have enjoyed considerable influence while Gainas was at Constantinople, and after Gainas' departure was able to act as an intermediary between the government of Eutychianus and the Goths.[93] Palladius was careful not to say anything about this in his biography of Chrysostom. He also fails to mention Chrysostom's opposition to Gainas' request to be given a church for Arian services. It had aroused criticism. It seemed arrogant[94] and opponents blamed Chrysostom for causing the break with Gainas by his intransigence.[95] It was left to Sozomen and Theodoret to write it up as worthy of praise, thirty or forty years after the event, when the controversy had died down. Chrysostom had petitioned Gainas on behalf of the exiles,[96] but he was also accused of having betrayed the *comes* John to them in some way or other.[97] So Palladius preferred to veil the subject of Chrysostom's relation with Aurelian and John in silence, even though the hostility of the returned exiles was to contribute to Chrysostom's downfall.[98] In short it served the reputation of none of the principal characters involved that the true story of Gainas at Constantinople should be known. We should no doubt know a little more if the contemporary *History* of Eunapius of Sardes had survived intact rather than in fragments[99] and in the abbreviated version of Zosimus. But to judge by what has survived, Eunapius was more interested in the sufferings of Asia than in politics at Constantinople. Thus the tradition about Gainas came to be distorted to an exceptional degree, and stories of conspiracy and divine intervention[100] took the place of genuine understanding.

---

[92] Socr. vi. 4 (673).

[93] *De Prov.* 1268 B; Theodoret *HE* v. 33; John Chrys. *Hom. cum Saturninus et Aurelianus acti essent in exsilium, et Gainas egressus esset e civitate* (PG lii. 4. 14–20); cf. above, p. 19.

[94] Socr. vi. 4. (673 B).

[95] 'Martyrius' answers the charge. See F. van Ommeslaeghe (1979) 152.

[96] Ref. above xx.

[97] Photius *Bibl.* 59 (17 b, 19).

[98] Zos. v. 23.

[99] Text, translation and notes in R. C. Blockley (1983) 2–150.

[100] Apart from the vision of soldiers that is said to have saved the palace (Socr. vi (677); Soz. viii. 4), the defeat of Goths in the city was attributed to divine intervention: *De Prov.* 1260; Eunapius fr. 78 = 68 Blockley; J. Kollwitz (1941).

De Providentia: How many editions?

De Providentia was certainly written in two stages. The first stage up to the 'oracle of the wolf' was recited while Typhos was in power.[101] The rest, that is Part II, is said to have been 'woven on'[102] at the request of the returned exiles, so that the work should not only contain accounts of their misfortunes but also include an account of how their affairs changed for the better.[103]

The question immediately arises whether the 'weaving' involved alterations to the older fabric. On the face of it a conscious artist in words, which Synesius certainly was, would be unlikely to be content simply to add a new conclusion to an existing composition. One would therefore suspect that at least the last section of Part I, concerned with the three oracles, has been emended to make it a better link between the old and the new. Besides, the first two oracles at least are so accurate in their forecast that they seem to have been written with knowledge of the outcome. But Alan Cameron has argued that it is unnecessary to assume that the oracles as we have them cannot have been part of the original version.[104]

Cameron's thesis is that Part I was written, not before the destruction of the Goths in Constantinople, but after it, during the last months of 'Typhos'' reign. The destruction itself is not described because there was no need to describe it. The end of the Goths is foreshadowed in the first of the oracles and the audience (or readers) would know from recent experience that the oracle had been fulfilled.[105] The 'oracle of the wolf' concluded the first version of the Egyptian Tale, as it does the telling of the original Egyptian myth by Plutarch, on which Synesius' work was based.[106] Its function was to justify Providence by forecasting the eventual triumph of good over evil—which was not yet in sight at the time of writing, since Typhos was still in power and Osiris–Aurelian in exile.

Alan Cameron's argument is very plausible as far as the circumstances of the writing of Part I are concerned—though it would not be difficult to suggest alternatives.[107] If his argument is accepted, it follows that the first oracle and the 'oracle of the wolf' were part of *De Providentia* from the beginning, very much as we read them now.

---

[101] 1209 A.   [102] ὑφάνθη.   [103] 1212 A.

[104] Alan Cameron, J. Lang, L. Sherry (1990) ch. VII. 6.

[105] *De prov.* praef. (1212 A) shows that from the start Part I included a recognizable divine prediction of the end of the German occupation of Constantinople.

[106] Praef. (1209); Plut. *De Is. et Os.* 19.

[107] e.g. it is conceivable that the original version included only the oracle of the wolf and a single oracle that Typhos and his barbarian allies would come to grief as a result of introducing religious (i.e. Arian) innovations.

This does not, however, apply to the explicit prediction of the fall of Typhos amid thunder and lightning.[108] This would have been redundant, since the 'oracle of the wolf' cannot be anything other than a prediction of the defeat of Seth–Typhos—at least if we interpret it in accordance with the original Egyptian myth as told by Plutarch.[109] The need for a second forecast of the fall of Typhos would only have arisen when it was seen that the downfall of the evil brother and the final triumph of good over evil would not happen at the same time. Aurelian had returned but had not been restored to the prefecture. Eutychianus had fallen from office but had not been permanently disgraced; quite the reverse. The complete vindication of Providence, through the full restoration of the good man and the final punishment of the bad, was yet to come. So I would suggest the second oracle was introduced into the concluding chapter of Part I at the same time as Part II was added so as to bring the oracular conclusion of Part I up to date.

A second passage in the *De Providentia* which has suggested *ex eventu* editing is the prophecy that in his old age Osiris would return to power and to rule the state amid greater consensus[110] and in effect bring back the golden age.[111] I have argued that this must be an allusion to Aurelian's second praetorian prefecture, which he took up in 414, and that *De Providentia* must therefore have been emended around that time.[112] The argument has been countered by Alan Cameron and T. D. Barnes. Can it be salvaged?[113]

The last section of *De Providentia* starting from Part II, chapter 5, is a very peculiar piece of writing, quite different in character from earlier sections. The Osiris myth has been practically abandoned. It had to be, because its Egyptian conclusion—only alluded to by Plutarch—ends with Osiris king in the underworld,[114] and this is not what Synesius would wish to forecast for his friend and patron. Synesius has also discontinued the narrative of very thinly veiled Constantinopolitan history of the first four chapters of Part II. In fact there is really very little concrete information about the exiles' better fortune, even though it is precisely this which Synesius tells us that they asked him to add to the older narrative.[115] What Synesius has

---

[108] 1256 D.

[109] In view of the Egyptian character of the tale it is more likely that 'the wolf' replaced the horse in Plutarch's oracle because Synesius follows the version of Diodorus i. 88. 6. See J. Long (1987).

[110] 1272 D μετὰ συνθήματος μειζόνος.

[111] Ch. 5 (1272–3).   [112] W. Liebeschuetz (1983).

[113] Alan Cameron, J. Long, L. Sherry (1990) ch. V. 6, T. D. Barnes (1986a).

[114] *De Is. et Os.* 19, the passage in Plutarch from which the 'oracle of the wolf' is derived is also the end of the narrative of the myth, cf. J. G. Griffiths (1970), 344 ff.

[115] 1212 A ταῖς βελτίοσιν αὐτῶν τύχαις ἐπεξελθεῖν.

provided is some loosely composed chat, with the author speaking in the *persona* of a man who has received a divine revelation. While solemn words are used, the mood is playful rather than solemn.[116] Three topics are treated: first the eventual return to power of Aurelian; secondly 'philosophical' arguments to the effect that it is indeed possible for two brothers to have totally opposite characters,[117] and to explain how the extraordinarily close resemblance between events of the Egyptian Tale and recent history could have come about;[118] and finally, scattered over the whole last section of *De Providentia* and in the whole concluding chapter, the wickedness of publishing sacred mysteries, and more specifically of revealing more detail of the future than Synesius has actually revealed.[119] The essay ends with the general advice that it is proper for human beings to wait and see. One might sum up the last section of *De Providentia* as a vague prophecy of future office for Aurelian, together with an extended apology for the author's reticence.[120]

One could construct a scenario which would explain why Synesius should have chosen to end nis pamphlet like this in 400/401. Providence had been vindicated as far as the Roman state was concerned, but Aurelian remained discontented, since he had not been restored to office as he hoped, and did not look like being restored in the foreseeable future.[121] Typhos–Eutychianus, his brother and enemy, had been dismissed from the prefecture, but was far from disgraced. In fact his prospects of office were much better than those of Aurelian.[122] It is perhaps not surprising that Synesius, writing to please Aurelian, had little definite to say about the present. So it is quite conceivable that this is why he finished *De Providentia* in the way he did.

Doubts remain. Was it necessary and tactful to pass quite so briefly over Aurelian's return to Constantinople and his consular celebrations?[123] Did Synesius have to insist that Aurelian would be an old

[116] Humour: Justice will return to earth if men give up seafaring and concentrate on agriculture (1274 B); elder sons are worthless (1276 D)—Synesius, like Aurelian, was a younger brother. [117] 1276.

[118] 1277. In fact the Egyptian Tale is an *ex eventu* 'typology' of the Gainas crisis. Synesius was surely aware of the resemblance between his Tales' anticipation of events at Constantinople, and the typological interpretation by Christians of the Old Testament. He will also have expected his readers to recognize the parallel. Synesius' 'homily' shows that he was familiar with the technique. Alan Cameron, J. Long, L. Sherry (1990), ch. VII. 6, demonstrate characteristics of an Apocalypse.

[119] 1272 C, 1274 C, 1277 C, 1980.

[120] Ch. 8, concluding with a warning to the man who, although found unworthy of initiation by the gods, wishes to know nevertheless (1280 C).

[121] *Ep.* 34 m = 47 (Garzya), if it dates from 401 or soon after; for possible later date see above, p. 138.

[122] Cf. above, p. 133. [123] 1272 B.

man before he could hold office again,[124] and that *several* men would
have to be prefect[125] before Aurelian would hold the office once
more? There is humour in the pretence that Synesius is in the position
of a priest of the mysteries who must not say all that he knows, but he
has developed his joke at excessive length.[126]

But there is a scenario in which features, awkward in a text
complimentary to Aurelian composed in 400/401, would become
assets: that is, if the text had been written in 414, at that instant when
Aurelian's return to the prefecture was known to be imminent, but
had not yet been officially published. Aurelian's age would simply
have been a fact. Synesius' unwillingness to talk about the future
would be a much better joke if everybody who was anybody knew it
already; so would the warning (to Aurelian personally?) against
excessive curiosity,[127] followed by the advice that a show of irritation
was unreasonable in a man about to receive what he deserved
shortly.[128]

So I would suggest that in 414, or thereabouts, Aurelian informed
Synesius that he was about to be given the prefecture of the East,
perhaps with a request for some literary celebration. Thereupon
Synesius got out his old piece and rewrote the last part of it, taking
it up to the present moment, but playfully refusing to refer to the
imminent prefecture as an accomplished fact. If this construction is
right, it follows that our version of *De Providentia* is the latest of
Synesius' writings, and evidence that he was still alive in 414.

---

[124] 1272 C γηρῶν τε Ὄσιρις κυδίων ἢ νέος.

[125] 1273 B ἔδει δὴ μεσιτεῦσαι τοὺς προκαθαίροντας.

[126] Is some definite work being parodied? See the acute chapter 'Oracles and Apocalypse' in
Alan Cameron, J. Long, L. Sherry (1990).

[127] 1280 C ὃν δὲ οὐκ ἀξιοῖ ὁ θεὸς εἶναι μύστην . . . μήτε ὠτακουστέτω.

[128] οὐδὲ τὸ ἀσχάλλειν εὔλογον τὸν μετα μικρὸν τῶν ἴσων τευξόμενον. Teasing of this kind would
surely have been tactless around 401 when there was so little prospect of Aurelian getting what
he thought he deserved in the foreseeable future.

Appendix II
The Column of Arcadius

IN 402/3 work was started on a column to commemorate the defeat of Gainas. In 421 a statue of Arcadius was unveiled on the top of the column.[1] The monument stood in the new Forum of Arcadius, on the Xerolophos. There it remained until it was demolished as a danger to the public in the early eighteenth century.[2]

Little survives of the column apart from its base, and that deprived of almost all its sculpture. But we can get a very full impression of its former appearance from a number of drawings, above all three drawings in the Freshfield folder in the Library of Trinity College, Cambridge.[3] These represent the column respectively from the west, south, and east.[4] A complete view from the north is lacking, but a seemingly very careful drawing of the column now in the Bibliothèque Nationale in Paris seems to record at least some of the carvings on the north side, notably part of Band 9, showing the Goths drowning in the Hellespont.[5]

The Freshfield drawings and the drawing in the Bibliothèque Nationale by and large support each other. The drawing on a 52-foot scroll preserved in the Louvre[6] presents serious problems. In 1702 C. F. Menestrier published it in 16 prints under the title *Description de la belle et grande colonne historiée dressée à l'honeur de l'empereur Théodose dessinée par G. Bellin.*[7] The theme of the drawing is the procession of a Roman army accompanied by barbarian prisoners. J. Kollwitz[8] has made a very strong case that this drawing too is based on the sculptural narrative of Arcadius' column (cf. S 6 and E 6 with Menestrier pl.18, and S 2 and E 2 with Menestrier pl.4 = our pl.IV).

---

[1] Marcell. Com. s.a. 421 (Mommsen ii. 751).

[2] On the history of the column J. Kollwitz (1941), 17–18. The sculptures interpreted as an oracle of the future of the city: G. Dagron, J. Paramelle, 'Un texte patriographique, le récit merveilleux, très beau et profitable sur la colonne des Xerolophes', *Travaux et Mémoires* (1979) 491–523, cf. G. Dagron, *Constantinople Imaginaire* (Paris, 1984), 74 ff.

[3] E. H. Freshfield (1921–2).

[4] Drawings reproduced in Freshfield (1921–2), plates xv–xxiii, Kollwitz (1941), Beilage 3–7. See also illustrations and full account in G. Becatti (1960), G. Q. Giglioli, *La colonna di Arcadio a Constantinopoli* (Naples, 1952).

[5] Invent. 6514, see Kollwitz (1941), Tafel 3/4. = our pl. 3.1.

[6] Invent. 4951.

[7] Another edition in 18 prints was published in 1765(?) under the title *Columna Theodosiana quam vulgo historiatam vocant ab Arcadio imperatore Constantinopolis erecta in honorem imperatoris Theodosii iunioris a Gentile Bellino delineata.*

[8] (1941), 21–2.

But the Louvre drawing was certainly not copied from the column directly. It seems to be a very free development of a drawing of the column which has been lost, for it was surely neither the Freshfield drawings nor the drawing in the Biblothèque Nationale. Furthermore it is agreed that the style of the Louvre drawing is mid sixteenth century or later. So it cannot be by Gentile Bellini,[9] though it may be that the lost drawing on which the artist composed variations was by Gentile Bellini. What the Louvre artist appears to have done is to transform a narrative of a campaign into that of a triumph, a procession of the same kind as Mantegna's Triumph of Caesar (around 1500).[10] Comparable scrolls showing a continuous narrative of the campaign of Trajan as carved around Trajan's column survive from the last quarter of the sixteenth century.[11] But they are essentially close copies of the sculptures, while our Louvre drawing is so free that it can be of very little help in reconstructing the lost carvings of the column of Arcadius.

Fortunately the evidence of the Freshfield and Bibliothèque Nationale drawings is sufficient to reconstruct the outline of the narrative with reasonable certainty. A difficulty arises with the start of the story. The lowest band of both the Freshfield and the Bibliothèque Nationale drawings shows a crowd standing under a row of states (W 1 and E 1). This cannot have been the actual beginning of the narrative bands since the weathered fragments still left on the stump of the column prove beyond argument that the lowest band showed a procession made up of horsemen, camel riders, carts, and pedestrians. Many individuals are shown wearing a '*chlamys*', some a long one reaching near the ankles, others a short form of that garment.[12] A sheep-skin *chlamys* was thought the characteristic wear of Germans.[13]

We do not know how exactly these surviving carvings linked up with the lowest band recorded on the drawings, but it is a plausible hypothesis that they are the beginning of the 'long march' of the men whose fate is represented on the higher levels of the column. Each of the copying artists omitted the lowest band of all, presumably

[9] Beccati (1960), 111–50, suggests B. Franco.

[10] A. Martindale, *The Triumphs of Caesar by Andreas Mantegna* (London, 1979). The Louvre drawing does not seem to have been influenced by Mantegna's work itself.

[11] C. Monbeig Goguel, 'Du marbre au papier, de la spirale verticale à la bande horizontale', in *Caesar Triumphans, rotoli disegnati e xilografie cinquecentesche da una collecione privata parigina*, ed. D. Arasse (Institut Français de Florence, 1984), 13–32.

[12] Kollwitz (1941).

[13] Alan Cameron, 'Earthquake 400', *Chiron* xvii (1987) 345–60, esp. 348. Illustrations of sheepskin cloaks: G. Bruns, *Der Obelisk und seine Basis auf dem Hippodrom zu Konstantinopel*, Istanbuler Forschungen 7 (Istanbul, 1935), pl. 43; R. Delbrück, *Die Consulardiptychen* (Berlin, 1929), nos. 46, 49.

because he was drawing the view as seen from ground level, from where the start of the narrative band would have been obscured by the base. It is, incidentally, unlikely that the artists actually worked at ground level: the copying is too detailed for that. We know that an artist who drew Trajan's column worked standing in a basket lowered from the top.[14]

The lowest band on the Freshfield and Bibliothèque Nationale drawings is unique in that it does not show men but monuments. There are a large number of statues, including one of an elephant, another of Heracles holding Cerberus (S 1), also a long two-gabled portico, and a diagrammatic view of a circular public space seen from above—probably the forum of Constantine (E 1). It would be interesting to establish the identity of some of the other monuments. The purpose of this band is clearly to identify the scene of the action as Constantinople.

Band 2 shows what is probably the key incident. On the western frame a mixed column of pedestrians and riders proceeds past some monumental buildings at Constantinople. One can recognize a two-towered gate, what looks like the narthex of a major church, and in the background a two-storeyed or even three storeyed colonade (W 2). Can these structures be identified? On the central frame the procession leaves the city through a two-arched monumental gate (only one column of the second arch is shown; (S 2). Something very significant is happening, for a winged Victory is hovering in the archway holding a wreath of some kind over the turned head of one of the departing men. At the same time a massive woman stands in the entrance, blocking it with the help of a horizontally held stick or sceptre. What does this mean? One plausible interpretation would be that the Victory is an angel and that the now blacked-out centre of the wreath once showed a Christian symbol. The image would thus illustrate the action of the divine power which has freed Constantinople from its unwelcome foreign visitors and will prevent any attempt of theirs to return. The woman is the *Fortuna* or rather, since this is a Christian monument, the personification of Constantinople,[15] and is

---

[14] Monbeig Goguel (1984), 15.

[15] On representations of personifications of Constantinople see J. Toynbee, 'Roma and Constantinopolis in Late Antique Art from 312–365', *JRS* xxxvii (1947), 135–44, pls. 1–13; id. 'Roma and Constantinopolis in Late Antique Art from 365 to Justin II', *Studies presented to D. M. Robinson* ii (1953), 261–77. I owe the references to C. Mango. Here the abstract figure could be interpreted as the *Fortuna* of Constantinople, or as the personification of Constantinople, or concretely as a symbol for the people of Constantinople who are defending their city. On the Christianization of the classical image of Victoria into that of an angel see H. Leclercq, s.v. anges, *DACL* (1924), 1.2, 2080–2162, esp. 2111–2121.

a more traditional image reinforcing the symbolism of the Victory-angel.

Bands 3–4 are remarkable for the absence of warlike confrontations. The views are topographical: the army is seen marching through forest and plain and into hilly country. It passes herds and nomad herdsmen and, most remarkable of all, a group of tent-like huts, their roofs resting on the ground occupied by near-naked families (W 5, S 5). These look like rustic dwellings depicted for their own sake. But it is more likely that they represent Gothic soldiers in a temporary camp. In fact comparison with *Ilias Ambrosiana* Miniatura xxvii makes it likely that the triangular structures are tents in which Goths are relaxing off-duty.[16]

Frame S 5 is split into two. It is likely that the upper half represents the imperial army, the lower half the Goths. It is likely, in fact, that both Goths and Romans are shown also on most subsequent frames, but unfortunately the drawings do not show enough detail to distinguish Romans from barbarians by dress and equipment. It is, for instance, impossible to tell whether either side wore armour. S 5 shows a suppliant prostrating himself before a horseman. This may represent a last attempt at negotiations, with the barbarian shown in suppliant position as appropriate.

Bands 6–9 show what might be described as the 'watch on the Hellespont'. Goths march along the edge of the water; Romans in boats prevent them from crossing. It may be that they are also being shadowed by a Roman force on the west bank (W 7). Eventually the Goths build rafts (S 8) and boats (E 8) and try to cross the straits. Their defeat by the combined action of God and the Roman fleet was shown in the north side and is not preserved on the Freshfield drawing. Part of it is, however, to be found on a drawing in the Bibliothèque National.

Bands 10–12 describe the final land campaign. There are three battles in each of which cavalry plays a decisive role. The first was fought on the banks of some water (E 10), perhaps on the south side of the Danube. There is nothing to identify the victorious cavalry as Huns. S 13 evidently shows the victorious emperor amid his grandees. But which is the emperor, and who is the sitting figure? No individual would be allowed to sit in the presence of the standing emperor. It seems that the artist has misinterpreted the scene he was copying. One suggestion is that the standing figure being crowned is in fact a statue, perhaps of Theodosius I, that the figure on the left of the statue which is taller than the other standing grandees represents

---

[16] Becatti (1960).

Arcadius, while the seated figure is a misreading of a representation of the personification of Constantinople.[17]

The column is a case of early classical renaissance. It revives a form of imperial art that was last practised in the Rome of Marcus Aurelius more than 200 years earlier. But times have changed and art has had to reflect the change. The column still shows a lot of traditional pagan imagery, winged Victories, *Fortunas* of cities, the chariots of sun and moon. But these have clearly lost their specific pagan significance. For the monument emphatically commemorates a Christian victory. This is proclaimed unmistakably on three sides of the base—the part of the monument which was most easily read by the passing public.

The role of the emperor too had changed. Arcadius was about as different from Trajan and Marcus Aurelius as it was possible to be. Far from leading his armies through the campaign he had scarcely left the palace. He was still the glorious head of the great empire, but he was not sole ruler. The Empire was divided between East and West and now had two emperors instead of one. All this had to be expressed. The emperors could not be shown campaigning. So they are shown in state, isolated from the events but inspiring their subordinates from a distance (Base, S 6, S 10, S 13). On one of the frames Arcadius may be shown on his own (S 6), but in two he is seen in the company of his brother Honorius (S 10, and probably S and E 13) who in fact was in Italy, hundreds of miles away.[18] It is evident that the men who built the column wished to emphasize the harmony and cooperation of East and West, a state of affairs which was the exception rather than the rule in those years.

I have assumed that the men whose defeat is shown on the column are Gainas' Goths. Although this has been doubted,[19] the likelihood is overwhelming. There remains the fact that the most celebrated episode of the Gainas affair, the destruction of the Goths inside Constantinople, is not shown. The reason must be that this episode was controversial. In the first place the outbreak of violence was fortuitous and should not have happened. It may well be that among the Goths killed were a lot of women and children. The column shows only a very few women and children among the marching Goths. Could it be that many had been killed in the city? Worst of all, the final massacre of by now unarmed Goths took place in a church and involved burning the church.[20] The events of 12 July 400 were

---

[17] Suggested by P. J. Casey, in whose view Arcadius and Constantinopolis on S 13 are paralleled by Honorius and Roma (standing figure with shield) in E 13.

[18] McCormick, *Eternal Victory*, (Cambridge, 1986), 115 ff. on collegial victory of emperors.

[19] e.g. Freshfield (1921–2), 90 ff. identified the drawings with events of 386 (Zos. iv. 38–9).

[20] G. Albert (1984), 172, and above 19.

soon after represented as a miraculous delivery in that the civilians of Constantinople had with divine help overcome and destroyed an army of occupation. This version eventually prevailed, but at the time there were thousands of witnesses who knew what really had happened. The whole truth was not suitable for commemoration on a column. It had to be covered up.

So what the artist has concentrated on is not the defeat of the Goths inside Constantinople, nor even the final defeat of the Goths beyond the Danube, but the peaceful departure of Gainas and a considerable part of his men which had preceded the massacre of 12 July 400. That was the real miracle proving that God favoured the emperor Arcadius and his capital city.

Bibliography

ABADAL DE VINYALS, R. D' (1958). 'À propos du legs visigothique en Espagne', in *Caratteri del secolo VII in Occidente*, Settimane di Studio del Centro Italiano di Studi sull' Alto Medioevo v, 541–85.

ACHELIS, H. (1900). 'Der älteste deutsche Kalender', *Zt. f. neutestamentliche Wissenschaft* i, 308–35.

ALBERT, G. (1979), 'Stilicho und der Hunnenfeldzug Eutropius', *Chiron* ix, 621–45.

—— (1984). *Goten in Konstantinopel: Untersuchungen zur oströmischen Geschichte um das Jahr 400 n. Chr.*, Studien zur Geschichte und Kultur des Altertums. Neue Folge, 1. Reihe, 2. Band, Paderborn.

ALBRECHT, R. (1986). *Das Leben der heiligen Makrina vor dem Hintergrund der Thekla-Traditionen*, Studien zu den Ursprüngen des weiblichen Mönchtums in 4. Jahrhundert in Kleinasien, Göttingen.

ALFÖLDY, G. (1974). *Noricum*, London.

—— (1979). *Römische Sozialgeschichte*, Wiesbaden.

ANSON, J. (1974). 'The female transvestite in early monasticism', *Viator* v, 1–32.

ARCE, J. (1980). 'La *Notitia Dignitatum* et l'armée romaine dans le diocesis Hispaniarum', *Chiron* x, 593–608.

ASAD, T. (1973). 'The Beduin as a military force', in Cynthia Nelson (1973), 61–73.

ASTIN, A. (1983). Observations on the *De rebus bellicis*, ed. C. Deroux, *Studies in Latin Literature and Roman History* iii, collection Latomus 180, Brussels, 388–439.

AUF DER MAUER, I. (1959). *Mönchtum und Glaubensverkündnis in den Schriften des heiligen Johannes Chrysostomus*, Paradosis xiv, Freiburg im Breisgau.

AUJOULAT, N. (1983). 'Les Avatars de la φαντασία', *Koinonia* vii, 157–77.

BACCHIELLI, L. (1981). *L'Agora di Cirene*, ii. 1 *L'area settentrionale del lato ovest della platea inferiore*, Rome, esp. pp. 188 ff.

BUGNALL, R. S., CAMERON, ALAN, WORP, K. A. (1987). See under Cameron, Alan.

BALFOUR, (1867). 'On the military conscription of France', *Journal of Statistical Society of London* xxx, 216–92.

BALZERT, M. (1974). *Die Komposition des Claudianischen Gotenkriegsgedichts*, Spudasmata 23, Hildesheim, New York.

BANDURI, A. (1729). *Imperium Orientale*, vol. 1, Venice.

BANG, M. (1906). *Die Germanen im römischen Dienst bis zum Regierungsantritt Constantins*, Berlin.

Banks, P. J. (1980). 'The Topography of the City of Barcelona, and its Urban context in Eastern Catalonia from the Third to the Twelfth Centuries', PhD thesis, Nottingham, unpublished.

Bardy, G. (1933. 'Le concile d'Antioche (379)', *Rev. Bén.* xlv, 196–213.

Barker, G. (1985). 'Agricultural organisation in classical Cyrenaica: the potential of subsistence and data', in G. Barker, J. Lloyd, J. Reynolds (1985), 121–34.

——, Hodge, R. (1981). *Archaeology of Italian Society*, London.

——, Lloyd, J., Reynolds, J. (1985) (ed.) *Cyrenaica in Antiquity*, BAR Int. Ser. 236, Oxford.

——, ——, Webley, d. (1987). 'A classical landscape in Molise', *PBSR* xlvi, 42–3.

Barkóczi, L. (1964). 'The population of Pannonia from Marcus Aurelius to Diocletian', *Acta Arch.* xvi, 257 ff.

Barnes, T. D. (1975). 'Patricii under Valentinian III', *Phoenix* xxix, 155–70.

—— (1976). 'The historical setting of Prudentius' contra Symmachum', *AJP* xvii c, 373–86.

—— (1979). 'The date of Vegetius', *Phoenix* xxxiii, 254–7.

—— (1986a). 'Synesius in Constantinople', *GRBS* xxvii, 93–112.

—— (1986b). 'When did Synesius become bishop of Ptolemais?', *GRBS* xxvii, 325–9.

Barnish, S. J. B. (1986). 'Taxation, land and barbarian settlement', *PBSR* liv, 170–95.

Batiffol, B. (1899). 'De quelques homélies de S. Jean Chrysostome et de la version gothique des écritures', *Rev. biblique int.* viii, 566–72.

Baur, P. C. (1929–30). *Der heilige Johannes Chrysostomus und seine Zeit*, 2 vols., Munich.

Bayless N. H. (1976). 'The Visigothic invasion of Italy in 401', *Class. Journ.* xxii, 65–7.

Baynes N. H. (1922). 'Stilicho and the barbarian invasion', *JRS* xii, 207–20 = (1955a), 326–42.

—— (1947). *The Thought World of East Rome*, Oxford = (1955a), 24–46.

—— (1949). 'The supernatural defenders of Constantinople', *Analecta Bollandiana* lxvii, 165–77 = (1955a), 248–60.

—— (1955a). *Byzantine Studies and Other Essays*, London.

—— (1955b). 'Alexandria and Constantinople: a study in ecclesiastical diplomacy', *Byzantine Studies and Other Essays*, London, 97–115.

Becatti, G. (1960). *La colonna coclide istoriata: problemi storici, iconografici, stilistici*, Rome.

Beck, H.-G. (1965). *Byzantinisches Gefolgschaftswesen*, Sitzungsberichte Bayerische Akademie der Wissenschaften, Phil. Hist. R. H. 5.

Bertolini, O. ((1968). 'Ordinamente militare e strutture sociali dei Longobardi in Italia', *Settimane* xv, 429–629.

Beševliev, V. (1970). 'Untersuchungen über die Personennamen bei den Thrakern', *Acta* VII FIEC congrès.

Bintliff, J. L., Snodgrass, A. M. (1985). 'The Cambridge/Bradford Boeotian Expedition: the first four years,' *J. Field Archaeology* xii, 123–61.

Biraben, J. N. (1976). *Les hommes et la peste en France et dans les pays européens et mediterranéens*, 2 vols., Paris.

Birley, E. (1961). 'Hadrian's wall and its neighbourhood', *Studien zu den Militärgrenzen Roms*, Beihefte der Bonner Jahrbücher 19, Cologne.

Blockley, R. C. (1980). 'The ending of Eunapius' History', *Antichthon* xiv, 170–6.

—— (1981). *The fragmentary classicising historians of the Later Roman Empire, Eunapius, Olympiodorus, Priscus and Malchus*, vol. I Liverpool.

—— (1983). *The fragmentary classicising historians of the Later Roman Empire*, vol. ii, text, translation, and historiographical notes, Liverpool.

—— (1985). 'Subsidies and Diplomacy: Rome and Persia in Late Antiquity', *Phoenix* xxxix, 62–135.

Boak, A. E. R. (1955). 'The population of Roman and Byzantine Karanis', *Historia* iv, 157–62.

Bognetti, G. P. (1966–8). *L'età longobarda*, 4 vols., Milan, esp. iii. 1–46, 'L'influsso delle istituzioni militari romane sulle istituzioni longobarde del secolo VI, e la natura della "fara"', and iii. 439–75, 'Tradizione longobarda e politica bizantina nelle origini del ducato di Spoleto'.

Böhme, H. W. (1974). 'Zur Chronologie germanischer Grabfunde des 4. bis 5. Jahrhunderts zwischen unterer Elbe und Loire', *Münchener Beiträge zur Vor- und Frühgeschichte* xix, Munich.

Böhme, J. (1757). *De pedum deosculatione imperatoribus Romanorum quondam praestita exercitatio*, Leipzig.

Bonsdorf, M. von (1922). *Zur Predigttätigkeit des Johannes Chrysostomus*, Helsingfors (Helsinki).

Borowski, M. J. (1974). 'Pulcheria Empress of Byzantium', PhD Univ. of Kansas, University Microfilms International, Ann Arbor, 1979.

Bouché-Leclercq, A. (1871). *Les pontifes de l'ancienne Rome*, Paris, repr. New York, 1975.

Bowman, A. K. (1985). 'Landholding in the Hermopolite Nome in the Fourth Century', *JRS* lxxv, 137–63.

Brändle, R. (1979). *Matth. 25. 31–46 im Werke des Johannes Chrysostomus*, Tübingen.

Braund, D. (1984). *Rome's friendly Kings*, London.

Bregman, J. (1974). 'Synesius of Cyrene: early life and conversion to philosophy', *Calif. St. Cl. Ant.* vii, 55–88.

—— (1982). *Synesius of Cyrene: Philosopher-Bishop*, Berkeley, London.

BROCK, S. P. (1982). 'Christians in the Sassanian empire: a case of divided loyalties', in S. Mews (ed.), *Religion and National Identity*, Oxford.

BROGAN, O. (1954). 'The camel in Tripolitania', *PBSR* xxii, 126–31.

BROWN, P. (1961a). 'Religious coercion in the Later Roman Empire', *History* xlvi, 83–100 = (1972), 301–31.

—— (1961b). 'The Christianisation of the Roman aristocracy', *JRS* li, 1–11 = (1972), 161–82.

—— (1967). 'The Later Roman Empire' (review of A. H. M. Jones), *Ec. Hist. Rev.* 2 ser. xx, 327–43 = (1972), 46–79.

—— (1969). 'The diffusion of Manichaeism in the Roman Empire', *JRS* lix, 92–103 = (1972), 94–110.

—— (1970). 'The patrons of Pelagius', *JThS* xxi, 56–72 = (1972), 208–26.

—— (1971). 'The rise and function of the holy man', *JRS* lxi, 80–101.

—— (1972). *Religion and Society in the Age of Saint Augustine*, London.

—— (1978). *The Making of Late Antiquity*, Cambridge, Mass.

—— (1981). *The Cult of the Saints*, London.

—— (1987). 'Late Antiquity', in P Veyne (ed.), *A History of Private Life*, Cambridge, Mass., 235–311.

BROWN, T. S. (1984). *Gentlemen and Officers*, Rome.

BROWNING, R. (1983). Review of G. E. M. de Ste Croix, *The Class Struggle in the Ancient Greek World*, in *Past and Present* c, 147–56.

BRUNT, P. (1971). *Italian Manpower 225 BC–AD 14*, Oxford.

BULLINGER, H. (1969). *Spätantike Gürtelbeschläge*, Archeol. Gandense 12, Bruges.

BURNS, T. (1973). 'The battle of Adrianople: a reconsideration', *Historia* xxii, 336–445.

—— (1978). 'Calculating Ostrogothic population', *Acta Antiqua Academiae Scientiae Hungariae* xvi, 457–63.

—— (1984). *A History of the Ostrogoths*, Bloomington, Indiana.

CADOUX, C. J. (1925). *The Early Church and the World*, Edinburgh.

CALLIES, H. (1964). *Die fremden Truppen im römischen Heer des Prinzipats und die sogenannten nationalen Numeri*, Beiträge zur Geschichte des römischen Heeres, *BRGK* 45, Mainz.

CAMERON, ALAN (1968). 'Theodosius and the regency of Stilicho', *Harvard Studies in Class. Phil.* lxxiii, 247–80.

—— (1970). *Claudian: Poetry and Propaganda at the Court of Honorius*, Oxford.

—— (1976). 'A quotation from Nilus of Ancyra in an iconodule text', *JThS* N.S. xxvii, 128–9.

—— (1981). 'The Empress and the Poet', *Yale Cl. St.* xxvii, 272.

—— (1987). 'Earthquake 400', *Chiron* xvii, 332–50.

—— (1989) 'A misdated homily of Chrysostom', *Nottingham Medieval Studies* xxxii, 34–48.

——, BAGNALL, R. S., WORP, K. A. (1987). *Consuls of the Late Empire*, Atlanta.

——, LONG J., with L. SHERRY (1990). *Barbarians and Politics at the Court of Arcadius*, Berkeley.

CAMERON, AVERIL (1976). *Corippus: In laudem Iustini Augusti Minoris*, London.

—— (1979). 'Images of authority, élites and icons in sixth-century Byzantium', *Past and Present* cxxxiv, 3–35.

—— (1985). *Procopius and the Sixth Century*, London.

CANNADINE, D. (1982). 'The transformation of civic ritual in modern Britain: the Colchester Oyster Feast', *Past and Present* xciv, 107–30.

CARNEY, T. F. (1971). *Bureaucracy in Traditional Society, Romano-Byzantine Bureaucracies Viewed from Within* (includes a translation of John Lydus, *De Magistratibus*), Lawrence, Kansas.

CARR, A. W. (1985). 'Women and monasticism in Byzantium', *Byzantinische Forschungen* ix, 1–16.

CARR, E. H. (1961). *What is History?*, London.

CATANI, E. (1983). 'Nota Sinesiana. *Epist.* cxxii; Katast. iii. 302 B', *Quaderni di Archeologia della Libia* xiii, 105–10.

CHALMERS, W. R. (1953). 'The *NEA EKΔOΣIΣ* of Eunapius' *Histories*', *CQ* xlvii, 165–70.

CHANTAL, V. (1979). 'Les juifs dans le Code Theodosien', in J. le Brun (ed.), *Les Chrétiens devant le fait juif*, Paris, 35–74.

CHAPELOT, J., FOSSIER, R. (1985). *The Village and House in the Middle Ages*, tr. H. Cleeve, London.

CHRISTIANSEN, P. G. (1970). 'Claudian and the East', *Historia* xix, 113–20.

—— (1966). 'Claudian versus the opposition', *TAPA* xcvii, 45–54.

CLARK, E. A. (1971). 'John Chrysostom and the *subintroductae*', *Church History* xlvi, 171–85.

—— (1979). *Jerome, Chrysostom and Friends: Essays and Translations* (includes translations of *Adversus eos qui apud se habent subintroductas virgines* and *quod regulares feminae viris cohabitare non debeant*), New York.

—— (1983). *Women in the Early Church*. Message of the Fathers of the Church 13, Wilmington, Delaware.

—— (1985). 'Authority and Humility: a conflict of values in fourth century female monasticism', *Byzantinische Forschungen* ix, 17–33.

CLAUDE, D. (1970). *Geschichte der Westgoten*, Berlin.

—— (1971). *Adel, Kirche und Königtum im Westgotenreich*, Sigmaringen.

CLAUSS, M. (1980). *Der magister officiorum in der Spätantike, 4.–6. Jahrhundert*, Munich.

CLEMENTE, G. (1968). *La Notititia Dignitatum*, Cagliari.

COLE, D. P. (1973). 'The enmeshment of nomads in Sa'udi Arabian society', in Cynthia Nelson (1973), 113–28.

CONSTANTELOS, D. J. (1968). *Byzantine Philanthropy and Social Welfare*, New Brunswick.

CONSTANTINESCU, M., PASCU, S., DIACONU, G. (1975). (ed.) *Relations between the autochthonous populations and the migratory populations on the territory of Romania*, Bucarest.

COURCELLES, P. (1967). 'Grégoire de Nysse lecteur de Porphyre', *REG* lxxx, 402–6.

COURTOIS, C. (1939). 'Les politiques navales de l'empire romain', *Rev. Hist.* clxxxvi, 17–47, 225–59.

—— (1964.) *Les Vandales et l'Afrique*, Aalen.

CRACCO RUGGINI, L. See under Ruggini, L. C.

CRAIK, E. M. (1983). *Marriage and Property*, Aberdeen.

CRITCHER, C. L. (1971). 'Football and Cultural values', in Stuart Hall (ed.), *Working Papers in Contemporary Cultural Studies*, Birmingham, 103–19.

CROKE, B. (1977). 'Evidence for the Hun invasion of Thrace', *GRBS* xviii, 347–67.

—— (1978). 'Hormisdas and Late Roman walls of Thessalonika', *GRBS* xix, 251–8.

—— (1981). 'Thessalonika's early Byzantine palaces', *Byzantion* li, 475–83.

—— (1987). 'Cassiodorus and the Getica of Jordanes', *Cl. Phil.* lxxii, 117–34.

CROOK, J. (1955). *Consilium Principis*, Cambridge.

—— (1971). 'Arnold Hugh Martin Jones', *Proceedings of the British Academy* lvii, 425–38.

CUNLIFFE, B. (1978). 'Settlement and population in the British Iron Age', in B. Cunliffe, T. Rowley (eds.), *Lowland Iron Age Communities in Europe*, BAR Int. Ser. 48, Oxford, 1–24.

Czuth, B. (1965). *Die Quellen der Geschichte der Bagauden*, Acta Universitatis de Attila Jozsef nominatae, Minora Opera ad Philologiam Classicam et Archaeologiam pertinentia ix, Szeged.

DAGRON, G. (1968). 'L'empire romain d'Orient au ive siècle et les traditions politique de l'hellénisme', *Travaux et Mémoires* iii, 1–240.

—— (1969). 'Aux origines de la civilisation byzantine: langue de culture et langue d'État', *Rev. Hist.* ccxii, 23–56.

—— (1970). 'Les moines et la ville. Le monachisme à Constantinople jusqu' au concile de Chalcédonne (451)', *Travaux et Mémoires* iv, 230–75.

—— (1974). *Naissance d'une capitale, Constantinople et ses institutions de 330 à 451*, Paris.

DANIÉLOU, J. (1967). 'Grégoire de Nysse et le néoplatonisme de l'École d'Athènes', *REG* lxxx, 395–401.

DANIELS, C. M. (1979). 'Excavations at Wallsend and the fourth century barracks on Hadrian's Wall', in W. S. Hanson, L. J. F. Keppie (eds.), *Roman Frontier Studies*, BAR Int. Ser. 71, Oxford 173–93.

DELEHAYE, H. (1912). 'Saints de Thrace et de Mésie', *Analecta Bollandiana* xxxi, 216–21.

DEMANDT, A. (1974). 'Saul (2)', *RE* Supp. xiv. 656.

—— (1980). 'Der spätrömische Militäradel', *Chiron* x, 609–36.

DEMOUGEOT, E. (1950). 'Note sur la politique orientale de Stilicon de 405 à 407', *Byzantion* xx, 27–37.

—— (1951). *De l'unité à la division de l'empire romain 395–410*, Paris.

—— (1956). 'Une lettre de l'empereur Honorius sur l'*hospitium* des soldats', *Revue historique de droit français*, xxxiv, 25–49.

—— (1958). 'La politique antijuive de Theódose II', *Akten des XI intern. Byzant. Kongr.*, 95–100.

—— (1960). 'Le chameau et l'Afrique du Nord romaine', *AES* cxv 209–47.

—— (1970). 'Àpropos des lètes gaulois du 4e siècle', in *Beiträge zur Alten Geschichte und deren Nachleben. Festschrift für F. Altheim*, Berlin, ii. 101–13.

—— (1972). 'Laeti et Gentiles dans la Gaule du ive siècle', *Annales litt. de l'Université de Besançon* cxxviii, 101–2 = Actes du Colloque d'Inst. Sociale, 1976.

—— (1974). 'Modalitiés d'établissement des fédéres barbares de Gratien et de Théodose', *Mélanges W. Seston*, Paris, 143–60.

—— (1975). 'La *Notitia Dignitatum* et l'histoire de l' Empire d'Occident au début du v siècle', *Latomus* xxxiv, 1079–134.

—— (1979). *La formation de l'Europe et les invasions barbares. De l'avènement de Dioclétien au début du VIe siècle*, Paris.

—— (1980–81). 'Restriction à l'expansion du droit de cité', *Ktema* v–vi, 381–93.

DIACONU, G. (1975). 'On the socio-economic relations between natives and Goths in Dacia', in M. Constantinescu (1975), 67–89.

DIESNER, H.-J. (1969). 'König Wamba und der westgotische Frühfeudalismus', *Jahrbuch der österreichischen Byzantinistik* xviii, 22 f.

—— (1972). 'Das Buccellariertum von Stilicho und Sarus bis auf Aetius 454–5', *Klio* liv, 321–50.

DITTRICH, U.-B. (1984). *Die Beziehungen Roms zu den Sarmaten und Quaden im vierten Jahrhundert n. Chr. (nach der Darstellung des M. Ammianus Marcellinus)*, Bonn.

DONNER, F. (1981). *The Early Islamic Conquest*, Princeton.

DOPP, S. (1980). *Zeitgeschichte in Dichtungen Claudians*, Hermes Einzelschriften 43, Wiesbaden.

DRINKWATER, J. F. (1983). *Roman Gaul*, London.

—— (1984). 'Peasants and Bagaudae in Roman Gaul', *Classical Views* iii, 349–77.

—— (1988). *The Gallic Empire, Separatism and Continuity in the North-Western Provinces of the Roman Empire 260–74*, Historia Einzelschrift 52, Stuttgart.

—— (1989). 'The Bagaudae: Revolutionary Movement, Social Institution or Loose Label?' in A. Wallace Hadrill (ed.), *Patrons and Clients*, London, 189–263.

DUBY, G. (1965). 'Démographie et villages désertés', in *Villages désertés et histoire économique, XIᵉ-XVIIIᵉ siècles*, Paris, 13–24.

DUMÉZIL, G. (1970). *Archaic Roman Religion* (tr. by P. Krapp of *La religion romaine archaique*, Paris, 1966).

DUMORTIER, J. (1951). 'Le valeur historique du dialogue de Palladius et la chronologie de saint Jean Chrysostome', *Mélanges de science religieuse* viii, 51–6.

—— (1953). 'La culture profane de S. Jean Chrysostome', *Mélanges de science religieuse* x, 53–62.

—— (1972). 'Une assemblée chrétienne au IVᵉ siècle', *Mélanges de science religieuse* xxix, 15–22.

—— (1982). 'A propos du commentaire sur Isaïe de saint Jean Chrysostome', *REG* xcv, 174–7.

DUNCAN JONES, R. P. (1978). 'Pay and numbers in Diocletian's army', *Chiron* viii, 541–60.

DVORNIK, F. N. (1934). 'The authority of the state in oecumenical councils', *The Christian East* xiv, 95–108.

EADIE, J. W. (1982). 'City and countryside in Late Roman Pannonia: the Regio Sirmiensis', in R. L. Hohlfelder (ed.), *City Town and Countryside in the Early Byzantine Era*, New York, 25–43.

ECK, W. (1978). 'Der Einfluss der konstantinischen Wende auf die Wahl der Bischöfe', *Chiron* viii, 561–85.

EGGER, R. (1948). *Der heilige Hermagoras*, Carinthia i, Mitteilungen des Geschichtsvereines für Kärnten, Klagenfurt.

EHRHARDT, A. (1964). 'The first two years of the emperor Theodosius I', *JEH* xv, 1–17.

ELMAYER, A. F. (1985). 'The centenaria of Roman Tripolitania', *Libyan Studies* xvi, 77–84.

ENSSLIN, W. (1947). *Theoderich der Grosse*, Munich.

FABRICIUS, C. (1962). *Zu den Jugendschriften des Johannes Chrysostomus: Untersuchungen zum Klassizismus des vierten Jahrhunderts*, Lund.

FERRILL, A. (1986). *The Fall of the Roman Empire*, London.

FIKHMAN, I. F. (1970). 'The Egyptian large estate in the 6th century', in D. H. Samuel (ed.), *Proc. XII Int. Congr. Papyrology*, Toronto.

FINLEY, M. I. (1976). (ed.) *Studies in Roman Property*, Cambridge.

—— (1980). *Ancient Slavery and Modern Ideology*, London.

—— (1983). *Politics in the Ancient World*, Cambridge.

Foss, C. (1977*a*). 'Archeology and the twenty cities of Byzantine Asia', *AJA* lxxxi, 469–86.

—— (1977*b*). 'Late Antique and Byzantine Ankara', *DOP* xxxi, 29–87.

—— (1979). *Ephesus after Antiquity, a Late Antique, Byzantine and Turkish City*, Cambridge.

Fowler, P. J. (1978). 'Lowland Landscapes', in S. Limbrey and J. G. Evans (eds.), *The Effect of Man on the Landscape in the Lowland Zone*, CBA Research Report 21, 1–12.

Foxhall, L., Forbes, H. A. (1982). 'Σιτομετρεία: The role of grain as a staple food in Classical Antiquity', *Chiron* xii, 41–90.

Frank, R. I. (1969). *Scholae Palatinae, The Palace Guards of the Later Roman Empire*, Monographs of the American Academy in Rome 23, Rome.

Frend, W. H. C. (1972). *The Rise of the Monophysite Movement*, Cambridge.

Freshfield, E. H. (1921–2). 'Notes on a vellum album containing some original sketches of public buildings and monuments drawn by German artists who visited Constantinople in 1574', *Archaeologia* lxxii, 87–104.

Frézouls, E. (1983). (ed.) *Crise et redressement dans les provinces européennes de l'Empire (milieu du IIᵉ–milieu du IVᵉ siècle ap. J.-C.)*, Strasbourg.

—— (1987). (ed.). *Sociétés urbaines, sociétés rurales dans l'Asie Mineure et la Syrie hellénistiques et romaines*, Strasbourg.

Fulford, M. G. (1985). 'Roman material in barbarian society c.200 BC–c.AD 400', in T. C. Champion and J. V. S. Megaw (eds.), *Settlement and Society: aspects of West European prehistory in the first millennium BC*, Leicester, 91–108.

Gallay, P. (1943). *La vie de saint Grégoire de Nazianze*, Lyon/Paris.

Galliou, P. (1981). 'Western Gaul in the third century' in A. King, M. Henig (eds.), *The Roman West in the Third Century*, BAR Int. Ser. 109 i–ii, Oxford.

Garnsey, P. (1970). *Social Status and Legal Privilege in the Roman Empire*, Oxford.

Garzya, A. (1981). 'Ai margini del neoplatonismo. Sinesio di Cirene', *Atti dell'Accademia Pontaniana* xxx, 153–65.

Gascou, J. (1976). 'L'institution des Bucellaires', *BIFAO* lxxii, 143–56.

Gaudemet, J. (1958). *L'église dans l'empire romain*, Paris.

Geffken, J. (1929). *Der Ausgang des griechisch-römischen Heidentums*, Heidelberg, tr. as *The Last Days of Greco-Roman Paganism*, by Sabine G. MacCormack, London, 1978.

Geppert, F. (1898). *Die Quellen des Kirchenhistorikers Socrates Scholasticus*, Leipzig.

GEROV, B. (1959). 'L'aspect ethnique et linguistique dans la région entre le Danube et les Balkans à l'époque romaine (Ic–IIIc)', *Studi urbinati di storia, filosofia e letteratura* N.S. B, xxxiii, 173–91.

GIBBON, E. (1787). *The History of the Decline and Fall of the Roman Empire*, cited from the edition of J. B. Bury which appeared in 1897.

—— (1814). *Autobiography of Edward Gibbon*, cited from B. Radice (ed.), *Edward Gibbon, Memoirs of My Life*, London, 1984.

GIGLI, G. (1947). 'Formi di reclutamente militare durante il Basso Impero', *Atti del Acad. Naz. dei Lincei* T 44, 268–89.

GILLES, K.-J. (1985). *Spätrömische Höhensiedlungen in Eifel und Hunsrück*, Trier.

GOFFART, W. (1974). *Caput and Colonate: towards a History of Late Roman Taxation*, Toronto.

—— (1980). *Barbarians and Romans: the Techniques of Accommodation*, Princeton.

—— (1981). 'Rome, Constantinople, and the barbarians', *American Historical Review* lxxxvi, 275–306.

GOODALL, B. (1979). *The Homilies of St. John Chrysostom on the Letters of St. Paul to Titus and Philemon*, Prolegomena to an Edition, University of California Publications in Classical Studies 20, B rkeley.

GOODCHILD, R. G. (1971). *Kyrene und Apollonia*. Zürich.

—— (1976). *Libyan Studies*, London.

GOULET, R. (1980). 'Sur la chronologie de la vie et des œuvres d'Eunapius de Sardes', *JHS* c, 60–72.

GRABAR, A. (1936). *L'empereur dans l'art byzantin*, Strasbourg.

GRADISH, S. F. (1980). *The Manning of the British Navy during the Seven Years' War*, London.

GRAVES, D. A. (1982) *Consistorium Domini: Imperial Councils of State in the Late Roman Empire*, 1973 PhD City University, New York, University Microfilms International, Ann Arbor.

GRÉGOIRE, H., KUGENER, M. A. (1930). *Marc le diacre, Vie de Porphyre évêque de Gaza*, Paris.

GREGORY, T. E. (1973). 'Zosimus V.23 and the people of Constantinople', *Byzantion* xliii, 61–83.

—— (1979. *Vox Populi, popular opinion and violence in the religious controversies of the fifth century AD*, Columbus.

GRIBOMONT, J. (1957). 'Le monachisme au IVe siècle en Asie Mineure: de Gangres au messalianisme', *Stud. Patr.* 2, TU 64, 400–15.

GRIFFITHS, J. G. (1970). *Plutarch's De Iside et Osiride*, text and commentary, Cardiff.

GRILLMEYER, A., BACHT, H. (1951–4). *Das Konzil von Chalkedon*, 2 vols., Würzburg.

GROSSE, R. (1920). *Römische Militärgeschichte*, Berlin.

GRUMEL, V. (1951). 'L'Illyricum de la mort de Valentinian 1er (375) à la mort de Stilicon (408)', *REB* ix, 546 ff.

—— (1958). *La chronologie*, Traité d'études byzantines i, Paris.

GUILLAUMONT, A. (1962). *Les 'Kephalaia Gnostica' d'Évagre le Pontique et l'histoire de l'origénisme chez les Grecs et chez les Syriens*, Patristica Sorbonensia 5, Paris.

GUNDERSON, G. (1976). 'Economic change and the demise of the Roman empire', *Explorations in Economic History* xiii, 43–68.

GÜNTHER, R. (1971). 'Laeti, Foederati und Gentiles in Nord- und Nordostgallien im Zusammenhang mit der sogenannten Laetenzivilisation', *Zt. f. Archeolol.* v, 39–59.

—— (1972). 'Die sozialen Träger der frühen Reihengräber-Kultur in Belgien und Nordfrankreich im 4/5. Jahrh.', *Helinium* xii, 268–72.

—— (1977). 'Einige neue Untersuchungen zu den Laeten und Gentilen in Gallien im 4. Jahrhundert', *Klio* lix, 311–21.

HAEHLING, R. VON (1978). *Die Religionszugehörigkeit der hohen Amtsträger des römischen Reiches seit Constantins I Alleinherrschaft bis zum Ende der theodosianischen Dynastie*, Bonn.

HALDON, J. F. (1979). 'Recruitment and Conscription in the Byzantine Army 550–950', *Sitzungsbericht Oest. Akad.*, Phil. Hist. Kl. 357, Vienna.

—— (1984). *Byzantine Praetorians*, Bonn.

HALKIN, F. (1977). *Douze récits byzantins sur S. Jean Chrysostom*, Subsidia Hagiographica lx, Brussels.

HALL, S. G. (1979). *Melito of Sardis: On Pascha and fragments*, Oxford.

HANDS, A. R. (1968). *Charities and Social Aid in Greece and Rome*, London.

HARRIES, JILL (1983). 'Treasure in heaven: property and inheritance among senators of Rome', in E. M. Craik (1983), 54–70.

HARRISON, M. (1963). 'Byzantine churches and chapels in central Lydia', *Anatolian Studies* xiii, 117–51.

HATCHER, J. (1977). *Plague, Population and the English Economy 1340–1530*, London.

HAWKES, S. (1961). 'Soldiers and settlers', *Med. Arch.* v, 1–70.

HEATHER, P. (1986). 'The crossing of the Danube and the Gothic conversion', *GRBS* xxvii, 289–318.

—— (1988). 'The anti-Scythian tirade of Synesius' *De Regno*', *Phoenix* xli, 152–72.

HEDEAGER, L. (1978). 'A quantitative analysis of Roman imports in Europe north of the *limes* (0–400 AD) and the question of Roman–Germanic exchange', *Studies in Scandinavian Prehistory and Early History* i, 191–216.

HEIL, W. (1966). *Das konstantinische Patriziat*, Baseler Studien zur Rechtswissenschaft 78, Basle.

HELD, W. (1974). *Die Vertiefung der allgemeinen Krise im Westen des römischen Reiches*, Berlin.

HEMMERDINGER, B. (1966). 'Les lettres latines à Constantinople jusqu'à Justinien', *Byz. Forsch.* i. 174 ff.

HENGEL, M. (1973). *Eigentum und Reichtum in der frühen Kirche*, Stuttgart.

HILTON, R. H. (1968) 'Villages désertés et histoire économique', *Études rurales* xxxii, 104–9.

HODGES, R., MITCHELL, J. (1985). *San Vincenzo al Volturno*, BAR Int. Ser. 252, Oxford.

HODGES, R., WHITEHOUSE, D. (1983). *Mohammed, Charlemagne and the Origin of Europe*, London.

HOFFMAN, D. (1963). 'Die spätrömischen Soldatengrabinschriften von Concordia', *Mus. Helv.* xx, 22–57.

—— (1969–70). *Das spätrömische Bewegungsheer und die Notitia Dignitatum*, Epigraphische Studien 7. 1–2, 2 vols., Dusseldorf.

—— (1974). 'Der Oberbefehl des spätrömischen Heeres im 4. Jahrhundert n. Chr.' in D. M. Pippidi (ed.), *Actes du IXᵉ Congrès International d'études sur les frontières romains*, Cologne, 381–97.

—— (1978). 'Wadomar, Bacurius und Heriulf: zur Laufbahn adliger und fürstlicher Barbaren im spätrömischen Heere', *Mus. Helv.* xxxv, 307–18.

HOLDING, P. A. (1982). *The Roman Army in Britain*, London.

HOLL, K. (1928). 'Die Zeitfolge des ersten origenistischen Streits', in *Gesammelte Aufsätze* ii, 310–50.

HOLUM, K. (1977). 'Pulcheria's crusade AD 421–22 and the ideology of imperial victory', *GRBS* xviii, 153–22.

—— (1982a). *Theodosian Empresses, Women and Imperial Dominion in Late Antiquity*, Berkeley.

—— (1982b). 'Caesarea and the Samaritans' in R. L. Hohlfelder (1982), 65–73.

HONORÉ, T. (1978). *Tribonian*, Cornell.

HOPKINS, K. (1978). *Conquerors and Slaves*, Cambridge.

HOPWOOD, K. (1983). *Policing the hinterland: Rough Cilicia and Isauria*, BAR Int. Ser. 156, Oxford, 173–8.

—— (forthcoming). 'Nomads or bandits? The pastoralist/sedentary interface in Anatolia', in M. Ursinus (ed.), *Proceedings of the 1985 Birmingham Byzantine Symposium*.

—— (1989). 'Bandits élites and rural order', in A. Wallace-Hadvill, ed. *Patronage in Ancient Society*, London, 171–87.

HUBBELL, H. M. (1924). 'Chrysostom and Rhetoric', *Cl. Phil.* xix, 261–76.

HUBEAUX, J. (1954). 'Saint Augustin et la crise eschatologique de la fin du IVᵉ siècle', *Bulletin de la classe des lettres, Académie royale de Belgique* xl, 658–73.

HUNT, E. D. (1972). 'Saint Silvia of Aquitaine, the role of a Theodosian pilgrim in the society of East and West', *JHThS* xxiii, 357–73.

—— (1973). 'Palladius of Helenopolis, a party and its supporters in the church of the late 4th century', *JThS* xxiv, 456–80.

—— (1982a). *Holy Land Pilgrimage in the Later Roman Empire*, Oxford.

—— (1982b). 'St. Stephen in Minorca: an episode in Jewish-Christian relations in the early 5th century AD', *JThS* xxxiii, 106–23.

IBN KHALDUN (1958). *The Muquaddimah, An Introduction to History*, tr. F. Rosenthal, 3 vols., London.

IONITA, I. (1975). 'The social-economic structure of society during the Goths' migration in the Carpatho-Danubian area', in M. Constantinescu et al. (1975), 77–90.

JAEGER, H. (1960). 'Justinien et l'episcopalis audientia', *Nouvelle Revue Historique de Droit Français et Étranger*, 4ᵉ sér. xxxviii, 214–62.

JAMES, E. (1980). *Visigothic Spain*, Oxford.

JANIN, R. (1964). *Constantinople Byzantine: développement urbain et répertoire topographique*, 2nd edn. Paris.

—— (1969). *La géographie ecclésiastique de l'empire byzantin*. Première partie: Le siège de Constantinople et le patriarcat œcuménique, les églises et les monastères, Paris.

JANSSEN, W. (1976). 'Some major aspects of Frankish and medieval settlement in the Rhineland', in P. H. Sawyer (ed.), *Medieval Settlement, Continuity and Change*, Norwich, 41–60.

——, LOHRMAN, D. (1983). *Villa-Curtis-Grangia. Landwirtschaft zwischen Loire und Rhein von der Römerzeit zum Hochmittelalter*, Munich.

JARNUT, J. (1982). *Geschichte der Longobarden*, Stuttgart.

JEEP, L. (1885). 'Quellenuntersuchungen zu den griechischen Kirchen-historikern', *JCPh* Suppl. 14, 53–178.

JIMÉNEZ GARNICA, A. M. (1983), *Origenes y desarrollo del Reino Visigodo de Tolosa (a. 418–507)*, Valladolid.

JOANNOU, P. P. (1972). *La legislation impériale et la christianisation de l'empire romain (311–476)*, Orientalia Christiana Analecta 192, Rome.

JOHNSON, A. C., WEST, L. C. (1949). *Byzantine Egypt: Economic Studies*, Princeton.

JOHNSON, D. L. (1969). *The nature of nomadism*, Research Papers 118, Chicago.

——, AL-AKHDAR, J. (1973). *Cyrenaica: an historical geography of settlement and livelihood*, Chicago.

JONES, A. H. M. (1940). *The Greek City*, Oxford.

—— (1964a). *The Later Roman Empire 284–602: an economic survey*, 3 vols., Oxford (abbreviated *LRE*).

—— (1964b). 'Collegiate Prefectures', *JRS* liv, 78–89.

—— (1968). *Studies in Roman Government and Law*, Oxford.

JONES, M. E. (1979). 'Climate, nutrition and disease: an hypothesis of Romano-British population', in P. J. Casey (ed.), *The End of Roman Britain*, BAR Brit. Ser. 71, 231–51.

JUNGCK, C. (1974). *Gregor von Nazianz, De Vita Sua*, Heidelberg.

JUSTER, J. (1914). *Les Juifs dans l'empire romain*, Paris.

KAEGI, W. E. (1981). *Byzantine Military Unrest 471–843*, Amsterdam.

KAISER, R. (1973). *Untersuchungen zur Geschichte der Civitas und Diözese Soissons in römischer und merowingischer Zeit*, Bonn.

KEAY, S. J. (1981). 'The Conventus Tarraconensis in the third century AD', in A. King and M. Henig (eds.), *The Roman West in the Third Century*, BAR Int. Ser. 109, Oxford, ii. 451–80.

KELLY, J. N. D. (1975). *Jerome*, London.

KENNEDY, D. L. (1977). 'Parthian regiments in the Roman army', in *Limes*, Akten des XI internationalen Limes Kongress, Budapest, 521–31.

KIENAST, W. (1968). *Studien über die französischen Volkstämme des Frühmittelalters*, Pariser historische Studien 7.

—— (1984). 'Gefolgswesen und Patrocinium im spanischen Westgotenreich', *Hist. Zeit.* ccxxxix, 23–75.

KIKHA, M. M. (1968). *Le nomadisme pastoral en Cyrénaïque septentrionale*, Aix en Provence.

KING, N. Q. (1957). 'The 150 holy fathers of the Council of Constantinople 381 AD', *St. Patr* 1 = TU 63, 635 ff.

—— (1961). *The Emperor Theodosius and the Establishment of Christianity*, London.

KING, P. D. (1972). *Law and Society in the Visigothic Kingdom*, Cambridge.

KOLLWITZ, J. (1941). *Oströmische Plastik der theodosianischen Zeit*, Berlin.

KOPECEK, T. A. (1979). *A History of Neo-Arianism*, Patristic Monograph Series 8, 2 vols., Philadelphia.

KÜHN, H. (1974). *Die germanischen Bügelfibeln der Völkerwanderungszeit in Süddeutschland*, Graz.

LACOMBRADE, CH. (1946). 'Synésios et l'énigme du loup', *REA* xlviii, 260–6.

—— (1949). 'Notes sur l'aurum coronarium', *REA* li, 54–9.

—— (1951a). *Le discours sur la royauté de Synésios de Cyrène à l'empereur Arcadios*, Traduction nouvelle avec introduction, notes et commentaire, Paris.

—— (1951b). *Synésios de Cyrène. Hellène et chrétien*, Paris.

LANE FOX, R. (1986). *Pagans and Christians*, London.

LATTIMORE, O. (1962). *Studies in frontier history: collected papers 1928–58*, London.

LEICHT, P. S. (1923). 'Gli elementi romani nella costituzione longobarda', *Archivo Storico Italiano* lxxxi, 5–24.

LEMERLE, P. (1954). 'Invasions et migrations dans les Balkans depuis l'époque romane jusqu'au viii^c siècle', *Rev. Hist.* ccxi, 265–308.

LEMOSSE, M. (1981). 'L'inscription de Walldürn et le problème de déditices', *Ktema* vi, 349–58.

LEONHARDT, R. (1916).'Inquilini', *RE* iv. 496.

LEPELLEY, C. (1967). 'Declin ou stabilité de l'agriculture africaine', *Antiquités Africaines* i, 135–44.

LIEBESCHUETZ, J. H. W. G. (1972). *Antioch: City and Imperial Administration in the Later Roman Empire*, Oxford.

—— (1977). 'The defences of Syria in the sixth century', *Akten des X Internationalen Limes Kongress*, Cologne, Bonn 487–99.

—— (1983). 'The date of Synesius' *De Providentia*, Actes VIIe Congr. FIEC, ii. 39–46.

—— (1984). 'Friends and enemies of John Chrysostom', in A. Moffatt (ed.), *Maistor*, Canberra, 85–111.

—— (1985*a*). 'The Fall of John Chrysostom', *Nottingham Medieval Studies* xxix, 1–31.

—— (1985*b*). 'Synesius and municipal politics of Cyrenaica in the 5th century AD', *Byzantion* lv, 146–64.

—— (1986). 'Why did Synesius become bishop of Ptolemais?', *Byzantion* lvi, 180–95.

—— (1987). 'The identity of Typhos in Synesius' *De Providentia*', *Latomus* xlvi, 419–31.

LIEU, S. N. C. (1985). *Manichaeism in the Later Roman Empire and Medieval China*, Manchester.

LINDNER, R. P. (1983). *Nomads and Othomans in Medieval Anatolia*, Bloomington, Indiana.

LIZZI, R. (1981). 'Significato filosofico e politico dell'antibarbarismo sinesiano. Il De Regno e il De Providentia', *Rendiconti dell'Accademia di Archeologia, Lettere e Belle Arti di Napoli* lvi, 49–62.

—— (1987). *Il potere episcopale nell' Oriente Romano*, filologia e critica collana divetta da Bruno Gentili, 53, Rome.

LLOYD, J., BARKER, G. (1981). 'Rural settlement in Roman Molise: problems of archaeological survey', in G. Barker and R. Hodges (eds.), *Archaeology and Italian Society*, 289–304.

LOUD, G. A. (1982). 'The Gens Normanorum—Myth or Reality?' in R. Allen Brown (ed.), *Proceedings of the Battle Conference on Anglo-Norman Studies* iv, Bury St. Edmunds, 10–46.

LONG, J. (1987). 'The Wolf and the Lion: Synesius' Egyptian Sources', *GRBS* xxviii, 103–15.

LOURIE, E. (1966). 'A society organised for war: medieval Spain', *Past and Present* xxxv, 54–76.

LÖWE, R. (1923). 'Gotische Namen in hagiographischen Texten', *Beiträge zur Geschichte der deutschen Sprache* xlvii, 407–33.

LUTTWAK, E. N. (1976). *The Grand Strategy of the Roman Empire*, Baltimore.

MacCormack, S. G. (1981). *Art and Ceremony in Late Antiquity*, Berkeley.

Macdonald, B. (1982). 'The Wâdi el-Hasa Survey 1971 and Previous Archaeological Work in Southern Jordan', *BASOR* ccxlv, 35–52.

MacMullen, R. (1963*a*). *Soldier and Civilian in the Later Roman Empire*, Cambridge, Mass.

—— (1963*b*). 'Barbarian enclaves in the northern Roman empire', *Antiquité Classique* xxxii, 552–61.

—— (1980). 'How big was the Roman imperial army?', *Klio* lxii, 451–60.

—— (1986). 'Judicial savagery in the Roman Empire', *Chiron* xvi, 147–66.

—— (1987). 'Late Roman slavery', *Historia* xxxvi, 359–82.

McNeill, W. H. (1976). *Plagues and Peoples*, New York.

Malingrey, A.-M. (1968). (ed.) *Jean Chrysostome, Lettres à Olympias*, seconde édition augmentée de la Vie anonyme d'Olympias, Sources Chrétiennes 13 bis, Paris.

—— (1981). 'La double tradition manuscrite de la lettre de Jean Chrysostome à Innocent', *Traditio* xxvii, 381–8.

Mango, C. (1984). 'A Byzantine hagiographer at work: Leontios of Neapolis', in I. Hutter (ed.), *Byzanz und der Westen*, Studien zur Kunst des europäischen Mittelalters, Österreichische Akademie der Wissenschaften, Phil. Hist. Kl. Sitzungsberichte 432, Vienna.

—— (1985). *Le développement urbain de Constantinople IVe-VIIe siècles*, Paris.

Mann, J. C. (1976). 'What was the Notitia Dignitatum for?', in R. Goodburn and P. Bartholomew (eds.), *Aspects of the Notitia Dignitatum*, BAR Sup. Ser. 15, Oxford, 1–8.

—— (1983). *Legionary Recruitment and Veteran Settlement during the Principate*, London.

—— (1986). 'A note on conubium', in W. Eck and H. Wolff (eds.), *Römische Diplomata*, Univ. Passau.

Mannino, V. (1984). *Ricerche sul 'Defensor Civitatis'*, Milan.

Mathisen, R. W. (1984). 'Emigrants, exiles and survivors, aristocratic options in Visigothic Aquitania', *Phoenix* xxxviii, 159–70.

Matthews, J. F. (1967). 'A pious supporter of Theodosius I: Maternus Cynegius', *JThS* xviii, 484–509.

—— (1974). 'The letters of Symmachus' in J. W. Binns (ed.), *Latin Literature of the Fourth Century*, London, 58–99.

—— (1975). *Western Aristocracies and Imperial Court, AD 364–425*, Oxford.

—— (1976). 'Mauretania, Ammianus and the Notitia' in R. Goodburn, P. Bartholomew (eds.), *Aspects of the Notitia Dignitatum*, BAR Sup. Ser. 15, Oxford, 157–86.

Mayerson, P. (1961). *The Ancient Agricultural Regime of Nessana and the Central Negeb*, London.

MEEKS, W. A. (1983). *The first urban Christians, the social world of the apostle Paul*, New Haven.

MELICHER, TH. (1930). *Der Kampf zwischen Gesetzes- und Gewohnheitsrecht im Westgotenreich*, Weimar.

MENESTRIER, C. F. (1702). *Description de la belle et grande colonne historiée dressée à l'honeur de l'empereur Theodose dessinée per G. Bellin . . . représentée en seize planches*, Paris. See also Appendix II, n. 7.

MEWS, S. (1982). (ed.) *Religion and National Identity*, Studies in Church History 18, Oxford.

MEYERS, E. M., KRAABEL, A. THOMAS, A., STRANGE, J. F. (1970–72). *Synagogue excavations at Khirbet Shema, Upper Galilee, Israel 1970–2*, Annual of American Schools of Oriental Research 42, Durham, N.C.

MIDDLETON, P. (1983). 'The Roman Army and Long Distance Trade', in P. Garnsey and C. R. Whittaker (eds.), *Trade and Famine in Classical Antiquity*, Cambridge, 75–83.

MIEROW, C. C. (1915). *The Gothic History of Jordanes*, Cambridge.

MIKESELL, M. W. (1955). 'Notes on the dispersal of the dromedary', *SW Journal of Anthropology* xi, 231–45.

MILAZZO, A. M. (1982). 'Le epistole di Giovanni Crisostomo a Innocenzo I e le epistole di Demostene', *Orpheus* iii, 200–27.

MILLER, J. M. (1979). 'Survey of Central Moab', *BASOR* ccxxxiv, 43–52.

MINOR, C. E. (1971). *Brigands, Insurrectionists and Separatist Movements in the Later Roman Empire*, PhD University of Washington, Facsimile copy University Microfilm International, Ann Arbor, London.

MÓCSY, A. (1964). 'Der Name Flavius als Rangbezeichnung in der Spätantike', *Akten des IV. internationalen Kongresses für griechische und lateinische Epigraphik*, Vienna, 257–69.

—— (1974). *Pannonia and Upper Moesia, a History of the Middle Danube Provinces of the Roman Empire*, London.

MOHAMMED, A. (1973). 'The nomadic and the sedentary: polar complements, not polar opposites', in Cynthia Nelson (1973), 97–112.

MOMIGLIANO, A. (1954). 'Gibbon's contribution to historical method', *Historia* ii, 450–63 = (1966), 40–55.

—— (1976). 'A.H.M. Jones' *The Later Roman Empire*', *Oxford Magazine*, 4 March 1965, 264 ff.

—— (1966). *Studies in Historiography*, London.

—— (1970). 'The ancient city of Fustel de Coulanges', *Riv. St. Ital.* lxxxvii, 81–88 (in Italian) = (1977), 325–43.

—— (1974). 'Historicism revisited', *Mededelingen der Koninklijke Nederlandse Akademie van Wetenschappen*, Afd. Letterkunde, N.R. xxxvii. 3, 63–70.

—— (1977). *Essays in Ancient and Modern Historiography*, Oxford.

MOMMSEN, TH. (1910). 'Das römische Militärwesen seit Diocletian', *Gesammelte Schriften* vi, Berlin, 206.

MONTESQUIEU, L. (1734). *Considérations sur les causes de grandeur des Romains et de leur décadence*, ed. C. Jullian, Paris, 1900.

MOORHEAD, J. (1986). 'Culture and Power among the Ostrogoths', *Klio* lxviii, 112–22.

MÜLLER, A. (1912). 'Das Heer Justinians nach Prokop und Agathias', *Philologus* lxxi, 101–38.

MURRAY, A. C. (1983). *Germanic Kinship Structure, Studies in Law and Society in Antiquity and the Early Middle Ages*, Studies and Texts 65, Toronto.

NELSON, CYNTHIA (1973). (ed.) *The Desert and the Sown: Nomads in the Wider Society*, Inst. of Int. Stud. Univ. of California, Berkeley.

NORDEN, E. (1898). *Die antike Kunstprosa vom VI. Jahrhundert v. Chr. bis in die Zeit der Renaissance*, 2 vols., Stuttgart, repr. 1958.

O'FLYNN, J. M. (1983). *Generalissimos of the Western Roman Empire*, Edmonton.

OBERMEYER, G. J. (1973). 'Leadership and transition in Beduin society', in Cynthia Nelson (1973), 159–73.

OPELT, I. (1965). 'Eunapius', *RAC*, cols. 928–36.

PALANQUE, J.-R. (1931). 'Sur la date d'une loi de Gratien contre l'hérésie', *Rev. Hist.* clxviii, 87–90.

—— (1933). *Saint Ambroise et l'empire romain*, Paris.

—— (1944). 'Collégialité et partages dans l'empire romain aux ive et ve siècles', *REA* xlvi, 47–64, 280–98.

——, BARDY, G., LABRIOLLE, P. DE (1936). *De la paix constantinienne à la mort de Théodose*, Histoire de l'église, (eds.) A. Fliche and V. Martin, Paris.

PARGOIRE, J. (1899–1900). 'Les homélies de S. Jean Chrysostome en Juillet 399', *Echos d'orient* iii, 20–25.

—— (1899). 'Rufinianes', *Byz. Zt.* viii, 429–77.

PARKER, H. M. D., WATSON, G. R. (1958). *The Roman Legions*, Cambridge.

PARKER, S. T. (1980). 'Towards a history of the Limes Arabicus' in W. S. Hanson and L. J. F. Keppie (eds.), *Roman Frontier Studies*, Papers Presented to the 12th International Congress of Roman Frontier Studies, BAR Int. Ser. 71, Oxford, 865–78.

—— (1986). *Romans and Saracens: a History of the Arabian Frontier*, American Schools of Oriental Research Dissertation Series 6, Winona Lake.

PASCHOUD, F. (1975) *Cinq études sur Zosime*, Paris.

—— (1985a). 'Eunapiana', *Bonner Historia Augusta Colloquium 1982/3, Antiquitas* xvii, Bonn. 239–93.

—— (1985*b*). 'Le début de l'ouvrage historique d'Olympiodore' in *Studia in honorem Iiro Kajanto*, Helsinki, 185–96.

PASQUATO, O. (1976). *Gli spettacoli in S. Giovanni Crisostomo: Paganesimo e christianesimo ad Antiochia e Constantinopoli nel IV secolo*, Orientalia Christiana Analecta 201, Rome.

PATLAGEAN, E. (1976). 'L'histoire de la femme déguisée en moine et l'évolution de la sainteté féminine à Byzance', *St. Med. Sr.* 3. xvii, 597–623.

—— (1977*a*). 'L'impôt payé par les soldats au vi^e siècle. Armées et fiscalité dans le monde antique', *Colloques Nationaux du Centre National de la Recherche Scientifique* 936, 303–10.

—— (1977*b*). *Pauvreté économique et pauvreté sociale à Byzance, 4e–7e siècles*, Paris.

—— (1981). *Structure sociale, famille, chrétienté à Byzance*, London, Variorum Reprints.

PAVIS D'ESCURAC (1980). 'Irrigation et vie paysanne dans l'Afrique du Nord antique', *Ktema* v, 177–91.

PEETERS, P. (1940–7). 'La vie géorgienne de S. Porphyre de Gaza', *Analecta Bollandiana* lviii–ix, 65–216.

PETERS, I. (1945). *Die Germanenpolitik der Kaiser Konstantius und Julian*, Diss. Heidelberg.

PETIT, P. (1951). 'Sur la date du *Pro Templis*', *Byzantion* xxi, 295 ff.

—— (1957). *Les étudiants de Libanius*, Paris.

PIETRI, CH. (1975). 'L'aristocratie chrétienne entre Jean de Constantinople et Augustin d'Hippone' in Ch. Kannengiesser (ed.), *Jean Chrysostom et Augustin*, Paris, 282–305.

—— (1976). *Roma Christiana*, 2 vols., Rome.

PIGANIOL, A. (1972). *L'empire chrétien (325–395)*, 2nd ed. by A. Chastagnol, Paris.

POHLKAMP, W. (1984). 'Kaiser Konstantin, der heidnische und christliche Kult in den Actus Silvestri', *Frühmittelalterliche Studien* xviii, 357–400.

POTTER, T. W. (1979). *The Changing Landscape of South Etruria*, New York.

PREGER, TH. (1901–7). *Scriptores originum Constantinopolitanarum*, Leipzig, repr. New York, 1975.

PRINGLE, D. (1981). *The Defence of Byzantine Africa from Justinian to the Arab Conquest*, BAR Int. Ser. 99, Oxford.

PROTASE, D. (1964). 'Considerations sur la continuité Daco-Romaine en Dacie post Aurélienne', *Dacia* viii, 177–93.

RAPHAEL, C. (1968). *The Walls of Jerusalem*, London.

RAWSON, B. (1986). *The Family in Ancient Rome*, London.

REICHARDT, K. D. (1978). 'Die Judengesetzgebung im *Codex Theodosianus*', *Kairos* N.F.. xx, 16–39.

REMONDON, R. (1961). 'Soldats des Byzance d'après un papyrus trouvé à Edfou', *Recherches de Papyrologie* i, 41–93.

—— (1965). 'P. Hamb. 56 et P. Lond. 1419 (notes sur les finances d'Aphrodito du vie siècle au viiie)', *CE* xl, 401–30.

—— (1974). 'Les contradictions de la société égyptienne', *Journal of Juristic Papyrology* xviii, 17–32.

RIDLEY, R. T. (1969–70). 'Eunapius and Zosimus', *Helikon* ix–x, 574–92.

RIST, J. M. (1965). 'Hypatia', *Phoenix* xix, 214–25.

RITTER, A. M. (1965). *Das Konzil von Konstantinopel und sein Symbol*, Göttingen.

ROQUES, D. (1982). 'Synésios évêque philosophe', *REG* xcv, 461–7.

—— (1983). 'Synésios et les migrations berbères vers orient, 398–413', *CRAI*, 660–7.

ROSENBAUM, E. A., WARD PERKINS, J. B. (1980). *Mosaic Pavements in Cyrenaican Churches*, Rome.

ROUCHE, M. (1971). *L'Aquitaine des Visigoths aux Arabes (418–781)*, Lille.

RUETHER, R. R. (1969). *Gregory of Nazianzus, Rhetor and Philosopher*, Oxford.

RUGGINI, L. C. (1959). *Ebrei e orientali nell'Italia settentrionale fra il IV e il VI secolo*, Studia et documenta historiae et iuris xxv.

—— (1980). 'Pagani, ebrei e cristiani: odio sociologico e odio teologico nel mondo antico', in *Gli Ebrei nell'alto medioevo*, Settimane di studio del centro italiano di studi sull'alto medioevo 26, Spoleto.

—— (1987). 'Intolerance', *Cl. Phil.* lxxxii, 187–205.

——, CRACCO G. (1977). 'Changing Fortune of the Italian city from Late Antiquity to the early Middle Ages', *Rivista di filologia* cv, 448–75.

RUNNELS, C. N. (1983). 'The Stanford University Archaeological and Environmental Survey of Southern Argolid', in D. R. Keller and D. W. Rupp (eds.), *Archaeological Survey in the Mediterranean Area*, BAR Int. 155, Oxford, 261–3.

——, VAN ANDELS, TH., POPE, K. O. (1986). 'Five thousand years of land use and abuse in the southern Argolid', *Hesperia* lv, 103–28.

RYAN, P. (1982). 'Chrysostom a derived stylist', *Vig. Chr.* xxxvi, 5–14.

SADDINGTON, D. B. (1982). *The Development of the Roman Auxiliary Forces from Caesar to Vespasian (49 BC–AD 79)*, Harare.

STE. CROIX, G. E. M. DE (1981). *The Class Struggle in the Ancient Greek World from the Archaic Age to the Arab Conquests*, London.

SANDER, E. (1958). 'Das Recht des römischen Soldaten', *Rh. Mus.* ci, 152–234, esp. 152–90.

SCARDIGLI, B. (1976). *Die gotisch-römischen Beziehungen im 3. und 4. Jahrhundert n. Chr., ein Forschungsbericht*, ANRW ii. 5. 1, 200–85.

SCHÄFERDIEK, K. (1977). 'Germanenmission', *RAC* x, col. 530 ff.

—— (1979a). 'Zeit und Umstände des Westgotischen Übergangs zum Christentum', *Historia* xxvii, 90–7.

—— (1979b). 'Vom Bischof von Gotien zum Gotenbischof', *Zt. f. Kirchengesch.* xc, 107–46.

SCHMIDT, L. (1941). *Die Ostgermanen*, revised ed., Munich.

SCHMIDT-WIEGAND, R. (1972). *Fränkische und frankolateinische Bezeichnungen für soziale Schichten und Gruppen in der Lex Salica*, Nachrichten der Akademie der Wissenschaften in Göttingen, Phil. Hist. Kl. no. 4.

SCHÖLLGEN, G. (1984). *Ecclesia Sordida. Zur Frage der sozialen Schichtung frühchristlicher Gemeinden . . .*, Münster.

SCHÖNFELD, M. (1925). 'Laeti', *RE* xii. 1, 446–8.

SCHOO, G. (1911). *Die Quellen des Kirchenhistorikers Sozomenos*, Berlin.

SCHOULER, B. (1984). *La tradition hellénique chez Libanios*, Lille.

SCHOVEY, D. J. (1984). *Chronology of Eclipses and Comets*, Bury St. Edmunds.

SCHWARTZ, E. (1921). 'Über die Reichskonzilien von Theodosius bis Justinian', *ZRG rom.* xlii, 208–53 = *G. Schr.* iv. 111–58.

—— (1935). 'Zur Kirchengeschichte des 4. Jahrhunderts', *Zt. f. neutest. Wiss.* xxxiv, 129–213 = *G. Schr.* iv. 1–110.

SCHWARTZ, J. (1951). 'Une forteresse construite sous Dioclétien, Qasr-Qârûm,' *CRAI* xci, 90–7.

SCOTT, L. R. (1972). *Magistri Militum of the Eastern Roman Empire in the Fifth Century*, Diss. Cambridge Univ.

SEECK, O. (1876). *Notitia Dignitatum*, Berlin.

—— (1883). *Q. Aurelii Symmachi quae supersunt*, Berlin, repr. 1961.

—— (1896). 'Arcadius', *RE* ii. 1137–53.

—— (1901), 'Colonatus', *RE* iv. 483–510.

—— (1910–20). *Geschichte des Untergangs der antiken Welt*, Berlin.

—— (1919). *Regesten der Kaiser und Päpste*, Stuttgart.

SHAW, B. D. (1982). 'Fear and loathing: the nomad menace and Roman Africa', in C. M. Wells (ed.), *Roman Africa*, Ottawa, 29–50.

SIEGERT, F. (1980). *Drei hellenistisch-jüdische Predigten*, Wissenschaftliche Untersuchungen zum Neuen Testament 20, Tübingen.

SNEE, R. (1985). 'Valens recalls the Nicene exiles and anti-Arian propaganda', *GRBS* xxvi, 395–419.

SOFFREY, M. (1939). *Recherches sur la syntaxe de S. Jean Chrysostome*, Paris.

—— (1947–8). 'Saint Jean Chrysostome et la litérature paienne', *Phoenix* ii, 82–5.

SOPRONI, S. (1985). *Die letzten Jahrzehnte des Pannonischen Limes*, Munich.

SORACI, R. (1974). *Richerche sui conubia tra Romani e Germani nei secoli IV–VI*, Catania.

STALLKNECHT, B. (1969). *Untersuchungen zur römischen Aussenpolitik in der Spätantike 306–395*, Bonn.

STAUFFENBERG, A. SCHENK VON (1948). *Das Imperium und die Völkerwanderung*, Munich.

STEIN, E. (1949). *Histoire du Bas-Empire*, Paris. 1st German edition Vienna, 1928.

STEINWERTER, A. (1956). 'Die Stellung der Bischöfe in der byzantinischen Verwaltung Aegyptens', *Studi in onore di Pietro de Francisci*, Milan, i. 75–99.

STREITBERG, W. (1908). *Die gotische Bibel*, Heidelberg.

STROHEKER, K. F. (1965). *Germanentum und Spätantike*, Zürich.

STUCCHI, S. (1965). *L'Agora di Cirene, i: I lati nord ed est della platea inferiore*, Rome.

—— (1975). *Architettura Cirenaica*, Rome.

SWIDLER, W. W. (1973). 'Adaptive processes regulating nomad–sedentary interaction in the Middle East', in Cynthia Nelson (1973), 23–41.

TCHALENKO, G. (1953). *Villages antiques de la Syrie du nord. Le massif du Bélus à l'époque romaine*, Paris.

TEALL, J. L. (1965). 'The barbarians in Justinian's army', *Speculum* xl, 294–322.

TEILLET, S. (1984). *Des Goths à la nation gothique*, Paris.

TEIXIDOR, J. (1987). 'Nomadisme et sédentarisation en Palmyrène', in E. Frezouls (1987), 49–55.

THOMPSON, E. A. (1948). *A History of Attila and the Huns*, Oxford.

—— (1956). 'The settlement of the barbarians in Southern Gaul', *JRS* xlvi, 65–75.

—— (1963a). 'Christianity and the Northern Barbarians' in A. D. Momigliano (ed.), *Paganism and Christianity in the 4th century*, Oxford, 72–5.

—— (1963b). 'The Visigoths from Fritigern to Euric', *Historia* xii, 105–26.

—— (1965). *The Early Germans*, Oxford.

—— (1966). *The Visigoths in the Time of Ulfila*, Oxford.

—— (1969). *The Goths in Spain*, Oxford.

—— (1982). *Romans and Barbarians, the Decline of the Western Empire*, Madison.

TODD, M. (1977). 'Germanic burials in the Roman Iron Age', in R. Reece (ed.), *Burial in the Roman World*, London, 39–41.

TOMLIN, R. S. O. (1979). 'Meanwhile in North Italy and Cyrenaica', BAR Brit. Ser. 71, Oxford.

TROUSSET, P. (1974). *Recherches sur le limes tripolitanus du chott El Djerid à la frontière Tuniso-Libyenne*, Paris.

TURNER, C. H. (1899 ff.). *Ecclesiae Occidentalis Monumenta Iuris Antiquissima*, Oxford.

VAGGIONE, R. P. (1987). (ed.) *Eunomius, the Extant Works*, text and translation, Oxford Early Christian Texts, Oxford.

VANANGS, P. (1979). 'Taxation and survival in the late fourth century' in M. W. C. Hassal (ed.), *De Rebus Bellicis Pt. I: Papers presented to E. A. Thompson*, BAR Int. Ser. 63, Oxford, 47–57.

VAN DAM, R. (1985). *Leadership and Community in Late Antique Gaul*, Berkeley.

VAN DE PAVERD (1970). *Zur Geschichte der Messliturgie in Antiocheia und Konstantinopel gegen Ende des vierten Jahrhunderts*, Orientalia Christiana Analecta 187, Rome.

VANDERSPOEL, J. (1986). 'Claudian, Christ and the Saints', *CQ* N.S. xxxvi, 239–55.

VAN OMMESLAEGHE, F. (1975). 'La valeur historique de la Vie de S. Jean Chrysostome attribué à Martyrius d'Antioche', *Studia Patristica* xii, 478–83.

—— (1977). 'Que vaut le témoinage de Palladius sur le procès de Jean Chrysostome', *Analecta Bollandiana* xcv, 389–414.

—— (1979). 'Jean Chrysostome en conflict avec l'impératrice Eudoxie', *Analecta Bollandiana* xcvii, 131–59.

—— (1981). 'Jean Chrysostome et le peuple de Constantinople', *Analecta Bollandiana* xcix, 329–49; xcv, 389–414.

—— (1989). (ed.), *L'oraison funèbre de S. Jean Chrysostome attribuée à Martyrius d'Antioche* (= *Subsidia hagiographica*, 71), Bruxelles.

VÁRADY, L. (1969). *Das letzte Jahrhundert Pannoniens 376–476*, Amsterdam.

VELKOV, V. (1962). 'Les campagnes et la population rurale en Thrace au ive– vi^e siècle', *Byzantino-Bulg.* i, 31–66.

—— (1976). 'Das Zeitalter Konstantins des Grossen in Thrakien', *Acta Antiqua Academicae Scientiarum Hungaricae* xxiv, 339–406.

—— (1980). 'Thrakien und die Thraker in der Spätantike', *Actes du IIe congrès international de Thracologie*, Bucharest, ii. 445 ff.

—— (1981). 'Thrace and Lower Moesia during the Roman and Late Roman period', *Klio* lxiii, 473–8.

VEROSTA, S. (1960). *Johannes Chrysostomus, Staatsphilosoph und Geschichtstheologe*, Vienna.

VEYNE, P. (1976). *Le pain et le cirque, sociologie historique d'un pluralism politique*, Paris.

—— (1983). *Les Grecs ont-ils cru à leurs mythes?*, Paris.

VIGNERON, P. (1968). *Le cheval dans l'antiquité gréco-romaine*, Nancy.

Villages desertés et histoire économique XIe–XVIIIe siècle, École pratique des hautes études—VIe section, Centre de recherches historiques, Les hommes et la livre xi, Paris, 1965.

VOLLWEIDER, S. (1985*a*). 'Synesios von Kyrene über das Bischofsamt', *Studia Patristica* xviii. 1, 233–7.

—— (1985*b*). *Neuplatonische und christliche Theologie bei Synesios von Kyrene*, Forschungen zur Kirchen- und Dogmengeschichte 35, Göttingen.

VULPE, R. (1961). 'La Valachie et la Basse-Moldavie sous les romains', *Dacia* v, 365–93.

WAAS, M. (1965). *Germanen im römischen Dienst im 4. Jahrhundert*, Bonn.

WALKER, S. (1981). 'The third century in the Lyon region' in A. King and M. Henig (eds.), *The Roman West in the Third Century*, BAR Int. Ser. 109, Oxford, ii. 317–42.

WALLACE-HADRILL, D. S. (1982). *Christian Antioch*, Cambridge.

WALLACE-HADRILL, J. M. (1971). *Early Germanic Kingship in England and on the Continent*, Oxford.

WARD, J. H. (1974). 'The *Notitia Dignitatum*', *Latomus* xxxiii, 397–434.

WELSBY, D. A. (1982). *The Roman Military Defence of the British Provinces in its Later Phases*, BAR Brit. Ser. 101, Oxford.

WENSKUS, R. (1961). *Stammesbildung und Verfassung. Das Werden der frühmittelalterlichen Gentes*, Cologne.

WERNER, J. (1950). 'Zur Entstehung der Reihengräberzivilisation', *Archaeologia Geographica* i, 23–32. Reprinted with revisions in F. Petri (ed.), *Siedlung, Sprache und Bevölkerungsstruktur im Frankenreich*, Darmstadt, 1973, 285–325.

WHITBY, M. (1985). 'The Long Walls of Constantinople', *Byzantion* lv, 560–82.

WHITTAKER, C. R. (1982). 'Labour supply in the Late Roman empire', *Opus* i, 171–9.

—— (1983). 'Trade and frontiers in the Roman Empire', in P. Garnsey and C. R. Whittaker (eds.), *Trade and Famine in Classical Antiquity*, Cambridge, 110–27.

WIEDEMANN, T. (1981). *Greek and Roman Slavery*, London.

WIGHTMAN, E. M. (1980). 'Depopulation in the Late Roman West', *Abstracts of Papers of 6th Annual Byzantine Conference*, Oberlin, 31–2.

—— (1981*a*). 'The fate of Gallo-Roman villages in the third century' in A. King and M. Henig (eds.), *The Roman West in the Third Century*, BAR Int. 109, Oxford, i. 235–43.

—— (1981*b*). 'The essential barbarian, comments on the deromanisation of Gaul', *Abstracts of Papers of 7th Annual Byzantine Conference*, Oberlin, 34–5.

—— (1985). *Gallia Belgica*, London.

WILD, J. P. (1976). 'Loanwords and Roman expansion in northwest Europe', *World Archaeology* viii, 57–64.

WILKEN, R. L. (1983). *John Chrysostom and the Jews*, The Transformation of the Classical Heritage iv, Berkeley.

WILKES, J. (1969). *Dalmatia*, London.

WIRTH, G. (1967). 'Zur Frage der foederirten Staaten in der späten römischen Kaiserzeit', *Historia* xvi, 231–51.

WOHLHAUPTER, E. (1948). 'Das germanische Element im altspanischen Recht und die Rezeption des römischen Rechtes', *ZRG rom.* lxvi, 135–264.

WOLFRAM, H. (1975–6). 'Gotische Studien', *Mitteilungen des Instituts für österreichische Geschichte* lxxxiii (1975), 1–32, 289–324; lxxxiv (1976), 239–61.

—— (1979). *Geschichte der Goten von den Anfängen bis zur Mitte des sechsten Jahrhunderts*, Munich.

—— (1983). 'Zur Ansiedlung reichsangehöriger *foederati*', *MIÖG* xci, 5–35.

—— 1987. *History of the Goths*, a new and completely revised edition of (1979) translated by Th. J. Dunlap, Berkeley.

WORMALD, P. (1977). '*Lex scripta* and *verbum regis*: legislation and Germanic kingship, from Euric to Cnut', in Sawyer and Wood (eds.), *Early Medieval Kingship*, Leeds, 105–38.

YPAS, J. (1969). 'Zur Tragweise frühfränkischer Gürtelgarnituren', *BROB*, xix, 89–127.

ZERFASS, R. (1963). 'Die Rolle der Lesung im Stundengebet', *Liturgisches Jahrbuch* xiii, 159–67.

—— (1968). *Die Schriftlesung im Kathedralofficium Jerusalems*, Münster.

ZEUMER, K. (1902). (ed.) *Leges Visigothorum*, MGH, Legum Sectio i, Hanover and Leipzig.

—— (1898–1901). 'Geschichte der westgotischen Gesetzgebung', *NA* xxiii, 419–516, xxiv, 39–122, 571–630; xxvi, 91–149.

Index

Italic numerals following names refer to articles in *PLRE* I–II.

Abundantius, general 96
Aemilius, bishop of Beneventum 226
Aetius 7, M. U. M. (West) 433–54, 64 n. 124
Africa, frontier defence 28
Agilo, general 8
agri deserti 18
alae 16 n. 52
Alamanni in army 8
Alans 31
Alaric, leader and later king, of Goths 51–8
　Roman friendships 39 n. 75
　checks Theodosius 51, 54
　turns against empire 55
　command in Illyricum 59
　invades Italy 60 ff.
　monarchy 62
　demands somewhere to live 70
　attempts crossing to Sicily 72
　election 78–9
　in *De Regno*? 107
　model for Tribigild? 101
Alatheus 27
Alexander, bishop of Basilinopolis 233–4
Alexandria, bishop of, rival of
　Constantinople 161–2
Anaunia, martyrs of 168 n. 12
A'nicii, family support Chrysostom 226
annona, attracts barbarians 40
Anomoeans 167
Anthemius, *PPO Orientis* 405–14, policy
　127; literary friends 139–40
　and Chrysostom 219
Antioch, Syria, dispute over *see* 160–1
　end of schism 225 n. 28
Antiochus 5, eunuch 134
Anysius 1, *dux Libyarum* 232
Anxomis, village in Pentapolis 231
Apions, *bucellarii* of 44, 45–6
Aquitaine, settlement of 418
Arbacius, general 124, 127
Arbogast 2, general 9–10
　inherits position 9
Arcadius' column 113 n. 13
　version of Gainas affair 120–1
　Freshfield drawings 273–7
　Louvre drawing 272–3
　themes and omissions 277–8
Ardaburius 3, general, defeats John 130
Arians, legislation against 147–8
　at Constantinople 152–3, 157–9, 163–5, 167

Arintheus, general 8
Ariovistus, composition of war band 77
　n. 241
Aristaenetus 2 134
Armenia, recruits from 27 n. 9
armour, reduction in use? 25
army, families 27
　size of army 40
　strength of units 41
　privatization 45–6
　inability to crush barbarian bands 52–3
　reorganized after defeat of Maximus 54
　corn consumption 73 n. 208
　consistent policy of East 94–5;
　　absenteeism 96; resents Eutropius 104–5;
　　in cities 117 n. 35; post-Gainas generals
　　126; reinforcements for West 127;
　　policy of Anthemius 128–9; Eastern
　　force deposes usurper John 129–30; re-
　　emergence of barbarian generals 130;
　　Eastern force against Vandals 130;
　　reduction in frontier forces 131; speed of
　　movement 265
Arsacius 3, general 126
Arsacius 1, bishop of Constantinople 207
ascetism, social effects 251–2
Aspar, son of Ardaburius 130
Aspendus 103
Athanaric, surrender of 28 n. 24
Athaulfus Gothic leader, joins Alaric 69, 71
　leads Alaric's Goths 72–3
Attalus 2, puppet emperor 71
Atticus, bishop of Constantinople 207
Augusta title 199
Ausurians 229
Aurelian 3, *PPO Orientis* II 414–16,
　prefecture of 399, 105–10
　family 133
　Christian 138, 141
　and Isaac 213
　opposition to Chrysostom 217 ff.
　when did he lose prefecture? 256
　consulate 259–61
auxilia 15, 16, 30
　raised by Theodosius 54

Bacurius, Armenian federate commander 30
bagaudae 17
　plunder Sarus 66
Balgritae, mounted archers 230

barbarians, attract outsiders 13, 17, 39, 61, 77, 101
  married to Romans 13
  fashions imitated 17 n. 65
  local agreements with 21
  nobles commissioned 23
  loyalty 25
  bands offered *annona* 27 n. 15
  tribally mixed bands 39–40
  veterans return home? 39 n. 75
  neighbours before entering empire 53
  influence of service in Roman army 77 n. 239
  mobile peasants 83
  absorb provincials 101
  settlement of 243
baritus 16
Bastarnians 52
Bauto, general 9
Basil, bishop of Caesarea 160
Basiliscus, usurper 82
Belisarius, *bucellarii* of 45
Bellini, Gentile 274
Biferno valley 19 n. 74
bishop, civic leadership 234–5
Bonifatius, *comes Africae*, demands troops 42
  bucellarii of 43 n. 109
Bonitus *1*, general 8
Bordeaux, Goths in 60
brigands 17
Brison, *cubicularius* 224
Britain, growth in population? 19 n. 76
bucellarii 7, 43–7
  of private individuals 44 n. 116, 47 n. 136

Caesarius *6*, *PPO Orientis* 395–7, 132–3
  wife, patron of monks 141
Callinicus, *Life of Hypatius* 211–12
camels 229
Cassian, ordained by Chrysostom 226
cavalry 27–8, 33–4, 37, 80
  of Greuthungi 38
  Alaric's 59
centenarium 28
Christianity, new scope for women 141–4
  allows literary paganism 150
  charity 187–8
  equalizer 173–4
Christianization 186–7
  effects discussed 249–52
Church, subject to law 151–2
  wealth of 200, 222
cities, break-up of territory 233
citizenship, intermarriage 13
  of recruits 14
  reduced meaning of 243, 244, 245, 247–8
civilians, self-defence 224, 231–2

Claudian, poet, attacks Eutropius 93
  a Christian? 150 n. 63
Clearchus *2*, 134
client peoples, provide units 34–5
cohortes 16 n. 52
coins, reduction in funds 62 n. 112
column of Arcadius *see* Arcadius' column
comes foederatorum 31
comitatenses of Pentapolis 230
commendatio, Visigothic 17
Concordia cemetery 32 n. 4
connubium 13, 30
conscription 19–20
consistorium, function 93–4
Constantine I, emperor 306–37, field army 7
Constantine III, Augustus 407–11, enters Gaul 66–7
Constantinople, massacre of Goths 117–18
  conspiracy-talk 122
  walls 128
  Macedonian monasticism 141, 145
  corn fleet 159
  Council of 381, 161
  second and third canons 163
  church of Paul 164
  monasticism at 211–14
  hospitals 222
  buildings on Arcadius' column 275
  personifications of city 275–6
  bishop, extent of jurisdiction 161–2, 171
Constantius *17*, Augustus 421
  agreement with Goths 74
  reconstructs field army 42
Constantius II, emperor 337–61, care for soldiers 17
corn, consumption 73 n. 208
  offered to Goths 73
Councils of Church, role and authority 162–3
curia and *curiales*, of Pentapolis 228–9, 248
  loss of control by 246–7
Cynegius, *PPO Orientis* 384–8, 136
Cyrenaica, nomad society 84
Cyrene 228, 232
  decline 232 n. 31

Dacia Ripensis, entrusted to Theoderic 82
Damasus, pope, opposes Gregory of Nazianzus 160–1
decurions see under *curiae* and *curiales*
dediticii 14, 36, 71
demilitarization 16–21, 23
  effect on citizenship 245
depopulation 11, 18–19, 243
  Jones' views 242
  population growth in East 247
deserted land 18

de Ste Croix, G. E. M., on fall of Roman
  Empire 242–7, 252
duces, of German origin 15
dux Libyae 230
dux Thebaidos, and *bucellarii* 45

Eleusius, founder of monasteries 212
emperor, relations with generals 23–4
  and church councils 162–3
Ephesus, deposition of bishop 171, 214
Epidamnus (Dyrrhachium) 82
Epiphanius, bishop of Salamis 204–5
Eriulf, Gothic leader, killing of 48, 54
estates 20–1
Eudoxia, empress 400–4, sister of
  Arbogast? 10
  marriage 24, 92
  images of 64
  silver statue 124
  supports Chrysostom 167–8
  break with Chrysostom 198–200
  public role 200–1
Eugenius, usurper 392–4, 33
  campaign against 54–5
Eunapius, historian, errors of 56–7
  date of *History* 119 n. 50
  on Fravitta 124
Eunomians, legislation against 147, 148–9
  Synesius attacks 234
Eugraphia 207
Eusebius 39, general 24
Eustathius of Sebaste, founder of monasteries
  209
Eutychianus 5 (thrice *PPO Orientis*), prefect
  of Illyricum 98–9
  replaces Aurelian 109
  policy of 116–18
  trial 122
  family 133
  and Chrysostom 218
  the Typhos of *De Providentia* 253–71
Eutropius, *praepositus sacri cubiculi* 92–108
  execution 108

Fall of Empire, causes discussed 236–51
federates, recruited through treaties 22–3
  in Maximus' campaign 36
  distinguished from regulars 32–3
  different kinds of 32 ff.
  of Stilicho 36
  families 36, 37 n. 50
  not in *Notitia* 33–4
  Procopius and Olympiodorus on 36
  of Gainas 37
  recruiting by commander 37
  turned into regular units? 42, 97

advantages of use 42–3
  close bonds with commander 42–7
field surveys 19 n. 74
Flavius, title 33
fortification 96, 128
  abandonment of frontier forts 131
  of towns and villages 231
  reduced size of forts 41 n. 86
Forum Tauri 133
Franks, in army 8
  migration 19 n. 73
  old homes left empty 19
  defend Rhine frontier 41
Fravitta, general, Roman wife 13
  campaigns in Thrace 61
  against Gainas 188–9
  death 123–4
Fritigern, leader of Goths, death 50
Fraomarius, Alamannic king 23
frontier civilization 22 n. 91, 39, 53

Gaatha 50 n. 17
Gainas 30
  commander of all *foederati* in 388, 31
  returns units to East 58
  and murder of Rufinus 92
  and Tribigild 100–3
  and Eutropius and Aurelian 3, 104–10
  fall 111–25
  massacre of Constantinople 117–18
  corresponds with hermit 144
  chronology of occupation of
    Constantinople 256–9
  his fall on Arcadius' column 275–6
  movements in autumn 399, 264–7
  in historical record 267–8
Gaiseric, king of Vandals, 'thousands' 14
Galla Placidia, daughter of Theodosius I 73
Gaul, army of 15
  good soldiers 16
  changes in population 18–19
Gaza, closure of temples 168
gentes annonariae 35 n. 34
gentiles 12–13, 15
George of Alexandria, *Life of*
  Chrysostom 200
Germans, not lineage based 13 n. 30
Germanus 226
Gerontius, bishop of Nicomedia 215
Gerontius 4, military commander, attacks
  barbarian band 27 n. 15
Gibbon, on decline and fall 238–9, 249, 251
Gildo, chieftain and commander 24, 91 n. 21
  transfers to East 98
Goffart, W., on treaty of 418, 74–5
Gomoarius 9
Goths, joined by outsiders 13, 17, 77, 101

Goths, joined by outsiders (*cont.*):
  Arianism 17, 49–50
  recruited 26
  treaties of 381 and 382, 27–30, 78 n. 245
  farm 28 n. 26
  custom of 29 n. 36
  share houses 29
  losses against Eugenius 33
  bucellarii 42 n. 102, 46 n. 128
  individually enrolled 37 n. 39, 50
  subdivisions 48
  oath 49
  non-Gallic names 49 n. 3
  several leaders 50 n. 11
  against Eugenius 55
  waggons 58
  cavalry 59
  migration resumed in 395? 56–7
  billeting 60
  monarchy 62 n. 108
  promised farmland 73 n. 211
  settled in Aquitaine 74
  defeat Asding Vandals 74
  ethnogenesis of Alaric's Goths 75–7
  numerical fluctuation of Alaric's band 75–6
Gothic place-names in Aquitaine 76
  clients 76
  language 76 n. 235
  Latin influence on Gothic 77 n. 240
  treaty of 382, 78 n. 245
  Lesser Goths 79–80
  Catholic Goths 80
  Theoderic Strabo's Goths depend on
    him 80
  between nomads and non-nomads 83–4
  depend on trade 84
  subject peoples 85
Gratian, emperor 367–83, agreement with
  Goths 27
  edict of tolerance 157
Greece, late sites more numerous 19 n. 74
Greek culture 134–40
Gregory of Nazianzus, at Constantinople
  158–63
Greuthungi 49
  defeated by Promotus 36
  of Tribigild 100–1, 102
guild of money lenders 224

hagiography, *Life of Paulus of
  Constantinople* 164
Hebrus [Maritsa], Theodosius checked 51
Helion *1, magister officiorum* 414–27, 134
Heradianus *3, comes Africae* 71, 72
heresy, legislation 146 ff.
  de facto toleration 152–3
Hierax *1* 123–4

honestiores 13, 243, 246
honorati 248
Honorius, emperor 393–423, letter to
  Arcadius 65
  oath 71
  death 129
Hosius *magister officiorum* 395–8, ex-
  cook 140
hospitalitas 60, 74–5
humiliores 13, 243, 246
Huns 61, 97
  invasion of 395, 55
  and Rufinus 90, 91
  defeated by Eutropius 99–100
  invade with Skiri 127–8
  invade Thrace 129
Hunsruck, depopulation 11
hymn-singing 168
Hypatia, philosopher, lynched 149
Hypatius, leader of monks 211–12

Ibn Khaldun, on adoption by tribes 78
Illyricum, field army 41
  division of 58
  Alaric military commander 59
  conflict over eastern Illyricum 65–7, 226–7
  prefecture 98 n. 28
inquilini 11–12
intermarriage 13
Isaac, monk 141, 207
  charges Chrysostom 210–11
  death of 210 n. 26
Isaurians, fighting qualities 17
  raids 124, 127
Isidore, priest of Alexandria 166
Italy, changes in population 19

Jews, in Minorca converted 149
  increased pressure on 149–51
  rights reaffirmed 150–1
  the patriarch 151
John the Baptist, head of 164–5
John Chrysostom, Eutropius sermons 104 n.
  4
  and fall of Eutropius 105, 188–9
  influence during Gainas crisis 109–10
  Hom. cum Saturninus etc. 110 n. 49, 191–2
  and burnt church 122
  election 166
  and Arians 167
  and mission 169–79
  and Goths 169–70
  administrative reforms 170–1
  extends jurisdiction of Constantinople 171
  commentaries 171–2, 183–4
  entertainer 172, 182, 185
  audience of 173

against élitism 173–4
and imperial family 174–5
and wealth 175–6, 188
generality of criticism 176–7
avoids political allusions 177–8
moral educator 178–9
views on women 179–80
on church finance 180–1
demands on congregation 181
educator 183–4
and shows 182–3, 185–6
effect of preaching 180
during Gainas crisis 188–93
and church for Arian services 190–1
fall of 195
sources 196–7
and political role of Eudoxia 201
in role of Ambrose 201
relations with clergy and monks 208–16
and Theophilus 203 ff.
and women 205
reforms 209–10
hostile bishops 214–15
lack of sociability 215–16
and rich 222–5
and poor 223
links with West 224–7
an exiled follower 235
prevented from leaving Constantinople
    260–1
John *1*, *comes*, opponent of Chrysostom 61,
    64, 217 ff.
hostile to West 123, 124
exile 108 n. 38
John, usurper 129–30
Jones, A. H. M., *The Later Roman
    Empire* 239–42, 249, 251
Jovian, emperor 263–4, election 9
Jovinus *2*, usurper in Gaul 411–13, 72–3
Julian *29*, Augustus 360–3, proclaimed
    emperor 15–16
Julius, *magister militum per Orientem* 371–8,
    29, 34

laeti 12
Latin, language of government 136
Lebanon, paganism 169
legions 15, 16 n. 54
legislation, not universally enforced 152–3
Leo *6*, emperor 437–74, against *bucellarii* 47
Leo *2*, general, against Tribigild 102–3
ex-wool worker? 140
Lesser Goths 83 n. 282
limes, evacuation of forts 131
limitanei, units with barbarian names 15
in Pentapolis 230

Lombards, influence of Roman army 40,
    77 n. 239
Lycia, disgraced 89
Lydia, devastated 103

Macetae 229
Macedonia, Goths stationed in 29
campaign in marshes 51–2
Zeno assigns cities to Goths 81
Macedonius, bishop of Constantinople 164,
    193
Macedonian clergy 165
and monasticism 209
magister officiorum 94, 219
magnates (*potentes*) of Pentapolis 228, 231–2
Malarich, tribune of gentiles 8
Marcomanni, stationed in Pentapolis 230
Mark, the Deacon 168–9
credibility of *Life of Porphyry* 199–200
Manichaeans, persecution 147
Mantegna 274
Marathonius, founder of monasteries 212
Martyrius and Marcian, relics of 164
'Martyrius', *Life of Chrysostom* 197, 223
Maximus, Christian Cynic, consecrated
    bishop 159
Maximus, Gothic bishop, theology of 50 n.
    11
Maximus *39*, usurper 383–8, 30–1
Melania the Younger 142, 225, 226
sells estates 222
Meletius, bishop of Antioch 158, 160–1
Merobaudes *2*, general, emperor-maker 9
Mersa, widow of Promotus 145
militarization 20
missionaries 170
Moesia, continued presence of Goths 79
Molise 19
Momigliano, A., on Jones' *Later Roman
    Empire* 240
on relevance of historical research 252
monasticism, patrons of 144–5
social effect 188, 251–2
Eustathius of Sebaste 209
Monaxius (twice *PPO Orientis*) 134
monks, against Chrysostom 211–14
Montesquieu, on causes of greatness of Rome
    236–8, 245
myth, importance of 76 n. 234

Nebridius *2* 136
Nectarius, bishop of Constantinople 160, 163
Neoplatonism, role of women 141 n. 81
Nevitta, general 9
Nicaea, Council of, creed 160
fifteenth canon 160

Nicopolis ad Istrum, and Goths 29
  Lesser Goths 79
Normans, ethnogenesis 76 n. 234
Notitia Dignitatum, omissions 32–4
  size of units 40–1
  peace-time armies 54
Novae, in Moesia II, centre of Theoderic's
  Goths 82
Novatians 171
  relative toleration 147
  co-operate with Nectarius 163
novi homines 137, 140–1
Numidia, frontier defence 28

obsequium 17
Olympias 224–5
  marriage 136
  Christian use of her property 142–4
  persecuted 221–2
Olympiodorus, on *bucellarii* 44
Optila, *bucellarius* 43 n. 110
Optatus *1*, urban prefect 134
  persecutes followers of Chrysostom 220
Orgetorix, following of 17 n. 61
Origenism, attacked 203–4
Origenists, link with Chrysostom 202, 213,
  225–6
Orosius, on sack of Rome 68–9
orthodoxy, definitions 158, 159, 160
  divided 158
Ostrogoths 30 n. 30, 48,
  created by shared campaigns 83
Ottoman Turks, ethnogenesis? 77

pagans, legislation against 150, 168–9
Paianius, urban prefect 220
Palladius, biographer of Chrysostom,
    reticence on Gainas 119, 267–8
  Dialogue on the Life of Chrysostom 197
  supported by Melania 225
Palmyra, centre of settled nomads 84 n. 289
Pamphylia, civilian self defence 103
Panhellenion 140
Pannonia, Alatheus and Saphrac's men 27
  location of Gothic federates 27
  pacified 55 n. 56
Pansophius, bishop of Nicomedia 214
Pataulia in Dacia Mediterranea 82
Paul, bishop of Constantinople 164
Paulinus, rival bishop of Antioch 161
peasants, temporary abandonment of land
    18 n. 71
  mobility 83
  loose part in *respublica* 244–5
Pentadia, widow of Timasius 224–5
Peter, bishop of Alexandria 158

peregrini 13 n. 29, 14
Perinthus, station of Goths? 27 n. 15
Persia, threats 127
  Pulcheria's war 129
Persians, as generals 126
Philippus 7, *PPO Orientis* 344–51, 133
Plintas, general 130
  Arian 153
Pollentia, battle of 63
population, growth 16, 247
  see also depopulation
Porphyry, bishop of Gaza 169
potentes 246
praesental armies not tactical formations? 31
    n. 44
Praetorian prefect of East, role 94
  not collegial office 253–5
prisoners of war enrolled 14
privatization of army 45–6
probatoria 37
processions 166–7
Proculus, son of Tatian 89
Promotus, general 24, 51–2, 90–1, 92
  patron of monks 144, 170
protectores, Roman names 15 n. 43
Ptolemais 232
Publicola, son of Melania the Elder 226
Pulcheria, Augusta 414–53, policies 129
  supports monasticism 149–50

Quartodecimans 171

Radagaisus 65–6
resistance by civilians 103, 118–19
relics support orthodoxy 164–5
Rehitah, son of Theoderic Strabo 81
recruiting 11, 16, 97
  beyond frontier 14
  citizenship on enlistment 14
  conscription 26
  resistance by landowners 20–2
  tax 19 n. 78
  before campaigns 34
  of Goths 29
retainers 102 n. 71
Rome, sacked 72
Rufinus, *PPO Orientis* 392–5,
    Christianity 90
  bucellarii 43, 45
  consequences of murder 59
  power and death 89–92
  treaty with Alaric 57–8
  treaty with Goths 52
Rua, king of Huns 130

saiones 17
Salvina, daughter of Gildo 24, 224

Samaritans, brigandage 17
Saphrax, Gothic leader 27–8
  succeeded by Athaulfus? 69 n. 169
Sardes, attacked by Gainas 111
Sarmatians in army 22
Sarus, Gothic leader, following 38–9
  bucellarii 44 n. 113
  campaign in Gaul 66–7
Sasima in Cappadocia 160
Saturninus *10*, general, treaty with
    Goths 28–9
  exiled 108
  patron of Isaac 144, 213
  opponent of Chrysostom 217
Saul, federate commander 30
scholae 8
  Roman officers 14 n. 41
  Germans in 15–16
  careers of officers 23
scutarii 15
sedes 68–9, 70, 74 n. 219
Segericus, Gothic leader 39
Selge in Pamphylia 103
Selenas, bishop, succeeds Ulfilas 80
Seleucia, wife of Rufinus of Caesarea 224
senate of Constantinople 135
  snobbery 137
senatorial order 135
  rank within 248
Serena, niece of Theodosius 24
sermon, a neglected topic 177–8
  effect of 186–7
settlement of barbarians 11–13, 73–4, 243
Severianus, bishop of Gabala 198–207
Side in Pamphylia 103
Silvanus, usurper 8
Simplicius, urban prefect 219–20
slavery 244
  slaves join Alaric 69
Socrates, ecclesiastical historian, on
    Gainas 112–14
Sozomen, ecclesiastical historian, on
    Gainas 112–14
  on defeat of Gainas 121
  supplements Socrates 196–7
Spain, decline of cities 19 n. 77
St Phocas of Pontus 168 n. 13
St Stephen, martyrium 141
  relics at Minorca 149
St Thrysus 141
Stilicho 10
  recruiting 37
  bucellarii 43
  first encounter with Goths 52
  guardian of Honorius 55
  returns units 58
  alliance with Alaric 65

  death 67–8
  claims guardianship of Arcadius 91
  in Greece 97
Studius, urban prefect 220
subintroductae 209
Suebi 74
Sueridus and Colias, band of 27 n. 15
Synesius, *De Regno*, tendency and date
    105–7
  De Providentia, the high priest 110
  De Providentia on Gainas 114–16,
  De Providentia on Typhos 115–16
  a miracle 116
  literary friends 137–41
  friendship of Aurelian 137–8
  De Providentia, role of Osiris 138
  Christianity of 141
  life and activities 228–35
  bishop 232–5
  accepts church discipline 233–4
  loss of influence 234–5
  De Providentia, editions 268–71
  De Providentia, a typology 271
Synod of the Oak 207

Tall Brothers 203–4, 207
Tatian *5*, *PPO Orientis* 388–92, 89
Taurus *3*, *PPO Ital. et Afr.* 355–6, 133
taxation, level of 247 n. 47
Teruingi 48
  treaty of 28–9
  regiment 29, 33
  Constantine's treaty 35
terra laetica 12
Theodemer, father of Theoderic 81
Theodore of Trimithus, *Life of Chrysostom*
    200
Theoderic, king of Ostrogoths, raises a
    following 29 n. 33
  history of his warband 81–3
Theodosius I, emperor, marriages of generals
    24
  enrols federates 26
  against Maximus 30–1
  return in 391, 51–2
  campaigns against Eugenius 53–5
  brings Westerners to East 136
  legislation against heresy 147
  imposes orthodoxy 157–65
Theodosius II, emperor 129
Theophilus, bishop of Alexandria 166
  and deposition of Chrysostom 203–7
  relations with Synesius 233
Thompson, E. A., on Gothic
    nationalism 48 ff.
Thrace, Goths settled after 382, 29
  settlements in 5th century? 80

Thracians, regiment, in Pentapolis 230
Timasius, general 90–1, 96, 225
Timothy, bishop of Alexandria 161
travel, speed of sea voyages 265
Tribigild, origins 38
  rebellion of 100–3
tribunus, rank given to local chiefs 28
Tripolitania, frontier defence 28

Uldin, king of Huns 119
  against Radagaisus 35
  invades Thrace 127–8
Ulfilas, primate of Goths 79–80
Unila, bishop of Goths in Crimea 170
Unnigardae 230

Valentinian II, emperor, vicissitudes 9–10
Vandals, joined by provincials? 14
  powers of recovery 17 n. 62

  force Rhine frontier 41
  start of migration 61 n. 105
  Asding 74
Varanes, general 126
Vegetius, on reduced efficiency of army 25
Verona, battle of 63
viaticum 35
Victor 4, general 8
  patron of Isaac 144
Videmer, brother of Theoderic 81
Visi, regiment 29, 33
Visigoths, use of name 48
  the making of, 75–6
widows, order of 144
women, Christianity offers new scope 141–5
  chaste cohabitation 209
  among supporters of Chrysostom 224–5

Zosimus, on Gainas crisis 111–12

PLATES

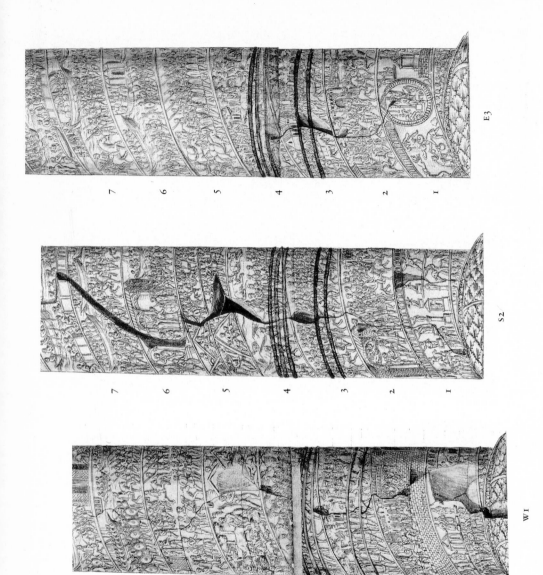

E3

S2

W1

1. 1–3. Freshfield drawings of narrative bands 1–7 of West, South, and East aspects of the column of Arcadius.

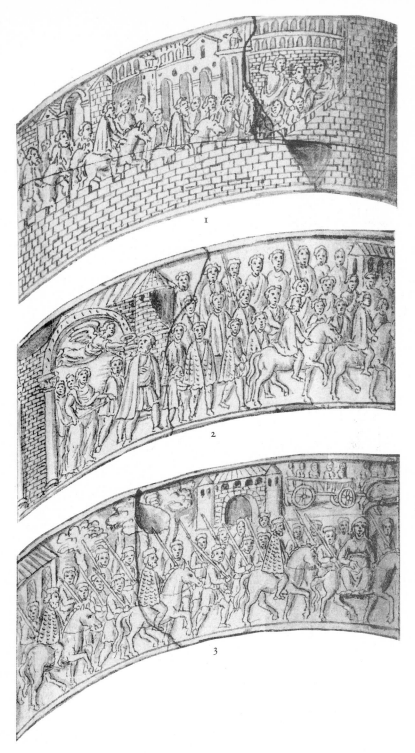

4. 1. Band 2 of Freshfield drawing showing Goths leaving Constantinople with intriguing view of buildings. 2. Within a gate an angel and a female figure prevent the Germans from re-entering. 3. Three Gothic riders with sheepskin cloaks.

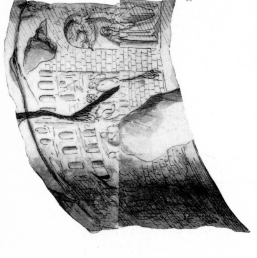

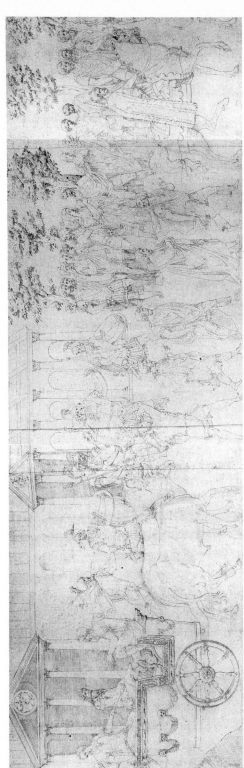

5. 1. Bibliothèque Nationale drawing of band 2, showing the angel and the standing figure in the gate. 2. Louvre drawing showing a scarcely recognizable variation on the South and East aspects of Band 2 (plate 4.2–3). Note the two figures between the temple facades, the five marching men, and the cloaked horseman, the first of three.

6. 1–2. Freshfield drawing of band 8 showing a Roman fleet patrolling the Hellespont and Goths building rafts or boats. 3. Bibliothèque Nationale version of part of the same carving as 1.

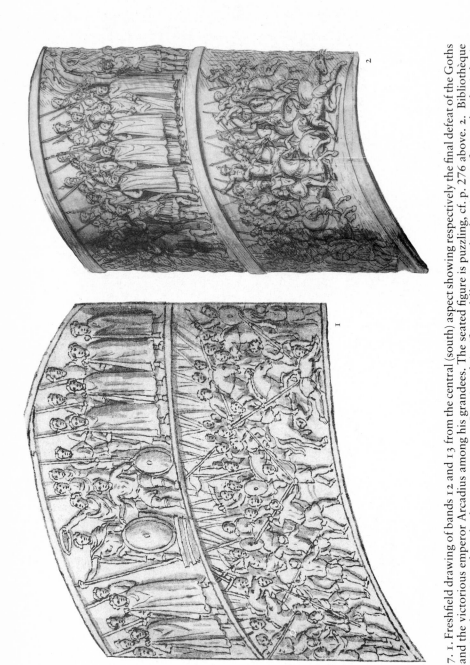

7. 1. Freshfield drawing of bands 12 and 13 from the central (south) aspect showing respectively the final defeat of the Goths and the victorious emperor Arcadius among his grandees. The seated figure is puzzling, cf. p. 276 above. 2. Bibliothèque Nationale version of surely the same 2 scenes. In spite of significant differences the drawings confirm each other's basic fidelity to the lost carvings.